POLITICAL TRADITIONS IN FOREIGN POLICY

Kenneth W. Thompson, Editor

The values, traditions, and assumptions undergirding approaches to foreign policy are often crucial in determining the course of a nation's history.
Yet, the interconnections between ideas and policy for landmark periods in
our foreign relations remain largely unexamined. The intent of this series
is to encourage a marriage between political theory and foreign policy. A
secondary objective is to identify theorists with a continuing interest in political thought and international relations, both younger scholars and the
small group of established thinkers. Only occasionally have scholarly cen-
ters and university presses sought to nurture studies in this area. In the
1950s and 1960s the University of Chicago Center for the Study of American Foreign Policy gave emphasis to such inquiries. Since then the subject
has not been the focus of any major intellectual center. The Louisiana
State University Press and the series editor, from a base at the Miller Center of Public Affairs at the University of Virginia, have organized this series
to meet a need that has remained largely unfulfilled since the mid-1960s.

Prophet of Decline

Prophet *of* Decline

Spengler on World History and Politics

JOHN FARRENKOPF

LOUISIANA STATE UNIVERSITY PRESS BATON ROUGE

Published by Louisiana State University Press
Copyright © 2001 by Louisiana State University Press
Manufactured in the United States of America

Designer: Melanie O'Quinn Samaha
Typeface: Galliard
Typesetter: Coghill Composition Co., Inc.

Library of Congress Cataloging-in-Publication Data:
Farrenkopf, John.
     Prophet of decline : Spengler on world history and politics / John Farrenkopf.
        p.   cm. — (Political traditions in foreign policy series)
     Includes bibliographical references and index.
     ISBN 978-0-8071-2727-8 (pbk. : alk. paper)
     1. Spengler, Oswald, 1880–1936. Untergang des Abendlandes. 2. Spengler, Oswald,
1880–1936. 3. History—Philosophy 4. Civilization—Philosophy. 5. Historians—
Germany—Biography. I. Title. II. Series.
     CB19.F32   2001
     909—dc21

                                                                                        00-054965

Frontispiece reproduced courtesy Bayerische Staatsbibliothek München

To my parents

CONTENTS

FOREWORD

THE LATE WILLIAM T. R. FOX, DIRECTOR
of the War and Peace Institute at Columbia University, lamented what he
called the absence of continuity in American social science research. In
comparison with the natural and physical sciences, social sciences were not
cumulative in the organization of research. In Professor Fox's view, especially younger social scientists were inclined to move from one subject to
another, sacrificing thereby the impact that experimental scientists
achieved. Natural scientists concentrated over long periods of time on
some fundamental and unexplained problem.

Whatever the merits of Fox's critique, John Farrenkopf is an exception.
From his first day in the Ph.D. program in the Department of Government
and Foreign Affairs at the University of Virginia, Farrenkopf made clear
his priorities. He was determined to make an enduring contribution to the
understanding of Oswald Spengler. His long-term interest was in the philosophy of history. His interest in Spengler paralleled mine in Arnold J.
Toynbee, so we enjoyed long and fruitful conversations. Through the
course of our discussions, I witnessed the sharpening of John's focus and
the deepening of his understanding. He left no stone unturned in the pursuit of the truth about Spengler's work. He related what Spengler had to
say to essentially every political theory course in his graduate studies. It
soon became clear that he was gaining the attention of the leading Spengler scholars and political theorists in Europe, and Germany in particular.
Some were quite willing to enter into correspondence. With others, Farrenkopf discovered that a period of residency in Munich and Eichstätt was
required.

Wherever Farrenkopf's research led him, he found that prominent scholars took notice and were pleased to supervise and advise on his research. What followed was a succession of high-quality articles that appeared in leading Western journals. As he became recognized in Europe, invitations to attend conferences and collaborate in research came his way. When his manuscript approached completion it seemed appropriate to invite him to submit the text to Louisiana State University Press. By then Farrenkopf was recognized by Spengler scholars, who recommended publication. We had no doubt that the book is worthy of recognition in a series on traditions and values. We are proud to include it as a contribution of significance in the philosophy of history.

Kenneth W. Thompson

ACKNOWLEDGMENTS

I WOULD LIKE TO THANK THE EARHART Foundation, the Germanistic Society of America, the Fulbright Commission for Educational Exchange between the United States of America and the Federal Republic of Germany, and the Fritz Thyssen Foundation for generously providing me with research grants for my work on Oswald Spengler. The Earhart Foundation sponsored preliminary research in the United States, while the latter three organizations funded four years of research in Germany. Without such institutional support, this book would not have been possible.

There are a number of distinguished scholars to whom I am indebted. Kurt Sontheimer of the Geschwister-Scholl Institut für Politische Wissenschaft of the University of Munich took me under his wing during my four years in Munich. Hermann Lübbe of the University of Zurich was most kind in facilitating the generous support of the Thyssen Foundation and in helping bring to fruition the idea of a Spengler symposium. Nikolaus Lobkowicz, president of the Catholic University of Eichstätt, and his colleague, Karl Graf von Ballestrem, supervised my research activities as a Thyssen fellow. Alexander Demandt of the Free University of Berlin further introduced me into the world of German scholarship; with the generous assistance of the Thyssen Foundation we organized an international symposium on Spengler hosted by the Werner-Reimers Foundation in Bad Homburg, Germany. The symposium papers have been previously published, with thanks again to the Thyssen Foundation. Here in the United States, I am deeply grateful to Kenneth W. Thompson of the University of Virginia, former director of the Miller Center of Public Affairs, for his mentoring and keen interest in this project over the years. He not only helped launch this work but has faithfully seen it through to completion. Along with the debts of gratitude owed these scholars, there are also ones to my editors. I would like to thank Maureen G. Hewitt, Editor-in-Chief of LSU Press, for her confidence in the book, and Christine N. Cowan for editing the manuscript with thoughtfulness and meticulousness. I also wish to express my appreciation to the staff of LSU Press and, in particular, John Easterly, Executive Editor, for his skillful oversight of the project and attention to detail.

Several academic journals have graciously granted permission to include in this book portions of articles originally published elsewhere. These articles include "The Transformation of Spengler's Philosophy of World History," in *Journal of the History of Ideas* (July–September, 1991); "Spengler's 'Der Mensch und die Technik': An Embarrassment or a Significant Treatise?," in *German Studies Review* (October, 1991); "The Challenge of Spenglerian Pessimism to Ranke and Political Realism," in *Review of International Studies* (1991; reprinted with the permission of Cambridge University Press); "The Early Phase in Spengler's Political Philosophy," in *History of Political Thought* (Summer, 1992); "Spengler's Historical Pessimism and the Tragedy of Our Age," in *Theory and Society* (1993); and "Spengler's Theory of Civilization," reprinted by permission of Sage Publications Ltd from *Thesis Eleven* (August, 2000), © 2000 by Sage Ltd. In addition, the Böhlau Verlag in Köln has kindly permitted me to make use of material from the essay "Klio und Cäsar: Spenglers Philosophie der Weltgeschichte im Dienste der Staatskunst," published in 1994 in *Der Fall Spenglers: Eine kritische Bilanz.*

Over the years I have benefited greatly from intellectual exchange both in the United States and in Germany about Spengler's controversial ideas on world history and politics. Whatever errors or inaccuracies this book may contain, they are the sole responsibility of the author.

ABBREVIATIONS

THE FOLLOWING ABBREVIATIONS ARE used in the footnotes. All of the abbreviations refer to material in German, except for the monograph on Spengler by H. Stuart Hughes ("H-Sp"). Except for the books abbreviated as "H-Sp," "K-Sp," and *KSA*, Oswald Spengler is the author of the material referred to by the abbreviation.

B	*Briefe 1913–1936* (Letters, 1913–1936). Ed. Anton Mirko Koktanek, in collaboration with Manfred Schröter. Munich: C. H. Beck, 1963.
DR	"Das Doppelantlitz Russlands und die deutschen Ostprobleme" (The Two Faces of Russia and the German Eastern Problems). In *PSch*.
EH	"Eis heauton." Autobiographical fragments, unedited. Spengler Archive, Bavarian State Library, Munich.
FdW	*Frühzeit der Weltgeschichte: Fragmente aus dem Nachlass* (Early Period of World History: Fragments from the Unpublished Writings). Ed. Anton Mirko Koktanek, in collaboration with Manfred Schröter. Munich: C. H. Beck, 1966.
H	"Heraklit" (Heraclitus). In *RuA*.
H-Sp	Hughes, H. Stuart. *Oswald Spengler: A Critical Estimate.* New York: Charles Scribner's Sons, 1952.
JdE	*Jahre der Entscheidung* (Years of Decision). Part I: *Deutschland und die weltgeschichtliche Entwicklung* (Germany and the World-Historical Development) Munich: C. H. Beck, 1933.

KSA   Nietzsche, Friedrich. *Sämtliche Werke. Kritische Studienausgabe* (Collected Works. Critical Studies Edition). Ed. Giorgio Colli and Mazzino Montinari. 2d ed. 15 vols. Berlin: Deutscher Taschenbuch Verlag de Gruyter, 1988.

K-Sp   Koktanek, Anton Mirko. *Oswald Spengler in seiner Zeit* (Oswald Spengler in His Age). Munich: C. H. Beck, 1966.

MuT   *Der Mensch und die Technik: Beitrag zu einer Philosophie des Lebens* (Man and Technics: Contribution to a Philosophy of Life). Munich: C. H. Beck, 1931.

NdR   "Neubau des deutschen Reiches" (Reconstruction of the German Reich). In *PSch*.

P   "Pessimismus?" (Pessimism). In *RuA*.

Politica I   "Politica I." Fragments from unpublished writings on political matters, unedited. Spengler Archive, Bavarian State Library, Munich.

Politica II   "Politica II." Additional fragments from unpublished writings on political matters, unedited. Spengler Archive, Bavarian State Library, Munich.

PP   "Politische Pflichten der deutschen Jugend" (Political Duties of German Youth). In *PSch*.

PSch   *Politische Schriften* (Political Writings). Munich: C. H. Beck, 1934.

PuS   *Preußentum und Sozialismus* (Prussianism and Socialism). Munich: C. H. Beck, 1920.

RuA   *Reden und Aufsätze* (Speeches and Essays). Ed. Hildegard Kornhardt. 2d ed. Munich: C. H. Beck, 1938.

UdA I   *Der Untergang des Abendlandes: Umrisse einer Morphologie der Weltgeschichte* (The Decline of the West: Sketch of a Morphology of World History). Vol. I, *Gestalt und Wirklichkeit* (Form and Actuality). Rev. ed. Munich: C. H. Beck, 1923.

UdA II   *Der Untergang des Abendlandes: Umrisse einer Morphologie der Weltgeschichte* (The Decline of the West: Sketch of a Morphology of World History). Vol. II, *Welthistorische Perspektiven* (World-Historical Perspectives). Munich: C. H. Beck, 1923.

Ufr   *Urfragen: Fragmente aus dem Nachlass* (Fundamental Questions: Fragments from the Unpublished Writings). Ed. Anton Mirko Koktanek, in collaboration with Manfred Schröter. Munich: C. H. Beck, 1965.

WW   "Das heutige Verhältnis zwischen Weltwirtschaft und Weltpolitik" (The Contemporary Relationship Between the International Economy and World Politics). In *PSch*.

NOTE ON THE SPENGLER ARCHIVE

THE FOLLOWING COMMENTS PROVIDE A glimpse into the Spengler Archive to those readers who may be unaware of its existence or contents. The archive, housed at the Bavarian State Library in Munich, has an extensive collection of material on the life and thought of Oswald Spengler. The wealth of documents, photographs and sketches, miscellaneous papers, interviews, and newspaper articles, accounts by third parties, original letters to and from Spengler, notes intended for an autobiography that was never written, and the papers and diaries of his sister, Hilde Kornhardt, were indispensable in Anton Mirko Koktanek's research of his biography. The largely biographical material is complemented by the collection of scholarly papers. Numerous aphoristic notes on metaphysics and world history in the archive were posthumously edited and published in two companion volumes, thanks to the research diligence of Koktanek (*Ufr* and *FdW*). Of further interest are Spengler's unpublished fragments on politics, including partial drafts of memoranda to the German kaiser and the nobility apparently composed during World War I, and notes for the projected continuation of *Years of Decision*, as well as unpublished poems, unfinished dramatic and epic compositions, and scattered reflections on questions of poetry and the visual arts.

Prophet of Decline

INTRODUCTION

HISTORICAL INQUIRY AND PHILOSOPHY
remain the means par excellence for denizens of the modern West to reflect on its origins, evolution, and future. The pantheon of modern Western historical thought is crowded with optimists. In the eighteenth and
nineteenth centuries, Johann Gottfried Herder, Immanuel Kant, the
Marquis de Condorcet, A. R. Jacques Turgot, Georg Wilhelm Friedrich
Hegel, Leopold von Ranke, Thomas B. Macaulay, George Bancroft, Karl
Marx, Auguste Comte, and Heinrich von Treitschke all expressed differently historical optimism. These luminaries prefigured the purported
progress of the modern West. In the twentieth century, despite its many
horrors, H. G. Wells, Arnold Toynbee, Karl Jaspers, and William H. Mc-
Neill also inspired hope for better times. Undoubtedly, these historical
minds have enriched our knowledge of the past and have stimulated our
historical imagination. Yet they have also arguably plotted a course to the
shallow backwaters of sanguinity instead of intrepidly charting the rendez-
vous of modernity with tragedy. The historical optimists have not provided us with penetrating insight into the crisis of our civilization in
contrast to their oft-ignored and, at times, reviled counterparts, the lonely,
searching spirits of historical pessimism: Karl Vollgraff, Ernst von Lasaulx,
Jacob Burckhardt, Brooks and Henry Adams, and, above all others, Oswald Spengler.

The terminal crisis of Communism, the end of the Cold War, and the
global enthusiasm for democracy and free-market economics precipitated
in the late 1980s a euphoric outburst of liberal optimism and Western tri-
umphalism. This self-intoxication with historical optimism, of which Francis Fukuyama's essay, "The End of History?," is the most striking

symptom, has already proven to be painfully premature. Historical pessimism cannot be ignored in our crisis-ridden age.

Today the pace of historical change and the interdependence and complexity of our fragile world are all simultaneously increasing. Under such disorienting conditions, on the cusp of a new millennium, it is most timely to contemplate where our civilization is heading from the perspective of Spengler's philosophy of world history and politics. To those receptive to the message of this leading twentieth-century philosopher of world history, he enhances our self-knowledge and self-consciousness as individuals and societies awash on the tidal flows of historical time.

Spengler, of the thinkers of the twentieth century, stands out as a historical pessimist. Indeed, the historian E. H. Carr went so far as to call him "the creator of the modern thesis of historical decline."[1] Moreover, retrospectively contemplating the twentieth century, the historical vision of this "pessimist extraordinary" appears to be largely confirmed by the horrors of economic depression, world wars, totalitarianism, and genocide; the emerging global environmental crisis; the decline of Western art; social fragmentation; and the crisis of the social welfare state.[2] Furthermore, American democracy, the bulwark of the West since 1941, not only seems to be incapable in recent years of providing effective leadership but is afflicted by political apathy, plutocratic tendencies, and fractious ethnic and interest-group politics. Anxiety mounts about the precariousness of modern civilization amid a disorderly post–Cold War world.

In this study I will investigate Spengler's ideas on world history and politics and their evolution, proceeding chronologically, beginning with biographical information. I then focus on his major work, *The Decline of the West*, and turn attention to Spengler's relationship to German historicism, before considering intellectual sources of and influences on his major work, as well as the critical reception of it. Spengler has been conventionally and simplistically depicted as a virulent antidemocratic thinker, but his politics were more complex than that and markedly changed. I uncover the early period in his political thought, advancing the novel argument that he advocated the quasi-democratization of Wilhelmine Germany. In light of his zeal for imperialism, I examine his intellectual relationship to the Neo-Rankeans as well as the Pan-Germans. I then discuss Spengler's

1. E. H. Carr, "Die Geschichte wiederholt sich nicht: Oswald Spengler und Arnold Toynbee," *Die Kultur* 5, no. 92 (1956–57).
2. "Oswald Spengler, Philosopher, Dies," *New York Times*, 9 May 1936, p. 15.

first political book, *Prussianism and Socialism*, before surveying his political phase during the 1920s.

Just as Spengler's interest shifted to prehistory and the antecedents of civilizations when he philosophized about the sweep of human history, so, too, do I redirect focus away from politics and back to the philosophy of world history. I reassess the slim book *Man and Technics*, showing that his philosophy of world history underwent a metamorphosis. This interpretation diverges sharply from that presented in *Oswald Spengler: A Critical Estimate*, the standard work on Spengler in the American scholarly community by H. Stuart Hughes (H-Sp). His treatise was first published in 1952, more than a decade before Anton Mirko Koktanek published four works in German indispensable to Spengler scholars: an edited volume of letters (*B*, which also appeared in an abridged English translation), the authoritative biography (K-Sp), and two tomes of notes selected from the voluminous material in his literary estate (*Ufr* and *FdW*). The provocative ideas on world history Spengler conceived in his twilight years, which remain to this day unknown to most of the scholarly community, deserve a serious hearing in the debate about modern civilizational, historical, and political development. In his late work, he emphasized the centrality of the struggle between man and nature in world history, adumbrating a global environmental crisis. Moreover, he argued that the destruction of modern civilization would ineluctably result from its irrationality, despite its extraordinary but ultimately superficial rationality, as epitomized in Western science and technology. Discourse with Spengler's "second" philosophy of world history illuminates the apocalyptic potential of modernity.

Spengler's interest in politics reawakened with the world economic crisis in the 1930s. Thus, I shift attention from his philosophy of world history, discussing his last work on politics, world affairs, and the crisis of the West, *Years of Decision*. A widely read book and belatedly banned by Nazi censors, it was one of few and the most sensational of the regime-critical works to appear during the Third Reich. Finally, I conclude with a discussion of the significance of Spengler as a philosopher of international relations, elucidating the ramifications of his tragic vision of world history and politics for the tradition of political realism.

Spengler's works, particularly his chef d'oeuvre, exhibit a literary power and beauty best conveyed in the original German. He himself commented in the introduction to the revised edition of *The Decline of the West* on the role of his prose style in gaining entry into his thought world. "[The book] is intuitive through and through, written in a language that attempts to reproduce symbolically the objects and the relationships, instead of replacing them with rows of concepts, and it addresses itself only to readers who likewise know how to reexperience the word-sounds and images."[3]

Heeding his words, in preparing this study, I have perused the corpus of his works in the original German, including substantial sections that remain untranslated. Moreover, I have utilized my own translations of the quotations selected from his publications and from his unpublished archival material in hopes of acquainting the reader with something of the beauty and power of his literary style.

3. *UdA* I, viii.

Heraclitus, the "Dark One"

OSWALD SPENGLER WAS BORN ON MAY 29, 1880, in Blankenburg am Harz in the Harz mountains of central Germany.[1] With the decline of the Harz mines, his father, Bernhard Spengler, had given up the family profession of mining technician and joined the ranks of the civil service as a postal official. In this respectable occupation Bernhard Spengler provided his family with the comforts and advantages of a middle-class existence. After he earned a promotion, the family moved from Blankenburg to Soest in the summer of 1886.

The family was Protestant on both sides, with the exception of Oswald's grandmother from Munich, who was Catholic.[2] His artistic propensities came from his mother's side of the family. His maternal grandfather, Gustav Adolf Grantzow, was a ballet master whose wife was a ballerina. Two of Oswald's maternal aunts were actresses; the third, Adele Grantzow, an acclaimed ballerina with gala performances in France and Russia. She left a small fortune in her will to his mother. This inheritance, a substantial portion of which was later transferred to the adult Oswald, who fortunately knew how to invest his money wisely, was to play a major role in his life.

The only surviving son, Oswald had three sisters, Adele, Gertrud, and Hildegard. His autobiographical fragments, consisting of 140 notes probably written between 1913 and 1919, and the diaries of his sister Hildegard paint a bleak picture of emotional life in his family. His father was

---

1. The following biographical information is extracted primarily from the authoritative biography by Anton Koktanek, to whom this author is indebted. See K-Sp.

2. August Albers, "Oswald Spengler," *Preußische Jahrbücher* 192, no. 2 (May, 1923): 131.

strict and cold; his mother, unloving. At the summit of Oswald Spengler's life, in a conversation with Hildegard, he traced the source of his success, like the Prussian general Helmuth Moltke before him, to his hard and joyless childhood.

Two features mark the childhood world of Oswald's emotions: deep anxiety and a powerful fantasy. As he himself observed as an adult, in autobiographical fragments presumably written in the years from 1913 to 1919, "When I contemplate my life, it is one feeling which dominated everything, everything—anxiety."[3] In his adult years, he productively channeled his deep anxiety into historical and political writings, as manifested in his solicitude for Germany in the arena of great-power rivalry. His lively fantasy was the psychical wellspring of his capacity for formulating fascinating historical analogies.

Spengler suffered throughout his life from bouts of anxiety and agonizing headaches. Three migraine attacks resulted in temporary memory disturbances. In his autobiographical reflections, he confesses to suicidal moments: "I never had a month without thoughts of suicide."[4] It is tempting to dismiss Spengler's disconcerting cultural pessimism as little more than the expression of psychological idiosyncracies. Yet one should treat skeptically this seductively simple and reassuring argument. Even if one were to demonstrate that there was a plausible psychological "explanation" for his pessimism (a supremely difficult task with a deceased subject), this would by no means cast doubt upon the potential validity of certain tenets of his world view. This is not to deny that psychological factors exert a formative influence upon an intellectual's Weltanschauung. However, it is eminently possible that certain psychological factors impelled Spengler to develop a pessimistic perspective that is arguably more realistic and insightful than the perspectives of more optimistically oriented thinkers. In the final analysis, his ideas, like those of any other thinker, must be judged solely on their own merits.

As a ten-year-old, Oswald regaled his sisters with fabulous tales of an Arabian imperial palace. As a fourteen-year-old, he drew maps and composed a two-thousand-year, pseudo-historical account of a fantasy archipelagic empire, which ended in revolution and dictatorship. As a sixteen-year-old, he labored for three years on a detailed, fifty-page history of the

3. EH, 78b; these autobiographical notes are collected under the caption "Eis heauton."
4. EH, 129.

phantastical empire *Afrikasien*. Presumably, shortly after conceiving his dream of an African-Asian empire, he developed his Greater Germany (*Großdeutschland*) fantasy, which foreshadows somewhat his vision as a mature historical philosopher of the emergence of an *imperium Germanicum* through world wars.

Oswald's parents read very little. His father actually reproached him for his omnivorous reading habits, deprecating his reading activities beyond those required by his school studies as nothing more than a waste of time. The son was supposed to grow up to be a dutiful government official, not a bookworm. As a child, Oswald was teased good-naturedly by his favorite uncle Julius that someday he would produce an epoch-making work. Little did his uncle realize then the prophetic accuracy of his playful, avuncular words.

Spengler, whose major work, *The Decline of the West*, has been described by H. Stuart Hughes as being "without equal" in the field of cyclical historical writing, showed literary creativity as a youth and worked on literary projects sporadically in the course of his life.[5] He conceived a drama entitled *Tiberius*, which he never completed, though he did not abandon the idea of someday finishing it. He never published his collection of poems. In his early twenties he worked on a series of Prussian dramas, *Friedrich Wilhelm I*, *Friedrich II*, and *Bismarck*. Thereafter, he presumably turned his attention to a cycle of North German tragedies. Anton Mirko Koktanek speculates that he burned many of his early literary efforts in 1911 and not only them but, according to Spengler's sister Hildegard, "numerous excerpts and sketches for his 'metaphysical, epoch-making' book" as well. She reports that her brother consigned the bulk of his early manuscripts to the flames with the explanation that he was happy he had never published any of the literary efforts of his youth. Later in his life, he invested considerable effort in an uncompleted dramatic composition on Jesus. The fateful encounter between Jesus and Pontius Pilate has been described as "the centerpiece" of the second volume of *The Decline of the West*. At the age of seventeen, he brought to completion the only drama he ever finished, *Montezuma*. Spengler managed to complete only two other literary products. One was a short story set during the Russo-Japanese War, *Der Sieger* (*The Victor*). The other was the libretto to the opera *Dianas Hochzeit* (*Diana's Wedding*), composed by Paul Strüver. Not surprising, this handful of finished literary efforts and several aborted ones yield insight into

5. H-Sp, 162.

Spengler's mind. Passages from the dramatic sketch *Maelstrom*, penned when he was sixteen, attest to the deep pessimism of the young thinker. As Koktanek appropriately observes, the piece strikingly demonstrates how Spengler's pessimistic Weltanschauung was internally generated and not simply derived from exposure to the works of Arthur Schopenhauer, Richard Wagner, and Friedrich Nietzsche.[6]

In the fall of 1891 the family moved from Soest to Halle an der Salle. There Spengler attended the *Latina* (a high school, or gymnasium, emphasizing the study of the classics) of the Franckean Foundation (*Franckeschen Stiftungen*). As a pupil at the gymnasium, he preferred geography and history. He venerated throughout his life his history teacher, Friedrich Neubauer, who had authored a famous history textbook.[7] He learned Latin and ancient Greek; the gymnasiast traditionally had to endure nine demanding years of the classical languages. Training in these languages provided a solid linguistical foundation for Spengler's life-long interest in classical antiquity. He also studied modern languages in school. Later, as a private scholar, he was to peruse essential literature on prehistory in French and English. Spengler picked Italian up after his school years on his frequent travels in the south and spoke it with acceptable fluency. As a private scholar, though, he exchanged ideas exclusively with German and German-speaking scholars and political figures, raising the question of why he never acquired the capability to correspond and converse with foreign scholars in their native languages. Koktanek's explanation is that the level of instruction in modern languages at the *Latina* was mediocre.

Politics were never discussed in Spengler's home. This passion he developed on his own. From the age of sixteen he immersed himself in cultural edification. At seventeen he began sneaking into the university library at Halle to indulge his multifarious reading interests. As a gymnasiast he studied all the works of Johann Wolfgang von Goethe, with the exception of those dealing with subjects from the natural sciences. The first part of *Faust* he knew by heart. Spengler familiarized himself with the ideas of his two famous predecessors in German cultural pessimism, studying zealously the works of Nietzsche and reading Schopenhauer's main work, *The World as Will and Idea*. Burying himself in *Thus Spake Zarathustra* was a particularly heady experience. He began to worship Wagner's music in his

6. K-Sp, 99–100, 67, 236, 44.

7. Armin Baltzer, *Philosoph oder Prophet?: Oswald Spenglers Vermächtnis und Voraussagen* (Neheim-Hüsten: E. Nicklaus, 1962), 265.

late teens, especially *Tristan*. Indeed, Spengler claimed years later, after being enchanted by a performance of this opera at Bayreuth, that his motive for learning to play the piano was so that he could play excerpts from Wagner. Spengler frequently attended various stage and operatic performances. His tastes in modern literature ranged widely. He read, for example, works by William Shakespeare, Gerhart Hauptmann, Henrik Ibsen, Maksim Gorky, Honoré de Balzac, Theodor Fontane, E. T. A. Hoffmann, Heinrich von Kleist, Friedrich Hebbel, Heinrich Heine, Friedrich Hölderlin, Lev Tolstoi, Ivan Turgenev, Fyodor Dostoevsky, August Strindberg, Émile Zola, Stendhal, and Gustave Flaubert.

The award of Spengler's gymnasial diploma in 1899 was capped by a *Kanonenrausch*, the only indulgence in excessive drinking Koktanek reports. Although the completion of a humanistic education signified membership in "the tiny educational elite" of Imperial Germany, the recent graduate still had to wrestle with the dreaded decision of choosing a future career goal.[8] He decided to study mathematics and the natural sciences at the University of Halle in order to prepare himself to be a gymnasial teacher. His keen interest in the thought of Charles Darwin and his German popularizer, Ernst Haeckel, played a key role in the decision. Despite concentrating on mathematics and science, Spengler's loosely structured education turned out to include as well courses in philosophy, politics, economics, and history. During his university studies, he vacillated between pursuing creative writing and science. His life-long fascination with Russian history, culture, and politics was stimulated by contacts with Russian students at Halle. He learned Russian autodidactically, enabling him to read his revered Dostoevsky in the original with the aid of a dictionary. Upon the death of Spengler's father in 1901, the family moved back to their original home in Blankenburg, which his mother had never wanted to leave in the first place. The young man decided to transfer to the University of Munich, attendance at more than one university being customary in Wilhelmine Germany, in order to escape his joyless existence at home. He fell in love with the vibrant metropolis of Munich, a cultural mecca and the gateway to the south. He matriculated at the University of Berlin in 1902 for only one semester. Berlin, which later in his historical philosophy symbolized the emergent megalopolitan world civilization, he found uncongenial.

8. Stefan Breuer, *Anatomie der Konservativen Revolution* (Darmstadt: Wissenschaftliche Buchgesellschaft, 1993), 28.

Spengler returned to the University of Halle to research and write his doctoral dissertation on the pre-Socratic philosopher Heraclitus. After his thesis was accepted, he failed his first attempt at the oral exam in the fall of 1903. The peripatetic student hadn't known any of his examiners, he had selected his dissertation topic without first checking with his professors, and, in the opinion of his examination committee, he insufficiently quoted specialized literature. In April, 1904, he passed the oral exam (*rigorosum*) on his second try, thereby fulfilling the requirements for his Ph.D. degree. Earlier that same year, he had taken his *Staatsexamen*, a series of exams that were a prerequisite for admittance into the teaching profession. Spengler passed them in the fields of zoology, botany, and philosophical propaedeutics in physics and chemistry (first level) and mineralogy and mathematics (second level). His required specialized study for his pedagogical career, "The Development of the Organ of Sight by the Main Levels of the Animal Kingdom" ("Die Entwicklung des Sehorgans bei den Hauptstufen des Tierreiches"), was unfortunately lost in later years.

Shortly after earning his doctoral degree, Spengler traveled to Lüneburg to assume his duties as a trainee teacher. After a quick look at the school there, he suffered a nervous breakdown. The notion of being a "mere" teacher was dismaying to the extremely ambitious intellectual. Bowing to reality and an indignant mother, Spengler filled in temporarily as a substitute teacher and soon accepted and carried out his next teaching assignment in Saarbrücken. Being near the French border, he made a number of trips to France, and his experiences in Paris he recalled throughout his life with great pleasure. During his first visit there, Spengler suddenly envisioned Berlin as the world city of an emergent phase of civilization and Paris, seen from the perspective of Versailles, as a declining, urban focal point of mature culture. The Baroque, personified in France of the *grand siècle*, represented for him the zenith of Western culture. Visits to the magnificent Gothic churches of France stimulated his ruminations that the Gothic era, not classical antiquity, constituted the true wellspring of West European culture.

The training year at Saarbrücken was followed by a probational period in Düsseldorf in 1906 and 1907. In June, 1907, Spengler passed a special examination certifying him for mathematics instruction at the upper class-level. That same summer he journeyed to Italy, a country that captivated him and became a frequent travel destination throughout his life. Although his heart condition never prevented him from indulging in one of his favorite pastimes, hiking, it sufficed to have him declared medically unfit for military service in December, 1907. Spengler was offered and accepted a position at a gymnasium in Hamburg in the winter of 1907. After being promoted in the spring of 1908, he transferred to a second gymnasium in Hamburg, where he taught the natural sciences and mathematics, as well as German and history, an unusually broad course offering. The ambitious young man never liked his profession, viewing it as beneath his desired level of status. However, Spengler sensibly planned to endure it, as it provided him with a reasonably good income and ample free time for private study and extensive traveling.

The illness and death of Spengler's mother in 1910, almost a decade after the death of his father, marked a turning point in his life. Already during her sickness, Spengler had requested and was granted a leave of absence; he traveled straight to Italy. It became clear to him that he would consider giving up the steady income and financial security of the teaching profession for a riskier, more fulfilling life. In March, 1911, he began an unpaid vacation in Munich and quickly made a major decision, boldly quitting his comfortable position as a teacher in order to embark on an uncertain future as a writer in this south-German metropole. Although the inheritance from his mother enabled him to abandon his former livelihood, he had to accept a markedly lower standard of living. Spengler's intention on arriving in Munich was not to produce a work of historical philosophy, as this idea had not yet germinated in his mind, but to pursue his literary ambitions. He aspired to write a major novel, first conceived during his student days in Munich, as well as sketches for a collection of novelettes. In addition, he entertained plans for a tragedy. Furthermore, his sister recorded in her diary that her brother was engaged as an art critic by two Munich newspapers. The charming city was to be Spengler's domicile for the remainder of his life.

Yet Spengler's literary activities in Munich ultimately climaxed in a break with his youthful dream. He came to the controversial conclusion that great poetry and drama had reached their end. The novel, he meditated, still had definite possibilities. Indeed, Spengler believed that a genius of his generation could write one that would "exhaust *the sum total* of the life of [his] *epoch*," as Goethe had done in *Wilhelm Meister* and Stendhal in *The Red and the Black*. The aspiring novelist dismissed the verbal pyrotechnics of Thomas Mann as a model worthy of emulation. Spengler yearned to see instead, as he put it during the war years, a "new German master prose," a "Hindenburg style," rise to command center stage in German letters. Such a prose would be "concise, lucid, Roman, above all *natural.*"⁹ He found himself unable to write a novel that would express his vision of the demise of the "old," nineteenth-century Germany of culture and the rise to hegemony of the "new," postcultural, imperial Germany of the twentieth century. It would be a century dominated not by cultural pursuits but by practical affairs: global imperialism, international economic competition, and technological advance. Plans for such a novel abandoned, he employed his literary talents instead in the composition of his speculative historical work.

Spengler was concerned about the growing diplomatic isolation of Imperial Germany following Otto von Bismarck's resignation in 1890 and the series of international crises that cast their dark shadow over Europe before the outbreak of World War I in 1914. The Agadir crisis of 1911, which suddenly raised the specter of a general European war and strikingly revealed the danger of Germany's "encirclement" by the Entente, crystallized Spengler's nascent vision of the future international political transformation of the West. In a stroke, his precious literary plans became of secondary importance. He was seized by the desire to write a short book dealing with the contemporary position of Germany in world politics, with the provisional title of *Liberal and Conservative*. It would apparently have focused upon the approaching war between England and Germany, portraying it as a struggle between antagonistic political cultures and foci of economic organizational and civilizational energy (England typified by liberalism, Germany by conservatism), and would have resembled *Prussianism and Socialism* (published in 1919).¹⁰ Yet this project acquired extremely broad, truly world-historical dimensions the year after the Agadir crisis.¹¹ The metamorphosis of the originally much more limited project into an ambitious, cross-cultural analysis of world history is symbolized by Spengler's coming into contact with the multivolume classic by Otto Seeck. After Spengler serendipitously saw Seeck's *Geschichte des Untergangs der Antike Welt* (*The History of the Decline of the Ancient World*) displayed in a Munich shop window in 1912, he thereupon conceived the title of his own budding work as a conscious parallel.¹²

---

9. Spengler to Hans Klöres, 30 January 1915, *B*, 35; Spengler to Klöres, 20 February 1917, *B*, 68; Spengler to Klöres, 14 July 1915, *B*, 45. In this and all subsequent quotations, unless otherwise indicated, the emphases belong to the author of the quotation.

10. See K-Sp, 233 ff.

11. See *UdA* I, 62 ff.

12. Interview of Oswald Spengler by Dr. Fritz Kopke, *Leipziger Neueste Nachrichten*, 22 October 1922, Spengler Archive, Bavarian State Library, Munich.

Composing the first volume of *The Decline of the West* was an exhilarating act of intellectual self-liberation. As the book took shape, Spengler anticipated the tremendous success it would have. He declared boldly in a letter in July, 1916, "it will, to be sure, arrive upon the scene of contemporary literature like an avalanche in a shallow pond."[13]

The war did not stimulate the production of the work. Instead, it complicated its composition by imposing privations on its author while delaying its publication. Spengler, a bit of a bon vivant, savored excellent food and wine, as well as fine cigars. During the war years he not only was compelled to eat unappetizing food but suffered from lack of nourishment. Many nights he was forced to work by candlelight because of the shortage of gas. The lack of heating fuel actually drove Spengler to resort to sitting on a chair on top of his desk so that he would be closer to the warmer air near the ceiling upon his makeshift platform.

The deprivation of the war years was overshadowed by personal tragedy. His sister Adele committed suicide in 1917 at the age of thirty-five. The following year the husband of his sister Hildegard, Fritz Kornhardt, fell on the field of battle. Spengler persevered under adverse circumstances. He finally wound up the manuscript of the first volume of *The Decline of the West* in early 1917. A long search for a willing publisher and the shortage of paper caused by the war delayed the book appearing in print by a year and a half.[14] Finally, after the well-known publishing houses in Germany had rejected the manuscript of the unproven author, the publishing house of Braumüller in Vienna accepted it and published it in April, 1918.[15] It is most fitting that *The Decline of the West* was first published in fin-de-siècle Vienna. As Karl Kraus, Vienna's preeminent satirist of the turn of the century, remarked, for many members of the artistic and literary community of the decaying metropole, the city was "the testing ground for the end of the world."[16]

The spectacular success of the first volume of *The Decline of the West* dramatically improved the position of its financially strapped author. Moreover, the Nietzsche Foundation awarded the Lassen Prize in November, 1919, to Spengler and two other co-winners, his former teacher, the philosopher Hans Vaihinger, and the philosopher and writer Hermann

13. Spengler to Klöres, 12 July 1916, *B*, 54.

14. Baltzer, *Philosoph oder Prophet?*, 267.

15. Albers, "Oswald Spengler," 132.

16. Quoted in Ian Buruma, "Anxiety in $^3/_4$ Time," *New York Times Magazine*, 8 November 1992, p. 54.

Graf Keyserling. The fame showered upon Spengler's controversial work gained him entry into important aristocratic, scholarly, and political circles in German society. He put the finishing touches to the second volume of his chef d'oeuvre in 1922. Spengler never married; his sister Hildegard ran his household from 1925 onward. He spent the rest of his life immersed in scholarly pursuits in Munich after failing to receive an important political appointment, despite a sustained effort from 1919 to 1924. In June, 1933, he declined an offer by Saxony's cultural minister of the prestigious Lamprecht Chair in Cultural and Universal History at the University of Leipzig. Shortly thereafter, the University of Marburg tried unsuccessfully to recruit him for their faculty. On the night between May 7 and 8, 1936, Spengler died unexpectedly of a heart attack.

Spengler once claimed that his "great book, *The Decline of the West*, was already emotionally conceived at age twenty."[17] Indeed, in his doctoral dissertation on Heraclitus, completed at the age of twenty-four, one can already recognize important features of his philosophy of world history. His first scholarly publication is of interest in this study, not so much for what we might learn about the philosophy of this pre-Socratic thinker, but rather for what we can see about Spengler's own intellectual evolution. Heraclitus influenced other German thinkers besides Spengler, including his forerunner, Nietzsche, as well as Hegel and the socialist Ferdinand Lassalle.[18]

In his dissertation on the enigmatic and aristocratic Greek philosopher of Ephesus, Spengler voices his preference for the use of insightful, imaginative powers in philosophy as opposed to cold, analytical rigor. He characterizes Heraclitus' intellectual approach as psychological, calling his philosophical system a "psychology of world-happening." This is indeed an appropriate description of the philosophy of world history Spengler himself was to elaborate in *The Decline of the West*. His contrastive study of cultures constitutes a psychological investigation of their disparate identities. The same expression that he used to epitomize the thought of Heraclitus can be most aptly applied to his own, namely, the "style of an imperator."[19] In "Heraklit" Spengler already shows his interest in what he understood to be the discontinuity in the intellectual tradition of Graeco-Roman and West European culture, the germinal source of his contrastive

17. EH, 113.
18. K-Sp, 70.
19. H, 10, 12.

study of these two high cultures in *The Decline of the West*. Moreover, he adumbrates in his dissertation the idea that high-cultural forms bear the imprint of their mother landscape.[20]

What Spengler later attempted as a philosopher of history is analogous to what he claimed Heraclitus had accomplished in Greek philosophy. In his estimation, the pre-Socratic thinker had painted with masterful strokes a picture of the universe in which cosmic laws permeate the constantly changing phenomenal world. There are striking similarities between his exaggerated depiction of Heraclitus' conception of the universe and Spengler's own maturing theory of how cultures cyclically develop. The determinism of his philosophy of history is foreshadowed in this description of Heraclitus' philosophy. "All the changes that happen in the cosmos are subjected to the same rules. We find the effects of the same one and eternal law in invisible becoming, in visible Nature, in life, in culture."[21]

Spengler never succeeded, like all other philosophers of history, in resolving the mysterious, omnipresent tension between freedom and necessity in history. Compared to other major philosophers of history in the Western tradition, like Herder, Hegel, Comte, Marx, and Toynbee, there is a tendency toward fatalism in his historical thought. Spengler's conviction of the tragic primacy of necessity in history is foreshadowed by his affirmation of the "powerful fatalism" inherent in Heraclitus' philosophy.[22]

The essence of the historical vision in *The Decline of the West* is that world history forms a magnificent cosmic spectacle, a grand harmony of perpetual struggle, of becoming and degeneration. Spengler previews this vision in his doctoral thesis. He regards as the great achievement of Heraclitus his formulation of "the idea of an eternal and never-ending struggle, which forms the essence of life in the cosmos, in which a master law governs and upholds a harmonious, elegant proportionality."[23] Not only are certain key ideas of *The Decline of the West* prefigured in his dissertation, but Spengler's conservatism is provided a forum as well. He voices his admiration for Heraclitus' aristocratic political orientation. Moreover, Spengler's critical attitude toward democracy and Nietzschean disdain for the masses are echoed in Heraclitus' fragmentary writings.[24]

20. H, 4, 10.
21. H, 45.
22. H, 45.
23. H, 46–47.
24. H, 6, 7.

In "Heraklit," which inaugurated his scholarly career, Spengler takes a big step forward in the development of his philosophy of world history, which is to be given mature expression later in *The Decline of the West.* More than is the case with most intellectuals, despite the transformation of his historical philosophy during the final decade or so of his life, Spengler as a young man emerges already with the groundwork of his philosophy firmly established—a philosophy to which we now turn our attention.

2

The Decline of the West

SPENGLER'S MONUMENTAL WORK, *THE Decline of the West*, is one of the most profound investigations of the nature, evolution, and future of Western civilization in intellectual history. He daringly attempted to illumine the tragic process by which the West will purportedly pass away. His philosophy of world history forms the foundation upon which he constructed the superstructure of his analysis of politics and world affairs, basic dimensions of his thought requiring our attention.

The Decline of the West provoked a storm of controversy, starting with the electrifying title. Referred to as "the most popular" one of the twentieth century, it has long since earned a place in the modern historical and political lexicon.[1] Some would argue that the title captures merely a transitory mood; others, the spirit of the twentieth century and beyond.

Spengler orchestrates a symphony of world history with magisterial, Wagnerian effect and Nietzschean, neologistical creativity. His major work is important in intellectual history because of six achievements. First, it made a seminal contribution to the liberation of modern historical thought from the limitations of its Eurocentricity. Well before Arnold Toynbee, Spengler expanded the scope of historical inquiry beyond Europe and classical antiquity to comprehend non-Western cultures, thereby contributing to the establishment in the twentieth century of the cosmopolitan orientation informing historical study both as a whole and in its specialties. Thus, Joseph Vogt paid this glowing tribute to Spengler: "Incontestable remains [his] service, to have made the breakthrough to a his-

---

1. Ludwig Marcuse, "Kultur-Pessimismus," in *Untergang oder Übergang*, 1. Internationaler Kulturkritikerkongreß in Munich, 1958 (Munich: Werk-Verlag Dr. Edmund Banaschewski, 1959), 113.

torical world that spans the planet, to a historical universe." He helped
spark the ongoing debate in contemporary historiography as to whether
progressive modernization or a fundamental equality in the cultural significance of diverse civilizations is a central theme of world history. Second, Spengler, perhaps more than any other intellectual in the early
twentieth century, helped shatter the illusory optimism and idealization of
the idea of progress so central to the Zeitgeist of the nineteenth century.
As Paul Costello observed, of all the major world-historical thinkers of the
twentieth century, Spengler "expressed most fully" in *The Decline of the
West* "the crisis in confidence in the meaning and direction of world history."[2] What is remarkable is that, in all likelihood, Spengler had forecast
and already, for the most part, analyzed the decline of the West before the
guns of August jarred Europe out of its complacency.

Third, Spengler masterfully exploited the possibilities of the cyclical
model for ordering the phenomena of history. This paradigm has been a
familiar one since Plato. As Karl Metz commented, "the cyclical theory of
history found in the twentieth century in Oswald Spengler its most influential representative."[3] Fourth, *The Decline of the West* broke new ground
in the comparative analysis of the crisis of the modern West and Roman
civilization. As H. Stuart Hughes noted, "At its center was the parallel—
frequently hinted at before but never developed in so great detail—
between our own time and the later centuries of the ancient world."[4] Here
Spengler followed in the footsteps of the obscure historical pessimist Ernst
von Lasaulx, who had left his mark on Jacob Burckhardt's *Reflections on
History.*[5]

Fifth, Spengler helped to blaze the trail for innovative social science research on civilizations. As Neil McInnes commented, *The Decline of the
West* "led directly to a new would-be science, the comparative sociology
of civilizations." Sixth, Spengler heightened awareness among social scientists of the interconnections between the various phenomena of a culture.

2. Joseph Vogt, *Wege zum historischen Universum: Von Ranke bis Toynbee* (Stuttgart: Kohlhammer, 1961), 73; Paul Costello, *World Historians and Their Goals:
Twentieth-Century Answers to Modernism* (DeKalb: Northern Illinois Univ. Press,
1993), 215.

3. Karl H. Metz, "Faust und Chronos: Das Problem der Technik in der Zivilisationstheorie Oswald Spenglers," *Archiv für Kulturgeschichte* 75, no. 1 (1993): 153.

4. H-Sp, 7.

5. See Hans Joachim Schoeps, *Vorläufer Spenglers: Studien zum Geschichtspessimis-
mus im 19. Jahrhundert* (Leiden: E. J. Brill, 1953).

As Felipe Fernández-Armesto remarked, "he anticipated one of the most brilliant trends in modern historical scholarship by wresting alarming and unsuspected connections between different aspects of a culture: its science and its politics, its social structure and its art, its music and its religion."[6] Finally, an ambiguous legacy of *The Decline of the West* is the contribution it made to the contemporary intellectual currents of multiculturalism and postmodernist relativism.

Whereas Edward Gibbon had been stimulated to begin his masterpiece by a visit to the Roman Forum, and Toynbee was inspired by an excursion to the ruins of Knossos, Spengler was galvanized into setting to work on his tome by a development in international affairs, the Agadir crisis of 1911. The following is a brief account of what happened. In response to the French dispatch of troops in April, 1911, to the capital of Morocco, the German government, in order to protect German interests in West Morocco, sent a gunboat, which anchored off Agadir on July 1. This provocative act precipitated an international crisis. In an age of European imperialist rivalries, Germany's action alarmed Britain, which resolutely backed its French ally, instructing the chief-of-staff, General Henry Hughes Wilson, to travel to Paris. The British cabinet authorized him to make arrangements for the dispatch of a British expeditionary army to France in the event war broke out on the Continent. Moreover, the prime minister, David Lloyd George, delivered a stern speech on July 21, signaling a readiness to go to war instead of caving in to the Germans to obtain peace at any price. The crisis was finally defused by the German government ignominiously backing down in exchange for minor concessions, but the Agadir crisis had raised the specter of a general European war. From the perspective of Berlin, the diplomatic debacle had thrown into dramatic relief the deterioration of Germany's diplomatic position since Bismarck's resignation. A general war in Europe would quite possibly find Germany encircled by a superior coalition. Germany, along with its comparatively weak allies of Austria-Hungary and Italy in the Triple Alliance, would have to square off against the imposing Triple Entente of Russia, France, and Britain. Although the great powers managed to avoid the outbreak of a general conflict in Europe in the tense summer of 1911, their success was short-lived. The Agadir, or Second Moroccan, crisis proved to be one of

6. Neil McInnes, "The Great Doomsayer: Oswald Spengler Reconsidered," *National Interest*, no. 48 (Summer, 1997): 65; Felipe Fernández-Armesto, *Millennium: A History of the Last Thousand Years* (New York: Scribner, 1995), 490–91.

several crises in European affairs, including the First Moroccan crisis of 1905–1906, the Bosnian crisis of 1908–1909, and the Balkan wars of 1912–1913, comprising the long fuse that finally exploded in August, 1914, in the Great War. The Agadir crisis, along with the ongoing German fleet-building program, solidified the Anglo-French entente into a military alliance and imparted momentum to the ominous arms race among the European powers. As one scholar observed, "it is difficult to overestimate the importance of Agadir in the chain of events leading up to July 1914."[7]

That a diplomatic crisis acted as a catalyst on Spengler's mind underscores the deep concern with power politics that informed his reflections on world history. Yet he suppressed the anxieties aroused in him by Agadir and by the ensuing crises that triggered World War I. He accepted without reservation the notion of the impending war as a necessary and giant step on the path to German global hegemony. Spengler styled his major work as a philosophical contribution to its attainment. Thus, he penned the curious concluding lines to the preface of the first edition. He expressed the hope that his "book would not stand completely unworthy alongside the military achievements of Germany."[8]

The Decline of the West, despite its philosophical profundity, recondite aesthetic preoccupations, and historical erudition, was envisioned by its author not only as a pathbreaking work of historical philosophy in its own right. Spengler also regarded it as a kind of unconventional textbook on the philosophy of statecraft. He hoped to generate enthusiasm among the German educated public for neoconservatism and imperialism. He sought to educate it in the vital art of statecraft in an age of global wars culminating in economic hegemony. Particularly the second volume, subtitled "World-Historical Perspectives," was intended to respond to the need of a foreign policy elite to cultivate an appreciation of the art of statecraft rooted in a universal historical philosophy and attuned to the imperialistic Zeitgeist. Imperialism and the achievement of a "suitable" position for the Second Reich in world politics had become a top priority of Max Weber and fellow German bourgeois intellectuals since Bismarck's dismissal in 1890. Bismarck's retirement signaled the abandonment by his successors of his cautious and "saturated" Continental policy in favor of

7. L. C. F. Turner, *Origins of the First World War* (New York: W. W. Norton, 1970), 25, and esp. 19; Gordon A. Craig, *Germany, 1866–1945* (New York: Oxford Univ. Press, 1978), 329.

8. *UdA* I, x.

an assertive and risky German *Weltpolitik*. As Spengler formulated it in the introduction, "[The second volume of *The Decline of the West*] proceeds from the *facts of real life* and attempts to obtain the quintessence of historical experience from the historical praxis of advanced humanity, on the basis of which we can take the shaping of our future into our own hands."[9]

Within the limits of this book, it is impossible to do full justice to the splendid detail and thematic richness of the almost twelve-hundred-page *Decline of the West*. Its main arguments, as well as some of its more interesting ideas, will be our central focus. The first volume, published in September, 1918, contained already the table of contents of the second volume in a form nearly identical to that actually published in 1922. This fact justifies consideration of both volumes of the work in combination, despite the interval of time separating their completion.

The publication of the first volume in 1918 and the second one in 1922 spanned some of the blackest years in German history, ranging from the devastating defeat in World War I to the disastrous inflation of 1923. The German public was psychologically ready to give a hearing to a "prophet of doom" who claimed to be able to make comprehensible the events of this chaotic period. Shortly after its publication, *The Decline of the West* sparked immense interest in Germany; sales were astounding for such a learned work. But it was also subjected to a barrage of criticism from both German academicians and foreign intellectuals.

Spengler grounded his conception of the decline of the West in a systematic, comparative, and contrastive historical analysis of Graeco-Roman and West European-American culture. As we have seen, his reflections on the Agadir crisis suddenly crystalized his thinking about the age he lived in. With stereotypical Teutonic thoroughness, he came to believe in the following months that a deeper understanding of this crisis and subsequent events required an extraordinary intellectual effort. "At last it was perfectly clear that no fragment of history could be truly illuminated, before the secret of world history, more precisely that of the history of advanced mankind, as an organic unity from regular structure was elucidated."[10]

The Decline of the West is an unconventional, multidisciplinary, and wide-ranging work on the philosophy of world history. Its author should be regarded not as an empirical historian, not as a narrator and self-

9. *UdA* I, 67.
10. *UdA* I, 63.

effacing analyst of chronologically ordered historical events, but instead as a philosopher of world history. Indeed, the book is a complex, integrated architecture of probing essays on a variety of historical-philosophical subjects. Hughes elegantly compared it to a "theme and variations, a complex contrapuntal arrangement" that produces a "sort of lofty cosmic harmony."[11]

Spengler sought to ascertain the forces responsible for historical change, the pattern of world history, and the meaning, if any, of world history. In his correspondence with scholars after the publication of the first volume of *The Decline of the West*, he never referred to himself as a historian but instead, on occasion, called himself a philosopher. Spengler, in the German historicist tradition of antipositivism, denies the existence of historical laws.[12] Yet his bold attempt to comprehend the nature of cultural and historical dynamics and ascertain the master pattern of world history certainly approximated the quest of historical positivists, like Henry Thomas Buckle, Hippolyte Taine, and Karl Lamprecht, to formulate historical laws.

The very first lines of *The Decline of the West* underscore the futurological quality of its author's reflections on world history and politics. "In this book is ventured for the first time the attempt to forecast history. It is a question of following the still unfinished stages in the destiny of a culture, and indeed the only one, which today is in a process of fulfillment on this planet—the West European-American."[13]

The major goal of his work, which Spengler boldly styled "*the* philosophy of the future," is to fashion a "comparative morphology of world history." This morphology is grounded in the "physiognomic" way of approaching historical reality: the ability with the artist's eye and intuitive power to view comprehensively the phenomena of world history, thereby gaining deep insight into their dynamics, spirit, and symbolism. According to Spengler, his comparative morphology reveals the organic structure of world history, fathoms the spirit of its diverse cultures, and simultaneously enables one to predict the grand lines of future historical development. Pragmatically, he aspires to determine "morphologically" the West European-American position in the period from 1800 to 2000.[14] He aims

11. H-Sp, 67.
12. *UdA* I, 127.
13. *UdA* I, 3.
14. *UdA* I, 6, 67, 61, 34.

to enhance his readers' understanding of the profound problems in international politics in the twentieth century through a process of philosophical deepening.

Spengler, like Marx, sought to put his intellectual labors in the service of an ambitious political agenda. An ardent German nationalist, he styled *The Decline of the West* as an attempt to forecast the future course of history in support of a visionary, imperialistically-oriented statecraft. "I teach here *imperialism*," the aspiring *praeceptor Germaniae* intones in its introduction. Spengler champions the creation of a German world empire controlled by a "socialistic" regime purged of the idealistic internationalism and class antagonisms of Marxism. "And with that, the task is set: it is imperative to free German socialism from Marx."[15] Spengler attempts to legitimize his imperialist program for Germany by arguing, as a historical determinist, the inevitability of Western empire-building but also by hammering home the putative Social Darwinist nature of world politics. He also arouses enthusiasm for imperialism by depicting the Western civilizational experience and its expansionary urge as intoxicating.

Spengler audaciously hails his new approach of comparative morphology as the correct method for comprehending the nature and direction of historical development in the twentieth century and beyond. Yet with uncharacteristic modesty he acknowledges the imperfections of *The Decline of the West*, describing it as "the preliminary expression of a new picture of the world, loaded with all the mistakes of a first attempt . . . incomplete and certainly not without contradictions."[16]

The introduction to the first volume opens with a discussion of basic questions of historical methodology, a major concern of German historiography since Johann Gustav Droysen's influential scholarship in the mid-nineteenth century. Central to Spengler's philosophy is the intriguing thesis that reality is dualistic. History represents a temporal, mutable form of reality every bit as real and significant as the world of physical reality. Drawing the fundamental distinction between "the *world as history*" and "the *world as nature*," he maintains that understanding history requires a special epistemological apparatus. Spengler argues that Kant advanced an epistemology that, in focusing only on the physical world, essentially ignores historical phenomena. "When he speaks of the innate forms of intuition and categories of reason, he never thinks of the completely differently

15. *UdA* I, 48; *PuS*, 4.
16. *UdA* I, 67.

formed comprehension of historical impressions." Spengler maintains that causal analysis is appropriate to the study of natural phenomena but that for illumining historical phenomena one must imaginatively formulate analogies. While causal analysis and the drawing of analogies continue to this day to be time-honored methods in historiography, the former is disparaged by him as "a piece of disguised natural science." Moreover, historians, he argues, have formulated historical analogies in a fragmentary, arbitrary, and unsystematic fashion.[17] The result is very often superficial instead of insightful.

Spengler identifies the source of the methodological error in applying the "scientific" causal approach to the study of history. Time, the dimension capturing change, dominates historical happening whereas, in sharp contrast, the world of the experimental scientist is a mechanistic, manipulative sequence of events in which time has no historical quality. For Spengler, historical events are suffused with *"the logic of time"* and embody the "organic necessity *of destiny.*"[18] Thus, the historian's task is not to parody the laboratory scientist, contenting himself with fact finding and superficial arrangement of his material according to a causal analysis scheme. Instead, the historian should strive to gain insight into the "logic of time" and apprehend intuitively the deeper meaning behind historical phenomena.

Spengler finds further fault with causal analysis: It is enslaved to optimistic visions of linear, civilizational progress. "Laws of a causal nature govern according to the materialistic historical view, with the result that one was permitted to apply utilitarian ideals like enlightenment, humanity, and world peace as the goals of world history, in order to achieve them through the 'process of progress.' "[19]

The architecture of analogies in *The Decline of the West*, often compelling in their power and beauty, does arguably enrich our understanding of the nature and direction of world history. However, one must view skeptically its author's audacious claim that he has developed a comprehensive and systematic use of the historical analogy that enables him to "lay bare the organic structure of history."[20] Reading his work reminds one of the immense difficulty, if not impossibility, of compressing the extraordinarily

17. *UdA* I, 6, 9, 7, 5.
18. *UdA* I, 9.
19. *UdA* I, 197.
20. *UdA* I, 5.

complex and variegated phenomena of universal history into a neat and tidy system, irrespective of its ingenious quality.

Leading German contemporaries in the field of historical thought, including Weber, Eduard Meyer, and Friedrich Meinecke, did not develop a historical philosophy as comprehensive and systematic as Spengler's. Yet they shared his interest in the utility of historical analogies for shedding light upon developments in world politics. Statesmen and analysts of world affairs prize history as an inexhaustible quarry of ideas, maxims, and analogies. From the simpler ages of Thucydides, Niccolo Machiavelli, or Leopold von Ranke to the present era of remarkable complexity in international relations, the field of history has traditionally been regarded as the great school of statecraft. Spengler believes that one of the virtues of his book consists in his ability, through a systematic approach, to improve upon the formulation of historical comparisons and analogies. Prior to the twentieth century, the study of history in relation to world politics was not pursued in a cross-cultural and world-historical-philosophical fashion. Spengler, on the eve of the firestorm of World War I, which served as the midwife of the discipline of international relations, saw himself as creating a revolutionary new philosophy of *Realpolitik*. This philosophy, the product of a systematic theory of world history, was intended to provide both practitioners and students of statecraft with an impressive vision of the future.

Spengler's goal of fathoming the general direction of international political change has deep roots in the German tradition of power politics. Heinrich von Treitschke was the most politically influential German historian of the Bismarckian era. In an imperialistic age when interstate interaction was increasingly assuming global dimensions, he provocatively asserted that the "political future of the earth has become discernible to the foreseeing eye." Spengler's bold approach is strikingly foreshadowed in the writings of Frederick the Great, the first major figure in the German school of power politics, who believed that a gifted intellect could comprehend the complex causal interactions in political history from the remote past onward and thereby glimpse the future. Refined historical vision was to aid greatly in designing a successful foreign policy. As he formulated this extremely ambitious idea, "It is a matter of cleverness, to know everything, in order to be able to judge everything and to take preventive measures against everything." Like Spengler after him, he prized analogical thinking. "No better means exist, in order to form a correct and exact idea of the things which happen in the world, than to judge them through comparison, to select examples in history, to place them in parallel with the things happening today and to observe their relationships and similarities."[21]

Spengler's historical philosophy has considerable anticipatory power. However, his daring claim that it enables him to forecast the future course of history is untenable. Not surprising, he backs away from this position in his later works. Yet one should differentiate between his goal of trying to foresee general civilizational developments and his even more ambitious corollary aim of anticipating major developments in world politics. He acknowledges more and more in his later years how extremely difficult it is to forecast major international political developments, especially the shifting alignments of the great powers and their ability to surmount crises in their history. Throughout his works, Spengler expresses more confidence in the capacity of his philosophy to illuminate the phases in a purported, grand process of organic civilizational development and decline. Initially, he certainly overestimated the specificity with which one can, at best, dimly perceive the major historical trends bridging the past and the future. Nonetheless, he did succeed arguably in discerning some of the contours of future historical and political change.

Great statecraft is and must be forward-looking, aspiring to divine as much as humanly possible the basic lines of development of the future course of history. Thus Hans J. Morgenthau, the grand theorist of American political realism, strikes what is very much a Spenglerian chord when he argues in *Politics Among Nations* that the ideal statesman should have a creative imagination "capable of that supreme intellectual achievement which consists in detecting under the surface of present power relations the germinal developments of the future, in combining the knowledge of what is with the hunch as to what might be, and in condensing all these facts, symptoms, and unknowns into a chart of probable future trends which is not too much at variance with what actually will happen."[22]

One can distinguish between two temporal orientations in the relationship of *Realpolitik* to history. There is the retrospective approach, which seeks to extract from the past the historical deposit of accumulated wisdom

---

21. Heinrich von Treitschke, quoted in W. Bussmann, "Treitschke als Politiker," *Historische Zeitschrift* 177 (1954): 255; Friedrich der Große, quoted in Friedrich Meinecke, *Die Idee der Staatsräson in der neueren Geschichte*, vol. I of *Friedrich Meinecke Werke*, ed. Hans Herzfeld, Carl Hinrichs, and Walter Hofer (Munich: R. Oldenbourg, 1976), 338, 340.

22. Hans J. Morgenthau, *Politics Among Nations: The Struggle for Power and Peace* (New York: Knopf, 1948), 116.

for the enrichment of the art of statecraft. There is the forward-looking approach, which aspires to delineate the international political milieu and anticipate trends shaping the future.

Spengler's contribution to the philosophy of statecraft consists of his argument that politically realistic policies in the twentieth century and beyond can only be formulated in conformance with a profound sense of what is conditioned by unfolding, grand-historical trends. Furthermore, given the phenomenal complexity and dynamic quality of historical change in the twentieth century and beyond, a grasp of what is historically possible cannot be the product of a fragmented study of history and international politics, no matter how energetically conducted it may be. Such a grasp can be best derived from an imaginative and systematically crafted universal historical philosophy. For Spengler, the study of the life cycles of past civilizations enriches statecraft because it illuminates the ineluctable trends of the future. "We learn there on another course of life to know ourselves, how we are, how we must be and will be; that is the great school of our future." He singles out the historical experience of Rome as being of supreme importance. "*Romanness* . . . will always offer to us, who are dependent upon comparisons, the key to understanding our own future."[23]

The Decline of the West is the first native work of historical-philosophical pessimism to achieve fame in the German-speaking world. While the works of historical pessimism by Spengler's nineteenth-century forerunners, Vollgraff and Lasaulx, remained obscure, Burckhardt's famous correspondence with Friedrich von Preen and his historical fragments were not published until 1922 and 1929. Spengler appropriated Nietzsche's tart denial of the idea of progress: " 'Progress' is merely a modern idea, that is to say a false idea." Faith in progress dominated the intellectual landscape of the West in the eighteenth and nineteenth centuries, being diversely expressed by such historical thinkers as Kant, Condorcet, Turgot, Herder, Hegel, Ranke, Comte, Macaulay, Bancroft, Treitschke, and Marx. J. B. Bury captured the essence of this vital, but debatable tenet of much of modern historical thought: "Civilisation has moved, is moving, and will move in a desirable direction." Spengler played a revolutionary role in challenging the traditional depiction of history as a Eurocentric process of progress. He attacked the conventional historical model of eighteenth- and nineteenth-century European thinkers. In their view, ancient, medieval, and modern history comprised a developmental sequence culminating

23. *UdA* II, 57; *UdA* I, 35.

in modern West European civilization. Spengler rejects this model. He argues that it underwrote an untenable vision of human progress, restrictively delimited the field of historical inquiry, and was erroneously Eurocentric.

> *Antiquity—the Middle Ages—the modern era:* that is the unbelievably inadequate and *senseless* scheme. . . . It restricts the scope of history, but worse is that it limits its theater of action. Here the landscape of Western Europe forms the stationary pole. . . . one doesn't know why, if this is not the reason, that we, the originators of this historical picture, are right at home here—around this pole rotates in all modesty millennia of the most tremendous history and far-away mighty cultures. . . . I call this, which is familiar to the West European of today . . . the *Ptolemaic system* of history and I consider it to be the *Copernican discovery* in the field of history, that in this book there appears a system in its stead, in which antiquity and the West do not take a position favored in any way alongside India, Babylon, China, Egypt, the Arabian and Mexican culture.[24]

The Decline of the West surveys in philosophical fashion world history from the emergence of advanced civilizations around 3500 B.C. to the first two decades of the twentieth century.[25] Spengler dismisses the vast period of prehistory as unimportant to his inquiry, like Hegel before him.[26] For these two thinkers, world history dawns with the rise of full civilization in ancient times. Spengler identifies and examines eight civilizations, or, in his terminology, cultures: Western, Graeco-Roman, Indian, Babylonian, Chinese, Egyptian, Arabian, and Mexican. In his theory, the rise and decline of the great civilizations of the past form the real theater of action in world history. The three cultures whose cultural styles and history Spengler investigates in depth, West European-American, Graeco-Roman, and Arabian, are given suggestive names, Faustian, Apollonian, and Magian. Subtitling his work, "Sketch of a Morphology of World History," he treats

24. Friedrich Nietzsche, *Der Antichrist, KSA,* vol. VI, 171; J. B. Bury, *The Idea of Progress: An Inquiry into Its Growth and Origin* (New York: Dover Publications, 1932), 2; *UdA* I, 20–23.

25. Spengler places the beginning of the early civilizations of Egypt and Babylon at about 3000 B.C. Contemporary historical knowledge indicates that civilization first emerged in southern Mesopotamia, in Sumer, at approximately 3500 B.C.; Egypt follows around 3100 B.C. (*UdA* II, 46; J. M. Roberts, *The Pelican History of the World* [Harmondsworth, England: Penguin Books, 1983], 58).

26. Georg Wilhelm Friedrich Hegel, *Vorlesungen über die Philosophie der Geschichte* (Frankfurt am Main: Suhrkamp, 1970), 82; *UdA* II, 38 ff.

the remaining five cultures with either modest attention to detail or cursorily. These cultures receive merely geographical appellations: Egyptian, Babylonian, Indian, Mexican, and Chinese. Spengler belatedly offers an explanation for the uneven treatment of these eight cultures in the second volume of *The Decline of the West*; there is an absence of serious, secondary scholarly literature on much of significance in non-Western world history because of the prevailing Eurocentricity.[27]

Impressed by the striking diversity in cultural traditions that archaeological discoveries had increasingly revealed since the mid-nineteenth century, Spengler conceived of world history as being culturally pluralistic. In searching for the reason for this, he appropriated the German historicist idea of the unique national spirit of a people, which Herder had advanced and Hegel had adopted, and applied it to the new macrohistorical unit of inquiry that he helped pioneer, the culture (the conventional term today would be "complex culture" or "civilization"). Thus, Spengler rejects the nineteenth century's preoccupation not only with Eurocentric history but with national history as well.

Spengler's selection of Greek and Roman antiquity as his primary analogical model for elucidating the decline of the West takes advantage of his training as a classical scholar. Moreover, the historical record of the Roman world fortuitously provides the clearest picture of decline of all the past civilizations.[28] Since the detailed analysis of Graeco-Roman and Western civilization forms the centerpiece of *The Decline of the West*, the following discussion will focus largely on their treatment.

We have seen that the analogy is Spengler's principal historiographical tool. He employs it in order to draw not only comparisons but contrasts as well. His comparative and contrastive analogy between classical antiquity and West European-American culture, the latter of which at times seems tantamount to an antithesis of the former, enables him to illustrate the irrational character and distinctive civilizational qualities of the West.

Spengler regards the problem of time, the mystery of why significant developments in a cultural cycle occur in a specific time and place and in a particular form and duration, to be of paramount importance in the study of history.[29] History is a grand, dramatic process in which time is often laden with meaning. History is not a bewildering chaos of interacting

27. *UdA* II, 44–45.
28. *UdA* I, 143.
29. *UdA* I, 66.

causes and effects but the symbolic unfolding of a deeper metaphysical reality. Spengler champions the idea of "destiny" (*Schicksal*), which, in combination with the analogy, he counterposes to the conventional historiographical method of cause-and-effect analysis.[30] "Destiny" conveys his conviction of the supremacy of necessity over human freedom in the course of history. For Spengler, man is less the autonomous creator of his history and more the vehicle for its expression. Just as an organism develops in a largely predetermined fashion complete with an average life-span, so do cultures exhibit the architectonic and teleological qualities of nature. Each culture is preprogrammed to pass through analogous phases; the basic character of each successive epoch within each cultural cycle is "necessary and predetermined." Thus, cultures experience history as a process of ascendancy and decline metaphorically comparable to the organic cycles of life forms. They pass through the stages of "childhood, youth, manhood, and old age."[31]

Determinism is a key feature of many philosophies of history; Hegel and Marx are two prime examples. Determinism is limited in Spengler's historical cosmos to the internal history of the life cycles of each of the cultures. The various cultures express the arbitrariness of nature in the sense that their emergence in a particular place and time is accidental. There is no identifiable cause or complex of causes that stimulates their birth. Moreover, the destruction of a civilization in the course of its historical cycle may be an externally imposed or "accidental" event, as was the overrunning of the Roman Empire and the utterly senseless devastation of Aztec civilization by Hernando Cortés.

Spengler does not content himself with the debatable proposition that the rise of a given culture at a specific time and place is more or less a random event. The very fact that human history transpires within a cultural framework, the emergence of the genus of culture itself, is accidental. "It was pure chance that the history of advanced mankind fulfills itself in the form of great cultures." It is also conceivable, he speculates, that this pattern of cultural cycles in world history will disappear and be supplanted by a new form of collective human existence. "It is also uncertain, whether a sudden occurrence in the existence of the earth will introduce a totally different form."[32] Yet this last statement appears to be merely idle speculation on Spengler's part, which he didn't take seriously.

30. *UdA* I, 9.
31. *UdA* I, 192, 139, 143.
32. *UdA* I, 188; *UdA* II, 42.

Each culture, Spengler argues, has a unique style expressive of its own spirit or "soul," the cultural expressions of which are symbolic. Culture is "a totality of spiritual expression." Each one realizes new possibilities of psychological self-expression, which appear, mature, wither, and never re-appear.[33] Spengler's concept of a cultural "soul" (*Seele*) may at first seem odd. It expresses in superannuated language the controversial but plausible idea that profoundly different psychological attitudes toward reality shape the style of each culture. The distinctive ethos and style of each culture reflect its prime symbol, a suggestive concept formulated in spatial terms. For example, the Graeco-Roman prime symbol is the sensuously-present individual body. That of Faustian culture is pure infinite space.[34]

That a culture is holistic is a thesis foreshadowed in Hegel's philosophy. He maintained that each particular national spirit "expresses concretely all sides of its consciousness and aspiration, its entire reality. Its religion, its political constitution, its customs, its legal system, its morality, also its science, art and technical skills, all bear its stamp." For Spengler, just as an organism is the sum of its integrated parts, so is a culture. Cultures manifest the various aspects of their essence in totalistic fashion: "High culture is the consciousness of a single colossal organism, which makes not only the customs, myth, technics and art, but also the peoples and classes it incorporates, the bearers of one unified form language with a unified history."[35]

The Graeco-Roman cultural "soul," which Spengler baptized Apollonian in imitation of Nietzsche, is comparatively unhistorical and completely oriented toward the present. It interprets reality as being a collection of distinct, separate bodies. The classical ethos arose dramatically around 1000 B.C., inspiring the anthropomorphic, mythological religions of ancient Greece and Italy. The Apollonian spirit manifested itself in the entire range of antiquity's cultural products: the idealized nude sculpture, the society of Olympian gods and the localized cult, the politically independent polis, Euclid's geometry, Democritus' theory of indestructible and indivisible atoms, and backgroundless fresco painting. Spengler, like Burckhardt and Toynbee, recognizes in Periclean Athens the apex of classical culture.

When interest in *The Decline of the West* soared in Germany in 1920, Weber publicly debated Spengler in the Munich *Rathaus*. Whereas Marx

33. *UdA* I, 213, 360, 28.
34. *UdA* I, 235, 431.
35. Hegel, *Philosophie der Geschichte*, 87; *UdA* I, 139; *UdA* II, 41.

disparaged religion as an instrument of class rule, Weber understood the importance of the great world religions to civilizational development as having consisted in their capacity to stimulate or retard the development of rationalized economic activity. Spengler ascribes an even greater role to religion: It is crucial to the whole spirit and style of a culture. The Gothic religion, or, alternatively, Germanic-Catholic Christianity, forms the wellspring of Western culture. This religion is radically different from early Christianity. This new religious ethos came into being suddenly, experiencing a sharp ascent.[36]

Clearly, Spengler interprets iconoclastically major historical varieties of the Christian faith, in his terminology, the Magian, the Faustian, and the Russian. Since early, or Magian, Christianity, along with Judaism, Manichaeism, and Islam, is one of the many religious expressions of the Magian, or Arabian, world, Magian Christianity constitutes a virtually completely different religion from Faustian Christianity, despite the extensive borrowing of external religious forms by Gothic Christianity from early Christianity. The conceptualization of the soul, the nature of immortality, and the fundamental ethos of early and of Faustian Christianity are profoundly different in Spengler's estimation. He anticipates that Russia will probably bring to full expression a third grand form of Christian belief.

Spengler depicts Gothic Christianity as a formative experience in West European culture. However, he persuasively argues, in opposition to Nietzsche, that Christian morality never seriously constrained West European man in giving free rein to his will to power. Gothic and later variants of Christianity in the West animate the Faustian individualistic, dynamic, transformative, and expansive ethos in its secular expressions as well. For the chief preoccupation of Faustian Christianity is the "continued existence of the soul as a pure center of force for all eternity."[37]

Spengler was fascinated by what he considered to be the psychological novelty of West European culture. For him, the linear-progressive thesis, pivotal to mainstream Western historical thought since the Enlightenment, inhibited an appreciation of the singular cultural qualities of Western Europe. We apply a tepid term, one borrowed from geography to our civilization: "Western." Spengler, a votary of Goethe, christens it with an evocative name: "Faustian." Faust, in the second part of Goethe's masterpiece, is regarded by Spengler as personifying the intense civilizational en-

36. *UdA* II, 351.
37. *UdA* II, 68.

ergy pulsating throughout the nineteenth and twentieth centuries. "Thus the Faust of the first part of the tragedy, the passionate researcher in the solitude of midnight, logically gives rise to the Faust of the second part and of the new century, the type of a purely practical, farseeing, externally oriented activity."[38]

Faustian culture arose "with the birth of the Romanesque style in the tenth century on the northern plains between the Elbe and Tagus." It achieved an early perfection of form with the Gothic. West European culture is not, Spengler provocatively argues, the heir to classical antiquity, which he portrays as virtually an enfeebled civilization. Instead, the West is a strikingly new departure in cultural development. Striving beyond "all limits of optically bound sensuousness," it overflows with expansive power and transformative energies. The newly-born Faustian "soul," in sharp contrast to the spirits of all other cultures, is driven by overpowering, goal-oriented energies, by the will to power.[39] This " *Willenskultur*" is "energetic, imperativistic, and dynamic," characterized by towering historical personalities without parallel in world history. The "intellectual will to power" animates holistically the West's magnificent artistic traditions and all other major aspects of its cultural and historical experience.[40] Like Goethe's Faust longing for the vitalism of the Earth Spirit, Spengler, the reclusive scholar sheltered in his dreary study from the drama and passions of the real world, celebrates in stirring language the vitalistic forces of world history, which he envisions as appearing in their most concentrated form in the West.

Spengler interprets dualistically the sources of these character traits he attributes to the West. At one level, they express the passions of the beast of prey that is West European man, of an "irrepressible life force" that pulses through the grand sweep of Western history since around 1000 A.D. Spengler rejects the Enlightenment argument that rationality is at the heart of Western culture. Instead, it drinks from the dark waters of human irrationality. Western culture reflects the "primary emotions of an energetic human existence, the cruelty, the joy in excitement, danger, the violent act, victory, crime, the thrill of a conquerer and destroyer."[41] Yet at a second level of analysis, Spengler regards the West as a sublime aesthetic

38. *UdA* I, 449.
39. *UdA* I, 235, 255, 118.
40. *UdA* I, 393, 444, 442–43, 395.
41. *UdA* I, 443, 411.

experience. The dynamism, yearning for infinity and transcendence, expansive energy, and transformative power of the West, as manifested in the entire range of its cultural creations, are profound, aesthetic responses to the experience of the prime symbol of Western culture, pure infinite space.

Alone among the denizens of past civilizations, Westerners view the world dynamically. They strive to expropriate nature thoroughly and reshape the world totally. The ethos of dynamism holistically expresses itself in Occidental cultural and historical development: soaring Gothic cathedrals, symphonic music, perspective oil painting, double-entry bookkeeping, differential calculus, cannon, machine technology, and the boundless expansionism of the Vikings, the Spanish conquistadores, and the empire builders of Britain. Animated by the "will to spatial transcendence," Western culture is not only by far the most dynamic culture that has ever existed. It is the most complex as well, "the most abstract of all," displaying the most esoteric qualities of all the cultures that have ever existed.[42]

The question arises: What are the origins of the cultural uniqueness of the West? Culture is not the product of race. Like Hegel, Spengler assigns to geography and climate a major role in history. Culture is powerfully molded by the "*mother landscape*" upon which it arises and matures.[43] However, this argument does not solve the mystery of cultural diversity and the cultural miracle synonymous with Western Europe. Although he persuasively argues that the West represents a new departure in human culture, his idealistic historical philosophy doesn't satisfactorily explain why.

The elemental, Western psychological drive to reshape totally the external world created the idea and reality of universal history and global politics. Since the dawn of the Age of Discovery, for the first time in human history, West European culture has been transforming the entire surface of the earth into the theater of an interconnected human history.[44] Because the West has hammered together the stage upon which the drama of modern world politics is played out, Spengler views the further evolution of international relations in the twentieth century to be dependent upon the organic process of Western civilizational development. Thus, understanding major international political phenomena in the twentieth century and beyond presupposes deep insight into the origin, evolution, and future of Western civilization. "The history of the present is nothing more than that

42. *UdA* I, 292, 157, 417 ff.
43. *UdA* II, 339.
44. *UdA* II, 31.

of Faustian civilization, spread over all the continents and seas," he provocatively argues.[45]

Spengler's affirmation of cultural pluralism is not without contradiction. In his critique of Eurocentricity he argued that non-Western cultures should be appreciated as very significant objects of historical inquiry and reflection. Yet with his exaltation of the spirit of the West, he ironically simultaneously creates an impression of its superiority. He thereby calls into question the very equality in cultural and historical significance he advocates.

The Decline of the West also constitutes a thoughtful reflection on the significance of classical antiquity for European culture and history. While Spengler falls into raptures about the purportedly superior cultural qualities and extraordinary spirit of Western history, he disparages the classical world. As Arthur Moeller van den Bruck noted, "a quiet hostility towards antiquity stirs throughout" *The Decline of the West*. Its author belittles antiquity as the culture of the "small, easy, and simple."[46]

Spengler took issue with the glorification of Greek antiquity in the German intellectual tradition, in which Herder, Goethe, Johann Joachim Winckelmann, Hegel, and Nietzsche engaged in diverse fashion. Spengler regarded German classicism and the cult of the Renaissance, with their questionable veneration of the ancient world, as inhibiting the recognition of the psychological novelty of modernity and the fundamental difference between the ethos expressed in the history and culture of Western Europe and that of ancient Greece and Rome. In his estimation, the classical world had not profoundly influenced West European culture. It had only superficially affected the external features of the cultural evolution of the revolutionary new ethos immanent in Western man since around 1000 A.D. Indeed, the dynamic ethos of the later medieval and modern West is totally foreign to the comparatively static spirit of the ancient world. The "form language" of antiquity is "almost the inversion of that of the West." Even such an otherwise hostile critic as R. G. Collingwood confessed, "the unforgettable things in the book are the passages in which the author characterizes such fundamental differences as those between classical things and their modern analogues."[47]

45. *UdA* II, 393.

46. Arthur Moeller van den Bruck, "Der Untergang des Abendlandes: Für und wider Spengler," *Deutsche Rundschau* 46, no. 10 (July, 1920): 56; *UdA* I, 262.

47. *UdA* I, 39, 36, 231; R. G. Collingwood, "Oswald Spengler and the Theory of Historical Cycles," *Antiquity: A Quarterly Review of Archaeology* 1, no. 1 (March, 1927): 313.

Spengler broke with tradition when he denied that the legacy of Greece and Rome formed an indispensable part of West European culture. According to him, the conventional idea of a Western civilizational tradition encompassing antiquity and West European culture is an illusion. In situating the genesis of West European culture in medieval times, he revolts, as did Romantic German historians before him, against the scornful treatment of the cultural and historical significance of the Middle Ages by Enlightenment historical thinkers.[48] The Enlightenment view has, indeed, been progressively overcome in historical scholarship during the twentieth century.

Spengler does get carried away, at times, in his attempt to differentiate the novelty of modernity from the character of classical times. He daringly maintains that Graeco-Roman culture is virtually inferior to non-Western cultures. He claims that "the magnificence of the spiritual conception" and "the power of the rise" of Indian, Babylonian, Chinese, Egyptian, Arabian, and Mexican culture "surpassed" by "many times" that of the classical world. Moreover, he audaciously asserts that the comparatively static spirit of ancient Greece and Rome is "more alien perhaps" to the dynamic, transformative ethos of the modern West than the "Mexican gods and Indian architecture."[49]

Spengler's depreciation of classical antiquity is, admittedly, too extreme. Yet it is a welcome corrective to the adulation of Graeco-Roman civilization in much of the Western intellectual tradition. More important, it illuminates how the modern West does represent, in many ways, a distinct break with antiquity, despite the obvious elements of civilizational continuity for which Spengler's theory of history fails to account. Predictably, the depreciation of classical antiquity has implications for his views on the Renaissance. While Spengler ascribes much significance to the Middle Ages, he shows little enthusiasm for the Renaissance, which, after all, raised antiquity to the status of an ideal. He asserts that the Renaissance "did not change at all the way of thought and the life-feeling of Western Europe."[50]

Given Spengler's unflattering portrait of the Graeco-Roman world, it comes as little surprise to discover that he found few things to be truly commendable in all of antiquity. However, it is notable that two things he

48. *UdA* I, 39.
49. *UdA* I, 23, 36.
50. *UdA* I, 300.

praised concerned Roman politics. First, he echoes the analysis of Machiavelli in his *Discourses* and interweaves it with the Rankean doctrine of the primacy of foreign policy. Spengler argues that Rome alone was able in ancient times to channel domestic political tensions into constructive political competition. This virtue enabled the state to excel in its wars and diplomacy. He fervently hopes that Wilhelmine Germany can duplicate Rome's success by transcending its political divisiveness and presenting a united front in the Great War. Second, Spengler delivers a panegyric to the Roman Senate's statecraft, which had laid the foundation of the Roman Empire. He believes that modern Germany will not merely emulate its role model, Rome, in empire building but surpass it, thanks to its Faustian expansive power.

According to Spengler, modernity is a completely fresh and original orientation toward the world, without precedent or preparatory phases in the history of defunct civilizations. In contrast, critics like Weber saw the West, despite its singular capacity for furthering human progress (or, in Weberian terminology, the process of secular rationalization), as nonetheless comprising a link in a chain of civilizational development and consequently dependent upon the prior advances of classical antiquity.

Spengler conceives the grand cycles of world history dualistically. Thus, the Greek and Roman worlds are integral phases in a vast, millennial, cultural cycle: Greece is the initial stage of culture; Rome, the concluding one of civilization. Although he stresses the sharp differences in cultural style between classical antiquity and the West, he also emphasizes the profound similarities that supposedly exist between the two historical worlds. Both cultures experience a cycle of cultural ascent and decline and an end phase of decadence, while exhibiting certain parallels in intellectual, cultural, economic, and political developments.

As adumbrated above, the phase in which a high culture displays vitality and creativity is the initial period of "culture" (*Kultur*). During the subsequent period of "civilization" (*Zivilisation*), symptoms of decline first appear and then multiply and intensify.[51] Culture is internally oriented, artistically creative, organic, authentic, intuitive, and religious. Civilization is externally oriented, inartistic, rootless, artificial, rationalistic, materialistic, decadent, and irreligious. Although a distinction had earlier been drawn in German thought between *Kultur* and *Zivilisation* by Kant and Wilhelm von Humboldt, the conceptual pair first truly acquired the kind

51. *UdA* I, 41.

of meaning attributed to it by Spengler in the philosophy of Nietzsche, later being formulated in this specific diachronistic terminology by Spengler. In Anglo-Saxon social-scientific thought, this interesting distinction does not exist. On the contrary, civilization continues to be frequently associated with the notion of ongoing human progress, as opposed to megalopolitan decadence, artistic sterility, and pervasive materialism as is the case in Spengler's work.

Zivilisation, drained of authentic cultural vitality and creativity, eventually degenerates into a state of petrifaction and senescence, an idea reminiscent of Hegel's speculations about historyless eras in world history. Spengler argues that a people only has real historical significance when it experiences a symbolically meaningful existence spanning the birth of a culture and its end phase of sterility. "Man is not only historyless before the birth of a culture, but *again becomes historyless*, as soon as a civilization has worked itself out fully to its definitive form."[52] Mandarinism, Egyptianism, and Byzantinism exemplify civilizational senescence, the languishing in a protracted phase of historical meaninglessness and changelessness.

The establishment of the Pax Romana ushered in this "historyless" period of history in antiquity. "Is not with Actium and the Pax Romana, ancient history at an end? Great decisions, in which the inner meaning of an entire culture concentrates, do not happen anymore. The meaningless, the zoology begins to become dominant." Yet the collapse of the Roman Empire in the West in the face of barbarian invasions prematurely terminated the development of an extended phase of senescence, or Mandarinism.[53]

Whereas the life-span of a culture is ideally fixed at a thousand years, the stage of civilization varies in duration from centuries to millennia. The epoch bridging the periods of culture and civilization forms the "climacteric." The culture-civilization cycle, a *"fundamental phenomenon,"* provides the framework not only within which the other defunct cultures expressed their essence but also within which world history would evolve in the future.[54] At this point in his intellectual career this Cassandra did not regard the decline of the West, notwithstanding the ominous-sounding title of his main work, as being tantamount to a catastrophic end of world history. The decline of Western civilization, traumatic as it would undoubtedly be to its denizens, would be followed by the rise of a new culture.

52. *UdA* II, 58.
53. *UdA* II, 60, 130.
54. *UdA* I, 147, 143; *UdA* II, 108; *UdA* I, 140.

The apparent brilliant success of Western civilization and its planetary expansion lend some credibility to the popular idea that the grand design of history is progress. Spengler's argument against this historiographical position is essentially twofold. First, what are commonly referred to as civilizational gains are not permanently transferred from culture to culture, given the striving for cultural autonomy. Second, modern Western civilization, despite its impressive scientific and technological achievements and increasing global diffusion, is not spared the experience of decline that befell all preceding civilizations. Civilizational decline is a statement of finality. The extinguishing of the vitality of a culture, including that of the West, is not compensated for by a grand process of progress that would permit the civilizational gains that had been won to be passed on to the future generations of another culture.

The future will not bring the consolidation of an enduring, modern, cosmopolitan civilization. Instead, modernity culminates in the decline of the West and the eventual regression of modernization in the non-West. "The civilization, which today has taken hold of the entire surface of the earth, is not a third era, but a necessary stage exclusively of Western culture, which distinguishes itself from every other one only by the power of its expansion."[55]

Cultures traverse a cycle conforming to a master pattern. Each culture, though animated by its unique spirit or leitmotif, passes through comparable or "homologous" phases. These phases are also "contemporary" in that they occupy the same temporal position in their respective historical cycles. Thus, with respect to classical antiquity and West European-American culture, we find "here a constant alter ego to our own reality, step by step, from the 'Trojan war' and the Crusades, Homer and the Nibelungenlied on through the Doric and the Gothic, the Dionysian movement and the Renaissance, Polyclitus and Johann Sebastian Bach, Athens and Paris, Aristotle and Kant, Alexander and Napoleon, up to the stage of the world city and the imperialism of both cultures." Homology and "contemporaneity" provide the basis for comparing Faustian civilization with the rise and decline of Roman civilization and other former civilizations in order to anticipate the basic outlines of the future of modernity. However, the pace of historical development varies significantly from culture to culture. Spengler, a passionate lover of Western music, maintains

55. *UdA* II, 43.

that the tempo of the Hellenic and Roman world is andante, whereas that of the dynamic, Faustian West is allegro con brio.[56]

Spengler's audacious claim that he can forecast the general lines of future historical development derives not merely from his quasi-positivistic theory of analogous, structurally comparable cultural cycles. It is also based on an argument about historical consciousness. *Historical consciousness* in the trans-epochal sense of the term is a creation of the West. Modern historical consciousness, which has summoned up an incredibly complex vision of the past, probing the most remote reaches of historical experience and bringing them into an active relationship with an evanescent present, has its counterpart in the cultural products of the West, which strive to transcend the limits of time and space. The tremendous power of modern historical consciousness, whose light radiates aeons backward in shedding light upon the past, also partially reflects forward to illuminate dimly the future.

Faustian man is extraordinarily historical in outlook; dynamic and extensive historical philosophy is unique to the modern West. The Western conception of history, in contrast to that articulated by historical thinkers animated by the comparatively static spirit of antiquity, is one of tense development toward a goal. "The sequence: antiquity, Middle Ages, modern era is a *dynamic* paradigm." Moreover, only Western culture has been capable of creating the consciousness of world history. The range in the levels of power and sophistication of individuals' historical consciousnesses is far more extreme in Western civilization than in those of any other.[57] The elite phenomenon of modern historical consciousness, which emerged in the eighteenth century, has but a couple of centuries left before it expires in the turmoil of the destruction of the culture that generated it.

> Just because today the force of our Faustian existence has formed a circumference of inner experiences, like no other men and no other time could acquire, just because for us the most remote events to a constantly increasing degree acquire a meaning and a relationship, which for all others and also for the closest contemporaries of these events could not exist, is today for us much that is history, namely has become life in unison with our life, which was not the case a hundred years ago. Although Tacitus perhaps "knew" the particulars of the revolution of Tiberius Gracchus, it no longer had any real meaning for him. Such is not the case for us. . . . For the world view of a

56. *UdA* I, 149, 35, 146.
57. *UdA* I, 462, 34; *UdA* II, 32–33.

civilization, whose stage has become the entire earth, there is ultimately nothing anymore that is completely unhistorical.[58]

World history encompasses not only the life cycles of the cultures but their relations with each other as well. Spengler criticizes cause-and-effect historical analysis because it implicitly denies that cultures have the capacity to burst forth as foci of pristine and nonderivative cultural creativity and vitality. According to the mechanistic, causal approach, "everything 'follows,' nothing is original," he complains. Spengler argues that the internal urge that suffuses a culture is of primary importance. This urge impels it to express holistically its grand theme, its spiritual essence. The impression made upon an active culture by the "influences" of foreign cultures past or present is ultimately of secondary importance. Active cultures, in reacting to the stimuli of alien cultural or civilizational influences, screen out the great majority of them and reinterpret those influences they do accept, reshaping them into means for expressing their own essential personalities.[59] Thus, culture is a unified and largely autonomous phenomenon.

Authentic cultural development can only transpire in the motherland of a culture. However, once a cultural cycle shifts into the phase of cosmopolitan and extensive *Zivilisation*, it diffuses widely its civilizational artifacts, tastes, and fashions.[60] The dynamic West will diffuse them globally, but it will be a transitory spectacle. For Faustian civilization will expire someday without transforming a successor culture. Modern civilization will not be perpetuated for millennia to come by the active cultures of the future integrating Western civilizational achievements into their personalities. Instead, these cultures will strive to create their own cultural architectures, expressing their own grand themes or ideas. Moreover, if the denizens of future cultures, each with its own unique ethos, were to look back and contemplate Faustian culture, they would find it "incomprehensible."[61]

Cultures follow, grow up alongside, and touch each other. They can also overshadow or even suppress another.[62] The suppression of a culture brings up Spengler's concept of pseudomorphosis, a term from mineralogy he uses to explain two major exceptions to his controversial argument

58. *UdA* II, 56.
59. *UdA* II, 62 ff.
60. *UdA* II, 128–30.
61. *UdA* I, 234.
62. *UdA* I, 140.

of limited cultural transmission. The term denotes the historical case wherein the intrusive presence of an older, alien culture or civilization in the motherland of an emergent culture impedes its attempts to develop its own pure, high-cultural form language. He argues that the first example of this phenomenon is Arabian, or Magian, culture, a novel historical construction of his.

Magian culture occupies a central position in world history. It is "geographically and historically the middlemost of the group of high cultures, the only one, which spatially and temporally is in contact with almost all the others." The lands between the Nile and the Tigris, the Black Sea and southern Arabia form its cradle.[63] The phase of *Kultur* spans roughly from the time of Christ to 1000 A.D. Magian culture—the culture of the three great monotheistic religions, algebra, golden glimmering mosaics, the arabesque, the centrally domed building, and sharia—has as its prime symbol, spatially formulated, the world as a cavern. The outward appearance of this fledgling culture is distorted initially by Hellenistic civilization since Alexander the Great's conquests and subsequently and more enduringly by Roman civilization once victory at Pydna heralded Roman hegemony in the East. Late in its evolution, Magian culture acquires the freedom to develop its personality.[64] Islam and the sword finally liberate Magian peoples, Persians, Jews, and Christians, from the culturally stultifying pseudomorphosis. United in an Islamic empire, the grand cultural trajectory ends in the Caesarism of the Seljuk Turks.

Russian history provides a second example of atypical cultural development. Instead of being initiated by foreign invasion, this pseudomorphosis is internally imposed by an exceptional statesman. Peter the Great, the avid Westernizer, is its prime mover. With the founding of the artificial city of St. Petersburg in the early 1700s, the "primitive" Russian soul is corsetted in the foreign forms of the High Baroque, then those of the Enlightenment, and subsequently those of nineteenth-century Europe.[65] Under such conditions, the Russian prime symbol of "*the endless plain*" and Russian spirituality have not yet found "sure expression."[66]

The question arises: If indeed the West is in decline and irreversibly so,

63. *UdA* II, 228; *UdA* I, 96.
64. *UdA* II, 228; *UdA* I, 274.
65. *UdA* II, 231. Until the spectacular collapse of the Soviet Union in 1991, Marxism-Leninism represented the latest form of the Russian pseudomorphosis. See DR, 120–21.
66. *UdA* I, 258.

can one already discern its likely successor? Spengler answers affirmatively; Russia, notwithstanding the travails of its pseudomorphosis, will bring forth the ninth culture of world history. For "the next millennium belongs to the Christianity of Dostoevsky."[67] However, the Russian high culture of the future, in eventually succeeding a moribund West, would not perpetuate its project of modernity.

With Russia mired in pseudomorphosis and Chinese, Indian, and Islamic civilizations exhausted, the only active civilization in the world is the Faustian. Its dynamism and transformative power produce an unprecedented planetary expansion and interdependent world. The non-West in the twentieth century and beyond will find the essence of its older civilizations slowly fading out as the Western civilizational style diffuses globally and predominates.[68] Thus, although cultural pluralism characterizes world history, the modern era attenuates this norm. Only with the collapse of the West and the rise of the new high culture of Russia will Western civilizational hegemony end.

Spengler's emphasis on cultural pluralism has implications for his thought on the meaning of history. There is a randomness inherent in world history. "The group of high cultures is not an organic unity. That they came into existence in just this number, at these places and time, is for the human eye, an incident without deeper meaning." Cultures develop to a large degree independently of each other. Each one is to a significant extent a self-enclosed cosmos, a world of cultural and historical meaning sufficient unto itself. Taken as a whole, mankind experiences no all-embracing history. Only various peoples, each with its unique form of culture, have their own histories. "But 'mankind' has no goal, no idea, no plan." Mankind is only meaningful as "a zoological concept." Categorically rejecting the Eurocentric vision of linear progress, Spengler maintains that there is no grand meaning or narrative, no telos to the whole of world history. The locus of meaning in world history is limited to the life cycle of each culture. "*There is not any meaning in human history*, there is only a profound significance in the courses of life of the individual cultures."[69]

In reflecting on history and meaning, Spengler converses with Nietzsche. In his radical and individualistic epistemology, Nietzsche advocated perspectivism and denied the existence of eternal truths in the stream of

67. *UdA* II, 237.
68. *UdA* II, 54–55.
69. *UdA* II, 43; *UdA* I, 27; *UdA* II, 52.

historical time. Carrying the German historicist emphasis on the diversity of social and cultural forms to its extreme and inspired by Nietzsche's perspectivism, Spengler denies that there is such a thing as absolute truth and standards of cultural value. Each culture has not only its own unique form of natural science and mathematics, art, and religious and philosophical truths but also its own morality. Consequently, history reveals no transcendental meaning. Echoing Nietzsche, he asserts that there are no eternal truths. The illusion of absolute truth and cultural standards disintegrates in the Heraclitean kaleidoscope of unending, cyclical change. With logical consistency, Spengler argues that his philosophy of world history is only valid as an intellectual expression of the civilization stage of the Faustian cycle. "My philosophy itself would accordingly be an expression and reflection *only* of the Western soul, as opposed to let us say the ancient or Indian, and to be sure, *only* in the civilized stage of today, whereby its content as a world view, its practical significance and its area of applicability are delimited."[70]

History as a whole is beyond value judgments of good and evil. The cyclical course of world history should be appreciated as an amoral spectacle of civilizational rise and decline without ultimate significance but wondrous, like the world of nature. As I adumbrated in my discussion of his dissertation on Heraclitus, *The Decline of the West* is a bold, aesthetic attempt to attribute to the grand, tragic process of world history awe-inspiring splendor and harmony. The dissonances within world history, the naturalistic, tumultuous cycles of the rise and fall of civilizations, are not mere anarchy. On the contrary, *sub specie aeternitatis* this rhythm of rise and decline forms a sublime cosmic order. World history mirrors that which reigns supreme over the awesome, agonistic world of nature: the equilibrium of the perpetual, organic cycles of life and death. The tragic nature of world history is defiantly transcended by Spengler through its vitalistic glorification. He poetically expresses his magnificent Heraclitean vision of the existence of a lofty harmony of vitalistic energies in the historical universe in the following passage: "[The cyclical course of world history] is a spectacle, which is sublime in its purposelessness, without aim and majestic like the motion of the stars, the rotation of the earth, the alternation of land and sea and of ice and primaeval forests upon her. One can admire or bewail it—but it is there."[71]

---

70. Friedrich Nietzsche, *Jenseits von Gut und Böse*, KSA, vol. V, 26, and *Menschliches Allzumenschliches* (vol. I), KSA, vol. II, 25; *UdA* I, 61–62.

71. *UdA* II, 543.

Hegel's famous dictum, that "world history is not the realm of happiness" could equally be applied to the vision of world history in *The Decline of the West*. Both Hegel and Spengler espouse anti-eudaemonism, rejecting personal pleasure and happiness as an end of life. In this regard they share an outlook common to virtually the entire tradition of German historical thought from Humboldt to Meinecke.[72]

Spengler maintains that the distinctive spirit or ethos of a culture can be comprehended by intuitive inquiry into its scientific paradigm, philosophical orientation, and aesthetic forms. Aesthetic reflection on world history serves two important functions. First, it places into sharp relief the rich cultural pluralism of world history. This pluralism strongly suggests that there is no overarching line of development and purpose in human history. His aesthetic approach enables him to challenge an implicit core assumption of linear-progressive historical thought, namely, that rationality and utility and not psychological individuation typify civilizational history. For if civilizational development in world history were indeed dominated by the pursuit of rationality and utility, then one would expect to observe far more uniformity in the cultural styles of diverse civilizations. The existence of profoundly different cultural styles demonstrates, according to Spengler, the diversity, not the unity, of human psychological orientation in civilizational development. Second, aesthetic analysis enables him to paint a compelling portrait of the West as being governed, not by an ethos of rationality, but instead by a spirit of irrational, intense dynamism.

Weber in his aesthetic reflections concluded that Western culture exhibited an unrivalled aptitude for rationalization. From his perspective, "rational" harmonic music, the "rational" use of the Gothic vault, the "rational" utilization of linear and spatial perspective in painting are all outstanding examples of profound rationalization in cultural forms. Spengler, by contrast, envisions Western culture as being suffused with a dynamic will to spatial transcendence. For him, the Gothic cathedral superbly captures the spirit of a revolutionary new psychological orientation to the world. "The interior of a cathedral draws upward and into the distance with primaeval power." For Spengler, as opposed to Weber, Western music is only superficially a "rational" cultural product, for it responds to powerful, irrational longings. The finest musical compositions of the Occi-

72. Hegel, *Philosophie der Geschichte*, 42; Georg G. Iggers, *The German Conception of History: The National Tradition of Historical Thought from Herder to the Present*, rev. ed. (Middletown, Conn.: Wesleyan Univ. Press, 1983), 47–48.

dent, from Bach to Johannes Brahms and Anton Bruckner, "constantly awaken" a "primaeval feeling of *resolution*, salvation, of the dispersion of the soul in infinity, a liberation from all material heaviness."[73] For Spengler, the advanced "rational" techniques incorporated in these artistic creations are nothing more than the highly sophisticated means selected by the artist for the masterful expression of the irrepressible, dynamic will to spatial transcendence, the essential spirit of Western culture.

Aesthetic reflection stimulated Spengler to reject the conventional idea of linear-progressive historical development. For if, as he contends, the arts do not undergo a trans-epochal and trans-civilizational process of advancement, why should this take place in other areas of civilizational endeavor? Spengler rejects as a fantasy of pedants the conventional idea that there was a separate, compartmentalized history of a branch of the arts, such as painting or music, that spanned the entirety of civilizational history. They focused on the superficialities of artistic techniques and not on the essential, the spirit of a culture that formed diverse branches of art into a living whole. "There is no branch of art which runs through all the centuries and cultures." Spengler concludes that one should avoid attaching undue significance to the merely externally similar antecedents one finds in foreign cultural traditions. What was of crucial importance in the study of art forms was to comprehend the unity in psychological orientation he claims he had discovered in West European music, painting, and drama. "The arts are living unities, and that which is alive does not permit itself to be cut up in little pieces."[74]

Spengler categorizes artistic creations, not according to different branches of the arts, but according to autonomous cultures. Each culture has a distinctive ethos that inspires all its artistic disciplines. Thus, the architecture of the Gothic cathedral expresses the Faustian will to conquer the heavens; Western symphonic music conveys the Faustian urge to conjure up a dynamic, transcendent, infinite space of sound; Western perspective painting mirrors the Faustian will to infinite distance; and the Western novel responds to the Faustian imperative to explore the inner depths of the human personality while extending outward with a comprehensive world view. Moreover, given the formative power of the Faustian ethos,

73. Max Weber, preface to *Gesammelte Aufsätze zur Religionssoziologie*, 4th ed., vol. I (Tübingen: J. C. B. Mohr, 1947), 2–3; *UdA* I, 230.

74. *UdA* I, 286, 285.

the successive periods in Western art of Romanesque, Gothic, Renaissance, Baroque, and Rococo "are only stages *of one and the same* style."[75]

Like Schopenhauer before him, Spengler worships music as the supreme art form. He esteems music as the outstanding cultural expression of the Faustian ethos because of its boundless energy and its drive to transcendence. The entirety of not just Western music but Western art itself achieved its zenith with the chamber music of Arcangelo Corelli, George Frideric Handel, and Bach, with their creation of *"an infinite space of tones."*[76]

A survey of world history does not yield absolute standards of beauty. However, within each culture, the standards of beauty that true connoisseurs treasure are experienced as being absolute, not relative. Moreover, Spengler's argument that the art forms of the West are far more complex than those of classical antiquity and can only be truly appreciated by a genuine connoisseur reinforces his proud conception of Western civilization and his elitist approach to politics. Art and statecraft, indeed all areas of achievement in Western culture, are the preserve of an elite. Spengler's aesthetic panorama of a plurality of autonomously developing cultural forms served not only to undermine the idea of a Eurocentric history. The transitory sublimity of the experience of art, *i.e.*, the exhaustion of a culture's creative energy, most dramatically expressed in the archaeological ruins of former civilizations, negated the idea of the progressive nature of history.

The aesthetic interpretation of a dazzling array of cultural products played a far more significant role in Spengler's philosophy of history than is the case with other speculative systems of history, those of Hegel, Marx, or Toynbee, for example. As William Dray observed, "Spengler's theory [of history] is by far the most aesthetic of the great speculative systems."[77] There are two fundamental questions, beyond the scope of this book to attempt to answer, that one must raise with regard to his challenging aesthetic theory of cultural individuation. First, do the various cultural products of the culture in question truly express the ethos Spengler attributes to them? Second, are cultural products more a matter of incidental, arbitrary ornamentation, or are they, as he maintains, necessary expressions of a fundamental cultural ethos?

75. *UdA* I, 260.
76. *UdA* I, 297–98.
77. William Dray, "A Vision of World History: Oswald Spengler and the Life-Cycle of Cultures," in *Perspectives on History* (London: Routledge & Kegan Paul, 1980), 104.

Spengler undoubtedly loved art and had a remarkable flair for its interpretation. However, he did not justify his appreciation of art by considering it to be a means to some recognized moral good or by maintaining that art is intrinsically valuable and an end in itself. Aesthetic reflection facilitated what Spengler deemed to be properly grounded political analysis. As he argues in the introduction to *The Decline of the West*, "It became obvious that a political problem cannot be comprehended from politics by itself, and that essential characteristics, which play a role at a deep level, often manifest themselves palpably only in the field of art, often even only in the form of very remote scientific and purely philosophical ideas."[78]

Spengler's preoccupation with aesthetic matters may strike the reader as being a bit perplexing on first thought, in light of his historicist conviction of the primacy in history of the clash of the great powers and his contempt for those who studied history primarily to indulge their romantic attachment to artistic golden ages long since past. Simplifying Ranke's doctrine of the centrality of great power rivalry to modern history and criticizing Burckhardt's devotion to cultural history, Spengler virtually militarizes the march of history. "Genuine history is *not* 'cultural history' in the antipolitical sense as is popular among philosophers and doctrinaires of every emergent civilization and therefore right now is again the case. But, quite the contrary, it is race history, military history, diplomatic history, the destiny of streams of existence in the form of man and woman, tribe, people, estate, state, which defend themselves and desire to overwhelm each other in the crashing waves of great facts."[79] However, the ultimate value of aesthetic appreciation in the heyday of European imperialism perversely lay in the fact that it cleared the path to a historical philosophy devoted to power-political ends. Contemplation of the Faustian spirit of European art, the dynamism and striving for infinity, translates into enthusiasm for the irrepressible energy and expansive power of modern Western imperialism.

The transition from *Kultur* to *Zivilisation* signals the beginning of the end of authentic artistic vitality and creativity. Spengler is a seminal figure in the twentieth-century debate about the death of Western art. The *Kulturpessimist* provocatively proclaims the decline of the West's superb artistic traditions, which hitherto composed the essence of cultivated existence. Cultural maturity had been epitomized in music by Bach. In painting, the

78. *UdA* I, 62.
79. *UdA* II, 417.

artistic apex was attained by masters such as Antoine Watteau and Francisco de Goya. The exhaustion of Western culture in music follows Wagner and Brahms and the Impressionists in painting. The architectural possibilities of the West ended with the Rococo. Only the novel as an art form still has great possibilities. With the extinguishing of Western culture, an appalling end phase of degeneration ensues. "*Art becomes arts and crafts, and to be sure in its entire range, in architecture and music, in verse as in drama.*" The sublime artistic traditions perfected and sustained by the great masters give way to a commercialized artistic sterility, wherein changing fashions conjure up the pathetic illusion of vitality. The impotence of artists expresses itself in their fruitless "chase after the illusions of a further artistic development, of a personal originality, of a 'new style,' of 'undreamt-of possibilities.' "[80]

Human freedom is impotent to prevent the death of art and the vulgarization of modern culture. Thus, Spengler envisioned the decadence of the modern West to be an inevitable process, in contrast to other leading cultural pessimists like Nietzsche; his friend and colleague at Basel, Burckhardt; and Paul de Lagarde. Nietzsche, who inveighed against Schopenhauerian pessimism in his later writings and proclaimed himself to be "a *bearer of good news,*" fervently hoped to see the rejuvenation of Western civilization through commitment to tellurian values.[81] Burckhardt, despite his alarming predictions, believed in an eventual rebirth of Europe through commitment to aesthetic and ethical norms, and Lagarde, in renewal through the Christian faith. Although Spengler was inspired by Nietzsche's penetrating analysis of the decadence of European culture, he dismisses his notion that cultural regeneration was possible. Here, he is arguably more realistic than Nietzsche in contending that modern Western man has no escape from the decadence of modernity. Spengler's controversial thesis of preprogrammed, cyclical cultural change deprives man of the requisite freedom to alter profoundly his future and to initiate cultural renewal. One can perhaps retard decline yet certainly not effectuate a regeneration.

Spengler's conviction that cultural renewal was an appealing but unrealistic aspiration meant that the only "realistic" course of action remaining was to embrace the present and its narrowly defined, historically determined possibilities. One should strive to live and act in a manner conform-

---

80. *UdA* I, 254, 376.
81. Friedrich Nietzsche, *Ecce Homo*, KSA, vol. VI, 366.

ing to the Zeitgeist, he advised. And the spirit of the age was, as Nietzsche had grasped, one of spreading decadence and materialistic, megalopolitan civilization and not one of venerable aristocratic tradition and urban cultural creativity and refinement. According to Spengler, the core tasks of the twentieth century and beyond are practical and extensive ones: global imperialism, international economic competition, and science and technology.[82]

Spengler was socialized in an age when Germany rapidly emerged as a major actor in world affairs. He believed fervently in a German mission, yet one of a power-political and "civilizational" nature, not a traditionally cultural one. The Prussians, the Romans of modernity, were to bring the postcultural phase of the West European-American cultural cycle to a glorious climax. The Prussians would hammer together in world wars a global empire that would supplant the far-flung empire of the declining dominant great power, Britain. The Pax Britannica would give way to a Pax Germanica. Imperial Germany would bring Western civilization to its final forms in science and technology, economics, and imperial politics. The German expansionary drive would be the motive force in Western civilization in the twentieth century and beyond. "But while this expansion oversteps all bounds, there takes place, and to be sure in magnificent proportions, the cultivation of the inner form in three clearly identifiable stages: the detaching from the culture—pure cultivation of the civilizational form—petrification. This development has already started for us, and to be sure I see in the copestone of the tremendous edifice the real mission of the Germans as the last nation of the West."[83]

Like Nietzsche before him, Spengler was a philosophical relativist. Yet he made no secret of his own values in *The Decline of the West*. His thought deviated from Nietzsche's on the decisive question of the German citizen's proper attitude toward the state and imperialism.[84] While Spengler appealed to his countrymen to devote themselves to the core tasks of *Zivilisation*, Nietzsche remained true to higher cultural values. "*So little state as possible!*—All political and economic matters do not deserve it, that precisely the most gifted intellects are allowed to and must concern themselves with them. Such a waste of the intellect is, after all, worse than a condition of distress." A radical individualist, Nietzsche decried the state

82. *UdA* I, 545.
83. *UdA* II, 129.
84. See Politica II, 131, B3–11.

as "the coldest of all cold monsters." Proudly regarding himself as "the last antipolitical German," Nietzsche took a jaundiced view of German unity and the accompanying upsurge in national sentiment following the founding of the Second Reich in 1871—sentiment he deplored as "political and national madness."[85] Spengler, in contrast, was very much a political German, swelling with pride when contemplating the founding of and the prospects for the expansion of the Second Reich. This German nationalist sang songs of praise to power politics, imperialism, and martial virtues.

The German tradition of power politics counseled realism and acceptance of the world as it is. Thus, it placed a premium on success. Spengler's aspiration to contribute to this tradition and his historicist affirmation of history induce him to portray the process of decline from ultimately irreconcilable perspectives. There are, in effect, two Spenglers present in the cyclorama of modernity in *The Decline of the West*. One, the nostalgic agrarian conservative, is a lover of cultural refinement and traditional social mores and laments the setting of the sun upon Western culture. The other is the resolute modernist and stern *Realpolitiker*. Inspired by Nietzsche's clarion call of the will to power, Spengler, as a historical determinist, readily accepts the decline of Western *Kultur*. For it heralds the dawn, the *Morgenröte* of a titanic age dedicated to the heady tasks of *Zivilisation*. It is an era when the overflowing Faustian energies of the West are pressed into the service of its final international political form, the *imperium Germanicum*. Spengler's passion for imperialism derives its strength from an aesthetic vision. Imperialism since the onset of the industrial revolution is the decadent but intoxicating concluding form of the dynamism, expansive power, and transformative energy of the West. His cultural despair yields an *amor fati* (love of fate) of power-political optimism and global imperialism. The preoccupation with the depressing idea of decline, which the arresting title *The Decline of the West* naturally gives rise to in the reader, should not prevent him from grasping the counterbalancing, affirmative qualities of Spengler's modernist perspective. Spengler is at one and the same time a sensitive aestheticist and nostalgic agrarian conservative and a resolute modernist and glorifier of the will to power.

85. Friedrich Nietzsche, *Morgenröthe*, *KSA*, vol. III, 157, and *Also sprach Zarathustra*, *KSA*, vol. IV, 61; Nietzsche, quoted in Hasso Hofmann, "Nietzsche," in *Klassiker des Politischen Denkens: Von Locke bis Max Weber*, ed. Hans Maier, Heinz Rausch, and Horst Denzer, 5th rev. ed., vol. II (Munich: C. H. Beck, 1987), 292; Nietzsche, *Morgenröthe*, *KSA*, vol. III, 163.

Aesthetic qualities of Spengler's writing support his imperialist agenda. The stentorian voice of the dramaturge of world history, the dazzling poetry, the boundless energy, the soaring flights of imagination are all orchestrated with magisterial Wagnerian effect to summon forth an intoxicating vision of power and destiny. The reader is to be so caught up in the exhilarating spectacle produced by the Occident's expansive power that he is to volunteer eagerly his services to help in forging at the anvil of world history the monumental imperial form of the West. "When men of the coming generation, due to the influence of this book, apply themselves to technology instead of poetry, to the navy instead of painting, to politics instead of epistemology, then they do what I wish, and one cannot ask for anything better for them."[86]

Bismarck created a united Germany and changed the map of Europe; Spengler aspired to be the prophet of a German universal empire. Spengler, the would-be inspirer and adviser of German statesmen, rightly views, as did Bismarck, the question of the relationship between freedom and necessity in history to be of supreme importance to statecraft. His philosophy of world history represents an attempt to solve, for the purposes of statecraft, the profound mystery of the omnipresent tension between the roles of freedom and of necessity in history, a central concern of Western historical philosophy. In a speech in 1895 Bismarck, whom Morgenthau called "the greatest practitioner of foreign policy in modern times," underscored the supremacy of necessity over freedom in the art of statecraft in a classic metaphor: "Man cannot create and direct the stream of time, he can only travel upon it and steer with more or less experience and skill, he can suffer shipwreck and run aground and also arrive in safe harbors." Spengler sees the powerful currents of the "stream of time," the primacy of necessity in history, as rendering infeasible the schemes of political idealists to improve radically the state of global affairs, compelling their rivals, realistic statesmen, to strive to ascertain the historically possible. Politics is "the art of the possible; that is an old saying and with it is almost everything said." The statesman stands in the midst of the mighty trends of history, and he must prudently estimate their nature, power, and direction. He must ensure that his foreign policy initiatives are consonant with emerging historical reality and do not run counter to it, for modern history will culminate in a universal empire of the West. Spengler believes that with visionary statecraft and a nation politically in form and committed to empire build-

86. *UdA* I, 54.

ing, the German ship of state can reach "the shoreline of the future." Indeed, he hopes for a great statesman capable of applying "the last, most careful pressure on the helm." He hammers home in *The Decline of the West* this central theme of the ramifications of the primacy of necessity in history for statecraft, concluding the tome with this ringing appeal: "We do not have the freedom to achieve this or that, but to do the necessary or nothing. And a task that the necessity of history has set up will be accomplished with the individual or against him."[87]

Whereas Nietzsche taught that the future was to a considerable degree open, Spengler contended that it was subject to profound constraints. The latter's philosophy was future-oriented, not in order to contemplate how the historical actor might exercise his reservoir of human freedom to shape decisively the emerging yet flexible contours of the future, but in order to apply the experience of the past in discerning the lineaments of the future face of time. "Henceforth it will be everyone's duty, to inform himself of what *can* happen in the future and therefore *will* happen with the inalterable necessity of destiny, and therefore completely independent of personal ideals, hopes, and wishes."[88] Spengler gives a new twist to Nietzsche's phrase *amor fati*. Spengler called upon man to love his fate, to summon up manly fortitude and heroic sacrifice to goals set, not freely by the individual, but by the tidal movements of history.

Spengler considers grand, deterministically flowing processes in world history to be of primary importance. Despite this romantic thinker's celebration of the great man, the role played by accident, circumstance, or personality in history, while not to be underestimated, is ultimately of secondary importance. Traditionally, a historical philosophy that leaves ample room for the actions of the great man idolizes him as a creative force who leaves his personal imprint on history. Spengler, in a manner reminiscent of Hegel, glorifies the great man of history as an agent of transcendent historical forces, as an expressive medium of what one might term the "march" of the cultural cycle.

Although Spengler's philosophy of history is largely deterministic, one should not overlook a residual area of conditioned human freedom. The

---

87. From the preface to the German edition of Morgenthau's *Politics Among Nations*; Hans J. Morgenthau, *Macht und Frieden: Grundlagen einer Theorie der internationalen Politik* (Gütersloh: Bertelsmann, 1963), 10; Otto Fürst von Bismarck, *Reden*, ed. Wilhelm Schüßler, 2d ed., vol. XIII of Otto Fürst von Bismarck, *Die gesammelten Werke* (Berlin: Otto Stollberg, 1930), 558; *UdA* II, 552, 537, 553, 630.

88. *UdA* I, 52–53.

individual presides over a measure of freedom circumscribed within the cyclically determined perimeters of historical action. The specific key events, as they actually transpire in a cultural cycle, are not the products of historical determinism. Thus, under different circumstances, France, not Spain, could have founded a great colonial empire in South America. Furthermore, the French Revolution was not fated to occur in the specific form it did. Yet in some manner or other, whether in Britain or in Germany, the "idea" of the French Revolution—the idea of "the transition from *Kultur* to *Zivilisation* and the triumph of the inorganic world city over the organic land"—had to be expressed in history.[89] What reflects historical determinism is that since every culture follows a pattern, some individual, group, or society will be induced to give concrete expression to the next act in the unfolding drama of a culture.

The decline of the West, we are told, is ultimately irreversible and will transpire in a manner basically comparable to the decline of Roman civilization. However, the exact way in which the decline of the West will be actualized is subject to individual volition. It is not the product of the interplay of mechanistic historical causes and effects. Spengler gives the reader the distinct impression that the decline of the West can be protracted to an extent if its denizens summon up the necessary will power. Moreover, the Germans can, if they strive to, ensure that the future *imperium mundi* (world empire) is animated by the noble spirit of "care and duty."[90]

If this dream of post-Bismarckian Germany forging the *imperium mundi* of the West had been achieved, then Berlin would have been its Rome. The crisis of modernity is most dramatically played out in its cities. Cities are of paramount importance to Spengler's vision of world history. Indeed, since all the cultures of the past have been "urban cultures," world history should be understood primarily as the history of city-dwellers. Each culture cyclically evolves from marketplaces to modestly-sized cultural cities (*Kulturstädte*) to the dominant world city, terminating in megalopolitan decay. In classical antiquity, the cyclical sequence is represented by a marketplace of Homeric Greece, *Kulturstädte* like Periclean Athens, and megalopolitan Rome; in the West, by a marketplace of Gothic Europe, *Kulturstädte* like Renaissance Florence, and megalopolitan New

89. *UdA* I, 191, 192.
90. *UdA* II, 629.

York.[91] Spengler forecasts that either New York or Berlin will emerge as the dominant world city of the twentieth century.[92]

Spengler predicts that the megalopoles of West European-American civilization stand at the threshold of immense growth. Urbanization will intensify, towering skyscrapers will be erected, and modern traffic management will become incredibly complex. "I see—long after 2000—urban settings for ten to twenty million people, which are spread over wide landscapes, with buildings, in contrast to which the tallest of the present appear dwarfish, and concepts of traffic, which would appear to us today as insanity."[93] Moreover, he accurately foretells a relative uniformity on a global basis in the physical appearance and amusements offered by cities within the *imperium mundi*. The above passage provides an interesting example of Spengler's failure to use properly his concept of the faster tempo of Western civilizational development in his analysis. What he brilliantly foresees occurred before 2000 A.D., not long after it.

The perennial question of decadence deeply interested Spengler, as it had Polybius, Ibn Khaldun, Charles Louis Montesquieu, and Gibbon before him. In the nineteenth century, decadence became a concern of Western historical and political thinkers amid urbanization, the acceleration of the industrial revolution, and secularization. Spengler argues that societal decadence befalls every civilization. As an agrarian romantic, he idealizes the peasantry and traditional values and views modern cities falling victim more and more to general, societal degeneration. Decadence is particularly insidious because it atrophies the ability of the population of the *imperium mundi* to remain in form for successfully meeting severe challenges in the arena of world politics. The atmosphere of *panem et circenses* (bread and circuses), of mass sensate culture, pervades the *imperium mundi*. Man is socially atomized and degenerates into a restless intellectual nomad, plagued with the *taedium vitae* reminiscent of imperial Rome. Society surrenders itself to sexuality as sport, to athletics, gambling, and mysticism as megalopolitan recreational pursuits. "Cinema, expressionism, theosophy, boxing matches, nigger dances, poker, and horse races—one will find all that again in Rome." There appears as a physical counterpart to cultural impotence the decline in the birth rate, the racial suicide of the advanced

91. *UdA* II, 105–6; *UdA* I, 42–51; *UdA* II, 597 ff.
92. *UdA* I, 43.
93. *UdA* II, 119.

civilized peoples.[94] Key aspects of Spengler's vision of the decadence of the West include the exhaustion of its cultural traditions, the atrophy of the formative power of social traditions, the breakdown of the family unit, a downward-sloping birth rate, quasi-pacifism, and hedonistic self-indulgence.

Symptomatic of societal decadence is the turning away from religion, which animates the cultural phase of a cycle. In an age of civilization, atheism would continue to spread among the peoples of the West. "The extinguishing of living inner religiosity, which also gradually forms and imbues even the most insignificant feature of existence—is that which manifests itself in the historical picture of the world as the change from culture to civilization, as the *climacteric of culture*, as I earlier called it, as the turning point, where the spiritual fecundity of a kind of being is forever exhausted and construction replaces creation." The cults and exotic religious beliefs that were emerging contemporaneously with the rise of atheism—beliefs such as occultism, theosophy, Christian Science, and "hypocritical, drawing-room" Buddhism—were not to be confused with authentic religious vitality. They were merely forms of amusement and recreation in the decadent West.[95]

A period of genuine "*second religiousness*," however, would dawn within several generations in the coming *imperium mundi*. Anticipating the spectacular rise of fundamentalist Christianity since the sixties, Spengler predicts that it would be a syncretic religion of the masses, simple and undoctrinaire, characterized by profound piety and a return to the certitude of Gothic Christianity. It would be comparable in form to the religion of the Seventh Day Adventists and similar sects.[96]

The crisis of Western civilization also convulses political life. When discussing the political ideas presented in the second volume of *The Decline of the West*, one should keep in mind that it was published in 1922, after some delay. By then its author had already abandoned his early political views—views that were supportive of the quasi-democratization of Wilhelmine Germany. Chapter 6 will explore in detail this early phase in the evolution of Spengler's political thought. The dismissive and more cynical stance toward democracy in the second volume of his major work, a posi-

94. *UdA* II, 117 ff., esp. 122; *UdA* I, 456. I apologize to readers who are offended by Spengler's language in the above quotation. However, I believe it important to translate the original accurately.

95. *UdA* I, 456; *UdA* II, 380.

96. *UdA* II, 380–82.

tion he embraced after the twin traumata of Germany's defeat in World War I and the overthrow of the Hohenzollern monarchy, attests to his bitterness toward the Weimar Republic.

Polybius and Machiavelli pioneered the idea of grand political cycles. Probably under their influence, Spengler argues that every culture undergoes a cycle of analogous political developments. The Western cycle can be briefly summarized. Feudalism, with its prime estates of the aristocracy and the church, witnesses a struggle between temporal power and the papacy, as well as wars among vassals and of vassals against the sovereign. Eventually the aristocratic state takes shape. Rooted in a robust aristocracy and peasantry, the West achieves its zenith with mature political forms, the dynastic monarchies of Europe. However, the third estate of the bourgeoisie rises to prominence with the growth of large cities. Antifeudal and critical of traditional privilege, the bourgeoisie asserts natural rights and champions democratization. The church, the ally of the throne, is put on the defensive by anticlerical elements of the bourgeoisie, which worship rationalism and the critical intellect. The politics of aristocratic tradition give way to party politics. The masses (the fourth estate in Spengler's terminology), warily regarded by elements of the bourgeoisie, nonetheless furnish the impetus to subvert the hierarchically organized monarchies. The French Revolution does not represent progress; on the contrary, it forms a watershed in the decline of mature political and social forms.

The standard-bearer of nationalism, the bourgeoisie devotes itself to imperialism and the wars of empire building. It champions commercialization; money soon permeates the social and political relations of democratizing polities. In the materialistic, civilizational late-period, the captains of industry and finance acquire tremendous political weight. The highly touted freedom of the press is in reality nothing more than its cynical manipulation by plutocratic powers. The population of the West will participate less and less in elections, which from quasi-civil wars turn into comedies. The West's most capable men will increasingly divorce themselves from politics and devote themselves to other pursuits. Democracy will degenerate into interest-group and money politics with an omnipresent press shaping public opinion.[97]

Towering figures arise, from Napoleon to the coming Caesars, who unleash the terrible wars of an imperialistic era. Parliamentarian government, only truly at home in England, is not an enduring triumph of the West but

97. *UdA* II, 577, 539, 517, 538, 572 ff.

is gradually reaching its end. Finally, democracy is overcome by Caesarism. Instead of government molded by tradition and experience and led by a capable elite, the West will be subjected to make-shift governments (*Zu-fallsregimente*) headed by Caesaristic individuals. Shallow intellect and money, the masses and elements of the bourgeoisie, and demagogues and plutocrats will have brought to ruin the old order of culture. Out of this turmoil there emerge the modern Caesars and their bands of followers. They will forge at the anvil of world history the final political form of the West, a universal empire.

Spengler's analysis of modern democracy sheds light on disturbing developments in the twentieth century in the United States, the world's model democratic polity. He accurately predicts what prevails in the 1990s and beyond: the dominant roles of interest groups, money, and the media in politics and growing political apathy, if not disgust. Fortunately, the key concluding phase of Caesarism does not appear on our horizon, particularly the authoritarianism and domestic political chaos of imperial Rome generated by the recurrent coup d'etats of military strongmen. Yet America as the core of the Faustian *imperium mundi* is already a reality.

Spengler does not gloss over the egoism and ruthlessness displayed in the struggle for power and plunder among the imperial aspirants of ancient Rome. Yet for all his talk of realism and his antipathy toward political idealism, he has a very idealistic conception of the nature of the Caesarism that he predicted for his native land. The modern German Caesar should serve a higher goal, that of the common good, which can only be guaranteed through a successful foreign policy. In opposition to Marxism, Spengler argues that the German Caesar should "call into being a mighty political-economic order over and above all class interests, a system of *noble* care and duty, that keeps the whole in fine form for a decisive struggle of history."[98] Spengler is not willing to accept the fact that his thesis of the ineluctable decline of aristocratic and monarchical forms of political order and the increasing vulgarization of political life in an age of mass politics and plutocratic tendencies conflicts with his romantic vision of the possibility of the founding of an imperialistic state animated by the lofty, selfless ethos of Prussian state service.

Yet the militarism of the Caesars will have to battle with pacifism. Amid the ferocious struggle to found the universal empire at the end of a cultural cycle, pacifism spreads. The widespread affluence and unrestrained

98. *UdA* II, 629.

pleasure-seeking of universal empire further encourage pacifism. The populace of the *imperium mundi* will grow weary of shouldering the burdens of imperial status. It will increasingly naïvely champion the ideals of world peace and the reconciliation between peoples and thereby condemn itself to impotence in power politics.[99]

Spengler's contemporary, Sigmund Freud, did not foresee the eventual atrophy of Western man's aggressive impulses in the arena of interstate relations.[100] By contrast, Spengler brilliantly predicts pervasive quasi-pacifism in the West following the conclusion of colossal internecine conflicts and the establishment of its final imperial form. Indeed, what is more quasi-pacifistic than the United States' obsession with waging a casualty-free war, as was the case in Kosovo in 1999? Spengler, in his discussion of pacifism, farsightedly warns the Western nations against adopting pacifistic attitudes vis-à-vis the non-West. In the twenty-first century and beyond, if the United States or Western Europe were to face a foreign policy challenge requiring that their societies overcome their quasi-pacifism, it would most likely originate in the non-West.

Spengler argues that war is a permanent feature of world history. He ridicules the idealistic orientation toward world affairs that had grown in popularity after the carnage of World War I, finding its greatest expression in the founding of the League of Nations. He derides pacifism, the ideals of world peace and international understanding, cosmopolitanism, and blueprints for improving the state of the world as symptoms of "European weariness," as a "flight from the struggle for existence." A true statesman must be a thoroughgoing realist. "The born politician despises the unworldly outlooks of the ideologue and moralist in the midst of his world of facts." Political realists understand, unlike idealists, that war cannot be transcended by civilized man. War remains the arbiter of the grim struggle that is world politics. History "permits *only* the choice between victory and defeat, not between war and peace."[101]

According to Spengler, the final creative task of statecraft is the establishment of a universal empire. As vital cultural development reaches its end in each cultural cycle, imperialism becomes an obsession and hegemonic struggle erupts among states. The struggle culminates in the estab-

99. *UdA* II, 222–24.
100. Sigmund Freud, *Civilization and Its Discontents*, trans. James Strachey (New York: W. W. Norton, 1961), 59.
101. *UdA* I, 454; *UdA* II, 262–63, 535.

lishment of an *imperium mundi*. The stormy transition from a multistate to an imperial system in classical antiquity, *i.e.*, the rise of the Roman Empire, is a historical phenomenon purportedly reproduced by each of the cultures. "Thus, the *imperium Romanum* no longer appears as a unique phenomenon, but rather as a normal product of a strict and energetic, megalopolitan, eminently practical mentality and as a typical end stage, which has already appeared many times, but has not till now been identified."[102]

The transition from culture to civilization ushers in the "Era of Warring States," named after the tumultuous period in Chinese history that culminated in the founding of the Chinese empire. This struggle for hegemony in Graeco-Roman history spans the legendary conquests of Alexander the Great and the battle of Actium. The creation by Augustus of the institutional foundation of Roman imperial governance, the Principate soon followed. Spengler estimates that the counterpart in the modern West to this turbulent period of antiquity would reach its end in the twenty-first century or later. Thus far, this phase has stretched from the climacteric of Western culture, signified by the French Revolution and the Napoleonic Wars, to World War I. In this manner, Spengler weaves into the fabric of his historical philosophy Nietzsche's alarming predictions that Europe would undergo wars of an intensity unparalleled in all of history and that the twentieth century would witness "a struggle for domination of the earth." Spengler maintains that World War I had its counterpart in the Second Punic War. "A comparative perspective yields the 'contemporaneity' of this period with that of the Hellenistic, namely, in particular, the correspondence of the present highpoint—designated by the Great War—with the transition from the Hellenistic to the Roman period."[103]

Spengler singles out Rome as the shining symbol of empire in the past. Yet he envisions German imperialism as being far more expansionary than that of ancient Rome. Indeed, the imperialism of the Caesars pales in comparison with that of the empire builders of the modern West, for their expansive drive is fed by the wellspring of the Faustian ethos.

[It is from a perspective conscious of the contrast between the Apollonian and Faustian ethos] that the easily misunderstood Roman expansion must

102. *UdA* I, 51.
103. *UdA* II, 522, 535; Friedrich Nietzsche, *Die fröhliche Wissenschaft, KSA*, vol. III, 609–10, and *Jenseits von Gut und Böse, KSA*, vol. V, 140; *UdA* I, 35.

be viewed. It is anything but an extension of the *Fatherland*. It confines itself exactly within the territory that had already been taken possession of by
cultural man and now fell to the Romans as booty. There was never any talk
of dynastic plans for world power in the style of the Hohenstaufen or the
Habsburgs or of imperialism of a fashion comparable with that of today. The
Romans never made the attempt to penetrate into the interior of Africa.
They waged their later wars only in order to *secure* their possessions, without
ambition, without the symbolic drive to expand, and they abandoned Ger-
mania and Mesopotamia without regret.[104]

The expansionism that repeats itself in the grand cycles of world history
reflects far more than simply the calculated pursuit of power and material
gain. In a deeper sense, expansionism attests to the psychological imperative of a civilization to attain its fullest and most powerful forms of self-
expression. Of Faustian culture, Spengler observes, "[It] was therefore
oriented in the extreme degree to *extension*, be it of a political, economic,
or intellectual nature; it overcame all geographical-material limits; it
strove, without any practical objective, and only for the sake of the Symbol, to reach the North and the South poles; it has finally transformed the
surface of the globe into a single colonial area and economic system."[105]
The first three and a half decades of Spengler's life coincided with the
golden age of European imperialism. Not surprising, late nineteenth- and
twentieth-century historical and political thinkers concerned themselves
with imperialism, a historical force to which Spengler assigns great importance. He proposes a primarily cultural interpretation of it, as opposed to
a more conventionally bourgeois or Marxian economic one, like those
propounded by his contemporaries, John Hobson, Rudolf Hilferding,
Lenin, and Rosa Luxemburg. Imperialism intensifies during the phase of
Zivilisation in every cultural cycle. The "civilized" peoples are helpless to
resist the imperialistic drive, which compels them to exploit the "barbarians" on the periphery. "The expansive tendency is a doom, something
daemonic and monstrous, which seizes the late man of the world-city
stage, presses him into its service, consumes him, whether he desires to or
not, whether he comprehends it or not."[106]
The spirit of Western culture provides the wellspring for the dynamism
and boundless expansionism of Western imperialism. One is tempted to

104. *UdA* I, 431.
105. *UdA* I, 430.
106. *UdA* I, 49.

criticize Spengler's analysis of the "causes" of Western imperialism as vague. However, it is instructive to note that a contemporary authority on theories of modern imperialism offered an explanation for its sources not dissimilar to Spengler's theory. "Imperialism was primarily the result of exuberant energies in the womb of European societies, in the economic as well as in the military and political area."[107]

The correlate to imperialism is materialism. The imperialism of the Pax Romana and, in my opinion, the neo-imperialism of the Pax Americana, facilitate the "bread and circuses," the materialistic and hedonistic life-styles of the megalopoles and the civilized "provinces." Spengler's cyclical theory of economic development envisions widespread but transitory affluence within a grand imperial structure exploitative of its periphery as forming the civilizational economic apex. This is an accurate scenario thus far. He anticipated on the eve of World War I the creation of a monumental imperial form of the West that would facilitate a widely diffused, but impermanent, affluent life-style. It would be analogous to the civilizational apogees of the past. "With the growth of cities, the standard of living becomes more and more artificial, refined, and complicated. The urban worker in Caesar's Rome, in Harun al Raschid's Baghdad, and in today's Berlin experiences much to be a matter of course, which to the wealthy peasant far away in the countryside appears to be insane luxury, but this standard of living is difficult to achieve and difficult to maintain."[108]

Imperialism incites a backlash. The subjugation of outlying lands by past civilizations, which was far less extensive than that by the modern West, provoked the increasingly stubborn and ultimately successful resistance of alien peoples inhabiting the periphery. The affluence and peace in which dominant civilizations luxuriated proved to be transitory. Past civilizations inevitably succumbed to the internal corrosion of societal sterility, *i.e.*, the atrophy of the formative power of social traditions, the breakdown of family structure, a downward-sloping birth rate, quasi-pacifism, and hedonistic self-indulgence, in combination with the external pressure of the revolt of the periphery. The West will also fall victim to this recurrent historical process of imperialistic or neo-imperialistic collapse through internal decadence and external revolt.

Undaunted, Spengler calls for eternal fidelity to martial values and im-

107. Wolfgang J. Mommsen, *Imperialismustheorien*, 3d rev. ed. (Göttingen: Vandenhoeck & Ruprecht, 1987), 139.

108. *UdA* II, 594.

perial vigilance. Nonetheless, in the long run, the historical fate of the peoples of the West remains to luxuriate in imperial affluence before finally succumbing to power-political impotence. The once-proud peoples of the West will eventually join the ranks of the "fellaheen," peoples that have already created magnificent but now senescent civilizations. These "fellaheen" peoples, like the Chinese, the Indians, and the Egyptians, are forever condemned to weakness in world politics.[109]

This argument of the power-political decrepitude of "fellaheen" peoples is problematic. On the one hand, it accurately reflects the fact that peoples of past civilizations have often been powerless in interstate relations in subsequent phases of their history. On the other hand, some of them have been rejuvenated in the twentieth century by nationalism and have summoned up civilizational energies in reaction to Western imperialism. Thus, Spengler has probably underestimated the ability of some former "fellaheen" peoples to reconstitute themselves as major actors in international politics in the second half of the twentieth century and beyond.

Spengler shed light on the crisis of imperialistic rivalry in the twentieth century. The same can arguably be said for the crises of capitalism. Weber described capitalism as "the most fateful force in our modern life." It figured prominently in Spengler's analysis of modern Western civilization. The significance of his ideas on political economy in helping to elucidate the economic crises of the twentieth century has not been appreciated in much of the critical literature on his thought. Theodor Adorno inaccurately stated that Spengler's "understanding of economic events remains helplessly dilettantish." Hughes echoed this critique, declaring that "the workings of the economic process escape him." Both zeroed in on the central role that Spengler assigned to money and the evolution of monetary values in the future development of the modern international economic system as opposed to the underlying productive forces. As Adorno put it, "He is so fascinated by the façade of money, by the 'symbolic power' of money, that he converts the surface symbol into the thing itself." Hughes unjustifiably dismissed Spengler's emphasis on monetary and financial factors in twentieth-century economics as an "intellectual limitation," an expression of uncultured, lower-middle-class German prejudice.[110]

109. *UdA* II, 49, 125, 224.
110. Max Weber, preface to *Gesammelte Aufsätze zur Religionssoziologie*, 4th ed., vol. I (Tübingen: J. C. B. Mohr, 1947), 4; Theodor W. Adorno, "Spengler nach dem Untergang: Zu Oswald Spenglers 70. Geburtstag," *Der Monat* 2, no. 20 (May, 1950): 125; H-Sp, 155; Adorno, "Nach dem Untergang," 125; H-Sp, 152.

Spengler's approach to political economy is, on the contrary, intellectually significant. Have not financial factors increasingly proven to be vital features of the contemporary global economy? The fine-tuning of monetary policy to control inflation without choking economic growth, the intimate relationship between interest rates and economic growth and international capital flows, the close relationship between exchange rates and export competitiveness, the critical problems stemming from the rapid movement of vast quantities of speculative funds, and the management with the aid of international financial organizations of crises like the Asian contagion are pressing concerns of the American government and the other G–7 countries. Perhaps the most striking illustration of the importance of money to economics in recent times is the European Union's adoption of a common currency.

Spengler would reject the neoliberal faith that the purportedly inherent, self-regulating or self-equilibrating nature of markets will help ensure the perpetuation of modern economic activity virtually ad infinitum. His unorthodox political economy of the decline of the West merits reexamination in light of the fragility of the post–World War II American-sponsored, liberal international economic order. Indeed, the global economic chaos of the thirties seemed to confirm his fascinating political economic thesis, that the spectacular rise of the modern world economy since the industrial revolution is "fantastical," "dangerous," and "almost desperate."[111] Similarly, the profound anxiety about the possible collapse of the international financial system during the early years of the Third World debt crisis and the shock waves in the international financial markets radiating from the epicenter of Wall Street on Black Monday in 1987 all lent some plausibility, despite the overcoming of these crises, to Spengler's remarkable thesis of the eventual breakdown of the global economy. Will another severer and less manageable crisis in the global economy, perhaps one foreshadowed by the alarming Asian contagion in the late 1990s, finally substantiate his position?

Spengler's political economy of the decline of the West is intriguing. Apparently, he developed its principal arguments in the years immediately prior to World War I. Thus, he was attentive to the problematic nature of capitalism long before many of the most serious economic problems that later confronted Western leaders had arisen: global depression, the rise of the welfare state with its crushing burdens upon fiscal policy, global infla-

111. *UdA* II, 583.

tion in the post–World War II period, oil crises, the Third World debt crisis of the 1980s, the Asian economic crisis of the 1990s, the intensification of economic competition from the non-West, the crisis of unemployment and / or underemployment in Europe since 1973, and the difficulties currently hindering the effective coordination of international economic policy.

Without question, Spengler's formal education in economics was limited. However, one does not know to what extent this largely autodidactic intellectual compensated for this by his own reading in the field. He did attend a regular series of lectures on economics at the University of Berlin. Interestingly, Spengler is believed to have also sat in on lectures in Munich by the distinguished German political economist Lujo Brentano, one of the leaders for a time of the Younger Historical School in German political economy, which had come to prominence in the 1870s.[112] As a young student Spengler may have been influenced in the development of his own political economic ideas by Brentano's critical position toward British classical economic theory. Spengler shares the main ethical and methodological objections to British classical theory raised by mainstream German political economists in the nineteenth and early twentieth centuries. As Tomas Riha noted in his study *German Political Economy: The History of an Alternative Economics*, both German economists and social scientists, with their firm attachment to an organic conception of society, were very critical of the classical school. Specifically, they found fault with classical theory for its promotion of the material interests of the individual, the abstract *homo oeconomicus*, as the basis of economic activity and its concomitant alleged neglect of ethical considerations in economic life. The methodological criticism directed against classical theory, which Spengler prominently incorporated into the opening pages of the concluding chapter of *The Decline of the West*, entitled "The Form-World of Economic Life," denounces its abstractness and ahistorical character and the associated claim of universal validity. This criticism of British classical theory had been voiced by Brentano, whose objections were representative of those of many figures in German political economy.[113]

The second volume of *The Decline of the West* contains quotes from Werner Sombart's *Der moderne Kapitalismus*, one of the most important

112. K-Sp, 67.
113. *UdA* II, 583–84; Tomas Riha, *German Political Economy: The History of an Alternative Economics* (Bradford, West Yorkshire: MCB Univ. Press, 1985), 35.

contributions to German political economy in the early twentieth century. Sombart was a guiding light, along with Weber and Arthur Spiethoff of the Youngest Historical School, which brought to a conclusion the Historical movement in German political economy. Members of the Youngest Historical School sought to illuminate the peculiar characteristics of modern capitalist society. They interpreted it as being a special "epoch," "historical individual," or "style" in the development of Western civilization. Sombart was deeply interested in delineating the unique spirits or states of mind active in historical cultures, envisioning these spirits as being at the root of diverse economic systems in different epochs.[114] As we will presently see, Spengler advances an extreme but nonetheless provocative theory of the relationship between culture and economic life.

According to Spengler, all cultures undergo a grand economic developmental cycle. Each cycle begins with the dominance of peasant agriculture, followed by a growing conflict between town and country. Finally, the cycle culminates in a dominant, imperialistic economic system with its center of gravity in the world city. The megalopolis exercises its hegemony through financial means. "But the economic life, just like the social, forms a pyramid. In the rustic substratum a completely primitive condition maintains itself almost undisturbed by the culture. The late urban economy, already the activity of a resolute minority, looks constantly down upon the early agricultural economy. . . . Finally the world city brings in a civilized world economy, which radiates from the extremely elitist circles of a few focal points, subjugating the rest as a provincial economy."[115]

Anglo-Saxon political economy sought to derive universally valid laws of economic interaction through deductive reasoning. Spengler rejects this as an unhistorical approach. He maintains that economic forms are historical and cultural phenomena. As such, they can only be understood by reference to the underlying cultural ethos that informs all historical manifestations of a given culture. Consequently, every culture has its "own economic style." Capitalism is "the objectification of something entirely spiritual, the translation of an idea into a living, historical form."[116] Modern capitalism in the West is the mechanistic, materialistic, and utilitarian expression during the phase of *Zivilisation* of the dynamism of West European culture earlier embodied in Germanic-Catholic Christianity during the Gothic age.

114. Riha, *German Political Economy*, 104.
115. *UdA* II, 594.
116. *UdA* II, 593, 59.

Weber celebrated the Reformation and argued that Catholicism was antagonistic to the emergence of the capitalistic spirit. Spengler, by contrast, considers the fundament of Germanic-Catholic Christianity to be indispensable to the rise of capitalism centuries later. Central to the dynamism of modern capitalism, with its unleashing of tremendous entrepreneurial energies and its facilitation of the comprehensive scientific-technological exploitation of the natural world, is the novel conceptualization of the soul introduced by Gothic Christianity. For Faustian Christianity, whether in the form of Catholicism or Protestantism, the decisive point is that the soul is esteemed as an eternal source of radiant energy. This religious conception captures the individualism, dynamism, transformative energy, and expansive power unique to the West.

Spengler's thesis that the key event in the history of modern capitalism, the industrial revolution, should be understood as being primarily an expression of the psychological and cultural idiosyncrasies of the West, not the product of material causes or the result of the desire to satisfy universal human material needs, opposes Marx as well as Weber. Interestingly, many of the outstanding examples of Western culture's dynamism, such as the Gothic cathedral, contrapuntal music, perspective oil painting, the printing press, and cannon, all antedate the onset of the industrial age in England around 1750. Spengler unearths the roots of the industrial age in the psychological subsoil of West European culture.

The striking divergence in the assessment by Weber and Spengler of the historical spirit of capitalism, Weberian superrationalism as opposed to Spenglerian irrational dynamism, can be illustrated by considering their interpretation of two major developments in modern capitalism, rational capital accounting and autonomous private enterprise. For Weber, modern accounting practices mean the more exact calculation of profit and loss and the rational systemization of business activities. For Spengler, double-entry bookkeeping is a uniquely dynamic, Faustian form of *"thinking in money."* From his perspective of cultural holism, *"Double-entry bookkeeping is a pure, spatial analysis of values relating to a system of coordinates in which 'the firm' is the origin."* For Weber, the development of the permanent business enterprise, which rationally utilized capital, means the creation of an economic entity with the capacity to increase productivity dramatically. For Spengler, the Western firm represents a "center of force conceived of being completely impersonal and incorporeal which radiates its effects in all directions into infinity."[117]

117. *UdA* II, 599, 611, 616.

Capitalism is also implicitly rational from the Weberian perspective because of its purported relative stability despite the intensity of economic competition and imperialistic rivalries. Spengler is more concerned about the negative effects of speculative activity since the onset of the industrial revolution than is Weber. Spengler regards speculative activity as being a central feature of the later stages of every civilization. The banks and stock exchanges of modern capitalism represent, not Weberian "rational" institutions, but institutionalized expressions of aggressive and dangerous dynamism. "Only high finance is *completely* free, completely intangible. Since 1789, the banks, and with them the stock exchanges have developed themselves upon the credit needs of an industry growing ever more enormous, into a power of their own and they will to be, as money does in *all* civilizations, the *only* power."[118]

As reflection on *The Decline of the West* from a contemporary perspective suggests, the advancing trend of "superficial," quintessential rationalism in Western civilization, as evidenced in capitalism by the introduction of robotics in industrial production and computerized information management, coexists uneasily with alarming symptoms of unstable dynamism. The inadequacy of macroeconomic policy coordination by the G-7 countries in the contemporary interdependent world economy, the Third World debt and Asian economic crises, and volatile exchange rates and massive shifts in speculative funds call into question the idea that capitalism on a global scale is as rational as Weber steadfastly maintained.

According to Spengler, the analogue of the West's modern economic system with its industrial technology is the extensive Roman slave economy. He also differentiates between the classical conception of money and the Faustian. The money of the ancient world was "corporeal," "the minted coin." In Faustian civilization, money is increasingly abstract and relational, "the booking of units of credit." This functional, dynamic form of money seeks to mobilize all things. Faustian man is relentlessly driven by the will to power: "The Faustian thinking in money 'opens up' entire continents, the water power of enormous river complexes, the muscle power of the population of vast lands, coal deposits, primaeval forests, laws of nature and transforms them into financial energy, which is applied somewhere in the form of the press, elections, budgets and armies in order to put into effect plans of domination."[119]

118. *UdA* II, 628.
119. *UdA* I, 447; *UdA* II, 593, 604–5.

Spengler predicts that the gold standard will be followed by a multiplying of the money supply and the creation of new financial instruments. His prediction appears to be consistent with inflation in most of the non-Communist world, particularly from 1965 to 1982, the innovation of financial derivatives, the Japanese bubble economy in the late 1980s, and asset inflation in the United States in the 1990s. "[There is] no more hindrance within the developed megalopolitan economy, to increase the supply of 'money,' to a certain extent to think in other dimensions of money. This has absolutely nothing to do with the possible increase in gold or with real values."[120]

The claim that each culture traverses a grand economic cycle of a uniform pattern is not without contradiction. On the one hand, Spengler argues that civilizations succumb to sterility and petrifaction and that the increasingly complex and refined economic interaction of a late civilization tends to stagnate. On the other hand, this argument conflicts with his more interesting one that the highly sophisticated economic interaction that every culture has generated in the final phase of civilization is inherently unstable. Spengler advances the challenging thesis, prophetic of the Great Depression and eerily disturbing in light of the global economic and financial turmoil precipitated by the Asian economic crisis as well as the anxious speculation that the United States may have a bubble economy, that the modern international capitalist system will someday collapse. "The quantity of work of all cultures grows by a monstrous amount, and so there develops at the beginning of every civilization an intensity of economic life which is excessive in its tension and constantly in danger and nowhere can be maintained for a long time."[121]

That is a provocative argument when specifically applied to the future evolution of the modern international economic system, whose feverish pace of global financial and economic interaction could culminate in an awful breakdown. But it is a dubious description of the economic systems of ancient China, India, and Byzantium, with their demonstrated capacity to continue functioning in spite of their relative stagnation.

Spengler didn't attempt to resolve this important ambiguity. However, he clearly believes that the global economy will eventually collapse. Despite his admiration for industrialists and the intimate contacts he cultivated with members of the German business elite during the Weimar years,

120. *UdA* II, 116.
121. *UdA* II, 594.

Spengler was gripped by the intriguing idea that the meteoric rise of the global economy since the beginning of the industrial revolution was, and his description merits repeating, "fantastical," "dangerous," and "almost desperate."[122] These words were published, it should be recalled, almost a decade before the onset of the most severe crisis to rock modern capitalism, the Great Depression.

Bourgeois economists typically expected capitalism and industrial civilization to endure more or less indefinitely. Marx regarded industrial civilization, when transformed for socialistically organized polities, as a permanent civilizational achievement. However, Spengler believes that capitalism and industrial civilization are transitory historical phenomena. Moreover, capitalism's tendency to instability is deeply and permanently rooted in the dynamic, spiritual fundament of Western culture. Furthermore, this tendency to instability would eventually become magnified and dangerous. His philosophy suggests that the eventual collapse of the international capitalist system will be a decisive event in the cataclysmic process of the eventual eradication of modern industrial civilization itself. Spengler considers international capitalism to be a Frankensteinian creation that will become increasingly more difficult for its human masters to control. It is totally incapable of ushering in a post-historical age. Industrial civilization will vanish amid the wreckage of the terrible anarchy of the final phases of modern Western civilization. Spengler declined to hazard a prediction when the modern global economy would collapse. He gives the impression that this ultimate crisis of capitalism would be a lengthy process, reaching its conclusion within a few centuries or so.

Whereas Spengler envisions the collapse of modern capitalism, Weber merely worried about the possibility of its stagnation. Weber optimistically believed that the cartelization of business firms eliminated the disruptive effect of ruthless competition and that large banks were able to regulate the availability of credit to moderate speculative activity. On a modestly pessimistic note, he speculated that a bureaucratically-run state would preside over a stagnant economy in the West, a historical situation foreshadowed in ancient China, Ptolemaic Egypt, the later Roman Empire, and Byzantium.[123]

122. *UdA* II, 583.

123. Max Weber, "Der Sozialismus: Rede zur allgemeinen Orientierung von österreichischen Offizieren in Wien 1918," in *Gesammelte Aufsätze zur Soziologie und Sozialpolitik* (Tübingen: J. C. B. Mohr, 1924), 507–8; Max Weber, *Parlament und Regierung im neugeordneten Deutschland: Zur politischen Kritik des Beamtentums und*

Spengler's intriguing argument, that the phenomenal dynamism of modern economic activity is inherently unstable, dangerous, and unsustainable, represents an important counterposition to the utopianism of Marx and, more important, to the cool optimism common to Weber and contemporary neoliberalism. The reassuring neoliberal faith in the self-equilibrating qualities, rationalism, and enduring nature of capitalism may prove unfounded if the increasingly interdependent global economy breaks down.

As we have seen, Spengler does not envision democracy or free-market capitalism offering an exit strategy from the cul-de-sac of the West's civilizational crisis. Then what of modern science and technology? These incomparable achievements of the West are often touted as the guarantors of its longevity and continuing success. Indeed, Leo Strauss asserted that the capacity of science to progress infinitely refuted both Spengler's analysis and prognosis of the decline of Western civilization.[124]

Spengler lived in an age of giant technological strides. Many intellectuals today cogently argue that a new kind of civilization based on high technology—called postindustrial, technological, neo-industrial civilization, or any of a dozen other names—has either already superseded industrial civilization or is in the process of doing so. Spengler's analysis of the fate of industrial civilization is equally applicable in its fundamentals to that of neo-industrial civilization, for he had a keen sense of the capacity of the West to make important technological advances in the coming decades.

Spengler, however, forecasts a bleak, long-term future for industrial civilization. He provocatively argues that this exceptional form of civilization will vanish because of the exhaustion of the intellect and spirit that befalls all civilizations. In *The Decline of the West* he does not consider the role of possible material factors such as the ecological poisoning of the planet, the population explosion, or the depletion of natural resources.

Spengler's distinctive aesthetic orientation informed his speculations on the future of modern science and technology. The twentieth century is an age of extensive, goal-oriented activity par excellence. The scientific and technological products of modernity, though they attest to our cultural bankruptcy, nonetheless demand aesthetic appreciation as quintessential

---

Parteiwesens, in *Max Weber zur Politik im Weltkrieg: Schriften und Reden 1914–1918*, ed. Wolfgang J. Mommsen, in collaboration with Gangolf Hübinger, vol. XV of *Max Weber Gesamtausgabe*, ed. Horst Baier *et al.* (Tübingen: J. C. B. Mohr, 1984), 462 ff.
124. Leo Strauss, *The City and Man* (Chicago: Univ. of Chicago Press, 1964), 2.

objectifications of the functionality, the *Zweckmässigkeit*, of our age. Despite Spengler's lamentations about the demise of the refinements of pre-industrial culture in the West, he borders on contradicting himself. He declares his love for the clarity and the ingenuity with which the dynamic spirit of Faustian culture expresses itself in the manifold creations of the industrial age. The true aesthete of modernity is a connoisseur of science and technology, and the museum of modernity is not an art gallery but a laboratory. "I love the profundity and refinement of mathematical and physical theories; faced with them, the aesthete and physiologist is a bungler. For the magnificently clear, highly intellectual forms of a fast steamship, a steel plant, a precision-lathe, the subtlety and elegance of certain chemical and optical procedures, I would give up the entire stylistic plundering by today's 'arts and crafts,' painting and architecture included."[125]

Every culture develops its own understanding of the natural world, its unique form of science. Western science and technology do not represent further advances upon the foundation of the prior scientific and technological achievements of the Graeco-Roman world, as is customarily argued. Instead, Spengler regards them as being distinctive expressions of the Faustian ethos of the West, which seeks to conquer time and space. "Something completely different is the Faustian technics, which with the full passion of the third dimension and, to be sure, from the earliest days of the Gothic era thrusts itself upon Nature in order to *hold sway* over her."[126]

Scientific theorization in the West serves technocratic and instrumentalist ends. Western scientific inquiry is not a manifestation of a passive, idle curiosity as it was for the savants of Chinese, Indian, Graeco-Roman, or Arabian culture. It is, instead, a highly energetic, goal-oriented intellectual process aiming at the mastery and exploitation of the natural world. "The Faustian inventor and discoverer is something unique." To underscore the singularity of the Western approach to science and technology, Spengler observes that whereas the Chinese made several important technological discoveries duplicated by the West, including the compass, telescope, printing, gunpowder, paper, and porcelain, because of their different cultural ethos they did not display profound technological aggressiveness in their approach to nature as did the West. Traditional Chinese culture "does not rape nature," as does Western culture.[127]

125. *UdA* I, 58.
126. *UdA* II, 622.
127. *UdA* II, 622, 622 n. 1.

Spengler has been recently described as "the first great prophet of the end of science." He provocatively argues that science has not developed in world history linearly and transculturally whereby it would progressively achieve a higher and higher level of insight into the ultimate nature of the universe. Scientific knowledge is not a cumulative but a cyclical phenomenon. Each culture develops its own distinctive paradigm of scientific knowledge as a comprehensive abstract critique of its preexisting religious world view. The science and technology of the West, grand and impressive to be sure, are nonetheless transitory, coming of age in the "autumn" and "winter" of the cultural cycle. The great period of scientific theoretical system-building was the nineteenth century; the twentieth century is one of "great harvests," the "final renderings." Spengler declares, "we are experiencing today the decrescendo of the brilliant latecomers, who arrange, collect, and wind things up like the Alexandrians of the Roman period." Moreover, he fears that the very industrial civilization that modern science and technology have made possible will someday cease to exist, as the young recruits to the intellectual elite of the West lose the motivation to devote themselves to scientific study, which grows ever more complex and demanding. "Science exists only in the active thinking of great generations of scholars, and books are nothing, if they do not become alive and potent in people who are equal to them." After two hundred years of an intense obsession with science, the soul of the culture is satiated. Industrial civilization is threatened by the danger of eventual alienation from it and will last perhaps "only for a small number of centuries."[128]

The West will fail to erect a permanent, universal structure of scientific truth. Moreover, modern scientific theories are not absolutely valid: They rest upon merely a "*working hypothesis*" and are "the *servant of the technical 'Will-to-Power.'*" Spengler's argument that the potency of Western scientific theories, as evidenced by successful technological applications, does not suffice to confirm their absolute validity finds some corroboration today. In his discussion of the epistemological crisis of modern science, Richard Tarnas concludes that as the twentieth century has progressed, science has "lost its long-secure claims to virtually absolute cognitive reliability." Gilbert Merlio notes that the scientific community has, for the most part, abandoned the traditional claim to objective truth in exchange for

128. John Horgan, *The End of Science: Facing the Limits of Knowledge in the Twilight of the Scientific Age* (New York: Broadway Books, 1997), 23; *UdA* I, 486, 544–545; *UdA* II, 625.

technological effectiveness, identifying scientific knowledge with technological know-how.[129]

Interestingly, while Spengler was predicting that pure science would undergo a decrescendo, applied science and technology had not yet peaked. For the twentieth century has been an age of extensive activity and of eminently practical pursuits: global imperialism, international economic competition, and the advance of technology. Nonetheless, ultimately the scientific theory-building and technological inventiveness that underwrite these pursuits will exhaust themselves. The scientific and technological creations of the modern West will disappear; they express the inner spiritual drive of Westerners—a drive that is transitory, as all that is historical is mutable. Moreover, the very peoples who summoned modern science and technology into existence will fade away as a vital civilizational force. "In a few centuries there will no longer be a West European culture, no Germans, no Englishmen, no Frenchmen, as at the time of Justinian there were no more Romans. . . . Transitory is every thought, every belief, every science, as soon as the spirits are extinguished, in whose worlds their 'eternal truths' were by necessity experienced as truth."[130]

Spengler's consequential cultural relativism induces him to claim dubiously that Russia, the apparent successor culture to the West, will someday articulate a cultural ethos that in some vague and unexplained fashion rejects Western science and technology.[131] He regards the modernization efforts of the Russian tsars since Peter the Great and of Lenin as ultimately a passing phase in Russian history. They have merely brought about a pseudomorphosis. It will eventually culminate in a rejection of Bolshevism and the reversal of the process of modernization, which is antithetical to the "true" Russian spirit. Such an argument certainly seems implausible given the enormous advantages Western science and technology conferred upon the former Soviet Union and other states in their struggles in power politics, to say nothing of the desire of the Russians and other peoples to enjoy the material benefits of modernization.

Concluding our discussion of *The Decline of the West* is a focus on Spengler's key concept of decline. The word *decline* ordinarily evokes an

129. *UdA* II, 367–68; Richard Tarnas, *The Passion of the Western Mind: Understanding the Ideas That Have Shaped Our World View* (New York: Harmony, 1991), 365; Gilbert Merlio, "Spengler und die Technik," in Peter C. Ludz, ed., *Spengler heute* (Munich: C. H. Beck, 1980), 103.

130. *UdA* I, 217.

131. *UdA* II, 626 n. 1.

image of a unilinear process. The familiar picture springing to mind is the decline of imperial Rome with a secular trend of societal decay and mounting internal and external crises. However, in order to appreciate properly Spengler's vision of the decline of the West, it is important to conceptualize it as a dualistic process. The decline of the West occurs in two related but distinct phases: first, as a decline in the Occident's cultural traditions—a decline that, in Spengler's view, had largely run its course by the outbreak of World War I; and second, as a deterioration in the military, economic, and political power of a universal Western empire and the concomitant exacerbation of societal degeneration, with a pacifistic West becoming mortally vulnerable to external pressure from non-Western peoples in revolt. This critical point would be reached soon after 2200 A.D.[132] In the first stage, that of cultural decline, magnificent artistic traditions give way to a commercialized artistic sterility. Furthermore, the diminution of cultural vitality signals the onset of the "Era of Warring States." With respect to the second stage, that of imperial decline, Spengler maintains that after one nation of the West gained ascendancy over the Western world and much of the remaining globe through victory in world wars, this *imperium mundi* would confront a mounting crisis. The entire West would subsequently experience moral and social decay, economic crisis, and eventually decreased competitiveness in power politics. Western societal degeneration would be characterized by three essential features: pacifism, the breakdown of the family unit and childlessness, and hedonism. Rome is the mirror image.

The Decline of the West presents a tragic vision of a macrohistorical process terminating with the end of modernity. This irreversible process manifests itself in art, religion, social mores, domestic and international politics, economic life, and science. The decline of the West does not have historical causes per se that can be isolated and studied so that the tidal flow of events can be reversed; at best, it can only be protracted. None of the vaunted achievements of the West, democracy, free-market capitalism, and science and technology, can arrest or reverse the process of deepening civilizational crisis. Perhaps some succor is provided by the expectation of the eventual rise of a new culture.

Writing in 1952, Hughes, in the concluding lines of his treatise on Spengler, remarked, "*The Decline of the West* offers the nearest thing we

132. This estimate is based on Table III, entitled " 'Contemporary' Political Epochs," in *UdA* I.

have to a key to our times."[133] Almost half a century later, his words still ring true. At the end of the Cold War and the dawn of the third millennium A.D., any thinker wrestling with the question of the future of humankind and modern civilization cannot ignore Spengler's pathbreaking inquiry into the crisis of modernity. In the following chapters, to understand better the complexity of his thought we will survey the thinkers, intellectual traditions, and ideas that influenced his major work, paying special attention to his relationship to the German tradition of historicism.

133. H-Sp, 165.

3

The Decline of the West: Spengler and the German Tradition of Historicism

DESPITE SPENGLER'S REPUTATION AS AN unorthodox figure in German historical thought, he actually sank deep roots in its mainstream tradition of historicism. He incorporated many of its cardinal tenets in his historical philosophy, though he revolted against fundamental ideas of the German historicist tradition and transformed others. Historicism was an influential body of ideas in Europe, achieving its most radical expression in German culture. Given the major impact of historicism on German intellectual life, particularly in the nineteenth and early twentieth centuries, it would be inconceivable that Spengler would have remained unaffected by it. Furthermore, it is a striking coincidence that the years of his birth and death spanned the culmination of the historicist movement in Germany.[1]

In any discussion of historicism, it is incumbent upon one to define the concept at the outset, for as Calvin Rand has noted, "A variety of definitions exists, and consequently, the concept is vague and ambiguous." In this study, I adhere to the definition of historicism in Georg Iggers' *The German Conception of History.* He examines the theoretical presuppositions and political values of historians of this major national tradition of historiography. As Iggers explains, historicism is "the main tradition of German historiography and historical thought which has dominated historical writing, the cultural sciences, and political theory in Germany from

1. Georg G. Iggers, *The German Conception of History: The National Tradition of Historical Thought from Herder to the Present,* rev. ed. (Middletown, Conn.: Wesleyan Univ. Press, 1983), 6; Calvin G. Rand, "Two Meanings of Historicism in the Writings of Dilthey, Troeltsch, and Meinecke," *Journal of the History of Ideas* 25, no. 4 (October–December, 1964): 504.

Wilhelm von Humboldt and Leopold von Ranke until the recent past."[2]
It should be noted that Iggers' analysis focuses on the historical thought
of German academics and consequently pays little attention to Spengler, a
private scholar.

Born in 1880, Spengler came of age when the study of history enjoyed
immense intellectual prestige in Germany. Like the leading German speculative philosophers of history before him, Herder, Hegel, and Marx,
Spengler embraces the historicist axiom that the study of history is the indispensable intellectual vehicle for comprehending man as both a social
and a political being. The cofounders of the German historical school of
jurisprudence, Friedrich Karl von Savigny and Karl Friedrich Eichhorn,
succinctly enunciated in 1815 this axiom: "History is by no means a mere
collection of examples but is the only way to true knowledge of our own
condition." Wilhelm von Humboldt poetically expressed the historicist
claim, "Like philosophy after the first cause of things, art after the ideal of
beauty, so history strives after the picture of the human destiny in perfect
truth, living fullness, and pure clarity."[3] Spengler envisioned man as simultaneously inhabiting two different but conjoined universes, that of nature
and that of history. In considering the latter to be of more importance,
he strove throughout his intellectual career to comprehend "the world as
history." Ironically, his historical relativism was interpreted by many contemporaries as undermining the status history had enjoyed in Germany in
the nineteenth century as the sovereign means to understanding the
human condition. Yet his historical relativism does not invalidate the proposition that history represented for him the pathway to understanding the
human condition.

The seminal works inaugurating the historicist tradition in Europe were
Giambattista Vico's *New Science* and Johann Gottfried Herder's *Also a
Philosophy of History*, appearing in 1774. Herder, a German theologian and
philosopher of history, presented an original formulation of historicist
principles. He sets forth three concepts of central importance to the entire
tradition of German historicism. First, there is the idea of individuality.

2. Rand, "Two Meanings of Historicism," 503; Iggers, *German Conception of History*, 4.
3. Friedrich Savigny and Karl Eichhorn, quoted in Iggers, *German Conception of
History*, 66; Wilhelm von Humboldt, "Über die Aufgabe des Geschichtschreibers," in
Schriften zur Anthropologie und Geschichte, 3d ed., vol. 1 of *Werke*, ed. Andreas Flitner
and Klaus Giel (Stuttgart: Cotta, 1960), 588–89.

Herder, in opposition to the teachings of natural law philosophy, theorizes that all values and cognitions are historical phenomena and individual in nature. History, which is in a state of constant movement, can only be comprehended through empathy, not through reason. Second, Herder affirms that history is governed by divine and benevolent purpose, that "Providence guides the theme of development onward."[4] Indeed, the divine is reflected in all of nature and history. Finally, Herder propounds the idea that nations have their own special cultural genius and value.[5]

In the late eighteenth century, biological analogies began to displace those derived from the mechanistic universe of Newtonian physics in historical and political thought. Herder, in exemplifying this trend, conceives of nations, within the flow of historical change, as organisms. They have a morphology; they are dynamic and alive. These organisms are not rational in character; they are things in themselves and not means. Like a person, nations have characteristics: a life span and their own spirit. His vision of the nation as the fountainhead of all truth implied the absence of objective criteria for determining truth. The resonances of Herder's historical philosophy in *The Decline of the West* are not limited to similarity in methodology, a common ground in historical relativism, and the conception of history as a morphology of "organisms." His idea that a *Volk*'s national culture is a unique product of its genius is suggestive of Spengler's that each culture is an expression of its distinctive soul. Like Spengler later, Herder also warned against a Eurocentric approach to the study of history.

Although the aforementioned conceptual affinities between the historical philosophies of Herder and Spengler are striking, there are significant differences. Herder enshrines the nation as the vehicle of historical development, whereas Spengler designates the culture-civilization cycle, which in the case of West European culture is multinational, as the vehicle of meaningful history and the key unit of analysis in historical philosophy. Moreover, in Herder's philosophy, each national culture stands in a meaningful relationship to both its predecessor and its successor.[6] Spengler interprets each culture as being essentially autonomous, as virtually a self-contained world. Cultures do not interact in a process of progressive enrichment, promoting the education or cultivation (*Bildung*) of their

---

4. Johann Gottfried Herder, *Auch eine Philosophie der Geschichte zur Bildung der Menschheit*, ed. Hans Dietrich Irmscher (Stuttgart: Reclam, 1990), 14.

5. On this phase in Herder's historical philosophy, see Iggers, *German Conception of History*, 34 ff.

6. *UdA* I, 140; Herder, *Auch eine Philosophie der Geschichte*, 16.

successors. The series of cultures does not manifest an overarching or higher meaning for Spengler as it does for Herder. The meaning of world history is fragmented and exists only in the limited context of each cultural cycle. Furthermore, he reverses Herder's relationship between the *Volk* and culture, demoting the proud *Völker* of Western Europe to mere products of the formative power of the "soul" of Western culture. "Peoples under the spell of a culture are, on the other hand, in view of their inner form and their entire manifestation, not the creators, but the *works* of this culture."[7] Finally and most important, Spengler's cultural pessimism and vitalistic celebration of the irrational energies in history stand in stark contrast to Herder's fervent faith in the providential nature of history.

Historicists believed in the operation of rational and ethical purpose in history. That is a highly debatable historical assumption when one reflects upon the tragic course of history in the twentieth century. Historicists believed that the diverse expressions of irrationality, individual spontaneity, and free will in human history were phenomenal manifestations of a transcendent ethical order. Thus, Humboldt claimed, "World history is not comprehensible without a cosmic governance." Ranke, the founder of the German historical school, wrote in one of his letters, "Over everything hovers the divine order of things." He sanguinely envisioned that Providence actively intervened in the temporal world when he asserted that "at the decisive moment there always enters something we call chance or fate which is God's finger." Johann Gustav Droysen, the inaugurator of the Prussian School of historical study, conceived a great scope for divine intervention, proclaiming, "we *believe* that in everything, down to the smallest detail, God's eternal guidance is powerful and full of care." Despite historicists' belief that Providence guided history, their outlook should not be confused with a shallow, utilitarian idea of progress. As Herder claimed, "The march of Providence goes also over millions of corpses to its goal!"[8] The entire tradition of historicism from Wilhelm von Humboldt to Friedrich Meinecke rejected happiness as an end of life, as did Spengler.

7. *UdA* II, 202–3.

8. Humboldt, "Über die Aufgabe des Geschichtschreibers," in *Schriften*, 600; Leopold von Ranke to Otto von Ranke, 25 May 1873, in Leopold von Ranke, *Das Briefwerk*, ed. Walther Peter Fuchs (Hamburg: Hoffmann & Campe, 1949), 518; *Zur eigenen Lebensgeschichte*, ed. Alfred Dove, Leopold von Ranke, vols. *LIII–LIV* of *Sämtliche Werke* (Leipzig: Verlag von Duncker & Humblot, 1890), 665; *Johann Gustav Droysen Briefwechsel*, ed. Rudolf Hübner, vol. I, *1829–1851* (Stuttgart: Deutsche Verlags-Anstalt, 1929), 103; Herder, *Auch eine Philosophie der Geschichte*, 100.

Although Nietzsche eschewed attempts at systematic thought, Spengler most certainly did not.⁹ Indebted to Hegel, whom Nietzsche had pointedly criticized, Spengler boldly pressed the complexities of history into a grand, methodical system like Hegel before him. Spengler's rejection of Christianity, which was never as stridently polemical as Nietzsche's, in combination with his pessimism, enabled him to develop a historical philosophy devoid of providential guidance and intervention in history. Spengler appropriated one of Nietzsche's antihistoricist ideas. Nietzsche had attacked with his customary wit the appealing historicist notion that human history conformed to a moral order of divine origin. "All of history is, to be sure, the experimental rebuttal of the thesis of the so-called 'moral world-order.' " Spengler, like Nietzsche, championed yea-saying to the *Diesseits*, the real world of sense experience, and dismissed the *Jenseits*, the realm of the ideal and of Providence, as a mere chimaera.¹⁰ For Spengler, history was not presided over by a Christian God, motivated by love and deep care for his creation. Despite the supposed nonexistence of God and history's putatively amoral nature, he affirmed history as did German historicists.

German historicists became increasingly concerned about the danger of the relativization of historical values consequent to the erosion of faith in a historical metaphysics. It was upon such a secure foundation that Ranke had composed his trailblazing work. Nietzsche had boldly denied the existence of eternal truths in the flow of historical time. Spengler, in turn, fashioned a historical philosophy that systematically grounded relativism, though diverse cultural orientations and not the individualistic thinker, as Nietzsche maintained, were held to be the ultimate source of relative truth and values. For Spengler, every culture gave birth to its own self-sufficient truth and belief system. He pictured putative eternal truths and cultural values as breaking down as the action of history was played out in the Heraclitean, kaleidoscopic pageant of civilizational rise and fall. Spengler's denial of absolute truths and eternal values also lent support to his abrasive, quasi-Social Darwinist approach to power politics, which prized realism and success and disdained idealistic commitment to a moral foreign policy.

Directing our attention to the basic question of historical methodology, we find again both significant affinities and differences between

9. Friedrich Nietzsche, *Götzen-Dämmerung, KSA*, vol. VI, 63.

10. Friedrich Nietzsche, *Ecce Homo, KSA*, vol. VI, 367, and *Der Antichrist, KSA*, vol. VI, 185.

Spengler's position and that of German historicism. As Iggers observes, "the core of the historicist outlook lies in the assumption that there is a fundamental difference between the phenomena of nature and those of history, which requires an approach in the social and cultural sciences fundamentally different from those of the natural sciences." As noted earlier, Spengler maintained that reality was dualistic. "Man is, as an element and bearer of the world, not only a member of nature, but also a member of history, a *second cosmos* of a different order and different content." Eduard Meyer, in an address before the German Historical Congress of 1924, argued that Spengler's dichotomization of reality into a world of nature and one of history and its implications for historical understanding were of "fundamental significance."[11]

Iggers cogently argues that Humboldt established the basic metaphysical and epistemological approach of German historicism. Humboldt's influential ideas on history resonate in *The Decline of the West*. He regarded history as being the theater of powerful forces, "ideas" striving to assume concrete form in the ebb and flow of historical change. Spengler adopts the term "idea" in his philosophy: In history, the "idea" that a culture personifies seeks to realize "the whole wealth of its inner possibilities." Whereas the individuality of nations (*Individualität der Nationen*) is a key feature of history for Humboldt, for Spengler, it is the individuality of cultures. Indeed, a culture is "a *person*," "a great individual"; in the plural, "world history is their entire biography."[12]

Humboldt maintained that different epistemological methods were required in the historical sciences and the natural sciences. History concerned itself with "living Nature," while scientists studied the physical world, or what Humboldt called "lifeless" nature. This "living Nature" could only be apprehended through the creative act of intuitively grasping its innermost character. Understanding the complex flux of the historical world requires more than simply dispassionate description. It demands the harmonious coordination of the faculty of, in Humboldt's words, "rational observation" and "poetic imagination." The latter is certainly the core of Spengler's conceptual apparatus. As he maintained, "Feeling for, intuiting, comparing, the immediate inner certainty, the precise perceptual imagination—those were his [Goethe's] methods to come closer to the se-

11. Iggers, *German Conception of History*, 4–5; *UdA* I, 65; Eduard Meyer, *Spenglers "Untergang des Abendlandes"* (Berlin: Karl Curtius Verlag, 1925), 6–7.

12. Iggers, *German Conception of History*, 62; *UdA* I, 142, 206, 34, 139.

cret of phenomena in motion. *And they are entirely the methods of historical investigation. There are no others.*"[13]

Ranke rejected mere empirical description and explanation; intuitive spiritual apperception, he argued, is indispensable to comprehending historical phenomena. In sharp contrast to Western positivism, German historicism held that the study of history necessitated intuitive approaches to understanding rather than causal explanation. Spengler identified with this position, roundly condemning granting causal analysis a role in philosophy of world history. "Therefore, in an inquiry like the one here presented, it cannot be a matter of accepting that events of an intellectual-political nature, which visibly develop from day to day, are simply surface happenings, of arranging them according to 'cause' and 'effect' and following them in their apparent, rationally comprehensible tendency. Such a 'pragmatic' treatment of history would be nothing more than a piece of disguised natural science."[14]

German historicists maintained that intuitiveness was of vital importance in historical comprehension. They emphasized the uniqueness, spontaneity, and individuality of historical phenomena. Such characteristics naturally rendered historical phenomena resistant to intellectual appreciation through generalizations or causal analysis. Thus, we find that positivism, as an approach to the study of history in the manner of Auguste Comte or Henry Thomas Buckle, did not have an important representative among German historians.[15]

The disparate nature of the German tradition of historicism and Western historical positivism was highlighted in the controversy surrounding Karl Lamprecht's work. The Lamprecht dispute erupted in German historical circles at the close of the nineteenth century. It revealed the passion with which the historicist tradition rejected the comparative study of cultures and the formulation of general historical laws, which Lamprecht espoused. Historicists insisted on the uniqueness and individuality of historical phenomena. Lamprecht's search for cycles of development within discrete units of mankind foreshadowed Spengler's own effort, though he didn't study Lamprecht's works prior to the completion of the first volume of *The Decline of the West*.[16] However, Lamprecht did not con-

13. Iggers, *German Conception of History*, 51; Wilhelm von Humboldt, quoted in *ibid.*, 51, 59; *UdA* I, 33.
14. *UdA* I, 7.
15. Iggers, *German Conception of History*, 130–31.
16. Spengler to Klöres, 1 September 1918, *B*, 107.

sider the basic units of comparative cultural study in history to be cultures as Spengler did. Instead, like Hegel before him, he saw them as nations, which were typically organized into states.[17] Spengler, like Lamprecht, Max Weber, and Wilhelm Dilthey, believed that comparative cultural study would yield profound insights into the nature of history and the spirit of one's own culture and epoch.

With his epistemological dichotomy between the worlds of nature and history, Spengler denied the capacity of the historical philosopher to derive scientific laws in imitation of the natural scientist. "Real history is heavy with destiny, but free of laws."[18] However, his daring project to uncover the master pattern of world history certainly bears some resemblance to the enterprise of historical positivists to discover historical laws. While German historicism was essentially idiographic in orientation, Spengler, his own protests to the contrary, with his methodical systematization and patternization of history, was largely nomothetic in approach, as were positivist historians. His aspiration to predictive powers also certainly places him in proximity to the positivist tradition. The famous epitome of Auguste Comte expressing the positivist relationship between knowledge and prediction as *savoir pour prévoir* ironically captures some of the quality of Spengler's philosophy of world history. He shares the interest of many positivist Anglo-Saxon and French social scientists in searching for significant regularities and recurrences in history and the desire of some of them to imbue social scientific study with a measure of predictive ability.

Spengler adopts historicism's methodology but applies it in an innovative fashion alien to mainstream German academic thought. His thesis that each culture undergoes analogous historical developments deviates from the historicist idea that every historical event is unique. Moreover, with his determinism he allows far less room for spontaneity and human volition in his historical philosophy than do his historicist counterparts. Nonetheless, he retains in modified form the historicist tenet of the individuality of history by maintaining that each culture has its own distinctive ethos. For Spengler, the cultural diversity of world history is reflected in its culture-civilization cycles. For Herder, Humboldt, and the German historicist tradition, cultural diversity expresses itself in national variation.

The nineteenth century was the golden age of historiography in the West. It bestowed on posterity magnificent products of national historical

17. Iggers, *German Conception of History*, 199.
18. *UdA* I, 153.

writing. However, the idea that the people, nation, or *Volk* was the fundamental unit of macrohistorical analysis, which largely dominated the
nineteenth-century historical horizon, was ultimately a limited one. Well
before his rival Toynbee, Spengler assisted historical thought in the twentieth century to progress beyond this narrow national perspective. He
championed a perspective where the, at times, multinational cultural collectivity, the culture or civilization, is appreciated as a basic category of
macrohistorical investigation.[19]

Spengler spans the traditions of historicism and of German systematic
and speculative philosophy of world history, which operated outside it, the
approach exemplified by Hegel and Marx. *The Decline of the West* is a creative effort to apply the key historicist principle of historical individuality
to cultures or civilizations. Historicism, however, conventionally restricted
the application of this principle to historical personalities, institutions, nations, and epochs. This core of historicist individuality, this cultural personality, spirit, or "soul," is then located by Spengler within a rigorous
world-historical schemata, in contrast to the antisystematic, antipositivistic
nature of historicist thought. And it was precisely the positivistic, systema-
tizing qualities of Spengler's major work that drew the sharpest criticism
from Meinecke.[20]

The Decline of the West is an ingenious attempt at synthesizing the historicist tenet of individuality and the relativity of values that historicism
inadvertently promoted with intellectual approaches lying outside the
mainstream German tradition of historicism, ones instead seeking underlying laws, structure, and system in history. Spengler's enthusiasm for systematization and generalization may reflect his passion for mathematics
and the natural sciences. This ambitious system builder, like Hegel before
him, rebelled against the antisystematic character of German historicism.
Spengler regiments the extraordinary complexity and diversity of world
history within the framework of a methodically constructed theory. He in-
vests the antinormative tendencies of historicism with a grand systematization. The historicist idea that all cultural values are culture-bound and
relative forms a fundamental tenet of his philosophy.

The German historicist tradition before World War I was Eurocentric.

19. See Gert Müller, "Oswald Spenglers Bedeutung für die Geschichtswissenschaft," *Zeitschrift für Philosophische Forschung* 17 (1963): 484.

20. Friedrich Meinecke, "Über Spenglers Geschichtsbetrachtung," in *Zur Theorie
und Philosophie der Geschichte*, ed. Eberhard Kessel (Stuttgart: K. F. Koehler, 1959),
194.

Spengler castigated historicism for its complacent assumption of the validity of what was an outmoded Eurocentric approach to world history. His expansion of historical study to include civilizations outside the Western tradition enormously enlarged the scope of historical inquiry. Moreover, his multidisciplinary effort at philosophy of world history ran counter to the predominant tendency toward extreme specialization in historiography in Wilhelmine Germany.[21]

History and politics perennially interact. Not only was historicism the dominant approach to the academic study of history in Germany, but it was of fundamental importance to the tradition of power politics in the nineteenth and twentieth centuries. German historicism, in its early stage of development, strongly favored a limited role for the state and cosmopolitanism instead of divisive nationalism. However, the stress and strain of French invasion and occupation and the enthusiasm generated by the Wars of Liberation influenced German historicism. These developments precipitated a transition from humanistic cosmopolitanism to antagonistic nationalism and the espousal of a more powerful state. Historicism became transformed into a constituent part of the national heritage. It provided a philosophical basis for German nationalism and power politics.

Beginning with Humboldt, the central role of politics in history becomes a tenet of historicism. Fundamental to the classical tradition of historicism is the idea that the state must be powerful and independent vis-à-vis other states. Statecraft should aim to preserve not merely the state's autonomy but its cultural vitality as well. Moreover, German power-political strength was optimistically interpreted as reinforcing an international order consistent with the promotion of European cultural richness and diversity.[22]

Ranke, the venerated founder of the German historical school, imparted to the German historicist tradition its preoccupation with foreign affairs. Ranke made the history of the modern European states system, at whose center the great powers stood, one of the most preferred themes of German historical studies and international political analysis. In his seminal essay, *The Great Powers*, he concentrates on the relations of the great powers, probing the ramifications for international order and cultural indi-

21. Iggers, *German Conception of History*, 131.
22. Wilhelm von Humboldt, "Denkschrift über die deutsche Verfassung," 2d Part, vol. II, *Politische Denkschriften*, ed. Bruno Gebhardt, in Wilhelm von Humboldt, *Gesammelte Werke*, vol. IX (Berlin: B. Behr's Verlag, 1903), 97.

viduality of their spirited competition. Spengler shared the keen interest of the historicist tradition in the rivalry of the great powers. Many of the figures in the historicist tradition preferred political and diplomatic history and focused on the actions of statesmen, generals, and diplomats. Spengler, by contrast, showed more attentiveness to social and economic forces at work in modern history, especially industrialization and the rise of mass politics.

A second hallmark of classic historicism, likewise originating with Ranke, is the idea of the primacy of foreign policy (*das Primat der Außenpolitik*). The term was purportedly coined by Dilthey in his reflections on Ranke's power-political ideas. It became axiomatic for many German philosophers of international politics and left its imprint upon American political realism. Ranke showcases this fundamental principle of German power-political thought in his influential essay *Political Dialogue*. He aspired to "relegate politics again to the field of power and foreign relations, where it belongs." Ranke maintained that the foremost duty of political leadership was to acquire the greatest possible measure of autonomy and power for the state in the arena of great-power competition. Thus statesmen, in conducting foreign policy, should be guided by sober and prudential considerations of the forces obtaining in interstate relations. Domestic political concerns should be ranked secondary to those of international politics. Paralyzing factionalism and political apathy must be overcome by the cultivation of the private citizen's willingness to assume his duties toward a monarchical state, thereby maximizing its powers in foreign affairs. It is well that the ordinary citizen know his place in the realm of politics, for the art of statecraft is the rare gift of an elite. This "difficult art" is "perhaps the most difficult" of all activities in life. The "supreme law" of the state is "to regulate its internal matters" in accordance with the goal of "maintaining itself" against its "rivals" and "enemies" in power-political struggles.[23]

Spengler endorses the doctrine of the primacy of foreign policy. In the section of *The Decline of the West* entitled "The Philosophy of Politics," he declares, "Finally, politics is the form in which the history of a nation is consummated within a plural number of nations. The great art is to keep one's own nation in form internally for external events." The supreme

23. Heinrich Heffter, "Vom Primat der Aussenpolitik," *Historische Zeitschrift* 171 (1951): 2; Leopold von Ranke, *Politisches Gespräch* (Leipzig: Insel-Verlag, 1941), 52, 58, 42 ff.

purpose of domestic politics is to serve the needs of foreign policy. For "the power relationship to other peoples and powers decide" the future of a nation.[24]

Germany's military collapse in 1918 and the establishment of the Weimar Republic caused Spengler to rethink his politics. Opposing Weimar, he held a conservative, corporatist, semi-authoritarian state to be best qualified to meet the formidable challenges of foreign policy. "But it is a grave error of modern doctrinaires, to regard the spirit of domestic history as that of history in general. *World history is the history of states* and it will always be so. The inner constitution of a nation always and everywhere has the purpose *to be 'in condition'* for the external struggle, be it of a military, diplomatic, or economic nature."[25]

Like German historicist thinkers before him, Spengler insisted that external moral norms, as well as utilitarian standards with respect to the liberty and well-being of its citizens, should not interfere with the conduct of statecraft. The leadership of the state must instead be motivated by *raison d'État*, by unswerving commitment to its power-political interests. Spengler's thought is steeped in the power-political orientation of Ranke and German historicism. However, Spengler, a radical imperialist, heretically rejected historicism's commitment to the balance of power as the ordering principle of interstate interaction.

In the Wilhelmine era, confidence in the beneficent strength of German culture was perhaps greater than in any other period in German history.[26] Spengler exhibits, at times, overweening pride in German civilizational achievements. However, he deviates from this predominant intellectual current with his alarming vision of cultural decline. The existence in modern Europe of a multiplicity of great powers, celebrated by Ranke in *The Great Powers*, was interpreted by the historicist tradition as guaranteeing cultural health and diversity in the West.

The years from 1890 to 1914 formed the apex of modern optimism. An almost boundless confidence in the achievements of science and civilization prevailed. However, during the Second Reich the fear that modern civilization was in profound crisis inspired the tradition of German cultural pessimism. Not surprising, this fear was not reflected in the works of German historians during this era. Not only academia but the general public

24. *UdA* II, 555, 556.
25. *UdA* II, 452.
26. Iggers, *German Conception of History*, 127.

remained relatively unaffected by the underlying currents of cultural pessimism among diverse artists and thinkers in Wilhelmine society. While
Spengler appreciated the self-destructive nature of mass society and the
dark side of modern technology, Iggers notes, "German historians were
amazingly unafraid of the developing technology and mass society."
Spengler's exposure to intellectual influences originating outside the academic field of history enriched his perspective, as German historical
thought in the decades after the unification of Germany remained "remarkably immune from the currents of pessimistic thought."[27] Although
sharing the historicist conviction that history is the essential vehicle for understanding the human condition, Spengler rejects its characteristic optimism through his assimilation of insights from the tradition of cultural
pessimism. Indeed, *The Decline of the West* is a creative and provocative attempt to synthesize certain tenets of historicism with ideas derived from
German cultural pessimism, whose chief figures, Schopenhauer, Burckhardt, and Nietzsche, had operated essentially in isolation from German
historicism. Spengler sought to deepen the analysis of the competition for
power in international politics by illuminating the major historical trends
that condition the milieu within which states interact.

Spengler's intensive study of Nietzsche provided him with much of the
intellectual ammunition for attacking the idea of progress. While Vollgraff
and Lasaulx, historical pessimists and precursors of Burckhardt and Spengler, were ignored for the most part by their contemporaries, *The Decline of
the West* electrified the educated classes of Germany. They had just experienced the carnage of the Great War. Thus, they were receptive to a work
that placed in question the traditional optimism of historicism about the
providential nature of history and the solidity of European international
political order.

The Decline of the West is, ironically, heavily indebted to the very tradition of German historicism that its author rebelled against. Adapting to
his speculative purposes its historical methodology, Spengler incorporates
fundamental elements of historicism into his historical philosophy: the
tenet of individuality, the idea of history as a meaningful human drama,
the rejection of happiness as an end in life, the focus on great-power rivalry, and the doctrine of the primacy of foreign policy. To be sure, *The
Decline of the West* has its flaws and shortcomings. Yet with its opposition
to historicism's optimism, congeniality to the idea of progress, and linger-

27. *Ibid.*, 129, 240, 129, 128.

ing faith in a transcendent order; its vision of impending cultural sterility, decadence, and widespread materialism; its pioneering critique of Euro-centric historiography; its displacement of the nation-state by the culture or civilization as a basic unit of historical inquiry; and its thesis of the destruction of the European balance-of-power system by world wars, *The Decline of the West* strongly challenged German historicism in the crisis years of World War I and its aftermath. As Othmar Anderle observed, professional historians "attempted to ignore [*The Decline of the West*], but were nevertheless unable to prevent that its effects were felt in almost all fields."[28]

28. Othmar F. Anderle, "Theoretische Geschichte: Betrachtungen zur Grundla-genkrise der Geschichtswissenschaft," *Historische Zeitschrift* 185 (1958): 14.

4
The Decline of the West: Diverse Intellectual Sources and Influences

EARLIER CHAPTERS TOUCHED ON VARIous intellectual sources of and influences on Spengler's philosophy. In this chapter we will fill in the gaps and more systematically treat these sources and influences. One of the strongest impressions *The Decline of the West* makes—an impression attested to by admirers and critics alike—is its author's erudition. Eduard Meyer acknowledged Spengler's "extraordinarily comprehensive, constantly present knowledge."[1] The tone with which Spengler made pronouncements about history and the future has been frequently commented on.[2] Many critics found his omniscient and peremptory tone somewhat irritating. Yet this literary pose had an important didactic function that has been frequently overlooked by his critics. It enabled Spengler to conjure up an exciting and highly charged atmosphere in which the reader could visualize and experience history as a drama of powerful ideas and forces. Admittedly, Spengler's pose of the omniscient dramaturge of world history has negative qualities. First, his refusal to acknowledge that he later changed his ideas complicates the scholarly effort to analyze the evolution of his philosophy of world history and politics in his subsequent writings. Second, Spengler's rhetoric unintentionally creates the false impression on the inattentive reader that he interprets all of history as being deterministic in nature. Finally, the intoxicating effect of his writing style makes it very difficult for Spengler early in his career to

1. Eduard Meyer, *Spenglers "Untergang des Abendlandes"* (Berlin: Karl Curtius Verlag, 1925), 5.
2. For example, see Joseph Vogt, *Wege zum historischen Universum: Von Ranke bis Toynbee* (Stuttgart: Kohlhammer, 1961), 52.

acknowledge humbly the profound difficulties one faces in gaining deep insight into the complexities of international relations.

Being the work of a polymath, *The Decline of the West* has diverse intellectual sources. It is unfortunately beyond the scope of this inquiry to touch upon the main ones more than briefly. It should be noted, too, that precisely tracing the intellectual influences on Spengler is a very difficult enterprise for two reasons. First, his thought is both creative and synthetic. Second, as Hughes notes, "his practice in citing authorities was distinctly haphazard."[3]

Spengler's interdisciplinary work deviated from the trend in German universities during the Second Reich toward increased specialization. His interest in marrying theory and praxis, philosophy of world history and statecraft, stood in contrast to the divorce between theory and practice, to the "abstract and sterile intellectualism" that characterized much of German scholarship during this period.[4]

Many of Spengler's critics appear to have been motivated at times by a desire to discredit a thinker who was not only an unwelcome oracle of decline but, even worse, one lacking professorial credentials. Thus, they immediately began to raise questions not only about the intellectual influences on his work but about its originality as well. At one point in a letter to his friend and editor, Oscar Beck, Spengler complained that if one were to compile a list of all the possible intellectual predecessors alleged by his critics, it would mushroom to over a hundred names.[5] His claim that Goethe and Nietzsche decisively influenced his thought cannot be contested. However, as we have already seen, the influence of the German tradition of historicism on his philosophy of history and *Realpolitik* was considerable.

In the introduction to *The Decline of the West*, Spengler states, "In conclusion I feel compelled to name those once more, to whom I owe practically everything: Goethe and Nietzsche." Goethe's influence on modern European thought has been enormous. The Goethe cult reached its zenith around 1900, when Spengler attained early manhood.[6] He credited Goethe with three things of particular importance to his philosophy of

---

3. H-Sp, 51.

4. See Kurt F. Reinhardt, *Germany: 2000 Years*, vol. II, *The Second Empire and the Weimar Republic*, rev. ed. (New York: Frederick Ungar Publishing, 1961), 593, 442.

5. Spengler to Beck, 18 September 1921, quoted in K-Sp, xx.

6. *UdA* I, ix; Gerhard Masur, *Prophets of Yesterday: Studies in European Culture, 1890–1914* (New York: Harper & Row, 1961), 46.

world history. Goethe provided the master image of Faust. For Spengler, Faust is identical with Western culture; he "is the portrait of an entire culture."[7] Moreover, according to Spengler, though this is debatable, he appropriated from Goethe the idea of organically developing cycles of culture. In addition, the intuitiveness of his intellectual approach was purportedly derived from Goethe.

Nietzsche's influence on Spengler's work was profound. A Nietzsche cult had acquired prominence since the turn of the century. Spengler paid Nietzsche the supreme compliment, remarking in 1921 in the letter to Beck, "it is not possible at all to express anything today that hasn't been touched upon in Nietzsche's posthumous works." At the impressionable age of sixteen Spengler discovered Nietzsche through his *Zarathustra*. Thereafter, its author assumed a highly visible role in Spengler's intellectual development, starting with his doctoral dissertation on the one philosopher whom Nietzsche revered, Heraclitus, then in his major work and, finally, in his late work (*Spätwerk*), much of it consisting of aphoristic notes patterned after those of Nietzsche. As Massimo Ferrari Zumbini fittingly observed, "Nietzsche is present almost everywhere in *The Decline of the West*."[8]

In the preface to the revised edition of the first volume of *The Decline of the West*, Spengler succinctly described his relationship to Nietzsche: "I have made from his outlook a commanding view." He boldly implied that he had raised Nietzsche's thought to a higher level by virtue of his worship of historical knowledge, in contrast to Nietzsche, who had once warned of the historical sickness. Moreover, Nietzsche held a dim view of almost any attempt at systematic thought, having never formulated his own philosophy in systematic form.[9] In disapproving of Nietzsche's distaste for systematic thought and his unwillingness to endorse historicism's celebration of historical knowledge, Spengler regarded himself as correcting these and other purported shortcomings of Nietzsche's philosophy.

Spengler is animated by that same powerful drive to write "for the fu-

7. *UdA* I, 136.

8. Spengler to Beck, 18 September 1921, quoted in K-Sp, xx; Massimo Ferrari Zumbini, "Untergänge und Morgenröten: Über Spengler und Nietzsche," in *Nietzsche Studien: Internationales Jahrbuch für die Nietzsche-Forschung*, ed. Mazzino Montinari, Wolfgang Müller-Lauter, and Heinz Wenzel, vol. V (Berlin: Walter de Gruyter, 1976), 217.

9. *UdA* I, ix; Friedrich Nietzsche, *Vom Nutzen und Nachtheil der Historie für das Leben*, *KSA*, vol. I, 329.

ture" and to philosophize "with a hammer" that inspired Nietzsche. Spengler ambitiously attempts to systematize in the form of a philosophy of world history Nietzsche's seminal diagnosis of the crisis of the modern West. Moreover, *The Decline of the West* is an effort at executing Nietzsche's project, announced in the famous preface to *The Will to Power*, of narrating "the history of the next two centuries."[10] *The Decline of the West* incorporates several fundamental Nietzschean themes: epistemological relativism, the distinction between culture and civilization, decadence, the transformation of all values, the will to power, the adulation of great men, *amor fati*, and the vision of the twentieth century as an age of struggle for world rule.

Nietzsche, despite his apoliticism, greatly influenced the tradition of international political thought in Germany in the twentieth century. Philosophers of international politics were trying to come to grips with the primacy of power in an age of imperialistic rivalries, revolutionary tensions and upheaval, and world wars. Nietzsche's paeans to power and to the men who grasped after power in world history appealed to them.

Both Martin Heidegger and Thomas Mann disparaged Spengler as being merely derivative of Nietzsche. Thus Heidegger, in contemplating the future of the West, showed little appreciation for the complexity of Spengler's critical evaluation and selective appropriation of Nietzsche's ideas. He condescendingly claimed that Spengler "calculated" the decline of the West on the basis of Nietzsche's "all too crudely understood philosophy." Yet despite Heidegger's sharp criticism of its author, *The Decline of the West* "affected him profoundly."[11]

Mann, who felt antagonism toward Spengler on account of political differences, labeled him Nietzsche's "clever ape." Such criticism is superficial and unjustifiable. For did not Spengler reject the fervent aspiration at the core of Nietzsche's thought to return modern European man to the ennobling spirit of classical Greece? Spengler criticized Nietzsche as the "last Romantic," as the "last victim of the South."[12] He strenuously objected

10. Friedrich Nietzsche, *Der Wille zur Macht: Versuch einer Umwertung aller Werte*, ed. Peter Gast (Stuttgart: Alfred Kröner, 1964), 3.

11. Martin Heidegger, "Der Spruch des Anaximander," in *Holzwege*, 3d ed. (Frankfurt am Main: Vittorio Klostermann, 1957), 301; Arthur Herman, *The Idea of Decline in Western History* (New York: Free Press, 1997), 336.

12. Thomas Mann, *Nietzsches Philosophie im Lichte unserer Erfahrung* (Berlin: Suhrkamp, 1948), 40; *UdA* I, 473, 39.

to Nietzsche's dubious claim that modern European man was inferior to the denizens of the classical world and of Renaissance Italy.[13]

Spengler is not a mere epigone of Nietzsche but an original mind who created a richer and more coherent vision of world history than his precursor Nietzsche did. Mann's shallow, simian sobriquet fails to recognize not only the quality of genius in Spengler's philosophy of history but also the considerable differences between the philosophies of Spengler and Nietzsche. First, in sharp contrast to Nietzsche, Spengler's attitude toward Christianity was ambiguous. While denying the claim of Christianity to absolute truth, he nonetheless respected Christianity as a fundamental expression of Western culture. Second, whereas Nietzsche expressed open hostility to the state, Spengler viewed it as man's highest ethical responsibility to serve the state dutifully and wisely in the terrible arena of power politics. Third, in sharp contrast to Nietzsche, who championed human volition, Spengler viewed the individual as being subjected to the imperious movement of transcendent historical forces. Moreover, he dismissed as utopian Nietzsche's key concepts of the *Übermensch* and the eternal return. Finally and most important, Spengler's writings on world history and politics greatly expand the boundaries of Nietzsche's confined historical cosmos. As Spengler observed, "Let us consider the historical horizon of Nietzsche. His concepts of decadence, of nihilism, of the revaluation of all values, of the will to power, which are deeply rooted in the essence of Western civilization and simply essential for its analysis—what was the foundation for their creation? Romans and Greeks, Renaissance and European present, the incorporation of a fleeting look sideways to a (misunderstood) Indian philosophy, in short: Antiquity, Middle Ages, modern era. Strictly speaking, he never moved beyond that and the other thinkers of his age as little as he."[14]

Nietzsche also provides the link between Spengler and the cultural pessimist Jacob Burckhardt. Burckhardt and Nietzsche, as colleagues at the University of Basel, enjoyed an intellectual association. Like a lone eagle gazing down upon the world below from his mountaintop aerie in Switzerland, Burckhardt brilliantly forecasted the impending vulgarization of Western cultural and political life. As he wrote, "We may all go under. . . .

---

13. As Nietzsche claimed, "We have, for example, with all the exertion of three centuries not yet reached again the *man of the Renaissance*; and on the other hand, the man of the Renaissance remained behind the *man of antiquity*" (Nietzsche, *Der Wille zur Macht*, 599).

14. *UdA* I, 31.

I will at least seek out the interest for which I shall go under, namely the culture of old Europe."[15] A seminal art historian, he anticipated Spengler's thesis of the exhaustion of the cultural vitality of Western culture. Moreover, Spengler shared, in some respects, Burckhardt's disdain, as a man of cultivation, for America. However, Burckhardt, who eschewed historical systems, did not offer a detailed system of historical philosophy elaborating the decline of the West as did Spengler.

Spengler's philosophy of world history has deep roots in German Romantic thought and idealism. Romantic thought generally reflects an intuitional character, central to his methodology. Romantic historians rediscovered the European Middle Ages, which Spengler interpreted as representing the true spiritual origins of West European culture. Influenced by the tradition of German idealistic philosophy, he similarly affirms spiritual principles of a pantheistic quality in the attempt to explain reality. He shares with his idealistic predecessors a conviction of the constructive power of the human mind, in combination with a relative disregard for experience and experimental science as sources of knowledge. Spengler portrays world history as a magnificent tableau of recurring totalities of historical reality, each expressive of a unique *Seele*, a cultural soul. He demonstrates here his affinity with the tradition of German idealistic philosophy of the Romantic period. It sought to reduce the sum total of reality to one fundamental principle: Johann Gottlieb Fichte with his "Transcendental Ego," Friedrich Wilhelm von Schelling with his "World Soul," Hegel with his "World Spirit," and Schopenhauer with his "World Will."[16]

Georg Simmel is reputed to have observed that the first volume of *The Decline of the West* was "the most significant historical philosophy since Hegel."[17] In a letter in 1919 to the philosopher Georg Misch, Spengler made it quite clear that he regarded his philosophy of history as a powerful counterposition to Hegel's. Yet Spengler also acknowledged a few years later his intellectual debt to Hegel, singling out his *Lectures on the Philosophy of History* along with the works of Gottfried Wilhelm Leibniz, Goethe, and Nietzsche as the "hidden prerequisites, which unconsciously lay at the basis of my style of thinking."[18]

15. Quoted in H-Sp, 17.

16. Reinhardt, *Germany*, 499 ff.

17. Spengler to Klöres, 18 December 1918, *B*, 114. See also Spengler to August Albers, 25 June 1919, *B*, 131; Georg Misch to Spengler, 8 November 1918, *B*, 109.

18. Spengler to Misch, 5 January 1919, *B*, 116–19; *P*, 66.

The philosophical speculation of the Romantic age and, indeed, of most of German philosophy in the nineteenth century is determined by its relationship to Immanuel Kant's seminal thought.[19] Despite his objection that Kant's epistemology fails to shed light upon historical phenomena, Spengler proceeds to make radical use of Kantian philosophical ideas concerning man's capacity to attain objective knowledge of reality. Kant had written in opposition to the empiricists John Locke, David Hume, and George Berkeley, who had maintained that knowledge is based on our external senses. For Kant, the seat of knowledge is not an objective one, the external world, but a subjective one, the mind. Kant argued that man is compelled to comprehend his experiences in the phenomenal world within the frameworks of space, time, and causation, which have their origin in the human mind. Spengler transforms this revolutionary idea, emplacing it as the centerpiece of his historical relativism, asserting that successive cultures create unique perceptual frameworks of space, time, and causation. They develop transitory modes for intellectually experiencing reality; it remains beyond the capacity of the human mind to grasp fully. The course of world history does not lead to an increasingly superior objective knowledge of the ultimate nature of reality. It merely generates various transitory, grand myths for its interpretation.

The intellectual pedigree of Spengler's cyclical model of world history is clouded. He credits Goethe, but doubts remain.[20] Spengler does not offer any details that would conclusively resolve the question of whether other thinkers besides Goethe may have influenced his conception of a cyclical historical model, which seems quite plausible. Vico's *New Science*, published in 1725, is generally recognized as the most developed, cyclical historical-philosophical work prior to the emergence of critical historical science in the nineteenth century. Vico, like Spengler after him, maintains that the methodology of the natural sciences is incapable of explaining human social phenomena. Vico also advances the idea, essential to Spengler and Toynbee, that a consideration of history on a comparative basis yields general principles.

Hughes suggests that the study of the cyclical historical thought of Joachim of Floris or of Vico possibly played a key role in Spengler's development of a cyclical model of history. He points out that Spengler revered Joachim of Floris as one of the great minds of the medieval world. More-

19. Reinhardt, *Germany*, 499.
20. *UdA* II, 43 n. 1.

over, Vico's ideas were "a familiar part of the German educational program" in Spengler's school years.[21] However, one could argue that he had
been exposed to much of the essence of Vico's cyclical model through his
meticulous study of the works of Nietzsche and Goethe, both of whom
were significantly influenced by the Italian thinker. Moreover, Spengler
held Machiavelli in high regard and, presumably, was familiar with his theory of cycles of political forms in *The Discourses*. Furthermore, as a well-
trained classical scholar, Spengler was conversant with the works of the ancient Roman historian Polybius, who had developed the mature concept
of a cyclical historical model.

The Russian naturalist Nikolai Danilevsky, the chief ideologue of Rus-
sophilism, published in serial form in 1869 a remarkable book, *Russia and
Europe*. A polemical work of historical philosophy, it bears some striking
similarities to *The Decline of the West*. Like Spengler's major work, *Russia
and Europe* is both a comparative world history and a "program for the
future." Although *The Decline of the West* ranges more widely and sees
more deeply into the future, this somewhat obscure yet nonetheless important work, more than any other historical-philosophical tome, directly
anticipates some of the major ideas Spengler presents almost fifty years
later. Danilevsky advances a cyclical philosophy of world history based on
the biological metaphor. In addition, he maintains, as Spengler did, that
Russia is the bearer of vital cultural forces different from those of the West
and will create a dominant culture in the future. However, it seems reasonable to conclude that Spengler acquired the latter idea from his study of
Dostoevsky, whom he held in great esteem and whose name he invoked
when he adumbrated his vision of Russia's future.[22] Moreover, the differences between the two works of historical philosophy seem to be as considerable as the similarities.

Danilevsky, in contrast to Spengler, regards science as a universal and
cumulative body of knowledge spanning the various cultures of world history. The taxonomy of cultures is significantly different; Spengler com-
bines Greek culture and Roman civilization into one grand historical cycle
and compresses what is for Danilevsky the separate cultures of Iran, the
Hebrews, and the Arab world, along with contributions from other socie-

21. H-Sp, 51, 53.
22. Cyril E. Black, "Russian Interpretations of World History," in James N. Rosenau, Vincent Davis, and Maurice A. East, eds., *The Analysis of International Politics*
(New York: Free Press, 1972), 373; Spengler to Klöres, 12 October 1916, *B*, 55.

ties to the west, into one cultural amalgam, Magian culture. Thus, two of the three cultures that were the focus of inquiry in *The Decline of the West* were treated much differently. Danilevsky's theory provided for the transmission of cultural influences that Spengler's virtually denied. Danilevsky maintained that the Slavic peoples would be the first nation in world history to excel simultaneously in all the major fields of cultural and social activity. This exaggerated nationalist claim is at odds with Spengler's thesis of the essential equality of value of cultures.[23] It seems rather likely that Spengler had not read Danilevsky's work in the original Russian prior to composing the first volume of *The Decline of the West*, especially when one bears in mind that he apparently would read his revered Dostoevsky in Russian, not with ease, but only with considerable effort. Danilevsky's work was not translated into German until 1920. It appeared only in the form of an abridged edition two years after the publication of the first volume of *The Decline of the West*.

The cyclicity of Spengler's philosophy is an echo from the classical world; his "irrationalism" is certainly very modern. As Hughes emphasizes, Spengler held the conviction, in common with many thinkers in the forefront of his time, that knowledge and ideas were rooted in "nonlogical preconceptions." His appreciation of the substratal, irrational qualities of world history finds its counterpart in psychology in Freud's investigation of the unconscious, in philosophy in Henri Bergson's reflections on the role of the élan vital, and in sociology in Vilfredo Pareto's study of reform ideals and political motivations.[24]

Spengler understood Western civilization and its future to be shaped, to a great extent, by human irrationality. Confidence in the rational and progressive nature of human history has been shaken in the twentieth century by the hammer blows of world wars, economic depression, genocide, the specter of nuclear annihilation, and a population explosion on an ecologically ravaged, resource-limited planet. Yet human optimism, far from being expunged, has proven resilient. After all, the twentieth century has been referred to, with some justification, as the American century. In the modern West, reassuring optimism, whether guarded or more robust, in the course of human history is conventional, whereas historical pessimism stirs up heated controversy. We direct our attention next to the critical reaction to the publication of *The Decline of the West*.

23. Black, "Russian Interpretations," 373–74; H-Sp, 48–49.
24. H-Sp, 22 ff.

5
The Decline of the West:
A Controversy Without End

ALTHOUGH THE CONTENT OF *THE DE-cline of the West* sparked great controversy, critics did not dispute its literary quality. Thomas Mann spoke of the "literary brilliance" of the work. The French professor of German literature André Fauconnet offered this supreme accolade: "La langue de Spengler est d'une richesse et d'une originalité incomparables."[1]

Praise aside, *The Decline of the West* remains one of the most controversial of all the classic books of the twentieth century.[2] The controversy that the first volume unleashed in Weimar Germany, which reverberated in the West and elsewhere as well, has long since abated but has never completely died down. The controversy will endure as long as the question of the fate of our civilization preoccupies mankind. The learned world has found it very difficult to approach Spengler's major work dispassionately, perhaps because it is virtually impossible to do so. *The Decline of the West* is, by its very nature, highly creative and speculative and thus quite properly invites searching criticism from those committed to traditional canons of scholarship. However, one cannot avoid the impression that the intensity and emotionalism of much of the criticism reflects antagonism toward Speng-

1. Gilbert Merlio, *Oswald Spengler: Témoin de son temps*, vol. I (Stuttgart: Akademischer Verlag Hans-Dieter Heinz, 1982), 16 n. 2; Thomas Mann, "Über die Lehre Spenglers," in *Gesammelte Werke*, 2d ed., vol. X (Frankfurt: S. Fischer, 1974), 173; André Fauconnet, *Un Philosophe Allemand Contemporain: Oswald Spengler* (Paris: Librairie Félix Alcan, 1925), v.

2. *Daedalus*, the Journal of the American Academy of Arts and Sciences, brought out an issue in 1973 entitled "Twentieth-Century Classics Revisited." Northrop Frye contributed the lead article on Spengler's major work. See *Daedalus* 103, no. 1 (Winter, 1973): 1–13.

ler's anti-Weimar neoconservatism and historical pessimism. W. Wolfradt in his book review in 1919 underscored the role of political prejudice in the impassioned controversy in Germany over *The Decline of the West* with these words of protest: "But I will not quietly tolerate, that here, out of political hostility, the man is condemned, to whom we owe the richest, most broad in outlook, most imaginative work of the epoch." Moreover, that an unknown, former gymnasial teacher authored a ponderous philosophical work that was a best seller as well could not help but arouse envy on the part of some of his German critics. As Hermann Lübbe noted, Spengler, like Nietzsche before him, presents "the rare case of a German philosopher who reached the broad public."[3] Particularly a number of university professors reacted enviously, viewing themselves as the mandarins of academia called upon to defend their sanctuary against Spengler's "dilettantish" intrusion.

Publication of the first volume of *The Decline of the West* coincided roughly with the defeat of Germany in World War I, the fall of the Hohenzollern monarchy, and the political, social, and intellectual disorientation of its educated elite. The book generated "the most excited and bitter literary controversy" of Germany in the interwar period. Ironically, the book's popularity resulted, to an extent, from a misunderstanding caused by the sensational title. Confused and dejected Germans were apprehensive that the demise of their glorious Reich meant the beginning of the end of Europe and looked to Spengler's book for orientation in a turbulent age.[4]

The luminaries of the German intellectual community, including Friedrich Meinecke, Ernst Troeltsch, Max Weber, Otto Hintze, Eduard Meyer, Kurt Breysig, Erich Brandenburg, Ulrich von Wilamowitz, Thomas Mann, Robert Musil, and Hermann Graf Keyserling, did not hesitate to take sides in the debate that raged around the philosopher of the hour. The reaction of the innumerable critics poured forth in a veritable flood of book reviews, newspaper articles, essays, and treatises. Criticism ran the gamut from the condemnation of Spengler as a charlatan to the extolling of his book as "*the decisive work of historical philosophy since Hegel's.*" Intellectuals to this day are hopelessly divided, and will remain so, on the signifi-

---

3. W. Wolfradt, review of *The Decline of the West*, by Oswald Spengler, quoted in Manfred Schröter, *Der Streit um Spengler. Kritik seiner Kritiker* (Munich: C. H. Beck, 1922), 8 n. 5; Hermann Lübbe, foreword to Peter C. Ludz, ed., *Spengler heute* (Munich: C. H. Beck, 1980), viii.

4. H-Sp, 1; K-Sp, 214.

cance of Spengler's work, particularly with respect to enhancing our understanding of the historical, political, economic, social, and cultural forces at work in the modern world. Bruce Mazlish scathingly remarks that "it is clear that [Spengler] does not understand either modern civilization or modern history. . . . It is Spengler's blindness to the important ideas and movements of his own time which marks the bankruptcy of his intuitive method." His colleague, H. Stuart Hughes, as we noted earlier, concludes his study of Spengler with glowing praise: "*The Decline of the West* offers the nearest thing we have to a key to our times."[5]

For the most part, Spengler prudently avoided becoming embroiled in a direct confrontation with his critics. The task of mounting a defense was left to a friend and admirer, the philosophy professor Manfred Schröter. In his career Schröter published two books on Spengler and collaborated with Anton Mirko Koktanek in posthumously publishing works from Spengler's literary estate in the sixties. Impressed by "the superior and daemonic strength" of the first volume of *The Decline of the West*, he exhaustively documented in a monograph the controversy in Germany surrounding the book. Convinced of the importance of Spengler's tome in assisting in deepening "the cultural-critical self-knowledge" of his era, Schröter complains that critics generally contented themselves with "pedantic and external criticism of details." Instead of evaluating the work in an integrated and comprehensive fashion, a host of specialists advanced a highly fragmented critique from the narrow perspective of their own disciplines. Schröter protests that the academic critics operated at a completely different level from Spengler's universal perspective, failing with their salvos of reviews and articles to generate a truly enlightening debate. As he eloquently remonstrates, "whoever does not feel stirring behind Spengler's violent constructions the spirit of a mighty, incomparably lively cultural comprehension, will always only be able to remain stuck in negative objections."[6]

An amusing anecdote about a scholar engaging in "pedantic and external criticism of details" concerns an American, Edith Wharton. Spengler's American publisher, Alfred Knopf, relates the incident: "[Wharton] wrote

5. Theodor W. Adorno, "Spengler nach dem Untergang: Zu Oswald Spenglers 70. Geburtstag," *Der Monat* 2, no. 20 (May, 1950): 115; Otto Braun, review of *The Decline of the West*, by Oswald Spengler, quoted in Schröter, *Streit um Spengler*, 96 n. 2; Bruce Mazlish, *The Riddle of History: The Great Speculators from Vico to Freud* (New York: Harper & Row, 1966), 350; H-Sp, 165.

6. Schröter, *Streit um Spengler*, iv, 7, 36.

Spengler upbraiding him for what she called his ignorance of Baroque art. He replied by citing in his support, among other sources, a study in an encyclopaedia of widely recognized authority. 'I know,' Mrs. Wharton wrote in reply, 'but I wrote that article, and at the time I was misinformed.' "[7]

Schröter observes that with a few exceptions, "all the critiques that deserve to be taken seriously, despite their feeling for the supreme significance and consequence of the work are nevertheless basically negatively oriented." He pinpoints "the condemnation of [Spengler's] forecast of our future," so unbearable to the critics, as the "reason for the almost universal opposition" by the intellectual community. It was as if "a deep and hidden wound had been painfully touched" by the author.[8]

The academic specialties of theology and musicology were the only exceptions to the otherwise virtually unanimous disapprobation of the German academic world. Protestant theological critics were the most sympathetic. However, they arbitrarily infused Spengler's vision of the future with their own idealistic aspirations. They hoped that Western civilization's decline would sweep aside all obstructions to the rejuvenation of Christian religious fervor. Musicologists reviewed *The Decline of the West* favorably, for, as one critic maintained, "it is Spengler's service, that he, for the first time, has correctly appreciated the significance of music for European history."[9]

Eduard Meyer, in an address before the German Historical Congress of 1924, in retrospectively surveying the reaction to the book, like Schröter before him, stressed the unfortunate tendency of many of his German colleagues to believe that they could dispose of the "great and lasting fundamental ideas" of the work by simply highlighting its errors in matters of detail.[10] It is obviously beyond the scope of this study to review the extensive body of criticism concerning specific minor details of *The Decline of the West*. I will concentrate on that which is ultimately of more importance, the major points of criticism, introducing arguments primarily but not exclusively voiced in the original controversy.

7. Alfred Knopf, "Biographical Note," in Edwin Franden Dakin, ed., *Today and Destiny: Vital Excerpts from "The Decline of the West" of Oswald Spengler* (New York: Knopf, 1940), 356.

8. Schröter, *Streit um Spengler*, 7, 9, 13.

9. *Ibid.*, 13, 55.

10. Eduard Meyer, *Spenglers "Untergang des Abendlandes"* (Berlin: Karl Curtius Verlag, 1925), 6.

One of the most bizarre but nonetheless fundamental objections to Spengler's work is that his philosophy of history offers nothing really new. R. G. Collingwood readily dismissed Spengler as a mere epigone of a long line of cyclical Western historical philosophers. Yet Collingwood fails to back up his dubious claim that "not only has the main thesis of Spengler's book been familiar to [me] all [my] life, but . . . the reading of it has not given [me] a single genuinely new idea."[11]

Major features of Spengler's treatment of the phenomenon of culture have been the object of much criticism. Critics focused on the idea that Western culture overshadows all its constituent national cultures, on his claim of being able to interpret authoritatively the characters of diverse cultures, on his depreciation of transcultural influence, on the analogy between a culture and an organism, and on his typology of cultures. Many prominent German contemporaries, including Arthur Moeller van den Bruck and Erich Brandenburg, the historian of German unification on the eve of World War I, with its inflammation of German national passions, found fault with Spengler's understanding of German culture. They rose to the defense of the traditional historicist perspective, which esteemed German culture as a distinctive phenomenon whose genius was a product of the German nation. Moeller van den Bruck and Brandenburg attacked Spengler's thesis of the individuality of German national culture being subsumed within a higher and more significant form of historical identity, the culture of Western Europe. Brandenburg complained sourly, "However, it appears even stranger to us, that undoubtedly spiritually so different peoples like the French, Italians, Spanish, Germans, and English, should likewise be bearers of a single cultural idea, emanations of the same cultural soul, the Faustian." Moeller van den Bruck concurred, "there is no uniform Occident."[12]

Thomas Mann argued that a contradiction exists between Spengler's assertion that the essence of cultural phenomena was so foreign to denizens of other cultures that it could not be thoroughly comprehended or appreciated by them and Spengler's purported ability, as a member of Western civilization, to be able to do so. This objection has limited value. First,

11. R. G. Collingwood, "Oswald Spengler and the Theory of Historical Cycles," *Antiquity: A Quarterly Review of Archaeology* 1, no. 1 (March, 1927): 314.

12. Erich Brandenburg, "Spenglers 'Untergang des Abendlandes' " *Historische Vierteljahrschrift* 20 (1920–21): 9; Arthur Moeller van den Bruck, "Der Untergang des Abendlandes: Für und wider Spengler," *Deutsche Rundschau* 46, no. 10 (July, 1920): 63.

Mann exaggerates when he implies that Spengler hubristically claimed a monopoly on this ability. "Only . . . Mr. Spengler is endowed with the intuition to understand all of them." Spengler describes this "entirely modern" gift as being "extremely rare" and shared by a few extremely historically oriented individuals. Second, Spengler stresses the limitations on him as well as others who seek to understand foreign cultures.[13] Third, his argument of the virtually mutually incomprehensible nature of cultures has value. It cautions us from making the glib assumption that an alien civilization is easily intellectually accessible. One cannot simply apply modern Western terms to the cultural products of other civilizations. Indeed, in the course of the twentieth century, researchers have become increasingly aware of the individuality of a wide variety of human cultures, ranging from the "primitive" to the "highly advanced," and the considerable barriers to mutual understanding.

Spengler's controversial thesis that cultural systems are to a large extent closed and his de-emphasizing of cross-cultural influence have justifiably been the targets of extensive scholarly criticism. He does exaggerate the discontinuity of history and largely ignores the existence of considerable scientific and technological progress before 1000 A.D. from which Western Europe since the Gothic Age has been able to profit. Although Spengler's position on cultural diffusion is too extreme, it is not without some insight. First, contact between early civilizations did not necessarily translate into significant cultural transmission. For example, even though the archaeological and historical record reveal that significant contact occurred between the ancient civilizations of Egypt and Mesopotamia, they exerted little influence on each other's cultural style. Second, Spengler's bold thesis that civilization developed entirely indigenously in the New World, an unorthodox one in the 1920s, corresponds to current expert opinion, which has finally rejected the popular theory of cultural diffusion positing that civilization in the New World was transferred from the Old. Third, and most important, Spengler's emphasis on cultural distinctiveness and plurality, exaggerated and pressed into a rigid framework as it is, remains to a degree justified by contemporary scholarship. The world historian J. M. Roberts observes that our present picture of past civilizations in world history is one of a multiplicity of "powerful, distinctive, often self-conscious and largely independent traditions at work," which probably achieved an apex of cultural diversification ironically at the very point that

13. Mann, "Lehre Spenglers," 175; *UdA* II, 64; *UdA* I, 214.

the Westernization of the globe and the destruction of traditional civilizational individuality began, with the Age of Discovery around 1500.[14]

According to his critics, Spengler erred when he denied that external cultural influences played a significant role in the development of Western civilization. Moeller van den Bruck argued that Spengler overlooked "that antiquity and the West merged into each other through the medium first of Hellenism, then of Christianity, and finally of the barbarian invasions." Meyer maintained that modern Western science depended on advances made in classical Greece. "Therefore every science that exists upon the earth goes back to the intellectual ferment that took place in the Greek world from the middle of the sixth to the close of the fourth centuries B.C." Brandenburg protested, "We work in all areas of knowledge with conceptions, technical terms, and discoveries that derive from the classical world and partially the Mesopotamian and Egyptian culture."[15]

One should place Spengler's heretical thesis of the absence of significant cultural transmission in its proper context. He sought to challenge the oppressive domination in the nineteenth and early twentieth centuries of Hegelian, Comtean, Marxian, Social Darwinist, and liberal visions of historical progress. He attempted to negate the idea of progress in two ways: first, by emphasizing the recurrent phenomenon of civilizational decline; and second, by denying the primacy of cultural transference, which in the progressivist view ensures the continuity of human civilizational achievement. Moreover, Spengler was profoundly conscious of the uniqueness of the West. He tried to fathom the essence of the modern civilizational experience, seeking to ascertain whether it was fundamentally an architecture of rationality built upon earlier "achievements of mankind," as the mandarins of historical progress maintained, or whether it was a wondrous, irrational experience.

The Decline of the West inadequately dealt with the complex question of the nature of transcultural influence. One must side with his critics when they affirm that West European-American civilization represents in certain respects a synthesis of the cultural achievements of advanced civilizations of the past. Yet, in defense of Spengler, it is extremely difficult to demon-

14. John A. J. Gowlett, *Ascent to Civilization: The Archaeology of Early Man* (New York: Knopf, 1984), 191; J. M. Roberts, *The Pelican History of the World* (Harmondsworth, England: Penguin Books, 1983), 309.

15. Moeller van den Bruck, "Untergang des Abendlandes," 50; Meyer, *Spenglers "Untergang des Abendlandes,"* 14; Brandenburg, " 'Untergang des Abendlandes,' " 11.

strate how the West simultaneously built upon the civilizational achievements of the past, infusing them with a new ethos, while making a tremendous leap forward in civilizational advancement. Furthermore, his exaggerated hypothesis of cultural individuality has considerable merit, which many critics fail to appreciate. It illuminates the uniqueness of Western culture, which has revolutionized the process of history unfolding on this planet like no other civilization. Western culture created modern science and technology. It has established a global economic and political system and transformed the planet into a theater of an interconnected world history. Moreover, Spengler's compelling portrait of the spirit of the West illumines its profound, subconscious, ultimately self-destructive, irrational qualities—qualities that are arguably ultimately of greater significance in determining the fate of the modern world than its rational qualities, which the Western high priests of the idea of progress have deified.

Many critics reviled Spengler's historical determinism: his emphasis on the primacy of historical forces and his corresponding de-emphasis of human freedom. Karl Joël complained that man was not recognized as the autonomous agent of his history. "It is perhaps the whole sickness of this significant book, that it has forgotten man with his creative doing and freedom." Benedetto Croce, taking issue with Spengler's denying Western man an open future, sanguinely argued that the decline of the West could be avoided through the exercise of human freedom. "Man is intellectuality, for that reason creativity, and carries within him infinite powers, which enable him to face all situations, to overcome and to transform them, no matter how difficult or desperate they also appear to be."[16] In Spengler's defense, many of the epochal developments in modern Western history do indeed seem to have been, when viewed retrospectively, virtually inevitable. The increased role of the masses in politics, the massive migration from rural to urban areas and the formation of world cities, secularization, the breakdown of the family unit, the decline in the artistic traditions of the West, the emergence of a materialistic world civilization, the rise of a world economy, the globalization of international politics, the continuing revolution in military technology, and the outbreak of the terrible struggle

---

16. Karl Joël, "Die Philosophie in Spengler's 'Untergang des Abendlandes,' " *Logos: Internationale Zeitschrift für Philosophie der Kultur* 9 (1920–21): 140; Benedetto Croce, "Oswald Spengler—'Der Untergang des Abendlandes,' " in Benedetto Croce, *Randbemerkungen eines Philosophen zum Weltkriege, 1914–1920*, trans. Julius Schlosser (Leipzig: Amalthea, 1922), 299.

for global hegemony are all landmarks in Spengler's panorama of modern cyclical historical change. Are not these landmarks perhaps necessary features of an organically developing, deterministic, world-historical process? Could the much-vaunted element of human freedom in history, the antipode of determinism, have truly enabled the peoples of the West to succeed in reversing any of these powerful historical trends? And can human freedom, as Croce affirms, enable modern man to direct the future course of civilizational change? Spengler raises the serious question of to what degree individuals or societies truly exercise free will in determining the general nature and direction of civilizational change.

Collingwood, in his posthumous work, *The Idea of History*, harshened his already negative evaluation of *The Decline of the West*. He grossly underestimated the value of Spengler's metaphorical conceptualization of a culture as an organism, subjecting it to scornful criticism. In using the analogy of an organism, Spengler tried to emphasize four things. First, he shows that man, despite his intellect and creativity, cannot transcend in his cultural activity the limits of the natural world, a world of growth and decay. Man's proud creation, his culture, grows, matures, and decays like all biological forms of life. Second, in history the process of cultural development is primary, and the freedom of the individual historical actor is secondary. Cultural developments, once initiated, take on a powerful life of their own. Third, the concept of an organism reinforces the argument that cultures not only have a life-span but are geographically delimited as well. There is an intimate relationship between a culture's physical environment and its ethos. Fourth, the concept of an organism, which is a unity of life energies, underscores the holistic nature of cultural expression and development. Finally, Collingwood ridiculed Spengler's biological analogy by comparing the life cycle of a culture to the lowly life cycle of an insect. He should have recalled that Spengler characterized cultures as "living things of the highest order," ones implicitly more complex and significant than the highest known actual biological form of life, man.[17]

One objection, which has acquired more weight as our knowledge of world history has grown, concerns the question of what macrohistorical phenomena should be considered to be cultures or civilizations. Although Spengler helped to expand the horizons of historical thought in the West, nonetheless the completeness of his taxonomy of high cultures, to say nothing of what the spatial and temporal limits of a given culture or civili-

17. *UdA* I, 28.

zation are, is open to serious question. Toynbee later classified for comparative analysis more than twenty civilizations in his *A Study of History*. Moreover, Spengler only subjects West European culture, classical antiquity, and the Arab world to in-depth analysis in his major work.

Understandably, readers are typically more interested in what Spengler had to say about the decline of their own civilization than that of the "fossilized" civilizations of the remote past. However, the question of the historical completeness and accuracy of his classificatory scheme of eight cultures cannot be ignored. The first volume of *The Decline of the West* was completed over seventy years ago. During the intervening decades, important additions to our knowledge of early civilizational history have been made. One example, Mohenjo-Daro, indicates how subsequent archaeological discoveries have rendered Spengler's survey of civilizations somewhat outdated.

Archaeologists started digging at the site of Harrapa, on a tributary of the Indus in 1921 and discovered Mohenjo-Daro in 1922. The archaeological evidence collected at these two sites demonstrates the existence of an important early civilization of the Indian sub-continent. It reveals "a society highly organized and capable of carefully regulated collective works on a scale equalling those of Egypt and Mesopotamia."[18] Harrapan culture was established around 2250 B.C. and appears to end approximately 1750 B.C. In the interpretation of cultural developments of the Indian sub-continent in *The Decline of the West*, its author naturally does not mention this important early civilization.

Spengler's understanding of the past was criticized; so was his effort to anticipate the future. Collingwood, as a staunch defender of the historical craft, caustically rejects Spengler's project of future-oriented historical philosophy as absurd. On the one hand, Collingwood is right when he stresses that no one can accurately forecast future events in detail. Spengler apparently grasped the fact that his audacious assertion in *The Decline of the West* that his philosophy enabled one to predict the future was unsustainable. In subsequent works he acknowledges the impossibility of anticipating major historical developments, particularly those in international politics, with anything approaching exactitude. On the other hand, Collingwood is unwilling to admit that a gifted intuitive and historical mind is capable of sensing to a degree and with varying success the dim outlines of future historical development. This is puzzling in light of his agreement

18. Roberts, *History of the World*, 133.

with Spengler that the modern West has an extraordinary historical sense in contrast to classical antiquity, which one would expect to translate into at least a modest measure of insight into future historical development.[19] Here, Collingwood is painfully out of tune with the twentieth and twenty-first centuries. Our entire economic and political life today is future oriented. Any sensible investor desires that the managers of his or her corporation attempt to anticipate major long-term business and market developments; any prudent citizen of a great power desires its leadership to ponder seriously lines of future development in international politics.

Many critics raised concern about the possibly deleterious impact of cultural pessimism on the West. For members of our civilization arguably need some hopefulness and guarded optimism in order to master the challenges in the present and future. Kurt Breysig objected to Spengler's argument of cultural decline and his advocacy of modernism. Breysig condemned his work as "aiming at the destruction of the courage and the strength for all works of deeper culture." Brandenburg feared that Spengler's pessimism would exert "a paralyzing effect upon many creative forces." Ernst Troeltsch sounded the warning that Spengler's book might function as "an active contribution to the decline of the West." In the preface to a special edition of the journal *Logos* on *The Decline of the West*, seven academic specialists united in their resolve to demolish the book through their criticism. They declared it their duty "to protect from a theory, through criticism of that undertaking, the already tortured psyche of the people" of Germany.[20] Here I must raise a dissenting voice. Should we not recognize the epochal philosophical necessity, which Spengler fulfilled, of bringing to full historical consciousness the shallowness of the faith of the eighteenth and nineteenth centuries in historical progress and the alarming reality of the decline of the West? This achievement outweighs the legitimate concern of critics with the possible impact of such a pathbreaking, yet admittedly disturbing, work on its readers. It is ironic and revelatory of the widespread need in the modern West to hope and entertain at least some measure of optimism that a work that appeared during the final stages of the most destructive war hitherto experienced in all of world history—a war that justified the systematization in a philosophy

19. Collingwood, "Historical Cycles," 313.
20. Kurt Breysig, "Der Prophet des Untergangs," *Velhagen & Klasings Monatshefte* 35, no. 7 (March, 1921): 270; Brandenburg, " 'Untergang des Abendlandes,' " 22; Ernst Troeltsch, review of *Der Untergang des Abendlandes,* by Oswald Spengler, *Historische Zeitschrift* 120 (1919): 291; *Logos* 9, p. 133.

of history of the counter-current of pessimism in Western intellectual history—should be roundly criticized on account of its pessimism.

Spengler's methodology was not spared criticism. Meyer justifiably took exception to his excessive reliance on the analogy as a methodological tool. "Certainly, the analogy, if really well-founded, is an essential device for historical comprehension; but the historical process is much too variegated, the sphere of possibilities much too large, that the analogy alone could be sufficient for a reconstruction of reality." Breysig gets carried away in his attempt to discredit Spengler when he lambastes his rejection of causal explanation. This "blocks the path to everything, but also all research into the meaning and essence of historical becoming."[21]

Contemporary social scientists, confronted by Spengler's unusual intellectual apparatus, might be tempted to side with Breysig. He argued that the rejection of causal analysis in *The Decline of the West* is a crippling methodological weakness. However, it should be remembered that Spengler is critiquing causal analysis in the context of the construction of a philosophy of world history. The value of causal analysis in historical inquiry diminishes the greater the time span and the complexity of the historical constellations one surveys. As the archaeologists Ruth Whitehouse and John Wilkins observed, "Our minds are so conditioned by human language and institutional beliefs that we tend to assume that causation exists 'out there' in reality. What we actually observe may be just one event following another; the causal link between them is always a matter of interpretation. In our practical everyday lives, however, the viewpoint of causation is a useful mental strategy. Transferred to a 'world stage,' with giant spectral agents and actions that can encompass hundreds or thousands of years, it has to be much more dubious."[22]

Spengler's ambitious effort to press violently the complexities of world history into a comprehensive, historical-philosophical system is not free from considerable errors and flaws. Yet this is inevitable in any effort to philosophize about world history. Its imperfections do not mean that *The Decline of the West* cannot be read with great profit by those seeking to understand better the nature of history. For Spengler has probed the dark side of modernity and enlightened us about the crises of our age as few

21. Meyer, *Spenglers "Untergang des Abendlandes,"* 12–13; Breysig, "Prophet des Untergangs," 265.
22. Ruth Whitehouse and John Wilkins, *The Making of Civilization: History Discovered Through Archaeology* (New York: Knopf, 1986), 196.

other thinkers have. There is considerable truth in Erich Heller's observation that "the history of the West since 1917 looks like the work of children clumsily filling in with lurid colours a design drawn in outlines by Oswald Spengler."[23] *The Decline of the West* endures as the most powerful statement of anti-Enlightenment historical thought yet produced.

23. Erich Heller, "Oswald Spengler and the Predicament of the Historical Imagination," chap. in *The Disinherited Mind: Essays in Modern German Literature and Thought*, 4th ed. (London: Bowes & Bowes, 1975), 182.

6

The Transformation of Spengler's Political Philosophy

WE HAVE INQUIRED INTO SPENGLER'S philosophy of world history, probed his relationship to the tradition of German historicism, treated the question of the intellectual sources of and influences on *The Decline of the West*, and discussed the controversy it generated. Now we direct our attention to his ideas on politics and statecraft.

Controversy swirls around the extent to which Spengler was a forerunner or precursor of Nazism. However, scholars unanimously agree that he was a virulently antidemocratic thinker. The epithet of "virulent opponent of Weimar democracy" is certainly well-deserved for the period in his political-philosophical development when he was famous, spanning 1919 to his untimely death in 1936. Yet what about the years immediately before the shocking military collapse of Imperial Germany and the outbreak of socialist revolution in the fall of 1918 aroused the hostility of the entire Right against Germany's first democracy? From 1911 to 1918 Spengler, as an unknown private scholar composing his major work, was politically inactive. Was he passionately antidemocratic before he became an embittered man? Drawing heavily on his private papers in the Spengler Archive, the following investigation of this rather obscure but important period in his thought surprisingly reveals that he was not vehemently antidemocratic during this time. He was, in fact, an opportunistic advocate of the quasi-democratization of the Second Reich.

This new interpretation of Spengler's early political thought is based primarily on careful examination of two unfinished, unsolicited memoranda he drafted, along with several related notes on political matters. He addressed one memorandum to the kaiser and the other to the German nobility yet apparently never submitted them. Although these interesting political documents are unfortunately undated, their context indicates that they were composed from around 1914 to 1917. Despite being fragmentary in nature, the memoranda and notes still amount in transcript form to sixty-five double-spaced pages. The archival material used in this controversial interpretation of Spengler's early political philosophy is supplemented by pertinent passages from his correspondence. Unfortunately, no details about Spengler's voting habits during the Wilhelmine period are available. Moreover, there is no correspondence extant before 1913.

Spengler scholars conventionally do not argue this novel position on his early ideas about democracy. The scholarly consensus is that no significant changes in Spengler's perspective on democratization in Germany took place in his intellectual career. Anton Mirko Koktanek argues that the fragmentary memoranda and related political notes "outline [Spengler's] in essence not further changed political position." Gilbert Merlio's discussion of the incomplete memoranda and notes is extremely abbreviated.[1] H. Stuart Hughes does not make use of them, as they were apparently unavailable to him when he prepared his monograph in the early fifties. He consequently does not discuss at all Spengler's political thought in the years before Germany's defeat in World War I.[2] Neither Ernst Stutz, Klemens von Klemperer, Horst Möller, nor Michael Thöndl uncover a phase in the development of Spengler's political philosophy when he advocated the quasi-democratization of the Second Reich.[3] In his discussion of Spengler's political ideas during this period, Walter Struve mentions the unfinished memoranda and related notes only in passing. He asserts, "there is no indication of an abrupt break in the development of his views." Detlev Felken interprets Spengler's political thought as being marked by continuity throughout the Wilhelmine, Weimar, and Nazi periods.[4]

1. K-Sp, 182; Gilbert Merlio, *Oswald Spengler: Témoin de son temps*, vol. II (Stuttgart: Akademischer Verlag Hans-Dieter Heinz, 1982), 613–15.

2. See H-Sp.

3. See Ernst Stutz, *Oswald Spengler als politischer Denker* (Bern: Francke Verlag, 1958); Klemens von Klemperer, *Germany's New Conservatism: Its History and Dilemma in the Twentieth Century* (Princeton: Princeton Univ. Press, 1968); Horst Möller, "Oswald Spengler—Geschichte im Dienste der Zeitkritik," in Peter C. Ludz, ed., *Spengler heute* (Munich: C. H. Beck, 1980); Michael Thöndl, "Das Politikbild von Oswald Spengler (1880–1936) mit einer Ortsbestimmung seines politischen Urteils über Hitler und Mussolini," *Zeitschrift für Politik* 40, no. 4 (1993): 418–43.

4. Walter Struve, *Elites Against Democracy: Leadership Ideals in Bourgeois Political Thought in Germany, 1890–1933* (Princeton: Princeton Univ. Press, 1973), 235; Detlef Felken, *Oswald Spengler: Konservativer Denker zwischen Kaiserreich und Diktatur* (Munich: C. H. Beck, 1988).

Ambivalence colors Spengler's position on the democratization of German political life before the Weimar period. On the one hand, he has a discerning eye for what are arguably democracy's weaknesses. On the other hand, this strength is more than outweighed by his disastrous enthusiasm for more authoritarian solutions to the problems of governance, an enthusiasm characteristic of the post–World War I phase in his political thought. His position is further ambivalent in that though he laments the rise of mass democratic politics, he regards it and imperialism as irresistible historical forces of the nineteenth and twentieth centuries. His understanding of democratization in the West as inevitable echoes one of Nietzsche's political pronouncements that "the democratizing of Europe is unstoppable." Spengler exudes confidence in the prospects for promoting a substantial measure of democratization of the monarchical regime of Wilhelmine Germany in a positive manner from a power-political perspective. The goal of substantially democratizing the political system of Wilhelmine Germany was not unrealistic. As one scholar has noted about its politics, "The existence of a parliament with budgetary powers and participation in legislation gave good reason to the assumption also to be able through parliament sooner or later to hold the reins of power."[5]

Adherence to the monarchical principle was quite typical of Spengler's era. It was not inconsistent with support for partial democratization of the Second Reich. The German monarchy was the target of guarded criticism, and a number of politicians called for its democratic modification. Yet none of the political parties during the Wilhelmine period actively opposed the institution of monarchy. Only the Social Democratic party was committed in its official program to the republican form of government.[6]

Of fundamental importance to Spengler's political philosophy is his largely deterministic historical philosophy. It conceives of history as unfolding "independent of ideals and hopes," responding to "a logic of history which is inevitable." Serenely unconcerned about the ideals of political actors, history "moves forward."[7]

Spengler can be categorized as a neoconservative, but the neoconserva-

5. Friedrich Nietzsche, quoted in Bruce Detwiler, *Nietzsche and the Politics of Aristocratic Radicalism* (Chicago: Univ. of Chicago Press, 1990), 171; Stefan Breuer, *Anatomie der Konservativen Revolution* (Darmstadt: Wissenschaftliche Buchgesellschaft, 1993), 15.

6. Walter H. Kaufmann, *Monarchism in the Weimar Republic* (New York: Octagon, 1973), 14.

7. Politica I, 79, 4.

tism of his early phase lacks reactionary features. It is complex, being flexible and adaptive, striving to adapt conservative aspirations to what he sees as the irresistible march of historical events.[8] While liberalism is doctrinaire and socialism is ideological for Spengler, traditional conservatism is provincial. German conservatism must liberate itself from its "provincialism" and learn to be, above all, practical. The program of conservatism is "dead" and must be completely reformed. The conservative politician and statesman must make use of the "most modern means with perfect expert knowledge" to achieve realizable goals. He must not vainly expend his energy in the service of obsolescent, romantic conservative ideals.[9] Conservatism must adapt to the new reality of the political mobilization of the masses, which set in after 1890 in Wilhelmine Germany.[10] Moreover, Spengler recommends borrowing ideas and policy proposals selectively from the two major political movements in Germany that his conservative, agrarian contemporaries energetically opposed, liberalism and socialism. "The genuine conservative, as I would like him to be, employs without hesitation liberal and socialistic measures, the moment he finds them expedient."[11]

Spengler counsels conservatives to abandon their antagonism to the idea of parliamentarism in Germany. Instead they should master its practices and customs. A wise conservative "should neither, like the stupid conservative, see in parliamentarism an enemy of the old, nor like the genuine liberal, a wonderful ideal, but merely an instrument of modern political life, which one must study as a machine and handle without prejudice and with virtuosity." Spengler understands and accepts the downside of this resourceful strategy of adjusting to changing historical conditions through compromising one's principles and adroitly utilizing the most modern methods of political practice. Inevitably, the ability to put into practice one's conservative values is ultimately destroyed by historical processes. "It is not sufficient to be an exponent of one's political ideals. One must also be capable of giving them up and opposing them, if one sees, that they are impossible. . . . We live—unfortunately—in the twentieth century." And at that, a politician in the twentieth century must content himself with achieving precious little of his ideals in an era of mass

8. *Ibid.*

9. *Ibid.*; Politica I, 79, 6.

10. Gerhard A. Ritter, *Die deutschen Parteien 1830–1914: Parteien und Gesellschaft im konstitutionellen Regierungssystem* (Göttingen: Vandenhoeck & Ruprecht, 1985), 23.

11. Politica I, 79, 5.

politics and rapid, relentless, historical change. "A party has a lot of luck, if it can achieve 10% of its ideals in the course of its existence, and even that it only achieves, by sacrificing for it 50%."[12]

The Junkers, Prussia's landed aristocracy, formed the bulwark of German conservatism in the nineteenth century. Prussia, in turn, was the dominant federal state in terms of size, population, and political power in the Second Reich. Spengler argues that German conservatism must be regenerated in order to adjust to Germany's rise to prominence in an age of global imperialism and economic competition. The Junkers must replace their provincialism with a pragmatic cosmopolitanism gained through wider experiences, if they want to play a major, constructive role in the future of their country. "Send your sons to the big international firms, to the fleet, to the colonies," he urges the patrician patriarchs. He hopes to see a Prussian Upper House of genuine distinction "in which no one sits who owes his seat solely to his birth."[13]

Spengler supports certain democratic ideas not out of conviction but out of expediency. He assigns a domestic political function to his quasi-Social-Darwinist, imperialistic aims. If Germany's imperialism during the Great War is successful and its economic upswing of the prewar era can be resumed, he argues, then a new social contract can be made. Under such conditions, imperialistic policies carried out by a strong alliance between the aristocratic and bourgeois elites will integrate the industrial working class in a conservatively democratic, monarchical state. Victory in World War I will help greatly to resolve the troubling social question and enormously enhance the prestige of the state in the eyes of the whole populace.

Spengler dreamed of Wilhelmine Germany forging the foundation of global economic hegemony through war. In his memorandum for Kaiser Wilhelm II, Spengler's soaring vision of Germany's future as the world's leading power is graphically depicted. "But today the Reich stands here, no longer Greater Prussia, the result of Sedan, but the world empire, the core of an *imperium Germanicum*. In this hour everything is decided. World history has here a turning point."[14]

Divisiveness characterized German politics from the founding of the Second Reich to the end of World War I. Spengler's tremendous faith in the capacity of the German people to overcome their divisions has two

12. Politica I, 79, 6; Politica I, 79, 7; Politica I, 79, 8.
13. Politica I, 79, 15.
14. Politica I, 79, 22.

sources. First, he overestimates the depth and longevity of the *Burgfrieden* (domestic peace), the interclass solidarity that arose in the euphoria of August, 1914. Contemplating the European scene, he boldly claims in May, 1915, in his correspondence that "the German people is the only unshakable political entity." Second, Spengler assumes that victory will reinforce national unity. He is grossly overconfident about Germany's ability to prevail in the Great War. Despite the disturbing failure of the Schlieffen plan in the pivotal battle of the Marne, Spengler wrote in a letter in October, 1914, "I am thoroughly optimistic." In 1915, Germany's success in the Gorlice campaign provoked the following outburst of confidence in German victory. He informs his close friend and his chief correspondent of the war years, Hans Klöres, that Germany is experiencing a "monstrous movement on the path towards world power, which only the Romans from 300 to 50 B.C. experienced" before them. His confidence in German victory waxes high in the spring of 1918 as General Erich Ludendorff launches his final drive toward Paris after the Treaty of Brest Litovsk confirmed Russia's staggering territorial losses, including the Baltic states, Poland, Finland, the Ukraine, and Transcaucasia. The war will end in the summer or fall, Spengler predicts, and the postwar years will witness the establishment of "the factual German protectorate over the Continent (up to the Urals!)."[15]

In his correspondence Spengler projected confidence about the prospects for German victory. Yet his confidence coexisted with extreme anxiety. His correspondence strongly suggests that he avoided closely following news reports about the war because of his suppressed anxiety that his country might lose the pivotal struggle, notwithstanding his overriding faith in German victory. Thus, he confesses to not having read a newspaper in weeks: "I also don't want to hear anything about politics now." A year later, he complains, "I have blocked my ears to all politics, in order to be able to do my work." This suspicion is confirmed when one turns to his autobiographical fragments. "Wartime. The insane anxiety. The avoidance of newspapers, shutting one's eyes. The passion: to rather die than to live in a humiliated Germany, therewith the certainty of victory."[16]

During the war, the parties of the Right were determined to frustrate

15. Spengler to Klöres, 24 May 1915, *B*, 37; Spengler to Klöres, 25 October 1914, *B*, 29; Spengler to Klöres, 14 July 1915, *B*, 42; Spengler to Klöres, 11 May 1918, *B*, 97.
16. Spengler to Klöres, 3 November 1915, *B*, 50; Spengler to Klöres, 20 December 1916, *B*, 59; EH, 21.

the aspirations of the Social Democratic party and the trade unions for democratic government and social reform. Rightists believed that the working classes could be fobbed off with an extravagant program of territorial expansionism. Spengler, however, espoused a program combining annexations and political reform. Quite optimistically, he believed that victory in World War I and success in imperialism and global economic competition in the decades after 1914 would legitimize to the masses the guiding role of the aristocracy and bourgeoise in a reformed constitutional monarchy. Consequently, he has no qualms about promoting the democratization of the Second Reich. "A conservative of political profundity and vision [should] readily accept and push through 'democratization.' " Chancellor Theobold von Bethmann Hollweg was persuaded that serious constitutional reform had to be postponed until after the war because traditional, conservative forces still had sufficient strength to block it.[17]

Spengler, by contrast, was convinced that the time for decisive action had come. Although the war had brought about a marked erosion in the power of the Crown, he believed that the Crown had to play a key role in initiating political reform. Such an act of monarchical benevolence would, in adapting to the regrettable, ineluctable, historical trend of democratization, be in the Crown's enlightened self-interest. He expresses his optimism, perhaps not well-founded, that the German state would retain its conservative character irrespective of the degree to which German national political life would be democratized. "If the parliamentary form is highly democratic, it will be offset by the conservative frame of mind of the house." Believing that the German people had attained a mature, coolheaded, and confident political orientation (something he most certainly didn't believe after crushing military defeat and socialist revolution in 1918), Spengler calls upon his emperor to grant Germany immediately a conservative-democratic political form. "Give to Germany today a democratic form, such as there has never been before, one interpreted by a people so maturely conservative." To be sure, he advocates, not a comprehensive democratization of German political life, but nonetheless substantial reform of it. Spengler's position was unusual, given his conservative and National Liberal sentiments. As one scholar notes, during the war, conservative groups "were vehemently opposed to any concession to par-

17. Politica I, 79, 10; Hajo Holborn, *A History of Modern Germany 1840–1945* (Princeton: Princeton Univ. Press, 1969), 466.

liamentarism," while the majority of the National Liberal party opposed parliamentary reforms.[18]

Partial democratization of Wilhelmine Germany certainly does not mean to Spengler that the people would truly govern their own affairs. "A dishonest characteristic runs through democratic theory from Rousseau on: [Its proponents] are silent about the organization of the government by the people, or they indulge in hollow words, because they do not have the courage to admit the utopian nature of the word 'self-government.' " Spengler's conception of political leadership was consistently elitist. Like Vilfredo Pareto, he contends that democratic rule by the people is an illusion, that a small elite governs. "In reality it is always a dozen gifted people who rule," Spengler notes.[19] Yet his elitism does not derive from a selfish desire to preserve the privileges of a select few in a polity. Indeed, this meritocratic bourgeois thinker celebrates the "self-made man." He advocates upward social mobility on the basis of talent and achievement. Social mobility will make a polity stronger and more capable of pursuing a successful foreign policy in an age of industrialization and abrasive competition between the imperialistic powers.

Elitism in matters of governance reflects Spengler's conviction of the tremendous complexity of modern statecraft and the perilous nature of great power rivalry. He supports this stance by expanding on the comparison between the intellectual accessibility of the culture of classical antiquity to the common man and the esoteric exclusiveness of West European culture that he had discussed in *The Decline of the West*.[20] While in classical antiquity, cultural forms are more or less readily apprehensible by ordinary citizens, he argues, in West European culture, "the more important, the more genuine and profound something is, the more incomprehensible it is to 'the people.' " Spengler echoes Ranke's teaching of the complex nature of modern statecraft. "Contemporary politics is incomprehensible to the people, though it is performed more than ever for the people. It is irrelevant what the condition of the education of the masses, the popular welfare, the newspapers is—politics presupposes connoisseurs, which, in terms of the level of intelligence and the extent of their education, only a few among thousands can come up to the standard."[21]

18. Politica I, 79, 75; Spengler to Klöres, 18 December 1918, *B*, 111; Politica I, 79, 24; Kaufmann, *Monarchism*, 35.
19. Politica I, 79, 57; Politica I, 79, 29.
20. *UdA* I, 417 ff.
21. Politica I, 79, 52.

Thus, not unlike Max Weber, Spengler considers the question of leadership selection to be a decisive problem in modern politics. Its solution will fortify Germany's position in the international arena. "It must be somehow possible that the relatively few intellectuals of statesmanlike talent and knowledge are at the same time 'the elected.' "[22]

The ascendant Social Democratic party was the largest party in the *Reichstag* in 1912. Spengler was interested in exploring ways to accommodate some of its aspirations. The Social Democratic party consistently rejected military, naval, and colonial policies during the Second Reich, yet it voted in 1914 for credits in support of the war effort. This epochal act of national solidarity with its peacetime antagonists in the *Reichstag* presumably encouraged Spengler to be receptive to the idea of favoring its further integration into the mainstream of German political life. The memoranda and related material reveal that his attitude toward the Social Democratic party was far more moderate and conciliatory than that of most conservatives. Indeed, the political parties of the Right and Center generally viewed the Social Democratic party as "a thoroughly pernicious force for whose destruction all resources were to be mobilised."[23] Spengler did not believe that the growing strength of the German industrial working class imperiled the internal status quo. On the contrary, he was optimistic about the prospects of its integration into German society.

The major issue in German politics in the decades before the war had been whether to preserve or reform the notorious Prussian conservative institution, the three-class electoral system.[24] The chief demand of the Social Democrats for years had been the reform of this undemocratic franchise, which had posed a formidable obstacle to the democratization of the Second Reich. Spengler supported this demand, calling for the elimination of this controversial feature of the electoral system in order to diminish German socialist antagonism to the state.[25] Under the influence of revisionism as propounded by the Bavarian party leader Georg Vollmar and the socialist theorist Eduard Bernstein, the Social Democratic party transformed itself from a party radically opposed to the state to one more like a loyal oppositional force. Cognizant of the reformist nature of mainstream social democracy, Spengler goes so far as to recommend assigning

22. Politica I, 79, 51.
23. V. R. Berghahn, *Modern Germany: Society, Economy, and Politics in the Twentieth Century*, 2d ed. (New York: Cambridge Univ. Press, 1987), 23.
24. Holborn, *Modern Germany*, 365.
25. Ritter, *Die deutschen Parteien*, 36; Politica I, 79, 6.

leading socialists ministerial portfolios. "Germany has more than one so-cialist who in large-scale organizational work has become mature and cool-headed enough to become a minister."[26] Yet there is one glaring weakness in his strategy of opening up the political process to greater par-ticipation by the industrial working class and their socialist leaders. He overlooks that the Social Democrats justified their support of the war only in so far as it could be considered to be a defensive effort. Most Social Democrats rejected grandiose schemes of empire building.

A wholesale housecleaning of the *Reichstag* is necessary to make it fit to help conduct the complicated and weighty affairs of this future German world empire. Spengler calls for removing from office "provincial wind-bags and local celebrities, climbers, and philistines." He criticizes the lead-ership of the Second Reich for its reluctance to award ministerial positions to bourgeois figures of proven ability. "When one sees what manner of significant men Germany possessed in the last thirty years . . . many inven-tors, organizers, and engineers of the highest quality, and how few of them were directly participating in the leadership of the state. . . . That [was] a mistake of the state." Spengler wishes at the same time to limit the power of the bureaucracy, which had traditionally resisted any increase in the power of the political parties. The superior organizational talents of bour-geois Germany, of men of accomplishment who have proven themselves through "magnificent practical life in great circumstances," must replace the bureaucrats of lesser niveaux of the past, he declares. Indeed, it is the best and the brightest of the bourgeoisie who had engineered Germany's vigorous economic growth during the Second Reich. The *Reichstag* should be composed of pragmatic and successful members from a cross-section of economic life. "And in this *Reichstag* our capable engineers, industrialists, businessmen and socialist secretaries, and commercial farmers and no bu-reaucrats, retired men of wealth, writers, and 'artists'—that is it."[27]

Flushed with wartime optimism, Spengler believes that German politi-cal life after the triumphant conclusion of World War I will be distin-guished by a truly superior level of political skill. Shortly before the passage of the Peace Resolution in July, 1917, he declares in a letter, "I at any rate believe here in a niveau of political thought and action in the *new* Ger-

26. Politica I, 79, 18.

27. Politica I, 79, 68; Politica I, 79, 61; *ibid.*; Politica I, 79, 21. The term *Reichstag* is not emphasized in the original but is italicized here simply to be consistent with previ-ous usage.

many, which will rank alongside that of the French in 1789, even if one appraises the latter very high."[28] One should not overlook here Spengler's implicit high regard for the political acumen of the early French revolutionary elite, not at all what one would expect from a vehemently antidemocratic thinker.

Upward mobility and new opportunities await members of the bourgeoisie in the coming German "superpower" of the twentieth century. Spengler desires to see the conduct of foreign affairs, the highest realm of politics in his philosophy and the traditional preserve of the Crown and the Junkers, placed in the hands of outstanding members of the bourgeoisie. "Here one courageously draws the consequences. Let's chance it that the nobility completely disappears from the diplomatic ranks. One lets in here only people who have put themselves to the test in a praxis of great style. The state, today, is a joint stock company, not a manorial estate." Of the military he writes, "We will get besides the nobility, a class of highly intelligent bourgeois officers, people like our engineers and industrialists, among whom organizational and technical abilities guarantee rapid advancement." He envisions a wide range of opportunities awaiting "self-made" men. "But I see also the time drawing near, when *other* positions of great responsibility, in government, the organization of commerce, industry, transportation, colonies, will be filled not any more by privy councillors, but by self-made men."[29]

The Germans face in the early twentieth century, from Spengler's perspective, a challenge similar to that which the English met the century before. In *The Decline of the West* he expresses his admiration for the foresight and flexibility of the English aristocracy in deciding to carry out prudent political reforms. It entered into a collaboration with the bourgeoisie, whose young talented men the aristocracy schooled in its exemplary tradition of statecraft, to govern Britain. He praises as "the greatest domestic political achievement of the nineteenth century" the democratization of Britain in a way consistent with the government remaining "strictly in form."[30] And in Victorian Britain, imperialism served as an integrative force in the democratizing country.

Skillful governance in the twentieth century and beyond presupposes familiarity with complex, international economic questions. Spengler rec-

28. Spengler to Klöres, 1 May 1917, *B*, 75.
29. Politica I, 79, 62; Spengler to Klöres, 7 September 1917, *B*, 47, 47–48.
30. *UdA* II, 512 n. 2.

ognizes that economics had become of decisive importance in world politics, as it had also in domestic politics. "International transportation, commerce, credit conditions, and heavy industry determine today the existence of states." He regards the *Reichstag* as "an administrative center for the most valuable economic system of Europe, perhaps in the world."[31]

Spengler's conviction of the critical importance of economics in world affairs is reflected in his conception of the kind of empire building Germany should engage in. His oracular pronouncements about Caesarism and his glorification of war and martial virtues have obscured the fact that his imperialism was primarily economic and secondarily territorial in nature. The economic character of his imperialistic program for Wilhelmine Germany is epitomized in the following lines from one of his memoranda: "But the spirit of the Germans, with their machines, billions of marks, railroads, and steamships will rule the world. . . . The new Germany will be present everywhere with its best powers—in Buenos Aires and Shanghai, in San Francisco and Capetown."[32]

One avoids being perplexed by what seems to be, in retrospect, the almost fantastical nature of Spengler's vision of German global hegemony if one bears in mind that he did not anticipate the emergence in 1917 of the United States as a decisive power in world affairs. Although his historical philosophy helped overcome the Eurocentrism of nineteenth-century historical thought, the same cannot be said for his international political thought during the Great War. It was Eurocentric, so much so that the implications of American entry in the conflict were never even discussed in Spengler's correspondence! He interpreted the Great War as a struggle for global economic hegemony between Germany and England, the leading world power in the nineteenth century. Thus, he wrote in a letter in December, 1914, employing an image from dueling, "This war intensifies to a decision between England and Germany: The other powers are merely the seconds."[33]

Although the fragmentary drafts of Spengler's two memoranda and related political notes are undated, it is clear that his attitude toward the future role of the *Reichstag* changes dramatically in the course of the war. In a few sections he assigns the *Reichstag* a central role, arguing that men of accomplishment from civil society can make major contributions to politi-

31. Politica I, 79, 69; Politica I, 79, 66.
32. Politica I, 79, 13.
33. Spengler to Klöres, 18 December 1914, *B*, 32.

cal decision-making. Spengler does not spell out what constitutional powers this legislative institution should have. He does not discuss the question of whether the chancellor's position should depend ultimately on the favor of the Crown or on the formation of a parliamentary majority. He conveys the distinct impression, however, that he wishes to see the marked expansion of the powers of the *Reichstag*, making the representative assembly rather than the monarch the center of political power. "One gives to the *Reichstag* a larger area of responsibility and demands at the same time, as 'good form,' that 'little people' (intellectually) do not get in." Elsewhere he writes, "But today the *Reichstag* is that which has become the organ of the whole. Everything else is in the shadows." In other places, a cynical attitude toward the *Reichstag* surfaces. He asserts, "the *Reichstag* will be merely a symbol"; for extraparliamentary forces will essentially determine affairs of state. It appears that this striking shift in attitude resulted from Spengler's reflections on the dramatic events of the summer of 1917, when the parties of the Left and Center-Left passed the Peace Resolution in the face of increasing privation on the home front. The controversial resolution called for a peace of understanding and permanent reconciliation among peoples. It renounced territorial annexation and political, economic, and financial oppression. The cooperation of the Center party, the Progressives, and the Social Democrats in support of the Peace Resolution was a significant development in German political history. It foreshadowed the active coalition of these political groups in the Weimar National Assembly of 1919. To Spengler, the Peace Resolution was a treasonous renunciation of the sacred cause of German imperialism. It "naturally" placed into question his earlier more accommodating stance on the role of the parliament in government. He terms the summer of 1917 the "debut" of the " 'German Parliament,' " complains of its "undignified scenes," and then, in an about-face, claims that the German people are not suited for parliamentarism.[34] The passage of the Peace Resolution precipitated a vigorous reaction from forces on the Right with the founding of the stridently imperialistic Fatherland party in September, 1917, by Admiral Alfred von Tirpitz and Wolfgang Kapp.

An idea basic to German conservatism and to Spengler's political thought is that each of the peoples of the West has a style of governance

34. Politica I, 79, 68; Politica I, 79, 21; Politica I, 79, 40. The term *Reichstag* is not emphasized in the original but is italicized here simply to be consistent with previous usage.

appropriate to its national ethos. He argues that Germany needs its own form of democracy. Writing after the Peace Resolution of 1917, Spengler asserts, with England in mind, "the German people have political instincts that are very democratic, but do not follow this 'Western' orientation." According to him, in this indigenous German form of "democracy," extraparliamentary interest groups, the unions, industrial organizations, agricultural organizations, the press, and the financial community, will powerfully influence the political decision-making process. Indeed, powerful economic interest groups had already acquired significant influence on the political parties in Germany in the 1870s. Spengler maintains that parliaments in Europe will progressively lose real political power. "The center of gravity of political decisions shifts to the tactics, hidden from public view, of large associations and interest groups, and to be sure, the more decisively the more that economic questions form the center of politics. . . . Parliaments will soon play a decorative role in comparison with economic factors."[35]

A letter that is revealing about Spengler's wartime political orientation is addressed to Klöres and is dated November 6, 1917. Spengler voices his hope that the National Liberals will rejuvenate themselves and expand their base of support and their political influence. He advises his friend,

> If you therefore—hopefully!—after the war think of political activity, so penetrate first into the party-political situation, where, in my opinion, the organization of the moderate liberals is the most important problem, because here industry, commerce, and higher intelligence must come together. The National Liberal party is inadequate in its present form and its connections to an absolutely reliable press are weak. However, the party could with some skill on the part of new personalities become a representative of the whole of property and a large part of the upper working class and with that take a decisive position. . . . And there you could, if you start from my ideas, also work for that, which I myself cannot, namely, draw the *practical* consequences.[36]

Much has been made about Spengler being a prophet of Caesarism and how Adolf Hitler's rise to power seemed to bear out his clairvoyance. Spengler, however, at the time he was composing the first volume of *The Decline of the West*, regarded himself as a prophet not so much of Caesar-

35. Politica I, 79, 40; Politica I, 79, 54.
36. Spengler to Klöres, 6 November 1917, *B*, 83.

ism as of a partially democratically-reformed German monarchy that would lay the foundation for a global economic empire through world wars. Caesarism would emerge after the egalitarian forces of the twentieth century had atomized society and plutocratic elements had thoroughly debased political life. Caesarism was a political phenomenon that belonged to the far shores of the future. Thus, he wrote in *The Decline of the West*, "[Cecil] Rhodes makes his appearance as the first precursor of a Western type of Caesar, whose time is still far off."[37]

The democratization of Wilhelmine Germany, as Spengler envisions it, would basically amount to an unavoidable manifestation of decadence. Democratization would be a lamentable movement away from the exercise of political power in Germany by the traditional ruling powers for most of the history of West European culture, the monarchs and the aristocracy. Thus, Spengler's nostalgic political ideal, which he explicitly renounces because it belongs to the past and is thoroughly unattainable in the present, is "the monarchy of the eighteenth century."[38] The decadence in political life that democratization signifies has its counterpart in the cultural decadence of Germany. Yet, on the positive side, substantial democratic reform of the Second Reich would supposedly markedly reduce socialist opposition to the state and finally give to the German bourgeoisie a very important voice in affairs of state and enable it to employ fully its talents for making Germany dominant politically, economically, and militarily in the world.

In contrast to virtually all the academic, historical thinkers of Wilhelmine Germany, Spengler was very pessimistic about its cultural future in the long run. He understood the decline of Western culture to be a comprehensive phenomenon that affected all the nations of this tradition. While many French and British intellectuals, including Toynbee, pictured their countries as being bulwarks of civilization against "German barbarism," it was customary among many German thinkers during World War I, in proclaiming the "ideas of 1914," to regard their nation as the champion of culture and the Western democracies as the protagonists of decadent civilization.[39] Like Werner Sombart and Thomas Mann, Spengler paid tribute to what he considered to be the distinctive national qualities

37. *UdA* I, 50. Spengler also refers to Rhodes as a precursor of "a very significant type of the twenty-first century" (*UdA* I, 445).

38. Politica I, 79, 7.

39. Fritz Stern, *The Politics of Cultural Despair: A Study in the Rise of the Germanic Ideology* (Berkeley: Univ. of California Press, 1961), 196 n.

of Germany and advocated an antagonistic nationalism. Nonetheless, he saw the entire West as inexorably moving toward cultural sterility and decadence. Thus, in this key respect, his position was the diametrical opposite of that of the exponents of the "ideas of 1914." Indeed, in a remarkable formulation, not surprisingly buried away discreetly in his correspondence instead of prominently displayed in his published works for consumption by the educated German public, many if not most of whom would have found such an idea repugnant, one discovers that he conceives Germany's future to consist in becoming "a second America." Spengler maintains that the transition in modern Germany from culture to civilization had already been completed by 1900. In the following passage from a letter written in October, 1914, when most German intellectuals were trumpeting the vitality of German culture in the desperate struggle of their country against the Western powers, Spengler bleakly assesses the future of German culture.

> What is in store for us is unfortunately not any more consoling, as long as one thinks and feels as a man of culture. Because the glimmer of inner culture, which the age of Goethe developed and which since Sedan, since the Berliner represents the new-German type, has lost the best, has been completely extinguished by this war. In the Germany that through technical intelligence, money, and an eye for facts has secured its great position in the world, a completely soulless Americanism will rise to ascendancy, which will reduce art, the nobility, the church, and Weltanschauung to a materialism, as only existed before in Rome in the earliest imperial period.[40]

Recognizing that the Germany of cultural achievement is becoming an anachronism as it rushes headlong into modernity, Spengler is capable of overcoming his nostalgia and regret. As a resolute modernist, he actually embraces the goal of Germany emulating America. In 1915, in a long letter in which he sets forth his vision of Germany's future on the world stage, he states,

> Let us be clear about it, that this Germany which today struggles against the world, is not Goethe's Germany, but a second America. For myself, I am sufficiently unprejudiced to regret that, while accepting it as a fact, and in the future, politically such as, for example, in educational issues, to set pre-

40. Spengler to Klöres, 14 July 1915, *B*, 44; Spengler to Klöres, 25 October 1914, *B*, 29.

cisely this fact as a *goal*. For Germany has, after all, nothing but this one thing to achieve. Also, I see in that *greatness*. Let us not forget that the Roman Imperium also was only an unscrupulous business enterprise and the great Romans were all speculators. However, beauty *envelopes* the Roman character.[41]

In summation, Spengler espouses for Germany after the Great War, which he confidently expects it to win, a partially democratically-reformed monarchy. In this postwar era, the nobility, particularly the Junkers, become more modern, flexible, and international in outlook. The nobility must be prepared, for the greater good of Germany, to enter into a full political partnership with the bourgeoisie. Indeed, the increasingly differentiated middle class will attain a prominent, if not leading, role in politics. Its role will be commensurate with its importance to the second most productive economy in the world and its growing contribution to the ranks of not only the officer corps of the fleet but the army as well. Finally, the industrial working class is better integrated. Spengler advocates the quasi-democratization of German political life for a variety of reasons. First, it is a historical stage in an ineluctable process. "This result is necessary in Germany, not in the sense of a party ideal, but naturally inevitable."[42] And if the Crown seizes the initiative, it can have some input in democratization, with advantages for the state amid the rivalries of world affairs. Second, the Zeitgeist demands some democratization. Because of the importance of political symbolism, it is necessary in an era in which mass politics increasingly predominate.[43] Third, democratization will purportedly reduce the antagonism of much of the Left to the power-political ambitions of the German state. Fourth, democratization elevates the bourgeoisie to numerous positions of great political responsibility and draws on their many talents for ensuring Germany's success both in global economic and power-political competition. Fifth, democratic reform will not alter the fact that the conduct of political affairs in Germany will not devolve to "the people." Governance will remain securely in the hands of an elite. However, this elite will be an expanded one, more capable of meeting the difficult challenges facing Germany in the twentieth century.

Obviously, the course of history completely frustrated the realization of

41. Spengler to Klöres, 14 July 1915, *B*, 44.
42. Politica I, 79, 34.
43. Politica I, 79, 29.

major aims of Spengler's early political thought. That he never conceded this in his publications or private papers does not discredit the argument of this chapter. A brilliant and flamboyant dramaturge of the grand movements and forces of history, Spengler never tired of trying to project an image of prophetic genius and infallibility.

Optimism about Germany's prospects for victory in World War I made Spengler psychologically unprepared for its shocking military collapse in 1918. Like Hitler, he broke down and sobbed on learning of Germany's defeat. It meant, in Spengler's words, "the collapse of everything that was deeply cherished and valued by me." He, like other conservative nationalists, blamed the debacle on the undermining of the home front by what were deemed to be disloyal groups. Crushing military defeat and socialist revolution in Germany transformed Spengler's political philosophy. Together, they destroyed his dream of carrying out a program of partial democratic reform of the Second Reich in order to help lay the foundation of a global empire. The parliamentary democracy that arose in 1919 on the rubble of his dreams was totally discredited at its birth in his eyes. In his opinion, its proponents had traitorously sapped the war effort. They bore responsibility for inflicting on their country humiliating defeat and the overthrow of the old order, which, despite its need for restructuring, should have served as a solid foundation on which to build. In 1919 he venomously declared, "Parliamentarism in Germany is nonsense or treason."[44] Spengler lent his support to the notorious, stab-in-the-back legend, according to which Germany's military didn't bear responsibility for the loss of World War I; instead, traitorous elements on the home front, deluded by the mirage of a Wilsonian peace, undermined Germany's morale and the will to persevere. With his new-found fame, he became active in political life. He advocated the founding of a semi-authoritarian state in the influential 1919 political tract *Prussianism and Socialism*, a polity combining Prussian authoritarian, corporatist, and socialistic features. An embittered man, he engaged in conspiratorial politics from 1919 to 1923, aiming to overturn Germany's fledgling postwar democracy. Subsequent chapters will analyze *Prussianism and Socialism* and discuss Spengler's political phase in the 1920s.

In retrospect, Spengler's confidence in the feasibility of the partial democratization he espoused for Wilhelmine Germany and his faith in the ability of its leaders to achieve grandiose, imperialistic plans appears to be

44. Spengler to Klöres, 18 December 1918, *B*, 111; *PuS*, 54.

unjustified. First, conservative forces were determined to maintain their political power and privileged position. Second, Spengler underestimated the powerful constraints under which German foreign policy operated. Even if the Second Reich had been blessed with better leadership after 1890 than that which was actually provided by Bismarck's successors, its chances of successfully carrying out an aggressive, expansionistic foreign policy were problematic to say the least. The Anglo-German antagonism, the breakdown of good relations with Russia, the historic rivalry with France, and America's perceived national interest in preventing German hegemony over the Continent were all factors conspiring to frustrate German imperialist ambitions. Even if Germany had somehow been able to win World War I amid such an unfavorable correlation of forces, it is very questionable that the country would have had an acceptable degree of social and political stability after the conflict was over. The realization of extreme war aims by Germany would have exacerbated the already-profound tensions between supporters of authoritarian rule and traditional privilege and the millions of ordinary citizens who, having sacrificed their blood and endured innumerable hardships on the home front, would now demand a thoroughgoing reform of German political institutions. Territorial annexations in Europe and the consequent need to hold down nationalistic peoples would have necessitated the maintenance of a very large peacetime military establishment. The resultant militarization of life would have worsened social and political tensions in German society. Moreover, the problems the Second Reich had encountered before 1914 in Alsace-Lorraine and the Polish provinces strongly suggested that the subjection of additional foreign peoples to German rule would have placed great strains upon the state. Finally, this enlarged German empire would have most likely become embroiled in further costly and destabilizing conflicts, as other great powers would not have tolerated such a revolution in world affairs.

It is conceivable that Germany, with much better leadership after 1890 and plenty of luck, could have won through force of arms domination of the Continent and possibly held on to its imperial gains. Nonetheless, such a very bold gamble would have entailed very substantial risks for the internal stability of the state and its external security as well. What would have served Germany's national interest best on the eve of the Great War was a foreign policy of patience, circumspection, and détente, not one audaciously aiming to establish a modern counterpart to the Roman Empire, as Spengler had advocated. Admittedly, in the pre–World War I atmosphere of heightened nationalist and imperialist sentiment not only in Germany but in the other European great powers as well, such a prudential foreign policy course would have been very difficult to pursue.

Our inquiry has shown that before his rise to prominence, Spengler was a neoconservative advocate of the quasi-democratization of the Second Reich. The Peace Resolution of 1917 seriously undermined his opportunistic interest in partially democratizing German political life; socialist revolution and Versailles destroyed it. For only the overthrow of the Weimar Republic, a regime illegitimate from its inception in his eyes, and its replacement with a more authoritarian one, would put Germany back on the path of power politics and imperialism in the grand style.

7

Spengler, the Neo-Rankeans, and the Pan-Germans

SINCE ITS FOUNDING IN 1871 THE SECOND
Reich experienced a population explosion and, after an initial economic
slowdown, a long boom from 1894 to 1912. This upsurge left its indelible
stamp on German historical and international political thought. In an age
of planetary imperial competition and accumulating German power resources, the desire for the pursuit of a *Weltpolitik*, a more assertive, globally oriented German foreign policy, naturally spread in bourgeois circles.
As Ludwig Frank remarked in 1911, "practically the whole bourgeoisie
. . . has become imperialistic."[1] As we shall discover, Spengler's brand of
imperialism exceeded in ambition that of the vast majority of his fellow
bourgeois intellectuals.

Wilhelm II's generation preened itself on the unification of Germany
through Bismarck's masterful diplomacy and Helmuth Moltke's military
genius and the rapid economic expansion. Yet the pride in Germany's
growing national power was accompanied by gnawing anxiety that Germany, as *die verspätete Nation*, having achieved national unity late in modern history, would be permanently left behind by the other imperial
powers in the mad scramble to gobble up the shrinking available territory
of the globe in the late nineteenth and early twentieth centuries. As the
German foreign minister, Bernhard von Bülow, colorfully expressed it in
a public declaration in 1897, Germany did "not wish to put anyone in the
shade, but we do demand our place in the sun." The post-Bismarckian

---

1. Ludwig Frank, quoted in Dirk Stegmann, *Die Erben Bismarcks: Parteien und
Verbände in der Spätphase des Wilhelminischen Deutschlands. Sammlungspolitik 1897–
1918* (Cologne: Kiepenheuer & Witsch, 1970), 113.

generation, overflowing with vitality, looked boldly ahead to the future. It was ready for new challenges and a global foreign policy, a *Weltpolitik*, that would abandon the cautiousness and restraint of Bismarck's postunification diplomacy and finally earn for Germany the position of equality she deserved among the great powers.[2] As Hajo Holborn observed about the generation of Germans at the end of the nineteenth century, they "believed that Germany's stunning rise as one of the three economic powers of the world would be followed by her acquisition of corresponding political position." In a similar vein, Gordon Craig noted, "This desire for [greater international] recognition, which was to be found in all sections of society, was the biggest political fact of the last years of the century. . . . The German people . . . desired the transformation of Germany from a continental to a world Power." *Weltpolitik* found ready spokesmen in bourgeoise intellectuals, indeed among the German intellectual elite as a whole, including all the leading historians.[3]

An understandable shortcoming of Leopold von Ranke's vision of the great powers was the circumscription of his analysis to the traditional European great powers and his failure to perceive the growing importance of states outside the immediate orbit of European politics.[4] Ranke's perspective as a historian was in the hitherto unchallenged Eurocentric tradition; his orientation in international politics also remained Eurocentric. This major shortcoming was overcome by intellectuals whom the renowned historian influenced in the so-called Ranke Renaissance.

Many of Germany's leading historical and political minds, including Max Lenz, Hans Delbrück, Hermann Oncken, Otto Hintze, Friedrich Meinecke, Max Weber, and Paul Rohrbach, trumpeted the new course of *Weltpolitik*. They championed a foreign policy whose central aim was the continued growth of German power within the context of a new international order. These thinkers optimistically expected that the European balance-of-power system would be naturally transformed into a truly inter-

---

2. Bernhard von Bülow, quoted in William Carr, *A History of Germany 1815–1990*, 4th ed. (London: Edward Arnold, 1991), 174; Winfried Baumgart, *Deutschland im Zeitalter des Imperialismus 1890–1914*, 5th ed. (Stuttgart: Kohlhammer, 1986), 46ff.

3. Hajo Holborn, *A History of Modern Germany 1840–1945* (Princeton: Princeton Univ. Press, 1969), 325; Gordon A. Craig, *Germany, 1866–1945* (New York: Oxford Univ. Press, 1978), 249; Werner Frauendienst, "Deutsche Weltpolitik: Zur Problematik des Wilhelminischen Reichs," *Die Welt als Geschichte* 19 (1959): 20.

4. Carsten Holbraad, *The Concert of Europe: A Study in German and British International Theory, 1815–1914* (London: Longman, 1970), 95.

national balance-of-power system. Such a transformation seemed logical and inevitable in an age of the increasing globalization of communication, transportation, and commerce. In their view, Germany was not a country on the verge of destroying the European balance-of-power system through the flagrant misuse of its rapidly expanding power resources. Quite the opposite, it was a responsible country finally assuming its legitimate place alongside other world powers, Britain, the United States, Russia, and Japan, in a new, global, international states system. Germany, they confidently believed, would at last break the confines of its Continental position and finally project its power globally. This emergent global balance-of-power system would maintain a respectable measure of international order and stability in the tense atmosphere of global imperialistic competition. Order and stability would be achieved, in conformance with Rankean principles, through the mechanism of the jealous rivalry of powerful sovereign states. War, it must be stressed, was not rejected by Wilhelmine historical and political thinkers as a legitimate means of accomplishing the well-deserved graduation of Germany to the coveted status of a world power among equals.

Ranke's ideas on power politics were particularly influential in Germany in the quarter-century prior to World War I. As Gerhard Ritter observed, "Ranke's idea of the secure existence of European culture based upon, in the end, the indestructible balance of power among the five great powers, dominated the entire historical conception."[5] Indeed, with the emergence of *Weltpolitik* after the dismissal of Bismarck, the decades after 1890, four years after Ranke's death, witnessed what was later termed a Ranke Renaissance.[6] Various German historical and political thinkers analyzed international politics in an imperialistic era by projecting onto the world scene Ranke's key concepts of the centrality to history of the struggle of the great powers and the operation of the balance of power, reinforced,

5. Gerhard Ritter, "Wissenschaftliche Historie Einst und Jetzt: Betrachtungen und Erinnerungen," *Historische Zeitschrift* 202 (1966): 579.
6. Georg G. Iggers, *The German Conception of History: The National Tradition of Historical Thought from Herder to the Present*, rev. ed. (Middletown, Conn.: Wesleyan Univ. Press, 1983), 89. For a discussion of the Ranke Renaissance, see also the following: Ludwig Dehio, "Gedanken über die deutsche Sendung, 1900–1918," *Historische Zeitschrift* 170 (1950): 479–502; Ludwig Dehio, "Ranke und der deutsche Imperialismus," *Historische Zeitschrift* 174 (1952): 307–28; Elisabeth Fehrenbach, "Rankerenaissance und Imperialismus in der wilhelminischen Zeit," in Bernd Faulenbach, ed., *Geschichtswissenschaft in Deutschland: Traditionelle Positionen und gegenwärtige Aufgaben* (Munich: C. H. Beck, 1974).

strange as it may sound to contemporary historical observers looking back at the tragic legacy of two world wars, through nationalism.

Ranke advocated the balance of power as the international ordering principle of Europe for two reasons: first, in order to secure the autonomy of the state in the balance-of-power system; and second, in order to ensure national cultural vitality, which requires that the state guard its freedom in the international arena. Ranke idealistically conceptualized power-political strength as an expression of moral and cultural energies. Thus, preserving an environment in European politics conducive to the prosperity of national culture in turn reinforces the internal mechanism that produces an effective balance of power in Europe. He was convinced that the competitive national individualism, the vitalism of national energies in the West, would preserve the states of Europe from external domination. The great powers would resist surrendering their freedom to a power striving for "universal monarchy." Such an international hegemony would have been analogous to that of ancient Rome. Ranke glorified metaphysically the capacity of the European states to safeguard their political independence and cultural individuality through a balance-of-power system. He regarded it as an expression of a transcendent "genius," as consonant with the "destiny of the world."[7]

Ranke's optimism in *The Great Powers* about the future international political evolution of Europe by no means abated in his later years. His sanguinity stood in sharp contrast to the visionary pessimism of his former student, Jacob Burckhardt, and his colleague Friedrich Nietzsche. Burckhardt observed with apprehension the rise of Prussia under Bismarck to become the leading great power of the Continent. He watched with despair the militarization of German life and predicted an era of wars.[8] Nietzsche shared his forebodings, anticipating the emergence of a new breed of tyrants and a struggle for world rule. Ranke, however, misinterpreted the founding of the Second Reich as reinforcing the European balance-of-power system. Instead, ironically, this historical watershed laid the power-political conditions for the destruction in two world wars of the European balance-of-power system that Ranke glorified.

Although the Neo-Rankeans adapted to their own purposes Ranke's

7. Leopold von Ranke, *Die großen Mächte*, ed. Friedrich Meinecke (Leipzig: Insel-Verlag, 1941), 58, 25, 59.

8. Jacob Burckhardt, *Force and Freedom: An Interpretation of History*, ed. James Hastings Nichols (New York: Meridian, 1955), 35–37.

ideas on power politics, their writings on international relations often lack the ethical high-mindedness one associates with the works of their master. This new historiographical school provided a theoretical underpinning for *Weltpolitik* and imperialism.[9] Prominent advocates of *Weltpolitik*, including Lenz, Delbrück, Rohrbach, Weber, Hintze, Oncken, and Meinecke, all manifested in varying degrees a Neo-Rankean orientation toward international politics.

The strident nationalist Heinrich von Treitschke, who filled Ranke's professorial chair upon his retirement, bridges the philosophy of history and politics of Ranke and the Neo-Rankeans.[10] Treitschke argued that Britain, with its sway over the oceans of the world and its sprawling empire, enjoyed an unnaturally privileged position vis-à-vis the other European great powers. This idea became the common property of Neo-Rankean adherents of *Weltpolitik*. The late nineteenth century was the golden age of the British Empire, until, as Lenz stressed in his epigonal work, *The Great Powers*, the Boer War raised the question of the solidity of Britain's impressive imperial standing. Delbrück maintained that, just as France's predominance had been eliminated at the close of the Napoleonic Wars by the institution of a concert of equally entitled European powers, Britain's superior position would be abolished by the creation of a balance-of-power system of world powers. Backing the controversial Tirpitz naval program, he aspired to eliminate the source of British international supremacy, its control of the high seas.[11] Rohrbach likewise supported the naval program with the aim of challenging the maritime hegemony of England and facilitating a global balance-of-power system. Weber, while not conventionally regarded as a Neo-Rankean, nonetheless embraced many of its aims. He espoused equality of status in world politics for Germany, complete with a powerful navy and a respectable colonial empire, in imitation of Britain.[12] Hintze argued that the goal of imperialism was not the forging of a modern world empire after the pattern of the Roman Empire but the transformation of the European balance-of-power system into a global one. This international balance-of-power system would facilitate coexistence within an international society of peoples and states, as it had

9. Iggers, *German Conception of History*, 130.
10. See Georg Iggers, "Heinrich von Treitschke," in Hans-Ulrich Wehler, ed., *Deutscher Historiker*, vol. II (Göttingen: Vandenhoeck & Ruprecht, 1971).
11. Dehio, "Ranke," 310, 312.
12. Dehio, "Gedanken," 483; Wolfgang J. Mommsen, *Max Weber und die deutsche Politik 1890–1920*, 2d ed. (Tübingen: J. C. B. Mohr, 1974), 147.

done for centuries in modern Europe. Oncken envisioned the old European balance-of-power system organically developing into one on a global basis. Meinecke maintained during World War I that the natural tendency of European history, in contrast to that of the ancient Roman era, would culminate in an international society of strong nations and not in a universal empire.[13]

Balance-of-power theory, to which the Neo-Rankeans made an important contribution, enjoyed a long tradition in Europe. As Herbert Butterfield noted, the balance of power had already become a highly developed doctrine in European international theory in the course of the second half of the seventeenth century, providing theoretical justification to European resistance to the hegemonic aspirations of Louis XIV. Eighteenth-century theorists of the balance of power looked back to the hegemony of Rome as an experience that Europe in the future must be spared. They argued that an international states system could be structured only in accordance with one of two ordering principles: first, a state of equilibrium, *i.e.*, a condition of an efficacious balance of power; or second, the establishment of a universal empire following the example of ancient Rome. The principle of the balance of power was not advocated solely because it safeguarded the territorial integrity and freedom of the state but because it provided an optimal environment in which the national cultures of Europe could prosper. The eighteenth century regarded the balance of power as virtually a law, one that comes into effect whenever there is an international states system, provided statesmen appreciated its moderation and wisdom.[14] Neo-Rankean thinkers naturally found attractive an organizing principle in international politics, the balance of power, that supported their normative aim of the enhancement of German cultural individuality and freedom of action in an age of imperialistic rivalry. The Neo-Rankeans, as heirs of the historicist tradition, viewed with a jaundiced eye the idea that the nations of Europe should be straitjacketed into a modern imperial form analogous to the Roman Empire. As Ranke sanguinely argued that nationalism would enhance international order, the Neo-Rankeans optimistically maintained that the twin forces of nationalism and imperialism could be constructively channeled to the end of international order by globalizing the European balance-of-power system.

13. Dehio, "Ranke," 315, 318, 319, 320.
14. Herbert Butterfield, "The Balance of Power," in Herbert Butterfield and Martin Wight, eds., *Diplomatic Investigations: Essays in the Theory of International Politics* (London: George Allen & Unwin, 1966), 139, 142, 147.

Spengler's philosophy of world history and politics dramatically exposed a fundamental weakness of the balance-of-power theory of Ranke and the Neo-Rankeans. They had a normatively rooted bias toward the maintenance of a multiplicity of independent and powerful nation-states and robust national cultures, goals admirably supported by the organizing principle in international politics of the balance of power. This bias prevented the Neo-Rankeans from recognizing, as Spengler did, that the unprecedented expansive power of Western civilization would destroy the European balance-of-power system and promote the international primacy of one Western power.

Ranke and the historicist tradition failed to appreciate the daemonic nature of nationalism and its capacity to lay in ruins the European balance-of-power system. Germany, like Italy, had achieved unification very late in comparison with the other European great powers. Nationalism and the instruments of power played indispensable roles in the long and difficult process of German unification. Consequently, these potentially highly destructive forces in international politics were regarded most approvingly in Germany. Spengler, in contrast to the Neo-Rankeans, understood on the eve of World War I the potential of nationalism, coupled with the might of industrialized societies, to demolish the European balance-of-power system. Yet despite his oracular vision of the destruction of this system through world wars, he gravely erred. Spengler believed that Imperial Germany would supplant the Pax Britannica of the nineteenth century by hammering together the foundation of a more impressive Pax Germanica in the twentieth century. He failed to foresee the approaching dawn of the American Century.

Bismarck's countrymen were elated with his achievement of German unification. They quickly came to esteem his diplomacy as exhibiting a mastery of the subtleties of power politics. His was a statecraft that had brought the course of Germany's development as a force in European politics virtually to its triumphant completion. A generation later, *Weltpolitik* critics such as Spengler and Weber, notwithstanding their appreciation of Bismarck's genius, criticized him. They found fault with Bismarck for not having pursued the strategic goal of expanding the power base of the Second Reich. For them, Bismarck had only satisfactorily answered the question of what a unified Germany's regional role would be. He had not answered the urgent question of what the Second Reich's role in the emerging world of globalized politics would be. The chancellorship of Bismarck stood at the end of an era. The European stage of high politics was being expanded and converted into a global one. The new and vital question was whether the European balance-of-power system that Bismarck had revolutionized would be projected onto a global level or transformed into a universal empire. For Spengler, whose imperialistic aspirations far exceeded those of Weber, the Little German "solution" (*Kleindeutsch-landlösung*) imposed by the Iron Chancellor was not the apex of German history as it had been for Bismarck's contemporaries. Bismarck's statecraft was only a transitional phase on the ascent to a German *imperium mundi*.

Spengler's radical imperialism sharply contrasts with that of the Neo-Rankeans, who called for a comparatively modest international role for Germany. The German historicist tradition recoiled in disgust at the thought that the proud nations of the West should be pressed into a modern, cosmopolitan empire reminiscent of Rome's, replete with the cultural deterioration foreign conquest would bring. Spengler, by contrast, championed the modern "Roman" imperial project as shown in the following passage from a letter dated July 14, 1915: "Follow Prussian history in its wonderful organic climb upwards: Fehrbellin 1675, Friedrich Wilhelm's organization of the state and army 1720, the Silesian Wars 1742–1763, Leipzig 1813, Sedan-Versailles 1870 and at last 1915, so you will find on the one hand a monstrous movement forward on the way to world power, as only the Romans from 300 to 50 B.C. have experienced."[15]

Before the founding of the Second Reich, the uppermost concern of German political thought had been the unification of Germany. Spengler's vision of Germany's power-political future responded to a major political tradition in nineteenth-century German historical thought known as Borussianism. The name of this tradition derives from Borussia, a feminine designation in New Latin for Prussia. Its founder, Johann Droysen, as well as its subsequent leading representatives, including Heinrich von Sybel and Heinrich von Treitschke, claimed that Prussia was responsible for accomplishing an important historical task, the Little German "solution" to the German question. Droysen, as a prominent historian of the unification movement, believed German unification under the leadership of Prussia to be its necessary historical task and to be morally right. As Friedrich Dahlmann had maintained in 1848 before him, only Prussia could promote Germany into the ranks of the great powers of Europe.[16] Treitschke as-

15. Spengler to Klöres, 14 July 1915, *B*, 42.
16. Wolfgang Hardtwig, "Von Preußens Aufgabe in Deutschland zu Deutschlands Aufgabe in der Welt," *Historische Zeitschrift* 231 (1980): 282.

serted in 1866 that the approaching unification of Germany would be "an act of historical necessity" conforming to the "movement of history" toward the formation of large nation-states. August Ludwig von Rochau, who coined the term *Realpolitik* after the debacle of the nationalist aspirations of German liberalism in 1848, declared in 1869 that the unification of Germany by Prussia was in accordance with a necessary "law of nature."[17] Borussian and most other German historical and political thinkers viewed Bismarck's Little German "solution" as reinforcing the European balance-of-power system and not establishing a precondition for its future destruction. Spengler, by contrast, envisioned Germany, united by Prussia in three short wars, to be the long-term destroyer of the European balance-of-power system. He regarded the creation of a universal empire by a Germany imbued with the Prussian spirit as responding to a historical necessity.

A stormy debate about war aims erupted in Germany in 1915. It echoes in Spengler's letters, in which he entertained various war aims. Yet he never drafted for private or public consumption a detailed strategic program or foreign policy plan according to which Germany could win global hegemony. He conceived this potential global hegemony, it should be stressed, to be an impermanent one and eventually overpowered presumably by Russia. One reason perhaps for his vagueness is that he argued that if Germany emerged victorious in the Great War, it would have to slug it out in one more war on a global scale to forge finally a German *imperium mundi*. Nonetheless, with this qualification in mind, his letters convey the distinct impression that he assumed that the attainment by Germany of Continental supremacy and the pursuit of its naval program in support of the global projection of economic and military power were sufficient to guarantee Germany's future as the dominant world power. To achieve German mastery of the Continent, he supported during the war a policy of limited annexations in Europe. Territorial expansion would improve Germany's security and enhance the access of its industry to crucial raw materials. Annexations would be complemented by economic satellitism. Beyond the Continent, he called for expanding Germany's African colonial holdings. Germany would thereby have a substantial overseas empire in emulation of

17. Heinrich von Treitschke, quoted in Karl-Georg Faber, "Realpolitik als Ideologie: Die Bedeutung des Jahres 1866 für das politische Denken in Deutschland," *Historische Zeitschrift* 203 (1966): 21; August Ludwig von Rochau, quoted in Hardtwig, "Preußens Aufgabe," 322.

Britain and France. However, even if Germany had achieved Continental hegemony and had gained a great African empire, it is most questionable that this admittedly very substantial power base would have sufficed for global hegemony. Such a German empire would still have had to coexist with the United States, which boasted the world's leading economy and a virtually impregnable position in the Western hemisphere. German domination of Europe would probably have resulted in a tension-filled German-American bipolarity in world affairs in the twentieth century.

The German battle fleet epitomized the imperialistic spirit of the Wilhelmine era; enthusiasm for its construction prevailed among the bourgeoisie. The Neo-Rankeans regarded the fleet as a shining symbol of Germany's new status as a leading great power and, if necessary, the means for winning equality on the high seas by force. Spengler, by contrast, viewed it as a strategic instrument for German global hegemony.

The second main group of bourgeois imperialist thinkers in Wilhelmine Germany were the Pan-Germans. The term *Pan-German* refers to intellectuals either directly contributing to or having a close affinity to the ideas of the Pan-German League. Founded in 1891, the league played an important role in the political system. "The most active and radical of all the major patriotic societies" of Imperial Germany, the league aggressively espoused imperialism.[18] Its members included such personalities as the historians Dietrich Shaefer and Georg von Below, the economist Ernst Hasse, the famous zoologist Ernst Haeckel, the founder of German geopolitics Friedrich Ratzel, and General Friedrich von Bernhardi.

With his grandiose vision of German global hegemony, Spengler is unquestionably one of the most imperialistic historical and political thinkers that the Wilhelmine age produced. Yet it would be mistaken to interpret his radical imperialism as originating in a shallow nationalistic adulation of German cultural achievements. Moreover, it would be an error to assign him automatically to the pole of Pan-German imperialist thought. For it is remarkable how his perspective deviates from many of the core ideas of Pan-German-oriented thinkers, who usually believed in the inherent superiority of things German. The Pan-Germans, as extreme nationalists, typically painted "a thoroughly negative" picture of the history of France; Spengler honored the ancien régime of Louis XIV and his heirs as personi-

---

18. Roger Chickering, *We Men Who Feel Most German: A Cultural Study of the Pan-German League, 1886–1914* (Boston: George Allen & Unwin, 1984), ix, 12.

fying "mature Western culture."[19] The Pan-Germans disparaged the supposed "perfidy and unscrupulousness" of British balance-of-power politics. For Spengler, Britain had produced, next to Rome, the most superb tradition of statecraft in world history. The Pan-Germans often conceptualized history in racist categories. Spengler, by contrast, denied race a role in cultural differentiation. Whereas they smugly looked down on the Slavs as "inferior" peoples, Spengler, drawing inspiration from his revered Dostoevsky, designated the Russians the bearers of the next great culture in world history. Extreme nationalists typically idealized German cultural achievements. Spengler, in contrast, viewed the cultural identity of the West as being more significant than that of its constituent national cultures. However, Spengler did share a few of the essential elements of Pan-German thought: the doctrine of the primacy of foreign policy, the glorification of war and Prussia, and the championing of radical imperialist goals.[20]

Spengler also advocated an imperialist agenda markedly different from Pan-German thought. The Pan-German League came very close "to treating *Lebensraum* as its central program element."[21] By contrast, one is struck by the absence of *Lebensraum* components in Spengler's thought. In the decades prior to World War I, the population of Germany had grown very rapidly. However, Spengler was already discussing in *The Decline of the West* how the Germans, and other West European peoples as well, would experience sharply reduced birth rates in the not-too-distant future, an astoundingly accurate demographic prediction. He did not expect the German people to increase substantially in numbers and viewed the urbanization of Germany as an irreversible historical trend. Thus, he logically did not urge annexation of agricultural lands for peasant settlement as advocates of *Lebensraum* imperialism typically did. While Spengler favored maintaining the integrity of German culture, he soberly recognized the inevitability of its deterioration. Thus, he did not advocate preserving the German national character (*Deutschtum*) through peasant

19. Hans Krause, "Die alldeutsche Geschichtsschreibung vor dem ersten Weltkrieg," in Joachim Streisand, ed., *Die bürgerliche deutsche Geschichtsschreibung von der Reichseinigung von oben bis zur Befreiung Deutschlands vom Faschismus,* vol. 21 of *Studien über die deutsche Geschichtswissenschaft* (Berlin: Akademie-Verlag, 1965), 196; *UdA* I, 194 n. 1.
20. Krause, "Die alldeutsche Geschichtsschreibung," 196–97.
21. Woodruff D. Smith, *The Ideological Origins of Nazi Imperialism* (New York: Oxford Univ. Press, 1986), 95.

migration. His fascination with martial virtues and Caesarism has obscured the fact that his imperialism incorporated significant economic features and was by no means exclusively territorial in nature. Indeed, as we have argued, Spengler was primarily an economic imperialist and secondarily a territorial imperialist. He built his imperialistic edifice upon the foundation of the Bismarckian *Kleindeutschlandlösung*. He did not espouse German imperialism for racial (*völkisch*) and *Lebensraum* motivations in the Greater Germany (*grossdeutsche*) tradition, which Hitler epitomized. In fact, Spengler argued after World War I, in the Bismarckian tradition, that Germany should have reached an understanding with Russia instead of blindly underwriting Austria's Balkan ambitions.[22] Nonetheless, despite the economic thrust of Spengler's imperialism and his lack of enthusiasm for *Lebensraum,* his vision of Germany achieving global hegemony was an extreme one. Perhaps, one must add, he was guilty of alleviating his cultural despair by intoxicating himself with dreams of radical power politics.

22. DR, 117–18.

Prussianism and Socialism and the Faustian Imperium Mundi

THE IMPERIALISTIC DREAMS OF THE bourgeois elite of Wilhelmine Germany, including Spengler's, turned into the nightmare in November, 1918, of humiliating defeat in World War I and socialist revolution. These events precipitated a heated political debate in Germany in which Spengler participated. Laying aside his work on the final draft of the second volume of *The Decline of the West*, he wrote his first political book, *Prussianism and Socialism*, in the summer of 1919. Published in December of that year, it offers additional insight into his political philosophy. Moreover, the little book illustrates the vision of international political change that originally inspired Spengler to compose *The Decline of the West*, though he did not elaborate this vision in it. As he wrote in the introduction to *Prussianism and Socialism*, "this small publication has emerged out of notes that were intended for *The Decline of the West*, namely the second volume, which were even partly the embryo out of which this entire philosophy has developed." *Prussianism and Socialism*, along with Arthur Moeller van den Bruck's *The Right of Young Peoples*, sounded the clarion call for the ideological assault on the political legitimacy of the Weimar Republic from the Right. The first volume of *The Decline of the West* and *Prussianism and Socialism* earned Spengler recognition as a leading philosopher of German neoconservatism. Along with him and Moeller van den Bruck, other "intellectually more significant representatives" of German neoconservatism, or what has been more frequently termed the "Conservative Revolution," included Ernst Jünger, Carl Schmitt, Hans Freyer, and Ernst Niekisch.[1]

---

1. *PuS*, 3; Arthur Moeller van den Bruck, *Das Recht der jungen Völker* (Munich: Piper, 1919); Klemens von Klemperer, "The Pessimism of Oswald Spengler," in *Germany's New Conservatism: Its History and Dilemma in the Twentieth Century*

Like his counterpart Max Weber, Spengler dreamed of an active role in politics, though both men were constitutionally better suited for intellectual life. Under the impact of the November revolution, Spengler, a disillusioned observer of the political scene in Germany, began a sustained effort to gain a significant role. Like many fellow conservatives, he believed for a long time in the possibility of the restoration of the Hohenzollern monarchy. Although Spengler stood on the right of the political spectrum during the interwar years, none of the parties met his political expectations or aroused his enthusiastic support. He devoted himself to politics from 1919 until the short-lived stabilization of the Weimar Republic in 1924. His objective was the creation of a network of elite personalities in important positions who were committed to German national resurgence. Modern means of political management were to serve his conservative goals. Spengler was also interested in organizing occupational groups in order to exert pressure on the political parties. In addition, he hoped to aid in the formation of a press empire with strong nationalistic leanings to shape public opinion. However, unlike the demagogue Hitler, Spengler, with his elitist orientation, shrank from immersing himself in mass politics. During this period of political involvement, he made important contacts, particularly with prominent industrial figures in the Ruhr and commercial leaders in Hamburg. He was sought after in these exclusive circles not only as a lecturer but behind the scenes, as an éminence grise, an advisor and intermediary.[2]

Prussianism and Socialism was published by the Beck publishing house in Munich, to which Spengler had granted in May, 1919, the rights for the third and all subsequent editions of *The Decline of the West*. The publication of *Prussianism and Socialism* marked the beginning of a long and mutually rewarding association between this respected publishing house and the controversial intellectual; the Beck *Verlag* published all of his subsequent works, establishing the Spengler Archive after his death.

The purpose of *Prussianism and Socialism* was twofold: first, to explain the historical significance of World War I; and second, to prescribe how the German polity should be renewed in order to enable Germany to triumph in the struggle for global hegemony that would resume in the coming decades. Spengler declares that the history of the German *Volk* is more

---

(Princeton: Princeton Univ. Press, 1968); Rolf Peter Sieferle, *Die Konservative Revolution: Fünf biographische Skizzen* (Frankfurt am Main: Fischer, 1995), 43.

2. K-Sp, 217 ff., 276 ff., 304 ff.

tragic than that of any other people. He identifies their modern history with the state of Prussia. "In the great crises all the others fought with victory or defeat at stake; we have always fought with victory or destruction at issue."[3] Germany will be confronted by this dilemma until the *imperium mundi* of the modern West is finally hammered together.

Spengler quickly grasped that "the war to end all wars" was the first phase of a revolutionary era in world politics. In a letter penned two months after the outbreak of World War I, he perceptively observes that the concept of European great power is obsolete. A new era of world powers is dawning. "The concept of great power comes to an end with this war; there are only world powers from now on." Four months after the opening shots were fired, he strikingly predicts in a letter, "This war is no concluding event, but the *beginning* of a colossal epoch, which will perhaps lead to completely different catastrophes." Spengler interpreted World War I as the modern counterpart to the Second Punic War, in which Rome, pushed to the limits of its endurance, prevailed over Carthage. He believed that just as victory in this existential struggle paved the way for Roman hegemonic expansion, so would the Great War for Germany because Germany was "the new power of the future."[4]

World War I was a momentous event of the "evening" phase of Western culture. Spengler provocatively argues that the war represented "the great struggle between both Germanic ideas": the Anglo-American political and economic system and the Prussian alternative. In the Great War "the last great spiritual question of Faustian man" had come to light.[5] Although formulated in superannuated language, his vision of a struggle between Western powers for economic hegemony of the world as centrally important to twentieth-century history is insightful. England and Germany championed antagonistic Germanic ideas, England standing for a vast, capitalistic trade empire, Germany striving to create a socialistic world empire.

The challenge of initiating national renewal after Germany's empire building ended in military collapse and political upheaval preoccupies Spengler. Appalled by the German socialist revolution of 1918, he asserts that the patriotic dedication of the German people to the war effort in Au-

3. *PuS*, 6.
4. Spengler to Klöres, 14 July 1915, *B*, 43; Spengler to Klöres, 18 December 1914, *B*, 32; Spengler to Klöres, 14 July 1915, *B*, 43.
5. *PuS*, 6, 7.

gust, 1914, represented a genuine German and socialist revolution, in contrast to the overthrow of the Hohenzollern monarchy in November, 1918. Although this "revolution" of 1914 was actualized in "legitimate and military forms," it transformed German social consciousness. After defeat in World War I, Spengler anticipates a national revival. He predicts that Germany's authentic revolution of 1914 "will slowly overcome the loathsomeness of 1918."[6]

Prussianism and Socialism critiques Marx's ideas and seeks to discredit them. Its author touches upon weaknesses of historical materialism. Although Marx's philosophy is a "magnificent construction," Spengler disputes "the validity of his economic constructions for the *entire* 'human society' " and his attendant claim that they are "the only substantial thing in the course of history." For Marx audaciously projects his political-economic interpretation of industrial England onto the whole of world history. Spengler asserts that Marx's thesis that high cultural achievements, such as religion, law, and art, are superstructurally dependent upon the economic base is only convincing to Marx's readers because of the decline of religion and traditions in a materialistic age.[7] With his enthusiasm for materialism, Marx's philosophy of history is bereft of insight into the primacy of the irrational, of psychological factors in history. "We do not believe any more in the power of reason over life. We feel that life dominates reason," Spengler proclaims. "As a man of the natural-scientific nineteenth century [Marx] was a good materialist and a poor psychologist."[8]

Marx's notion of international proletarian solidarity, already exposed as superficial and illusory by the debacle of the Second International in 1914, arouses Spengler's scorn. Although Marx expected conflict among states to remain a reality until the dawn of international socialism, he believed that the growing global economic intercourse stimulated by capitalism was significantly diminishing national antagonisms. Thus he did not anticipate warfare of the magnitude of the two world wars, which destroyed the primacy of Europe in world politics. Spengler certainly did not suffer from any of Marx's illusions about the role of nationalism and armed conflict in global politics in the twentieth century.

Spengler rules out the possibility of a triumphant revolution led by the working class in Germany, the elusive dream of Marx and Friedrich Eng-

6. *PuS*, 12.
7. *PuS*, 69, 78–79.
8. *PuS*, 79, 69.

els. Spengler correctly predicts that the socialist leadership, indecisive in 1918, had forever lost the necessary momentum for victory. Instead of the millenarian, proletarian seizure of power, there would be merely inconsequential fisticuffs. He caustically observes, "Out of leaders of a great movement they will one day sink to being verbose heroes of suburban riots."[9]

The great political task is "to free German socialism from Marx." This will be accomplished by a three-pronged strategy: first, by overcoming the centrality of class struggle in socialist thought; second, by implanting a vigorous nationalistic spirit through the emphasis of the Rankean primacy of great power rivalry, which Marx's utopian internationalism discounts; and third, by awakening consciousness of the innately socialistic ethos of German society. German socialism as a magnificent national form "stands at the beginning, but socialism as a separate movement of the German proletariat is at its end." Despite his hostility to the Weimar Republic, Spengler argues that German socialism will be democratic, for politics must conform to the irresistible tendency of the twentieth century. "Democracy, one may regard it as one wants to, is the form of this century, which *will* prevail. There is for the state only democratization or nothing." However, German socialism will be ennobled by its constitutional monarchical structure and the Prussian ethos of hierarchy and communality. Realizing the goal of a strong German socialist state and fulfilling its mission of global hegemony in the struggle against the Anglo-Saxons is virtually exclusively a matter of power. Echoing Treitschke's famous dictum that "the essence of the state is first of all power, in the second place power, and thirdly, once more, power," Spengler declares, "socialism means power, power, and again and again power."[10]

Discourse on domestic politics alternates with international relations analysis. Spengler sees the remarkable imperialistic energies of the West profoundly shaping modern history. Since the French Revolution and the Napoleonic Wars (the transition from culture to civilization), the elemental Faustian instinct of the will to power and the will to the infinite lives on "in the terrible will to total world domination in the military, economic, and intellectual sense, in the fact of the world war and the idea of world

9. *PuS*, 13.

10. *PuS*, 4, 98; Heinrich von Treitschke, "Bundesstaat und Einheitsstaat," in Heinrich von Treitschke, *Historische und Politische Aufsätze*, 8th ed., vol. II (Leipzig: G. Hirzel, 1921), 146; *PuS*, 98.

revolution, in the determination through the means of Faustian technology and inventiveness to forge the swarms of mankind into a whole."[11]

The modern Western drive to establish a universal empire aims at the transformation of the planet. Being more dynamic than the Babylonian, the Chinese, or the Roman, West European-American empire building recognizes no boundaries. This awesome, Faustian transformative urge has sought to remake the world in its image in the nineteenth and twentieth centuries. It will persist in striving to realize this tragic longing. "We have occupied all the continents with cities of our type, subjugated them to our thought and to our life-styles."[12]

The Spanish, British, and Germans personify this insistent, imperialistic impulse of the West. The creation of a global economic system is one of the deepest spiritual necessities of Faustian culture. Each of these nations has contributed to its realization. Despite his hero-worship of Napoleon, Spengler rejects French candidacy to this elite triad, perhaps because of bitterness after French victory over Germany in World War I. "The state of Louis XIV is an isolated case like the Napoleonic Empire, not a system of permanence."[13]

The British and Prussian expansionism of the nineteenth and twentieth centuries, which sets the tone for the phase of civilization in the West, was foreshadowed by Spanish imperialism. During "the Spanish Century," from 1527 to 1659, Spain expressed, in the phase of culture in the West, the Faustian drive to empire in magnificent forms. The modern state was created in the *Escorial;* refined power politics and exemplary cabinet diplomacy originated in Madrid. "The Spanish spirit desires to conquer the planet, an empire in which the sun never sets. . . . The Spanish were the ones who transformed the entire surface of the earth into an object of West European politics."[14]

Germany and Britain are the chief rivals in the contest to found the culminating imperial form of the West. With the benefit of hindsight, it is clear that the main deficiency in Spengler's application of his model of world-historical change to the twentieth century, at this stage in his intellectual development, is his misjudgment about the exact nature of the struggle for global hegemony. Spengler, along with many of his contem-

11. *PuS,* 23–24.
12. *PuS,* 24.
13. *PuS,* 51, 59.
14. *PuS,* 27.

poraries in Germany in 1914, misinterpreted the British position. They exaggerated Britain's strength and did not fully grasp its motivations. Nonetheless, in their defense, one should bear in mind that despite the onset of decline in the 1880s, Britain was still probably the paramount world power in August, 1914.[15] Simultaneously, they initially largely overlooked the United States as a potentially decisive force in the revolutionary transformation of the international states system. As will be shown later, Spengler eventually developed a sound appreciation of the decline of British industrial and imperial power. Moreover, he came to acknowledge, albeit in a limited and ultimately inadequate fashion, the ascendancy of the United States to world-power status.

In the years leading up to World War I, Britain was a status-quo-oriented power. It was preoccupied with preserving its insular security and imperial supremacy. British foreign policy, despite imperial pride, was not aiming to aggrandize aggressively Britain's already-vast imperial possessions. In 1917, the United States sought to prevent German Continental hegemony by basically upholding the existent distribution of power in the international system, one already quite favorable to American economic and security interests. The United States under Woodrow Wilson did not seek to alter radically the power relations in the world but aspired, preferably through the principle of collective security, largely to preserve the existing framework. The distribution of power Wilson favored was naturally very conducive to the further development of America's enormous economic potential.[16]

While Spengler compared World War I to the Second Punic War, other leading German historical minds also interpreted World War I by drawing comparisons with the history of classical antiquity. Weber wrote with resignation in a letter in November, 1918, "It's all over with a *world*-political role for Germany: the Anglo-Saxon world domination . . . is a fact." Employing a historical analogy that envisions World War I like Spengler's analogy did, as the counterpart of the Second Punic War, he continues, "America's world domination was as inevitable as that of Rome in antiquity after the Punic War." Eduard Meyer feared that the United States was

15. Paul Kennedy, *The Rise and Fall of the Great Powers: Economic Change and Military Conflict from 1500 to 2000* (New York: Random House, 1987), 231.

16. "No previous American administration had worked so hard to promote American economic interests abroad" as that under Wilson (C. J. Bartlett, *The Global Conflict: The International Rivalry of the Great Powers, 1880–1970* [New York: Longman, 1984], 97).

assuming the imperial role of ancient Rome. Just as Rome, the power on the periphery, had undergone a cultural process of Hellenization in order then to Romanize the ecumene politically, so had the peripheral power America been Europeanized in order now to proceed to Americanize the world. In 1919 Friedrich Meinecke voiced the fear that the Allied victory may have facilitated a "*Pax anglosaxonica.*" It would mean world domination by an American and British "dyarchy," underwritten by American economic preeminence, comparable in historical significance to that exercised monopolistically by Rome.[17]

Germany's failure in World War I to hammer together the foundation of a global empire came as a rude shock to Spengler. He became aware that it was unrealistic to expect any historical philosophy to anticipate unerringly the basic contours of international political change in the future. Thus, one witnesses in *Prussianism and Socialism* and in later works his growing awareness of the immense obstacles to forecasting change in international politics with any degree of precision.

In *Prussianism and Socialism* Spengler compares the political cultures of Germany and Britain to illuminate their hegemonic rivalry. It should be noted that much of his analysis here of Britain is arguably applicable to America. Spengler attributes the fundamental differences between the English and Germans to geopolitical causes. An insular existence molded the "soul" of the English people. Guardianship of border lands, which, lacking natural boundaries, were exposed to foreign threat from all sides, profoundly shaped the German people's "soul." The English personify the "Viking" spirit; the Germans, the spirit of knighthood. Distinguishing characteristics of the English include individualism, democracy, and capitalism. Commonality as a *Volk*, Prussian authoritarianism, and hierarchical socialism are hallmarks of the Germans. The orientation toward work differs in both cultures. The Englishman and American value the result of work, the success, money, and wealth it yields. The Prussian, with a genuinely socialist ethic, views work as a duty.[18] The decisive question of Western civiliza-

17. Weber to Friedrich Crusius, 24 November 1918, Max Weber, *Gesammelte Politische Schriften* (Munich: Drei Masken Verlag, 1921), 483; Alexander Demandt, "Eduard Meyer und Oswald Spengler. Lässt sich Geschichte voraussagen?" chap. in *Eduard Meyer: Leben und Leistung eines Universalhistorikers*, ed. William M. Calder III and Alexander Demandt (Leiden: E. J. Brill, 1990), 166; Friedrich Meinecke, "Weltgeschichtliche Parallelen unserer Lage," in *Nach der Revolution: Geschichtliche Betrachtungen über unsere Lage* (Munich: R. Oldenbourg, 1919), 98, 80–85.

18. *PuS*, 32, 41.

tion since Napoleon arises. Will the "capitalist" powers, the United States and England, or will Germany, revitalized by semi-authoritarian and imperialistic socialism, win control through world wars over the organization of the global economy?[19] Spengler's thesis of the tendency in modern history toward the establishment of global economic hegemony was foreshadowed by Nietzsche, who had spoken of the "inevitable, impending total economic administration of the earth."[20]

Spengler traces the spiritual origins of British capitalism to "the piratical instinct of an island people." In a trenchant description he captures the raw competitiveness and exploitativeness of capitalism. "The generation of *individual* fortunes, of *private* wealth, the victory over the competition, the exploitation of the public through advertising, through pricing strategies, through the stimulation of needs, through the mastery of the relationship between supply and demand is the goal, not the planned raising of the national living standard."[21]

Significantly, Spengler underestimated America's chances to prevail in the struggle for global hegemony. This is perhaps best illustrated by a characteristically romanticized passage describing the settlement of the American West. Late in Western history, the Viking idea "had expelled onto the American prairies, English, Germans, Scandinavians . . . a monstrous movement of Germanic peoples with the extreme longing for distance and limitless spaces, adventurous bands, out of which *another* people of Saxon stamp arose, but separated from the motherland of Faustian culture and therefore without the 'inner basalt,' to use Goethe's expression, with characteristics of the old prowess and the old noble blood, but without roots and therefore without a future."[22] Spengler imprisons himself in an inflexible, organic view of modern history. Select nation-states of Europe, arising on the mother soil of Faustian culture, are the logical and rightful contestants for the establishment of the Faustian *imperium mundi*.

Spengler attacks the Weimar Republic. It is an alien political-cultural form, a hothouse of careerism, interest-group politics, and corruption. Weimar is incapable of responsibly conducting domestic and foreign affairs. The prerequisite for the regeneration of German national strength is

19. *PuS*, 50–51.
20. Friedrich Nietzsche, *Der Wille zur Macht: Versuch einer Umwertung aller Werte*, ed. Peter Gast (Stuttgart: Alfred Kröner, 1964), 590.
21. *PuS*, 47–48.
22. *PuS*, 32.

to purge the fatherland of the vitiating English parliamentarian and democratic influences implanted on German soil by the intermediation of Napoleonic France. The quasi-parliamentarian nature of German politics from 1871 to 1914 was contrary to the true character of the German body politic and had impaired political-cultural maturation. Spengler praises August Bebel's well-organized and disciplined socialist party as a product of Prussia par excellence. The strength of genuinely German national instincts was displayed in the illiberal and antiparliamentarian tendency of the German conservatives and socialists in Wilhelmine Germany. Both groups rejected private and party-political governmental leadership, desiring to subordinate the conduct of the individual to the general interest.[23] This he conceives as the Prussian alternative to British individualism and democracy.

German socialism is unique. It has essentially nothing in common with French or British socialism, to say nothing of Russian socialism. Spengler dismisses French socialism as a political philosophy of putschism and sabotage, of mere social revenge, and English socialism as reform capitalism; only German socialism constitutes a genuine world view.

Although Spengler does not use the word *Dolchstoß*, he basically accepts the notorious *Dolchstoß-Legende* ("stab-in-the-back" legend), which found credibility in conservative-nationalist circles. Most notably, Paul von Hindenburg had lent his authority to it. The legend, as discussed earlier, misrepresented the causes for Germany's loss of World War I. Its defeat was not attributed to deficiencies in German leadership or the United States' pivotal entry into the war but to the collapse of the home front, strained by privation and demoralized by leftist agitation. Spengler, too, argues that domestic political opposition to the strategic aims of the military dictatorship of Ludendorff and Hindenburg grievously undermined the war effort. Thus, the democratic and parliamentarian spirit of England, transplanted to German soil, had helped precipitate the preliminary act of the German socialist revolution of 1918, the famous Peace Resolution of July, 1917. This resolution, passed by the parliamentarian majority comprised of the Socialists, the Center party, and the Progressive Liberals against conservative opposition, sapped German war morale and secured final victory for the "external England" of the Entente powers.[24] How-

23. *PuS*, 63.
24. *PuS*, 65.

ever, it should be noted that five years later, Spengler backs away from this indefensible position.[25]

Germany, after it experiences the national renewal Spengler yearns for, will have to contend with determined Anglo-American resistance to its efforts at reassertion in foreign affairs. He argues that France, the United States, and Britain will not hesitate to intervene if developments in Germany take a turn deemed counter to their national interests. Indeed, although France acted unilaterally, three years later, Raymond Poincaré sent troops to occupy the Ruhr.

In a letter written in September, 1918, Spengler had first shown that he anticipated that struggle between huge economic systems would characterize world politics in the twentieth century and beyond. He envisions the history of modern international politics as revealing a significant evolutionary pattern. "With the murder of [Albrecht von] Wallenstein, French culture triumphed over the Spanish in Europe, Bourbon over the Habsburg. 1800 the struggle has turned from the dynastic into the national form: English against French nationality, 1900 into the economic: Berlin against London-New York."[26]

Pursuing this line of argument, we would say that World War II decided the outcome of the struggle between huge spheres of economic power in the West in favor of New York. We are witnessing the continuance of the primacy of economic struggle in the twentieth century and the beginning of the twenty-first. The United States through the North American Free Trade Agreement (NAFTA) and the European Union through the single market and Economic and Monetary Union (EMU) have both regrouped to respond to the East Asian economic challenge spearheaded by Japan, while China continues its radical economic modernization program in its bid to emerge as a leading power.

Anglo-American capital seeks to establish global trusts, Spengler asserts in *Prussianism and Socialism*, aiming at the economic enslavement of the globe. "Its means is today *the League of Nations, i.e.*, a system of peoples, who possess 'self-government' according to the English style, that means in reality a system of provinces whose populaces are to be exploited by a business oligarchy with the aid of purchased parliaments and laws."

25. See NdR, 191, for Spengler's bleak description of Germany's strategic position before the outbreak of World War I, which conflicts with the notion basic to the stab-in-the-back legend, that defeat was avoidable.
26. Spengler to Klöres, 1 September 1918, *B*, 108.

English-American capital will brook no obstacles in its drive to attain "absolute world-economic domination."[27]

In sharp contrast to interwar political idealists, including Alfred Zimmern, G. Lowes Dickinson, James T. Shotwell, and Arnold Toynbee, Spengler grasped the inevitability of another world war. He accurately predicts in superannuated, romantic language the inability of the League of Nations and international law to contain the explosive power vented by Germany and the Anglo-Saxon world in a titanic struggle for global hegemony. "Let our trivial enthusiasts for peace and reconciliation between peoples idly talk: the *ideas* will never be reconciled; the Viking spirit and the spirit of the Teutonic Knights will fight it out to the bitter end, may the world emerge exhausted and broken from the streams of blood in this century."[28]

Radicalizing Ranke's doctrine of the centrality of great-power rivalry to modern history, Spengler elevates war to the sovereign position in world history. *"World history is the history of states. The history of states is the history of wars."* He reformulates in militaristic language the Rankean doctrine of the primacy of foreign policy. Joining the ranks of Hegel, Moltke, Nietzsche, Treitschke, and Bernhardi, he glorifies war. "War is the eternal form of higher human existence, and states exist for the sake of war; they are an expression of the readiness for war."[29]

In a letter written in June, 1920, Spengler succinctly describes the period of peace after Versailles as a "breathing-space in the World War." In *Prussianism and Socialism* he moderates his optimism about Germany's power-political future. No longer does he prophesy victory for Germany in this struggle for global hegemony. And Spengler wonders whether the Russians will overpower the emergent Western universal empire, after internecine wars have exhausted the peoples of the West.[30]

This is indeed an astonishing thought when one considers that Spengler recorded it at a time of extreme Russian weakness. The pathetic performance of the Russian army in World War I and the devastation occasioned by the Civil War and Allied intervention clearly indicate that this was a nadir of Russian power. Furthermore, the scenario he sketches captures much of the essence of the history of the international states system in the

27. *PuS*, 89, 88.
28. *PuS*, 52.
29. *PuS*, 52, 53.
30. Spengler to Klöres, 21 June 1920, *B*, 165; *PuS*, 52.

twentieth century: the bloodletting of the West in two immense conflicts, the supplantation of the European concert of great powers by a neo-imperialistic reorganization of the Western states and affiliated, non-Western territories under the hegemony of one Western power (which, contrary to Spengler's nationalistic aspirations for Germany, turned out to be the United States), the outbreak of the Cold War, and Soviet expansionism.

The irreconcilable antagonism between the Prussian and Anglo-American versions of universal empire, of global "socialist" organization as opposed to international finance capitalism, is presented in a discussion of British and German political culture. However, Spengler does liberally season his analysis of British political culture with references to America, and he clearly identifies the British and Americans as collaborating to organize an *imperium mundi*. Despite his failure to recognize the United States' power-political potential in the twentieth century, I believe that the framework of his historical philosophy is consistent with the thesis that America established an *imperium mundi* in 1945. One must, of course, purge his philosophy of world history of the organicity that inflexibly prescribes that the universal empire of the West must arise on the exhausted cultural soil of Europe.

The question arises: Why did Spengler, in the first two decades of the twentieth century, overestimate the power-political potential of Germany while underestimating that of the United States? The sources of Spengler's optimism about Germany's future as the leading power of the world and his underestimation of the United States are manifold. Europe, as the motherland of Faustian culture, and not the United States, was to be granted the privilege of bringing forth the crowning imperial form of the West. To be sure, it would be under German leadership. Spengler matured intellectually in an age in which German power grew by leaps and bounds, rivaling that of Britain, the premier power of the nineteenth century. Notwithstanding cosmopolitan features of his philosophy, he was to a substantial degree chauvinistic in an age when chauvinism was prevalent in Europe. He glorified the values of "Prussianism," developing an exaggerated picture of the achievements of German society. His overoptimistic forecast of German international supremacy was compounded by his inability to appraise properly the phenomenal power-political potential of the United States in the twentieth century, for which four basic reasons exist. First, the United States prior to 1917 was an isolationist power, despite the foreign adventure of the Spanish American War. Second, Spengler had a widely shared, European cultural disdain of the United States. Europe was for him the fountainhead of cultural energies that had created the foundation for a global hegemony and civilization. Third, basic social values of America, egalitarian democracy, individualism, and the emphasis on private gain, grated against his sensitivities. Such values were the opposite of his conceptualization of Prussian values: order and hierarchical corporatism, the primacy of social obligations, and the rejection of materialism. Fourth, Spengler suffered from a lack of first-hand knowledge of conditions in the United States comparable to that of his colleagues, Weber and Meyer. Both men had insightfully recognized the potential of a country that Spengler often injudiciously regarded as little more than a European offshoot and not as the colossal civilizational successor to the Old World it was.

What is more Faustian than the United States of America? What is more expressive of the Faustian will to power than American history, if one strips away the veneer of high-sounding ideals with which Americans love to embellish their national history and acknowledges its true character? What one sees is the annihilation of the Indian tribes, the plundering of the vast natural treasures of this virgin continent, and the economic exploitation of the periphery to sustain life-styles of unrivaled materialism and hedonism. What is more dynamic than American history, which in the course of a few centuries transformed a handful of scattered coastal settlements into the mastery of a once-pristine continent and the political and economic leadership of much of the globe? It is through the irresistible will to power immanent in Western civilization that a country that, in its infancy, held it to be its mission to develop a new existence isolated from the power-political machinations of Europe became so extraordinarily enmeshed in international relations that today virtually everything that transpires globally can be conceived as impinging on American "national" security.

Curiously, although Spengler firmly believed that Germany would establish the Faustian *imperium mundi*, he declared in a letter in July, 1915, that America epitomized the character of the coming empire! He should have perhaps drawn the obvious conclusion, that the United States, in light of its personification of the essence of modern Western civilization and endowed with a geopolitically secure position, continental resources, and a large, industrious populace, would in fact win global hegemony. Instead of recognizing that America incarnated the final form of Western civilization both culturally and power-politically, Spengler contented himself with his chauvinistic faith that the *imperium Germanicum* would be established. Moreover, thanks to its Prussian ethos, this empire would bestow upon the closing phases of Western civilization a grand aura. "The best Germans . . . would represent a new kind of American, [yet] more refined, nobler."[31]

Spengler's philosophy of statecraft was initially decidedly Eurocentric. Although it was common among educated Europeans on the eve of World War I to view Europe as the center of world politics, this was a key deficiency of his early philosophy of statecraft that must be underscored. *The Decline of the West* was written years before the idea that the West fully embraces both the Old World and the New World had gained widespread acceptance. It was after his death with the founding of the Pax Americana and the integration of the Federal Republic of Germany into this Occidental world order that the concept of the West has come to encompass the Old World and the New.

The original, undiluted Eurocentricity of Spengler's thought on international politics is most clearly demonstrated by comparing the first edition of the first volume of *The Decline of the West*, published in 1918, with the final revised edition, which appeared in 1923. We read in the opening paragraph of the first edition, "It is a question of following the still unfinished stages of the destiny of a culture, and indeed the only one, which today on this planet is in a process of fulfillment, that of Western Europe." In the revised edition, Western culture, instead of being narrowly defined as that "of Western Europe," is broadly conceived as "West European-American."[32] This change was clearly made in order to take into account the United States' tremendous weight in world affairs, so strikingly revealed for the first time in its pivotal role in turning the tide against Germany in World War I. Failing to foresee in 1914 the assumption by the United States three years later of a paramount role in international affairs, Spengler believed that Imperial Germany could defeat its archrival Britain either in the Great War itself or at least in its sequel, thereby laying the groundwork for German primacy. Thus we read in the original edition, "After Madrid, Paris, London, follows Berlin." These metropolises function as symbols for what Spengler envisages as successive phases in Western culture. In succession, Spanish culture, the French Rococo, and English civilization are to be followed by Prussian "Roman-style" imperial civiliza-

31. Politica I, 79, 13.
32. Oswald Spengler, *Der Untergang des Abendlandes*, vol. I (Munich: C. H. Beck, 1920), 3; *UdA* I, 3.

tion. Now, we read in the revised edition, "After Madrid, Paris, London, follow Berlin and New York."[33] Each of the two alternatives for the concluding economic and civilizational imperial form of the West, Prussian or American "Roman-style" civilization, has its locus in its dominant megalopolis.

The juxtaposition of Berlin and New York also signifies Spengler's reassessment, in the years following the publication of *Prussianism and Socialism*, of the prospects of the United States for attaining global hegemony. Indeed, early in World War I he had actually excluded the United States from the elite club of world powers, Germany, Britain, and Russia.[34] In the early 1920s, no longer does Spengler, as he did in *Prussianism and Socialism*, regard Britain, with the United States lending its support, as representing the chief rival of Germany for world paramountcy. The United States is promoted to a higher position than Britain. Indeed, in the second volume of *The Decline of the West*, Spengler goes so far as to toy with the idea that the United States instead of Germany itself might attain global primacy, symbolized by New York's ascent after Northern victory in the Civil War to the status of a world city.[35] Archival material (unfortunately, undated) indicates that he gradually developed the insight that the United States could supplant Britain as the principal rival of Germany in the struggle between the Anglo-Saxon powers and Germany for world hegemony. "England or more correctly expressed, the Anglo-Saxon element, whose maritime bases today are spread over the whole world, and which could have its center of gravity one day in North America instead of in London. It is the only opponent that necessarily stands in the way of the Pan-German future because only undivided rule is possible. Russia is in comparison with it only a local North-Asiatic power."[36]

Seven years after the publication of *Prussianism and Socialism*, Spengler foolishly passed up a golden opportunity to visit the United States, where he could have gained direct knowledge of conditions in this ascendant superpower. Regrettably, the universal scope of Spengler's historical mind, for the most part, did not determine his choice of travel destinations. It is surprising that, though he was financially independent, he never traveled beyond the borders of Europe. He was invited by the philosopher Eduard

33. Spengler, *Der Untergang des Abendlandes*, vol. I (1920 edition), 45; *UdA* I, 43.
34. Spengler to Klöres, 14 July 1915, *B*, 43.
35. *UdA* II, 117.
36. Politica II, 116, V2-48.

Spranger at the request of Professor John Coss of Columbia University and Herr Friedrich Schmidt-Ott, President of the Emergency Society of German Science, to address the international philosophical congress to be held in Cambridge, Massachusetts, in 1926. Coincidentally, the first volume of *The Decline of the West* had appeared in translation in English that same year. The congress organizers hoped that Spengler would participate in the conference section entitled "Philosophy of History" and engage in a lively intellectual exchange with H. G. Wells. The novelist had published in 1920 a best seller on world history, *Outline of History*. Wells offered historical orientation in world affairs in the form of "a plain account of the whole human drama" with the progress of mankind as the grand theme.[37] If Spengler had decided to journey to the United States and had attended the conference, expanding his itinerary so that he would have traveled through this vast, populous, and dynamic country, he would have given himself the opportunity to form a more perceptive appraisal of America's capacity to challenge Germany for global hegemony and to prevail.

Spengler's failure to appreciate fully the power-political potential of the United States also exemplifies the Eurocentricity of German historical and political thought during the Second Reich. In the fifty years prior to the outbreak of World War I, the *Historische Zeitschrift*, Germany's leading journal of historical studies, published only five articles on North America, most of them reviews. Ernst Fraenkel lamented that Germany never produced a great book on America comparable to Alexis de Tocqueville's *Democracy in America*.[38] A negative attitude toward the United States reigned in Wilhelmine Germany. The liberals of the *Vormärz* (the period 1815–1848) and the Revolution of 1848 had shown a thoroughly positive attitude toward the young vigorous republic, a beacon of democratic ideals. Burckhardt's condemnation of America's purported materialism and culturelessness highlighted a profound reorientation in the attitude of German historical and political thinkers toward the ascendant world power. Spengler did share with Burckhardt and with numerous European men of culture their undisguised contempt for many features of American culture and society. However, in his resolute modernist moments he pas-

37. Eduard Spranger to Spengler, 26 December 1925, *B*, 427; Christopher Dawson, "H. G. Wells and the Outline of History," chap. in *Dynamics of World History*, ed. John J. Mulloy (London: Sheed & Ward, 1957), 366.

38. Hans W. Gatzke, "The United States and Germany on the Eve of World War I," in Immanuel Geiss and Bernd Jürgen Wendt, eds., *Deutschland in der Weltpolitik des 19. und 20. Jahrhunderts* (Düsseldorf: Bertelsmann Universitätsverlag, 1973), 277.

sionately espoused social mobility and also admired, in sharp contrast to Burckhardt, the economic prowess of American capitalists, viewing it as representative of the nineteenth and twentieth centuries. Spengler's sketchy knowledge of American history is symptomatic of the atrophy of interest in the political ideals and social forms of the United States prevalent in Germany since 1871. The relative lack of interest in the United States and the swollen sense of national pride that developed in Wilhelmine Germany, which Spengler reflects, sowed the seeds of the extraordinary underestimation of the weight of the United States in world affairs in the years before World War I, contributing greatly to errant foreign policy and military decisions.[39] Spengler came to acknowledge the tragic consequences of the German elite's relative unfamiliarity with American history and politics during the Second Reich. He complained in 1924 that the German secondary school system had failed to impart knowledge about key events in American history and their implications for America's entry into World War I.[40]

I champion the idea that the Pax Americana, which the United States established in 1945, is the Faustian *imperium mundi* forecast by Spengler. Arnold Toynbee would object to applying the Spenglerian historical paradigm in this way. In *A Study of History*, Toynbee rejects the idea that the United States, given the constraints imposed by the nuclear age on the use of force in world politics, is capable of creating an *imperium mundi*, or a "universal state," to use the term he borrows from Meyer. "In the Atomic Age, into which the West—and, with it, the World—has entered in our lifetime, it now looks as if a universal state could not be established again."[41] However, since a universal state has never existed in all of world history in the literal sense of the word, the inability of Western civilization to bring forth a truly universal empire does not signify that the American, post–World War II, international order does not deserve to be acknowledged as the Western *imperium mundi*. As Toynbee well understood, every "universal state" that has arisen in the course of world history has either encountered redoubtable opponents who delimited its boundaries or exhausted its expansive energy. Rome was never able to duplicate Alexander's conquest of the Middle East up to the Indus River; Rome failed to

39. Wolfgang J. Mommsen, "Die Vereinigten Staaten von Amerika im politischen Denken Max Webers," *Historische Zeitschrift* 213 (1971): 358–59.

40. *NdR*, 235.

41. Arnold J. Toynbee, *Reconsiderations*, vol. XII of *A Study of History* (London: Oxford Univ. Press, 1961), 518.

subdue Persia under both Parthian and Sassanid rule. Furthermore, the Sinic universal state Toynbee refers to existed essentially as an expression of the cultural arrogance of the literati of the Chinese Empire. Where did the rest of the planet fit into the schema of the Sinic universal state? Thus, contra Toynbee, the "free world" under American leadership, obviously an informal empire of limited, non-global territorial dimensions, constitutes a universal state, or *imperium mundi*, in a manner fully comparable to that of its historical predecessors. The term *imperium mundi* dramatically and economically expresses the idea of the fulfillment of the expansive essence of an internationally dominant civilization. The West, the creator and perfecter of a civilization that has dominated the globe politically, culturally, and technologically since the Age of Discovery, has achieved with the *imperium Americanum* its final, extensive form. The stunning collapse of the Soviet Union in 1991 has accentuated the primacy of the American universal empire for a time, not created it.

Toynbee dismisses the idea that the Pax Americana represents the universal state of Western civilization mainly because he considers it to be a great historical possibility that an ecumenical civilization with an attendant, global, central political authority may evolve. As Toynbee speculated in 1961, "This progressive cultural and social unification of the whole human family is bound to find some expression on the political plane. . . . The most likely nucleus of a future political world order is perhaps a central authority exercising an effective world-wide control over the use of atomic energy."[42] Indeed, the Spenglerian and Toynbeean perspectives demarcate the parameters of debate on civilizational development and affiliated international political scenarios in the twentieth century and the new millennium. At one pole, one envisions the crisis of the West and the adoption of elements of its civilization and technology by the non-West as instruments for eventually staging a successful revolt against a transitory, neo-imperial order. At the other pole, one speculates about the evolution of an ecumenical civilization with Western qualities embracing the developed and developing worlds and the flowering of a relatively peaceful, international order.

Another objection that can be made against the argument that the post–World War II American world order is an "imperial" one is that the United States clearly does not exercise direct control over the territories within its far-flung spheres of influence. Reflection on Spengler's ideas

42. *Ibid.*, 309.

suggests that the dynamic ethos of Western civilization permits the articulation of unique modes of indirect neo-imperial domination over foreign peoples. The decisive force for consolidating the Pax Americana has been economic. While the economies of Germany, Japan, the Soviet Union, Britain, and France were all either devastated or weakened by World War II, the American economy boasted record growth rates. The United States emerged in 1945 as the undisputed economic power of the globe. With its control of sources of capital, technology, and market access, it found itself in a commanding position to lay the ground rules for postwar international economic intercourse and to penetrate the Third World through American-based multinational corporations. This exploitation of the periphery has been intensified by the inroads of international bank capital in Third World economies since the first oil crisis in 1973. Moreover, when the International Monetary Fund (IMF), an international organization responsive to American wishes, imposes austerity programs, and has done so since 1982, upon scores of developing countries, is this not a form of imperial penetration of societies, as intrusive as that of Roman fiscal administration?

Reflecting on *The Decline of the West* today, one cannot help but wonder at how remarkably prophetic of the crisis of Western civilization it is. World War I is the watershed demarcating the decline of European political and cultural primacy and heralding American power-political and civilizational dominance, the American Century, which achieved full expression with American victory in World War II. Surveying the course of history in the twentieth century, it can be plausibly argued that the United States forged an *imperium mundi* in 1945. With the military and political "disciplining" of Japan and Germany, its massive economic mobilization during World War II, and its nuclear monopoly, it assumed undisputed global supremacy economically, politically, and militarily. Moreover, American dominance was confirmed by its triumph in the Cold War. Yet the decline of American hegemonic power is inevitable as twilight begins to spread its shadows over the Pax Americana. This American neo-imperial world order will prove in the twenty-first century to be a transitory affair. In its home country the signs of sociological decay are already unmistakable in the breakdown of the family structure and growing social pathologies, the spread of quasi-pacifism, and the unabashed excesses of our sensate culture. Despite the remarkable economic prosperity of the 1990s, causes for anxiety abound. The fiscal burdens of the welfare state compounded by an aging society, the massive current-account deficits, frenzied speculation, and the recurrent instabilities of the global economy portend an eventual economic crisis for the United States. Effective governance already faces the multiple challenges of interest groups subverting the public interest, plutocratic tendencies, the necessity of coping with unprecedented ethnic diversity, and growing political apathy, if not disgust. The erosion of America's ability to exercise leadership in world affairs and manage world order is only a matter of time. The fragile Pax Americana will not have the impressive staying power of the Pax Romana.

Spengler's Political Phase in the Twenties

AS WE SAW IN CHAPTER 6, SPENGLER FA-
vored the quasi-democratization of the Second Reich. However, Germany's agonizing defeat, the myth that democratic elements on the home
front were mainly responsible for it, and the onerous Versailles Treaty induced him to rethink fundamentally his politics. Embittered, Spengler opposed the Weimar democracy.

Fame as a philosopher of world history never completely overshadowed
Spengler's notoriety as a neoconservative. Posterity has not forgotten that
his strident opposition to the Weimar Republic inadvertently helped to
clear the path for Nazi totalitarian rule. Several factors motivated Spengler
to engage in political competition and conspiracy from 1914 to 1924: his
admiration for the philosophers of the past who involved themselves in
practical affairs, his sense of political ethical responsibility, his nationalistic
pride and hostility toward the Weimar Republic, and his solicitude about
Germany's future in the dangerous arena of power politics.[1] In this chapter, we will examine his most important publications and lectures during
his active political phase, which was inaugurated by the publication of
Prussianism and Socialism in December, 1919.

Spengler responded to the hostile critical reception in Germany of the
first volume of *The Decline of the West* with the essay "Pessimismus?," published in 1921. Although *The Decline of the West* was obviously in many
respects pessimistic, Spengler rejected the label of pessimist for several reasons. The term had a pejorative connotation and downplayed his resolute
modernism. Moreover, it implied he lacked confidence in his defeated

1. *UdA* I, 55–58.

country to confront the challenges before it. He claims that his philosophy of world history has been misunderstood, largely because of the "completely new way of looking at things" and "the method" that his book showcases. Spengler believes that the tendency to regard him as a pessimist is partly due to the "dismaying" title of the book. He emphasizes that his deterministic vision of decline is by no means a "catastrophic" one. The transition from culture to civilization means that the West has reached its final organic stage of development and may magnificently achieve its extensive possibilities. Indeed, one could say "perfection" (*Vollendung*) instead of "decline" (*Untergang*). He insists, "No, I am not a pessimist. Pessimism means: to not see any more tasks."[2] Instead, he had affirmed a modernist agenda of economic modernization, imperial politics, and applied science and technology.

The Decline of the West arguably enhances modern Western man's conscious relationship to his history. Spengler views it as his "service" that he has stimulated greater awareness of the power of necessity in world history and the major tendencies operant in modern history.[3] In addition, he expresses his conviction of the primacy of power politics in human history. The essay concludes with a resounding avowal of political realism and a rejection of political idealism. "Toughness, Roman toughness it is, which now begins in the world. There won't be any more room soon for anything else. . . . Politics yes, but from statesmen and not from starry-eyed idealists."[4]

After the publication of *Prussianism and Socialism*, Spengler went back to finishing *The Decline of the West*. He had worked out the contents of the second volume as early as 1917. However, it was not published until May, 1922, after entreaties from the public and some pressure from his publisher. In the meantime, the first volume, after several reprintings, had again gone out of print by the end of 1920. Spengler, who had been revising the first volume since the end of 1920, refused to permit its reprinting in its unrevised form. He insisted on this, despite the continued keen interest in his book. In early 1923 the final revised version of volume one appeared, "very much changed in its outward form, but unchanged in its basic ideas."[5] The composition and revision of his major work had spanned over a decade.

2. P, 63, 63–64, 75.
3. P, 70 ff.
4. P, 76, 79.
5. August Albers, "Oswald Spengler," *Preußische Jahrbücher* 192, no. 2 (May, 1923): 132.

Earlier I pointed out that in the revised edition of volume one of *The Decline of the West* its author reformulated the concept of Faustian culture from a culture encompassing solely Western Europe to one embracing North America as well. Otherwise, the emendations in the first volume for the most part appear to be minor. Spengler cut the reworked tome by approximately eighty pages. Manfred Schröter observed that revisions can be seen on almost every page. Nonetheless, as he noted, the "structure and arrangement of all chapters, sections, and paragraphs remain exactly the same."[6] Spengler, in contrast to many contemporary academicians, did not enjoy the luxury of having the original manuscript of the first volume circulated among a small private audience of critical scholars before submitting it for printing. He incorporated in the revised volume many of the suggestions and corrections of his critics.

The second volume of *The Decline of the West* did not provoke a stormy debate as did the first one. The journal *Wissen und Leben* (*Knowledge and Life*) brought out a special issue on Spengler. Interestingly, the scholar who was invited to contribute a review of the recently published work observed, "But before this new volume [the public] shows itself to be conspicuously silent, and while a flood of publications, articles, and debates poured over the earlier one, I have hardly read or heard an opinion on the second one."[7] The second volume, subtitled "World-Historical Perspectives," dealt primarily with more concrete topics of a political and economic nature. The book also examined Spengler's conceptualization of a Middle-Eastern high culture, the Magian. He expands on themes that had been only briefly touched on in the first volume. The major topics he handles include his biologically colored metaphysical speculations, Christianity, historical pseudomorphosis, Magian culture, Caesarism and the second religiousness, his philosophy of politics, political economy, and industrial civilization and technology. The chapters entitled "The State" and "The Form-World of Economic Life" were both republished as separate slim volumes.

The reading public was divided in its opinion of the book. Many considered the second volume to be almost more important than the first. Others were somewhat disappointed, seeing the second volume as essen-

6. Manfred Schröter, "Zwischen den Fahrten," *Wissen und Leben* 16, no. 12 (April, 1923): 599.
7. Karl Joël, "Zum Zweiten Band Spengler: Kritik an seinen Begriffen," *Wissen und Leben* 16, no. 12 (April, 1923): 561.

tially an expansion on the sensational themes of the first.[8] From a contemporary perspective, the second volume is significant. For Spengler advances the challenging thesis of the breakdown of the global economy, of importance in the 1990s and beyond, as it had been earlier in the 1930s. Moreover, he adumbrates what will later emerge as a bold vision of the highly destructive impact of industrial civilization on the environment.

Earlier, Spengler had interrupted his work on the emendation and completion of *The Decline of the West* in order to deliver in February, 1922, a lecture, "The Two Faces of Russia and the German Eastern Problems." Along with Weber, he had been one of the few German scholars in the early twentieth century to concern himself with the study of the Russian language, history, politics, and culture. As Gary Ulmen notes, given the overall deficit of expertise on Russian history and source material in Germany then, it is "remarkable" that Spengler "understood so much about Russian history and culture."[9] This interest was to remain a lifelong one.

Two months before the signing of the sensational Rapallo Treaty, Spengler gave his lecture. A decade later, he characterized Rapallo as "the first autonomous act of German foreign policy in years."[10] The treaty shocked the Western victors of World War I because the two pariah states of Germany and Soviet Russia normalized their relations, thereby breaking out of their diplomatic isolation. In his talk Spengler assesses the historical significance of the Communist revolution. He also explores the possibility of reshaping German relations with the Soviet Union to alleviate the pressure by the Western powers on Germany. Spengler builds his foreign policy analysis upon the foundation of his philosophy of world history. He views the Russians as a unique people, the bearers of an emergent high culture that will eventually supplant that of the decadent West.

The Russians are profoundly culturally different from the peoples of the West. Russia west of the Urals only geographically belongs to Europe; "the real Europe ends on the Vistula." Spengler maintains that the Russian people naturally tend to submit to authoritarian rule. "The endless plain created a softer national individuality, meek and melancholy, also spiritually merging itself with the flat expanse, without real personal will, prone to submission. That is the precondition of great politics from Genghis Khan to Lenin."[11]

---

8. K-Sp, 254 ff.
9. DR; G. L. Ulmen, "Metaphysik des Morgenlandes—Spengler über Rußland," in Peter C. Ludz, ed., *Spengler heute* (Munich: C. H. Beck, 1980), 146.
10. *PSch*, viii.
11. DR, 110.

Peter the Great is the towering historical figure who distorted Russia's nascent, indigenous high culture by his labors to Westernize it. "Petrinism was and remains a *foreign body* in the Russian nationality." Peter divided Russian society in two. The "official," superficially Westernized Russia of the aristocratic elite coexisted uneasily with the "real" and "subterranean" Russia of the backward and devout peasantry.[12]

Spengler interprets the turbulent events of 1917. In the February revolution the peasantry revolted against their despised foreign masters, the Europeanized Russian aristocracy. But the October revolution betrayed the peasantry. The Bolsheviks skillfully harnessed the peasantry's elemental energies to seize power as a "second" form of Westernizing elite; the Communist ideology "is a revolt against the West" with Western ideas. Yet Spengler predicts the eventual collapse of Soviet Communism. The Bolsheviks, he maintains, will be unable to suppress the power of the peasantry. "The creation of Lenin is Western, is Petersburg, is alien and hostile to the great majority of Russians, an object of hatred, and it will disappear one day in some way or other."[13]

Spengler was writing, of course, before Lenin's death in 1924 and Joseph Stalin's triumph in the succession struggle. In retrospect, Spengler underestimates the ability of the Bolsheviks, equipped with the omnipotent instruments of modern totalitarian rule that Stalin perfected, to repress brutally the peasantry and to suppress their religious aspirations. During the twenties, the Bolshevik leadership debated how they could hold on to power while modernizing Russia, a vast and backward country with a predominantly rural population. Spengler accurately predicts, when one reflects on Stalin's program of collectivization, that the Bolsheviks would exploit the Russian peasantry more ruthlessly than the Mongols or the tsars. However, Spengler errs when he argues that, despite the inhuman oppression that the peasantry will suffer, it will prove stronger than its sinister master, Stalin. For Spengler, the teeming Russian peasantry is the irrepressible carrier of a new ascendant culture, a "new unborn religion." "It is the nationality of the future, which doesn't let itself be smothered or falsified, which without a doubt and even if yet slowly, will replace, transform, dominate, or destroy Bolshevism in its present form." While Spengler's analysis of Bolshevism is thought-provoking and he did prophesy the fall of Soviet Communism, its main thesis is clearly errone-

12. DR, 113.
13. DR, 120–21.

ous. Bolshevism has not performed the historical function he assigned to it, namely, of making the way free for a new culture, "which will someday awaken between 'Europe' and East Asia."[14]

It should be noted that two years after giving this lecture, Spengler distanced himself from his dubious claim in *The Decline of the West* that Russia would someday evolve a nontechnological, nonscientific culture, which, indeed, logically flowed from the premises of his historical philosophy. In an interview in the fall of 1924, he commented on how he envisioned the emergent Russian culture. "What kind of culture it will be remains to be seen. However, I do not believe that Russia can do without Western Europe's industrial and technical apparatus, but, in the beginning, Germany's, England's, and America's technology and capital must certainly serve in the establishment of the economic basis for that culture, which later must refashion the alien organs according to its own essence."[15]

In foreign policy matters, Spengler maintains that the proper management of German foreign policy toward the Soviet Union in the future will require "the entire tactical skillfulness of a great statesman and connoisseur."[16] This statement is a cruel irony of history when one recalls Hitler's barbarous and dilettantish Eastern policies. Spengler hopes that Germany can make common front with Bolshevik Russia against Britain and France. Moreover, Germany must scrupulously avoid arousing Russian expansionary tendencies toward the west, accommodate any surge of Russian power toward the straits of Bosporus, and explore developing advantageous economic ties. Moreover, a Western crusade against Bolshevism, which later emerged as a central foreign policy goal of Nazi Germany, would be disastrous.[17]

Spengler's foreign policy analysis has become soberer. He criticizes Wilhelmine diplomacy for sacrificing its freedom of maneuver by blindly supporting Austria's Balkan ambitions.

And finally Germany became the object of this deep [Russian national] hatred, which could not be influenced through practical considerations. For from being an ally it became more and more since 1878 the protector and

14. DR, 111, 122, 121.

15. "Das russische Problem. Eine Unterredung mit Dr. Spengler," *Münchner Neueste Nachrichten*, 9 November 1924, Spengler Archive, Munich.

16. DR, 124.

17. DR, 123 ff.

preserver of the decaying Habsburg state and unfortunately thereby, despite Bismarck's warning, of its Balkan plans as well. Finally Germany did not understand the idea of Count [Sergey] Witte, the last pro-German diplomat, of choosing between Austria and Russia. But it could have won Russia again as a genuine ally, as soon as it gave up its close ties to Austria. A new orientation of the entire German policy was perhaps still possible in 1911.[18]

Here one encounters again a striking example of the complex nature of Spengler's historical determinism. Cultural developments, in the broad sense of the word, are seen as conforming to a cyclical pattern. Yet alternative lines of action are available to the statesman in the arena of world politics.

In the preceding passage, Spengler gives clear expression to his attachment to the old school of Prussian diplomacy, which advocated friendship with Russia. Bismarck regarded good relations with Russia as being indispensable to Germany's security. Spengler was not aware, as recent historical scholarship has revealed, that Bismarck had, in fact, contemplated taking extreme measures in order to remain in Russia's good graces. Bismarck dreaded the possibility of a two-front war, with Germany sandwiched in between Russia and France. He believed that the "Empire of the Russian nation" was indestructible and that if Germany ever initiated hostilities against Russia, his country would "never be able to recover from it." Thus, as Andreas Hillgruber observes, "In a dire emergency . . . Bismarck was prepared not only to cede large parts of Southeastern Europe to Russia, but, as an ultima ratio, was also obviously prepared to sacrifice the Habsburg Empire."[19]

On February 26, 1924, the very same day that Hitler's trial began for his failed putsch, Spengler gave an address to students at the University of Würzburg. The lecture, "Political Duties of German Youth," focused on foreign policy. Spengler was later to complain that "the 'young generation' had not understood" his talk.[20] He begins his speech by presciently underscoring the transitory nature of the economic stabilization in Germany after the Ruhr crisis. Indeed, it was to last only five years or so. Moreover, he emphasizes the weak position of Germany among the great powers. In addition, he recognizes the dangerous and transitional nature

18. DR, 117–18.
19. Otto von Bismarck, quoted in Andreas Hillgruber, *Deutsche Großmacht- und Weltpolitik im 19. und 20. Jahrhundert* (Düsseldorf: Droste Verlag, 1977), 73; *ibid.*
20. PP; *PSch*, x.

of the interwar period in world politics. The arena of international politics is rife with "enormous tensions," as World War I has "postponed and transformed the great questions but not solved them."[21]

Spengler echoes Ranke's teaching of the primacy of foreign policy. He tells his young audience that the internal constitution of the state is decisive in determining its success in "the struggle for international self-assertion, which is becoming constantly harder and harder." He abrasively asserts the impossibility of transcending the international struggle for power. This transcendence was the fundamental goal of interwar political idealism and remains an elusive dream to this day. The decisions of history are "hard and cruel, and he who believes that in this matter he can avoid them through understanding and reconciliation is not fit for politics."[22]

Spengler endeavors to counteract the enthusiasm of German youth for National Socialism. He minces no words in emphasizing the need for Germany's young people to overcome their political immaturity. "National politics has been understood in Germany since the war as a sort of intoxication. Youth enthused itself in droves for colors and insignia, for music and marches, for theatrical pledges and dilettantish proclamations and theories." He provides his youthful audience with, as Otto Hintze expressed it, "splendid lessons for self-education to political tasks." Spengler stresses that statecraft, as it was for Ranke in his *Political Dialogue*, is "an *art* that is difficult and difficult to learn."[23] Statesmanship is the "art of fencing with intellectual weapons" and "requires an extraordinarily high degree of practice and knowledge." Modern statecraft must be forward-looking and anticipatory, rich in *"knowledge of the facts, forces, and tendencies of contemporary world politics."* He challenges Germany's youth to toss aside all the party programs and literature and to study attentively diplomatic documents from the preceding decades, the speeches and letters of distinguished politicians, and the relationship between international economics and world politics.[24] Only in this way can they educate themselves to serve great leaders.

The serious study of international affairs is imperative because of the

21. PP, 129, 130.
22. PP, 143, 147.
23. PP, 148; O. Hintze, review essay of *Der Staat (Das Problem der Stände, Staat und Geschichte, Philosophie der Politik), NdR*, and PP, by Oswald Spengler, and *Die Staatslehre Oswald Spenglers: Eine Darstellung und eine kritische Würdigung*, by Otto Koellreuter, *Zeitschrift für die gesamte Staatswissenschaft* 79 (1925): 544; PP, 130.
24. PP, 151, 155.

vulnerability of Germany to the designs of foreign powers. "We cannot solve any German question, whichever one you wish, if we do not know exactly into what relationship it immediately enters with the political combinations in England, Russia, and the United States."[25] These are ominous words, when one recalls that Hitler's defiant attempt to solve on his own terms the question of Germany's future as a force in world affairs resulted in the formation of the Anglo-American-Soviet Grand Alliance and the destruction of Germany as a traditional great power.

Spengler poignantly expresses his mounting anxiety about Germany's future in world politics. In the coming years his anxiety will increasingly displace the optimism that pervaded his international political thought before Germany's defeat in 1918. He warns that it is necessary for the Germans, who achieved unity and statehood as a people late in their history and thus are still immature in international politics, to grasp that politics is a "high art." "But if we do not learn this now, so I am afraid that also the future will not give us another opportunity."[26]

The essay "New Forms of World Politics" was first presented by Spengler in lecture form in 1924 at the Overseas Club in Hamburg. The piece was written in the aftermath of the Ruhr occupation by France. Like many other contemporary German political and historical thinkers, Spengler fears, with the prostration of Germany, the establishment of French hegemony on the Continent. "Here emerges first of all the phenomenon that certainly dominates these days the politics of Western Europe, the hegemony of France." He insightfully realizes that its partner Britain is perhaps already undergoing irreversible power-political decline. And this comes at a time when world history is rushing onward with "catastrophic tempo."[27]

Spengler grasps that a new revolutionary era of history, one of profound unrest, is dawning. The traditional primacy of Europe in international politics is being severely challenged. The entire world is becoming integrated into one complex, interdependent, international political system. "We see how all around the entire world is becoming *for the first time politically active as a whole* and not playing a passive role as the background of European entanglements. Indeed, things are being driven, in a completely new arrangement, and with growing restlessness, toward unknown goals and

25. PP, 154.
26. PP, 155.
27. Oswald Spengler, "Neue Formen der Weltpolitik," in *PSch*, 160, 171–72.

in surprising new forms toward unknown explosions." The world war "introduces . . . an epoch of immense decisions, of whose greatness and terribleness nobody today dares to make a picture, even if he should be able to sense the future."[28]

Disparagingly referring to most twentieth-century politicians as "agitators," Spengler ponders the crucial problem of leadership selection and grooming in an age of mass politics. He draws an important distinction, differentiating between the skills that politicians cultivate in domestic political competition and those that politicians-suddenly-turned-"statesmen" must have in order to succeed in the highly complex arena of international politics. There, the fate of nations hangs in the balance. He recommends that the leaders of all great powers should be required to master the intricacies of statecraft through diplomatic service, long before an electoral victory suddenly catapults them into office. "The political school that the politician goes through in popular assemblies is not that which the diplomat abroad needs. A talented agitator is practically never able to think like a statesman."[29]

As the struggle for empire intensifies, Caesaristic figures will come forth and dominate the stage of world politics. In the totalitarian states Hitler and Stalin were to rise to power. And in the Western democracies Franklin Delano Roosevelt was elected to an unprecedented four presidential terms. He completed the transformation of the United States from an isolationist republic with limited government into a welfare state and superpower with an "imperial Presidency." Spengler believes that "we are entering now into an era where also foreign policy in the form that suprapersonally and for centuries has organically developed and that we can somehow characterize with the words legitimacy, constitution, political tradition, diplomatic style, changes into forms that originate in the character of individual personalities." Interestingly, Spengler no longer maintains that Germany may emerge as the dominant world power as he did in *Prussianism and Socialism*. However, he sees the possibility of Germany, under gifted leadership, of regaining its status as a world power. "In this age . . . a conquered and half-destroyed land too can attain enormous significance overnight."[30] Tragically, Hitler turned these words into prophetic ones.

28. *Ibid.*, 159.
29. *Ibid.*, 171.
30. *Ibid.*, 182, 183.

One month after this lecture in Hamburg, Spengler addressed the annual gathering of the German nobility in Breslau. Hughes observes, "from a social standpoint this address marked the high-point of his career."[31] It underscored the esteem in which many in elite circles held this representative of the educated classes (*Bildungsbürgertum*). For the offspring of a middle-class family, a nostalgic romantic conservative, and a great admirer of nobility and social hierarchy, it must have been extremely gratifying to have been invited to speak before such a select group.

A self-styled *praeceptor Germaniae*, Spengler focuses on the political "tasks" of the German nobility. He declares that world history teaches that the nobility traditionally functioned as the most politically gifted social order. The socialist revolution of 1918 was a severe blow for Germany in that respect. "Through the revolution just about everything has been destroyed that belongs to the preconditions of a successful statecraft."[32] The nobility is of particular importance for Germany's future because Germany lacks a grand bourgeois society in the manner of England or France. Like Rome in antiquity, England, the architect of a splendid empire, exemplifies how a noble class is the treasurehouse of the political acumen of a nation. Spengler argues that despite the relative rarity of an outstanding leader in the past two hundred years, British statecraft retained its excellence because of the cultivating force of a robust aristocratic tradition and ethos.[33]

This encomium to the political role of the nobility in history modulates into constructive criticism. He argues that Germany's severe setback in World War I is due in large part to its rapid transformation from a collection of disunited petty states into a great power. The German people failed to replace the limited political horizon of their particularistic heritage with a profound, international political perspective equal to the exigencies of power politics on a global scale. This grave weakness in German political culture persists after the war. "However, a German policy is since Bismarck only still possible if it is anchored in the entire range of contemporary international relations, and if the leading class considers it to be its most lofty duty to educate itself for *this* statecraft of vast horizons and superior methods." The task of the German nobility is to be modern. For "world politics destroys countries that are not intellectually equal to it."

31. H-Sp, 114.
32. Oswald Spengler, "Aufgaben des Adels," in *RuA*, 89.
33. *Ibid.*, 90.

He exhorts them to "strip off the last remnants of the rural exceptional position and the distaste for world horizons, world trade, and world industry." If the nobility realizes that the conservative politics of 1860 and 1900 are outmoded and commits itself to cultivating zealously the political acumen that Spengler sees as imperative, then Germany can "conquer again a decisive position in world politics."[34]

The political tract *Reconstruction of the German Reich* was published in May, 1924, the same month as Spengler's speech to the German nobility.[35] The short book is noteworthy because he first gives unequivocal public expression to his abandonment of his earlier optimism about Germany's capacity to become the dominant world power. *Prussianism and Socialism* was written in the heat of political passions provoked by the bitter loss of World War I. Thus, Spengler initially defiantly refused to give up hope that Germany enjoyed good chances to win global hegemony. Five years later, he is soberer.

Spengler came to appreciate that the founding of the German Empire in 1871, in a very insecure geopolitical location, placed the German nation in a most problematic situation in the struggle for world hegemony. His soaring optimism in the prewar and war years about Germany's international political future has given way to sobriety and anxiety. Interestingly, he suggests that Germany's strategic position was perhaps already hopeless on the eve of the Great War. "The German people before the war were ignorant of their terribly endangered, and perhaps already hopeless position; they were unaware of it during the war *and they are today just as far removed from being so.*"[36]

Indeed, historical research is increasingly bringing to light the gravity of the problem of Germany's relationship with the great powers that it faced after unification in 1871. Originally, the traditional view among scholars was that Bismarck displayed rare genius in creating a power-politically *secure* Germany and that the fruits of his statecraft were destroyed by the incompetence and aggressiveness of epigones. This view has given way to a more insightful and balanced analysis. The revisionist view continues to acknowledge the diplomatic genius of the Iron Chancellor. Nonetheless, it underscores the profound insecurity of the Second Reich's half-hegemonic position on the Continent that his diplomacy established.

34. *Ibid.*, 93, 95.
35. NdR.
36. NdR, 191.

This significant change in interpretation is exemplified by the scholarship of Gordon Craig, a leading expert on modern German diplomatic history. Whereas Craig in his work *From Bismarck to Adenauer*, published in 1965, speaks of "the security of Bismarck's Reich," he adopts a completely different perspective in his later work *Force and Statecraft*. There he observes, "Even if the chancellor had remained in office after 1890, it is impossible to believe that it [the Bismarckian model of balance of power] could have stood the strain of his manipulations much longer."[37]

Craig is very pessimistic that the German leadership could have reached an understanding with Britain, of fundamental importance to the security of Wilhelmine Germany. "Even had William II, Bülow, and Tirpitz been wiser and more responsible leaders, it is difficult to believe the British apprehensiveness about Germany would have been different than it was. . . . Basically, it was the transformation of Germany from a cluster of second-rate states under insignificant princelings to a united empire with a population greater than Britain's, impressive industrial resources, and advanced technology that was the root cause of the deterioration of its relations with Great Britain."[38]

Spengler significantly improves the analysis of German political culture he had originally put forth in *Prussianism and Socialism*. In searching for the reasons for Germany's stinging defeat, he reflects on the relationship of political culture to foreign-policy leadership selection during the Second Reich. He identifies essentially two causes for the debacle of 1918: first, the aforementioned geopolitical dilemma; and second, the deficient process of foreign-policy leadership selection.

The myopic optimism prevalent in German society prior to August, 1914, according to Spengler, was a primary cause of Germany's foreign policy disaster. This optimism derived from an antebellum naïveté about international politics, which, in turn, resulted from Bismarck's failure to cultivate an elite tradition in foreign policy and from the pedantic classicism of German historical education. It is imperative, Spengler argues, to improve substantially the foreign policy skills of present and future German elites, for the ferocious struggle for universal empire will continue to dominate world politics.

---

37. Gordon A. Craig, *From Bismarck to Adenauer: Aspects of German Statecraft*, rev. ed. (New York: Harper & Row, 1965), xii; Gordon A. Craig and Alexander L. George, *Force and Statecraft: Diplomatic Problems of Our Time* (New York: Oxford Univ. Press, 1983), 40.

38. Craig and George, *Force and Statecraft*, 41.

An echo of Spengler's shattered wartime dream of an imperialistic, quasi-democratic German Reich returns in *Reconstruction of the German Reich*. He finds fault with Bismarck and the Hohenzollerns for their unwillingness to confer bona fide governmental responsibility upon leading members of bourgeois society. It was a critical factor in fostering German society's disastrous, shortsighted assessment of the international political situation in the years before the Great War. Bismarck's consummate mastery of foreign policy did not compensate for his failure to educate politically the German people. He did not establish a tradition of political maturity and realism so that his achievements could be secured and built upon. Here, Spengler finds himself in agreement with Weber, who had earlier complained that Bismarck "left behind a nation *without any political education at all*." Spengler does not concede, of course, that the imperialistic plans he concocted for Germany during the Great War were excessive and unrealistic. Thus, he moderates his celebration in *Prussianism and Socialism* of the Prussian ideal of an authoritarian state. He reverts to the critical tone toward the leadership of the Second Reich that he had already shown in his wartime memoranda for the nobility and the kaiser. According to Spengler, the period in European history when Bismarck established an authoritarian state was "the last splendid era of West European parliamentarianism." The success of the conservatives in England under Benjamin Disraeli attested to the possibilities open to Germany if Bismarck had chosen to expand the inner circle of power to include talented and promising members of German society. The Iron Chancellor missed a golden opportunity in the first decade of the Second Reich. He should have extended to the political parties in the *Reichstag* "the sharing of responsibility for the administration and leadership of the powerfully rising country and the difficult tasks of its foreign policy."[39] Here Spengler directly contradicts the argument he previously made in *Prussianism and Socialism*. There he argued that the quasi-parliamentarian nature of German politics from 1871 to 1914 was contrary to the true character of the German body politic and had impaired political-cultural maturation.

Interestingly, Spengler notes that the unfavorability of the Central European position of Germany, whose geopolitical vulnerability had given birth to an ethos of authoritarianism, was in this respect "disastrous." The leadership of the Second Reich suffered from arrogance. It falsely believed

39. Max Weber, *Gesammelte Politische Schriften*, 3d rev. ed. (Tübingen: J. C. B. Mohr, 1971), 319; NdR, 188.

that with its superb administration, bureaucracy, and army it alone knew the correct policies to implement. The leadership refused to cultivate and utilize the expertise and sound judgment of leading figures of society.[40] It is a surprising argument by a man simplistically and invariably condemned in the literature on German history and politics as a thoroughgoing anti-democratic thinker. His argument that the development of a mature, monarchical-parliamentary government during the Second Reich would have enabled Germany to manage better its difficult and complex foreign policy problems tends in the direction of Weber's position.

Spengler contemplates how German political life can be rejuvenated to enable its citizens to confront the challenges of world politics. He voices his unqualified opposition to anti-Semitism. He criticizes the slogan "Clear out the Jews!" as "petty, shallow, narrow-minded, and undignified." Spengler responds to the Nazi propagandistic charge that the Jews, because of their alleged anti-German qualities, undermine the strength of the German state. He observes, with his characteristic, unflinching commitment to power politics that "the most dangerous anti-German qualities, the urge to international and pacifistic foolishness, the hatred for authority and the successes of power, are deeply rooted right in the *German* character." A sound philosophy of power politics cannot be based on racism. Racial sentiment does not represent "a foundation for high politics, with which a country should be governed or saved."[41]

Mastery of the art of statecraft is a necessity that flows from the exigencies of world history. World history is unsentimental and terrible in its judgment: It can either raise a people to the height of greatness or destroy them. If Germany does not succeed in producing an elite that can develop the requisite capabilities for the conduct of statecraft, Spengler anticipates Germany's destruction.[42]

The former gymnasial teacher turns his attention to the problem of properly educating German youth in the art of statecraft. He strongly criticizes the classicism of German education for being "thoroughly *antihistorical*."[43] As he wittily puts it, "Also by Caesar was his use of the accusative with an infinitive more important than the conquest of Gaul itself." Not only did the pedantic classicism of German education militate against the

40. NdR, 188–89.
41. NdR, 203 n. 1, 203.
42. NdR, 205.
43. NdR, 228.

study of antiquity from the enriching perspective of *Realpolitik*. What was more important, it precluded a rigorous study of the great international political events of the modern age as well. "The political unworldliness of the nineteenth century derived from the gymnasium, which through Plutarch forgot the American Civil War and knew Roman weapons better than Japan's objectives as a world power. We were educated for everything possible, for theology, philology, and philosophy, yet only not for the dangers of our world position, which all around us lay in ambush for us, because the teacher himself knew nothing of it."[44]

Spengler calls for the introduction of the study of international relations into the classroom, not as a minor elective, but as a central part of the curriculum. Moreover, in the finest tradition of political realism, he identifies the study of history as the great school of international politics. He eloquently expresses, from the perspective of German conservatism, the terrible primacy of power politics in human existence and the necessity of studying history from a perspective of *Realpolitik*.

> Instruction in history *or the political education of a people through the school,* who would have earlier realized that both were one and the same? . . . What we need is a strong, daily, profound education of our national consciousness, as a prudential attitude, but with the foundation of a grim realistic portrayal of modern history with its great powers and power-political aims, its political, military, economic, and propagandistic instruments, with the geographical conditions for sea trade and naval war, raw material provisioning and export. . . . To know that all politics is power politics, that weakness means destruction; to know that every individual must live, think, and conduct himself, with every living breath as an essential member of his nation; and to know where and how History prepared the great events of the preceding decades and prepares the future ones—to bring that to full comprehension is what I call teaching history.[45]

His discussion shifts to the modern international states system. Spengler underscores that the Great War was a watershed in the evolution of the international states system. "The forms in which the fate of the world is being propelled since the Great War are changing quickly and have already displaced the system of equal great powers with its network of tensions and

44. NdR, 228.
45. NdR, 235–36.

alliances that underlay politics in the era from 1815 to 1914, just as Napoleon overturned the multistate system of the ancien régime."[46]

International politics in the coming years would be characterized by growing tensions and increasing complexity. With the decline of the mature traditions of parliamentarianism, power would be increasingly concentrated in the hands of Caesaristic individuals. They would dramatically reshape the map of the world.[47] World history has been impelling the West irresistibly toward the struggle for global supremacy ever since Napoleon. Under such circumstances, the cultivation of a mature and prudential knowledge of power politics by Germany's foreign-policy elite has become a matter of national survival.

Reconstruction of the German Reich found little resonance in conservative circles and the general public. With astonishing suddenness Spengler abandoned his unrealized political ambitions.[48] His efforts at founding, in collaboration with conservative notables, a nationalistically oriented press empire had been in vain. His political intrigues had yielded nothing. The attempt by right-wing figures to encourage General Hans von Seeckt, head of the *Reichswehr*, to lead a coup d'etat against Gustav Stresemann's government, which had terminated passive resistance against the French occupation of the Ruhr to the infuriation of the Right, had been unsuccessful. Seeckt did toy with the idea of supporting a conspiracy to establish a civilian authoritarian government. It would have been comprised of conservative notables; Spengler, with whom Seeckt personally negotiated in Berlin, had been under consideration as a minister of culture or minister of science and scholarship (*Wissenschaftsminister*) for it. However, the general ultimately remained loyal to the Weimar regime. Plans were then hatched by an elite political network in Bavaria, with which Spengler was in contact. The plotters aimed to restore the monarchy after the overthrow of the democratic government. Yet this monarchist intrigue was crossed up by Hitler's own failed putsch. Spengler had never been so near nor would he again come so close to grasping political power.[49]

Spengler beat a hasty retreat from the difficult arena of political competition and cabal to the familiar world of scholarship. He channeled his energies into research in the fields of prehistory, early civilization, philoso-

46. NdR, 292–93.
47. NdR, 287, 295.
48. K-Sp, 309–10.
49. K-Sp, 287 ff.

phy, and historical philosophy. In the summer of 1924, he establishes a correspondence with leading historians, political scientists, archaeologists, prehistorians, ethnologists, Assyriologists, Indologists, Sinologists, Egyptologists, and philologists.[50]

Spengler undertook a six-week tour from October to December, 1924, of Lithuania, Latvia, Estonia, Finland, and Sweden. Fascinated with Russia, he desired to travel there also. Moreover, as one scholar comments, "Spengler exercised a great power of attraction on the Russian intelligentsia." *The Decline of the West* had been the subject of lectures and publications, both by emigres and by intellectuals who remained in Bolshevik Russia. However, his visa request was denied by the Soviet authorities, who had forbidden the publication of a Russian edition of the second volume of *The Decline of the West*, apparently because of its discussion of religion. Already in May, 1922, Lenin had lambasted Spengler in *Pravda* as a "Philistine." Although he proceeded with a shortened itinerary, Spengler's trip to the Baltic region and Scandinavia was a triumphal march. "Everywhere there was lively interest and packed auditoriums, the presence of the leaders and pillars of society and friendly press reports."[51] Two vacations in Italy followed in 1925.

In a lecture delivered in November, 1926, "The Contemporary Relationship Between the International Economy and World Politics," Spengler briefly returned to political analysis.[52] This lecture illuminates how he significantly changed his ideas on the transformation of international politics in the twentieth century—ideas that he had expressed in the period from 1911 to 1922, when he composed *The Decline of the West*.

Spengler stresses that a country's level of industrial development is a decisive factor in the struggle in international politics in the twentieth century. He acknowledges the central role of economic considerations in the formulation of foreign policy, a very sophisticated view. "And just as little is it possible to formulate even the slightest national political goal, if one leaves out economic imperatives."[53]

50. K-Sp, 306, 312–13.

51. Xenia Werner, ed., *Der Briefwechsel zwischen Oswald Spengler und Wolfgang E. Groeger* (Hamburg: Helmut Buske Verlag, 1987), 16 ff., esp. 16, 45; Lenin, quoted in Hans-Christof Kraus, " 'Untergang des Abendlandes': Rußland im Geschichtsdenken Oswald Spenglers," chap. in Gerd Koenen and Lew Kopelew, eds., *Deutschland und die Russische Revolution, 1917–1924* (Munich: Wilhelm Fink Verlag, 1998), 301 n. 74; K-Sp, 370.

52. WW.

53. WW, 325, 314.

Between the wars, political idealists embraced the reassuring illusion of the underlying harmony of national interests. They also believed in the capacity of increasing international economic interdependence to ameliorate the traditional abrasiveness of great-power rivalry. Spengler counters with the argument that the world economy will never constitute an integrated, rational system of economic interaction. He evaluates the global economy in terms of the Rankean image of the great powers, as an interaction of egoistic and competitive states. "The world economy always consisted and will always consist *of a number of national economies*, and the history of the world economy will always be composed, to a large extent, of the moods and events that develop *between* these bodies as a consequence of their own powerful life."[54]

Spengler's ideas on political economy stand in marked contrast to those of post–World War II Anglo-Saxon economic theorists. They evidence a proclivity for ahistorical abstraction, deify economic rationality, and express confidence in the possibility of "solving" tremendous economic problems through manipulative, national macroeconomic policies and international economic policy coordination. Spengler views economic reality as characterized by historically organically-changing forms, a process in which the thorny problems of the past are simply superseded by new ones. "The great problems that the world economy throws up in the course of its development are of a *secular* nature. They need decades in order to develop, and decades, not in order to arrive at a 'solution,' but in order to achieve an organic form, in which thereupon new problems arise."[55]

According to Spengler, the international states system and the global economy are being profoundly transformed in the late nineteenth and twentieth centuries. Amid the imperialistic rivalry of the late nineteenth century, a few great powers have transformed themselves into world powers. World War I is ominously described as "the first of the great decisive wars.[56]

Geoffrey Barraclough observed that until the division of Europe into two blocs by the extra-European superpowers, the United States and the Soviet Union, most people were of the opinion that Europe formed the center of international politics. The retreat of the United States into isolationism after the repudiation of Wilsonianism and the debilitation of Rus-

54. WW, 316.
55. WW, 315.
56. WW, 330, 331.

sia following defeat in World War I, revolution, and civil war confused many political observers. They erroneously concluded that Europe had remained the center of gravity in world affairs. Spengler did not share this illusion. "The unconditional preeminence of Europe has been lost," he flatly states. In the interwar period he becomes conscious of the power-political weakening of Europe owing to the debacle of 1914, the continued globalization of world politics with the increasing power of extra-European states, and the rise of foreign economic competition to the European economies. The traditional primacy of Europe was being undermined by the non-European world.

> I see in that historically the most important revolution that the Russo-Japanese War paved the way for and the world war brought to its height: In contrast to prior centuries, the great powers of Europe no longer arrive at decisions exclusively among themselves. The colored world has itself become a great power, in Africa, in East Asia, in the Islamic world, in Central America. That corresponds to the turning point in Roman history, as the provinces became more important than Rome. . . . The United States has acquired a position that is more and more favorable for organizing the American continent into a world of its own.[57]

The growing economic rivalry with the non-West poses a grave challenge to Europe's standing in international politics. Vigorous economic competition, originating already from Japan, will emanate from much of the non-West. "It cannot at all be foretold how long it will take yet until South America, China, and Persia have entered into the ranks of countries with heavy industry." Spengler's recommended policy response to Europe's loss of international political primacy through World War I is neo-imperialism. "A new form of association between a European country as the center of gravity and some kind of relations to other continents must be achieved as a foundation, one that is scarcely foreshadowed today in the British Empire or in Russia's attempt to annex in Asia a circle of states."[58]

Spengler recognizes that the United States is a world power on the rise. However, in a conspicuous omission he fails to discuss the significance of its overwhelming lead in industrial production for its power-political future. For the first time he expresses his respect for Benito Mussolini, who

57. Geoffrey Barraclough, "Europa, Amerika und Russland in Vorstellung und Denken des 19. Jahrhunderts," *Historische Zeitschrift* 203 (1966): 280; WW, 337, 334.
58. WW, 333, 337.

was admired by many foreigners in the twenties. Notwithstanding his words of praise for Mussolini, he recognizes the impossibility of Italy achieving *il Duce's* grandiose foreign policy ambitions. Italy "can never become a world power."[59]

Perhaps unduly influenced by the devastating hyperinflation in Germany in 1923, Spengler makes a wildly inaccurate prediction. He advances the excessively pessimistic and erroneous idea that the developed world would not achieve again the high standard of living it had enjoyed thanks to its economic expansion during the two decades before World War I. "We are not permitted to indulge any doubt about the fact that the standard of living, which for example was held to be normal in Germany during the last twenty years before the war, will never be achieved again. It was unnatural and would have demanded in exchange an amount of work from the individual that he was neither willing nor capable to assume permanently. The same holds also, of course, for England and America, to say nothing at all of Russia and other countries."[60]

This statement certainly ranks as one of the most egregiously false predictions Spengler ever made. Interestingly, he ascribes the inability of the developed world to regain its prewar high standard of living to a slackening of the work ethic. Yet the motive force in the capacity of advanced economies to achieve higher standards of living has largely been technological innovation and the resultant increases in productivity. In the essay "Pessimismus?," Spengler had correctly maintained that "technology has, in practically all areas, its pinnacle ahead of it."[61] In light of his conviction of the bright prospects for continued technological advancement in the twentieth century, his gloomy economic forecast is puzzling.

The above-quoted passage highlights his growing skepticism about the capacity of a great power of the West to create a modern counterpart to the Pax Romana. In antiquity the Pax Romana had facilitated the attainment and diffusion of a comparatively affluent standard of living.[62] This economic development was a momentous one, and, as Spengler had maintained in the second volume of *The Decline of the West*, the Occident would likewise experience it.[63]

59. WW, 336.
60. WW, 327–28.
61. P, 75.
62. See Werner Dahlheim, *Geschichte der Römischen Kaiserzeit* (Munich: R. Oldenbourg, 1984), 54 ff.
63. *UdA* II, 594.

The optimism Spengler exuded during the Wilhelmine period of his thought about Germany's capacity to become the paramount world power has been reduced to mere hopefulness. Nonetheless, he cannot resist indulging in occasional outbursts of immoderate pride in German achievements. His analysis concludes with words of encouragement for his countrymen: "My hope for Germany is based on the fact that we are the one people that have produced for a century the strongest, distinct personalities in technology and science and in business organization, army, and administration and obviously this power of generation has not yet been exhausted by far."[64] It comes as no surprise that he overlooks in this passage luminaries in American technology and economic organization such as Thomas Edison, Andrew Carnegie, and Henry Ford. His chauvinistic contentment with the purported preeminence of Germany in technological, scientific, business, administrative, and military achievement illuminates his corresponding inability to assess properly American capabilities. The United States, with its large population, superior human capital, cornucopia of natural resources, and comparative geopolitical security, was destined in the early post–World War II period to consolidate its position as the greatest economic power in world history.

64. WW, 338.

Man and Technics: A Reassessment

AS WE HAVE SEEN, 1924 WAS A WATERSHED
in Spengler's life. With the Weimar Republic stabilizing, he suddenly
shifted gears. He abandoned his intrigues and failed dreams of gaining a
prestigious political appointment and being an éminence grise. Spengler
now reaffirmed the vocation of private scholar. At the same time he began
what Koktanek described as "the second phase of Spenglerian thought."
In *The Decline of the West* he had dismissed prehistory as unimportant to
his inquiry.[1] A little more than a year after the revision of the first volume
in November, 1922 (and approximately two years after the composition
of the second volume), Spengler redirected his study of civilizational development away from high cultures. Except for brief interruptions when
his passion for politics reasserted itself, he increasingly and ultimately almost exclusively fixed his attention on new interests, prehistory and the
periods antecedent to various high cultures or civilizations. Some of the
greatest discoveries hitherto made in archaeology, prehistory, and ethnol-
ogy stimulated Spengler's enthusiasm for prehistory.[2] Moreover, his close
relationship with the brilliant and unconventional ethnologist, Leo Frobenius, was pivotal. Frobenius had cogently criticized his superficial treatment of early man in *The Decline of the West*. Association with Frobenius
motivated Spengler to broaden his inquiry to include prehistory and early
civilizational history. In a letter to him about this, Manfred Schröter
wrote, "Only now do I comprehend your contact or crossing, so full of

1. K-Sp, 363; *UdA* II, 38 ff.
2. Anton M. Koktanek, introduction to *FdW*, vii, xiv.

destiny, with Frobenius' world. It is indeed the 'continuation toward below' [deeper into the past]."[3]

This second major phase in Spengler's thought extended from 1924 to his death in 1936. During these years he developed what one can arguably call his "second philosophy of world history."[4] The metamorphosis in his philosophy occurred after he absorbed the criticism of *The Decline of the West* and expanded the scope of his inquiry. As Koktanek observes, "Even though he does not expressly respond to important objections to his philosophical and historical conception, being proud of his apparent immutability, they nonetheless affect him and induce him, to depart from his first philosophy toward a new, more universal conception."[5] Interestingly, Spengler was not the only major philosopher of world history in the twentieth century to recast his thought. Indeed, Toynbee went so far as to transform his philosophy of world history in the middle of his massive work *A Study of History.*

The abrupt shift in Spengler's interest from politics and intrigue to the study of prehistory and the antecedents of civilizations was highlighted by two events in the fall of 1924. In October of that year, at a conference of the German Oriental Society, the mature scholar who had loved cartography as a school boy eloquently pleaded for a collective, interdisciplinary cartographical effort by German scholars. He recommended that they assemble a comprehensive collection of maps as an essential tool in the study of prehistory and world history. Spengler argued that students of prehistory and early civilizations were doubly hindered, both by the absence of maps for important periods and by the tardiness with which available maps were updated. His appeal for a major cartographical effort highlights his changing views on cultural interaction. Spengler's daring thesis of the autonomous character of civilizations, their relative insulation from external civilizational influences, continues to receive deservedly much criticism.[6]

3. Anton M. Koktanek, introduction to *Ufr*, xvii–xviii; Schröter to Spengler, 13 December 1920, *B*, 176.

4. This striking phrase, a "second philosophy of history," is borrowed from Merlio, who wrote of "la deuxième philosophie de l'histoire de Spengler." See Gilbert Merlio, *Oswald Spengler: Témoin de son temps*, vol. I (Stuttgart: Akademischer Verlag Hans-Dieter Heinz, 1982), 455–61.

5. Koktanek, introduction to *Ufr*, xiv.

6. Although sometimes the criticism goes too far; for example, see Detlef Felken, *Oswald Spengler: Konservativer Denker zwischen Kaiserreich und Diktatur* (Munich: C. H. Beck, 1988), 64.

However, in discussing his "Plan eines neuen Atlas Antiquus" ("Plan For a New Atlas of Antiquity"), he showed a strong interest in going beyond his thesis of cultural individuality to explore the role of cultural interaction in universal history. Spengler visualizes primitive cultures engaging in dynamic interplay. "The primitive cultures encompass the entire earth, they have used all the seas along the coasts and island chains as go-betweens and form, with their spheres and currents a living whole, without which one is not able to survey the origin and prior history of the great cultures." He now conceived civilizations to be involved in significant cultural interchange. Thus, the Sassanid Empire is characterized as "a most decisive creation at the crossroads of four high cultures." One week after this lecture, Spengler completed a five-page sketch entitled "Altasien" ("Ancient Asia").[7] The outline attests to his ambition of developing a new vision of universal history. It would encompass prehistory, the historical antecedents of civilizations, and the interactions of these "precivilizations" in recorded history, key topics ignored in *The Decline of the West*.

After this watershed year, 1924, Spengler went on to develop his second philosophy of world history, a development he interestingly kept to himself. The reader may wonder why he never conceded that he significantly remodeled his philosophy of world history. *The Decline of the West* was, of course, the claim to fame of a proud man who had previously been an obscure secondary school teacher. An admission by Spengler that he had found it necessary to revise substantially his historical philosophy might have precipitated a storm of ridicule from already-unsympathetic critics. Furthermore, as a prominent ideological opponent of the Weimar Republic, he earnestly desired to maintain the myth of the infallible prophet and dramaturge of world history and politics. This myth invested him with an aura of authority to propagate more advantageously his controversial political ideas and proclaim the primacy of necessity in world history.

That Spengler produced a second philosophy of world history has not been recognized in the Anglo-Saxon intellectual community and is not widely known in the intellectual community of Germany, despite significant advances in Spengler scholarship since the 1960s. In his monograph on Spengler, Hughes presents a much different picture from what is shown in this book. He does not make the crucial argument that Spengler made major changes in his philosophy of world history. Other scholars in

7. Oswald Spengler, "Plan eines neuen Atlas Antiquus," in *RuA*, 100, 103; Oswald Spengler, "Altasien," in *RuA*.

the English-speaking world besides Hughes, including such experts in historical philosophy as R. G. Collingwood, Bruce Mazlish, and William Dray and two authors of monographs on Spengler, John F. Fennelly and Klaus P. Fischer, also do not argue that Spengler profoundly changed his philosophy of world history.[8]

The corollary to the question of why Spengler never acknowledged that he had made major changes in his philosophy of world history is why numerous scholars did not realize it. First, he fell far short of his goal of completing his companion volumes on prehistory and the antecedents of civilizations and the metaphysics of world history. He failed to present his new philosophy of world history in a large-scale, systematically organized work, which would have made the transformation of his historical philosophy plain for all to see. Second, as previously mentioned, Spengler was unwilling to concede either to the public or to his circle of intimates that his philosophy required substantial revision. He helped create the myth that he had not changed his philosophy of history, a myth easy to perpetuate because his monumental book, *The Decline of the West*, had attracted the lion's share of the critical attention devoted to his works. For many years scholars were typically predisposed not to challenge the then-orthodox view that *The Decline of the West* contained virtually everything of importance its author had to say about world history.

As far as I can determine, Hughes did not rededicate himself to the study of Spengler after publishing his fine monograph on him in 1952. As a result, he did not make use of Koktanek's painstaking research in the Spengler Archive, which yielded, in the decade before his death in 1978, four works, all of which, as mentioned earlier, are indispensable to Spengler scholars: a volume of letters, a definitive biography, and two stout volumes of edited archival material. In producing this seminal scholarship, Koktanek collaborated with his "generous friend and adviser," Manfred Schröter.[9]

8. See in this regard the influential, posthumous work, R. G. Collingwood, *The Idea of History* (London: Oxford Univ. Press, 1956), 181–83; Bruce Mazlish, "Spengler," chap. in *The Riddle of History: The Great Speculators from Vico to Freud* (New York: Harper & Row, 1966); William Dray, "A Vision of World History: Oswald Spengler and the Life-Cycle of Cultures," chap. in *Perspectives on History* (London: Routledge & Kegan Paul, 1980); John F. Fennelly, *Twilight of the Evening Lands: Oswald Spengler—A Half Century Later* (New York: Brookdale Press, 1972); Klaus P. Fischer, *History and Prophecy: Oswald Spengler and the Decline of the West* (New York: Peter Lang, 1989).

9. Koktanek, introduction to *Ufr*, viii.

192 / *Prophet of Decline*

Particularly the latter two books, *Urfragen (Fundamental Questions)* and *Frühzeit der Weltgeschichte (Early Period of World History)*, enrich our understanding of the transformation of Spengler's historical thought. However, one can still perceive many of the changes in his historical philosophy without reference to them by attentively perusing the entirety of his published works, particularly *Man and Technics*.[10] Most scholars who have written on Spengler in English since the mid-sixties have either ignored *Fundamental Questions* and *Early Period of World History*, for whatever reason, or, in cases where they have utilized them, have not appreciated their significance. For example, while Fennelly denies the importance of these two books, Fischer does not make the argument that Spengler developed a catastrophic vision of world history.[11]

In *Man and Technics*, we will explore not only the central question of the metamorphosis of his philosophy of world history but other noteworthy features of this brief work as well. The significance to historical philosophy of this little book has frequently not been appreciated by scholars writing about him, to say nothing of the general intellectual community. The latter is not surprising when one considers that the work is completely ignored in many discussions of his philosophy of history.[12] The unusual, short volume deserves a reassessment, which is one of the main purposes of this chapter. Since *Man and Technics* is the one published work, brief as it is, whose careful reading offers insight into the remarkable transformation of his panorama of a virtually eternal series of independent cultural cycles into a tragic, catastrophic vision of world history as a largely integrated process, and has been not properly interpreted as such by important students of Spengler, we will discuss it first.[13] We will then draw upon germane, posthumously published material and delineate a fuller picture of his second philosophy of world history in the next chapter.

Predictably, *Man and Technics* has suffered at the hands of critics who had been unfavorably disposed to *The Decline of the West*. Harry Elmer

10. In this regard, *Man and Technics* (*MuT*) should be ideally read in conjunction with the selections in Spengler's *RuA*, which pertain to world-historical topics, as well as with Oswald Spengler, "Achäerfragen" (second part of "Zur Weltgeschichte des zweiten vorchristlichen Jahrtausends"), ed. Hildegard Kornhardt, *Die Welt als Geschichte* 6 (1940).

11. See Fennelly, *Twilight*, 23–24; Fischer, *History and Prophecy*, 232–33.

12. See, for example, Mazlish, "Spengler"; Dray, "Spengler and the Life-Cycle of Cultures."

13. See H-Sp, 120 ff.; Fennelly, *Twilight*, 24.

Barnes, a leading expert on Western historiography, belittled the slim volume. He confidently declared that the Spengler "bubble" had been burst as a result, in part, of its publication.[14]

But even scholars who think highly of Spengler often do not attach any real importance to *Man and Technics*. Hughes and Fennelly adopted a highly critical stance toward this book as a contribution to the study of prehistorical and civilizational development. They also did not show any appreciation of the fundamental changes in Spengler's philosophy of world history that it helps illuminate. Hughes' discussion of *Man and Technics* is abbreviated, a mere three pages. Fennelly's is even more cursory. The former labels the work "a kind of anthropological fantasy." This characterization is echoed by Fennelly. For Hughes, the work amounts to an embarrassment that offers very little that is new to the reader. "The charitable reader might note an occasional new idea; he might detect a more pessimistic tone than in any of Spengler's other works. But even this was largely a question of emphasis."[15] However, not only is the overall tone of *Man and Technics* far more pessimistic than that of *The Decline of the West*, as will become readily apparent, but one can perceive the adumbration of a new vision of world history.

Hughes desired to produce, as the subtitle of his monograph indicates, a "critical estimate" of Spengler's thought. It was understandably very difficult for him to reach firm conclusions about *Man and Technics*. He conveys the impression of not being sure where it fits in the Spengler corpus. I can sympathize with Hughes' predicament, for the voluminous material from Spengler's literary estate had not been edited for publication at the time and no biography existed. Thus, Hughes states, "Of all Spengler's works, it is the hardest to classify and, as an intellectual construction, the least successful." To be fair to Hughes, decades later he revised his low opinion of the unconventional essay and came to value it. In 1990 he wrote that *Man and Technics* "has gained rather than lost in relevance as the years have passed."[16]

To be sure, this gem of a little book, Spengler's brief philosophical sketch of prehistory and early civilization, is marred by a number of major

14. Harry Elmer Barnes, *A History of Historical Writing*, rev. 2d ed. (New York: Dover Publications, 1963), 205.

15. H-Sp, 120, 122.

16. H-Sp, 120; H. Stuart Hughes, preface to *The Decline of the West* by Oswald Spengler, an abridged edition by Helmut Werner, trans. Charles Francis Atkinson (New York: Oxford Univ. Press, 1991), xii.

flaws that cannot be glossed over in an analysis. The shortcomings of the essay are to be expected from a scholar who was obviously not a professionally trained prehistorian, though one well-read in German, English, and French scholarly literature in the field. Yet in an age of suffocating academic specialization, a bold attempt at synthesis, even if it appears to posterity to be at times a bit awkward, is refreshing. Its flaws and disappointing brevity should not lead us to ignore the Olympian vision of world history, in an age of potential apocalypse, that this unusual book offers to the receptive reader.

As noted earlier, Spengler failed to produce the major work on prehistory and early civilizational history on which he had expended years of research energy. However, when the opportunity to expound his views to the public on these subjects, albeit in very compact form, fortuitously presented itself, he took it. On March 13, 1931, Spengler was invited to become a permanent member of the managing committee of the Deutsches Museum, one of the most prestigious technological museums in the world. He promised to deliver an address entitled "Kultur und Technik" at the museum's annual meeting. To the surprise and perhaps disappointment of many of the prominent guests, who apparently expected a lecture on the modern age and technology, Spengler used the evening as an opportunity to adumbrate his new vision of world history.[17] Shortly after giving the lecture, he expanded the text into a short book, which he published in July, 1931, with the title *Man and Technics*.

Spengler addresses one of the most fundamental questions of the twentieth century and the new millennium: What are the origins, character, and fate of science and technology and their significance for human history, including their global environmental impact? He gives his answer in the context of a very sketchy, yet nonetheless intriguing, portrait of the history of man's development of technics from early prehistory to the present. He also handles at the end of the essay a second important question. Amid economic crisis in the 1930s, Spengler asks: What are the prospects of the West for upholding its traditional position of technological and economic preeminence?

Man and Technics was extracted from a projected, larger work that remained unfinished. That tome was to survey "*the history of man from his origin onwards*," complementing the overview of civilizations in *The Decline of the West*. Conscious of the extraordinary complexity of the subject

17. K-Sp, 399 ff.

and the brevity with which he treats it, Spengler aspires in *Man and Technics* "to provide a preliminary impression of the great secret of the destiny of man."[18]

At the very outset, as the above quotation from the preface clearly shows, Spengler expresses his belief that mankind, irrespective of the variable nature of culture and the discontinuities in history resulting from the rise and decline of civilizations, ultimately shares a historical destiny. In *The Decline of the West* his position had been diametrically the opposite. He asserted that the concept of mankind had only a zoological and not a historical significance. For the early Spengler, world history only displayed its meaning in fragmented fashion within autonomous high cultures. The late Spengler no longer maintains, from the position of methodical, philosophical relativism set forth in *The Decline of the West*, that his philosophy of world history is only valid for denizens of Western civilization. Now, he declares in bold Hegelian fashion at the beginning of the work that world history has finally achieved the necessary stage of maturity that permits the comprehension of its essence. "The twentieth century has finally become mature enough to penetrate to the ultimate meaning of the *facts*, out of whose entirety the *real* world history consists."[19]

Prehistory tells the story of mankind during the immense stretch of time before the invention of writing. This discipline deals with a period of time that dwarfs that of recorded history because "99.8 per cent of the time for which we have an archaeological record" belongs to prehistory.[20] It is this period that now engages Spengler's interest.

Like Nietzsche, Spengler was interested in biology and had a lifelong interest in the subject of human evolution. In autobiographical fragments he records that he read Darwin and his enthusiastic German popularizer, the zoologist Haeckel, during his school days.[21] And Spengler was, apparently, so keenly interested in the works of the two scientists that it induced him to concentrate initially on mathematics and the natural sciences in his university studies. In *Man and Technics* he rejects the idea that the human species has undergone a gradual and extended process of biological evolution. Spengler, like Nietzsche, opposes Darwinian thought. He disparages Darwinian evolutionary theory for supporting the notion of "gradual,

18. Oswald Spengler, preface to *MuT*.

19. *MuT*, 4.

20. John A. J. Gowlett, *Ascent to Civilization: The Archaeology of Early Man* (New York: Knopf, 1984), 9.

21. EH, 8.

phlegmatic change," a scientific conclusion that "conforms to the English temperament." Instead, he champions the mutation theory of Hugo de Vries, arguing that profound changes in biological forms transpire suddenly and dramatically. Spengler's rejection of the idea of the gradual biological evolution of man and his belief that the pace of civilizational development accelerates in world history influence him to conclude erroneously that the human species is only a comparatively recent biological phenomenon. "Since when man exists, we do not know. The number of years is also of no importance, though today it is still assumed much too high. It is not a matter of millions, not even of several hundred thousand; nevertheless, a substantial number of thousands of years must have elapsed." In his private papers he is more precise, fixing the appearance of the human race at approximately 100,000 B.C.[22]

Spengler composed his slim book in the early thirties. Since his death in 1936 a veritable revolution in our knowledge of early man has occurred. The discovery of important paleontological and archaeological sites and the development of new methods for dating the material they have yielded have enabled scientists to push back greatly the time when early man emerged in the process of evolution.

The theory of human evolution encompasses vast stretches of distance and time. Yet, as the archaeologist John A. J. Gowlett notes, it is based on "very few known sites." Controversies over important questions remain unresolved to this day. Nonetheless, the following basic picture has taken shape. Modern man belongs to the order of primates, which includes apes and chimpanzees. The ancestors of modern man, members of the hominids, or the family of man, branched off from the ape line from 6,000,000 to 12,000,000 years ago, pursuing an evolutionary path much different from that of apes. There is still a significant gap in the fossil record for the span of time when this critical divergence in evolutionary trajectories took place.[23] Human evolution witnessed important anatomical changes. They include the development of a skeletal structure permitting ambulation for long periods of time, the virtual complete loss of an original coat of hair, the development of a distinctive body cooling system, the refinement of the hand, various dental modifications, and most importantly, changes in the size and structure of the brain. The first solid evidence showing modern man as fully formed dates this event to around 40,000 years ago.[24]

22. *MuT*, 19, 26; *FdW*, #72, p. 76.
23. Gowlett, *Civilization*, 28, 14, 18.
24. *Ibid.*, 14, 120.

Today, the idea of a relatively gradual biological evolution of modern man from his primate ancestors is widely accepted. Whereas Spengler insists that all the basic anatomical features of modern man emerged dramatically and simultaneously, paleontological evidence indicates otherwise.[25] For example, the famous Lucy skeleton discovered in the 1970s at Hadar in Ethiopia, the most complete skeleton yet found at any early site, reveals that an early hominid's body had attained almost entirely human form at least 3,000,000 years ago, long before the evolution of the modern cranial form about 100,000 years ago. The emergence of man can be viewed from a biological or, alternatively, from a cultural perspective. According to a biological definition, the evolution of the first *Homo* species about 2,000,000 years ago signals man's appearance. According to an archaeological definition, the first stone tools, decisive early forms of human material culture, attest the presence of man. The oldest collection of stone tools, discovered in 1976 also at Hadar, are roughly estimated to be 2,600,000 years old. According to the contemporary picture of human prehistorical development, mankind has experienced a very long process of cultural development during 2,000,000 years of the Stone Age.[26]

A further deficiency of Spengler's views on prehistory is his notion that Paleolithic and Mesolithic man was a lone wolf, an isolated struggler in a cruel world. "Every man lives his own life, produces by himself his own weapon, carries out alone his own tactics in daily struggle. No one needs anyone else." He does soften slightly the harsh lines of this picture. He notes that very small groups of prehistoric men, women, and children formed extremely loose associations he terms "packs." Based on the study of contemporary hunting and gathering peoples, archaeologists conclude that in spite of their low population density, prehistoric hunters and gatherers spent sufficient time together as a small, functioning society to enhance chances of survival.[27]

Prehistoric civilization arose with the transition from hunting and gathering to farming and animal domestication and the development of organized village life. Spengler maintains that this transition occurred suddenly and dramatically. An explosion in technical expertise and cooperative undertakings took place, facilitating the emergence of the first early civilizations.[28] In his estimation this transition is a second, epochal event in

25. *MuT*, 19.
26. Gowlett, *Civilization*, 26–27, 43, 39, 6.
27. *MuT*, 27, 23; Gowlett, *Civilization*, 11.
28. *MuT*, 26 ff.

human history comparable to the earlier one of the abrupt biological appearance of man. His position basically conforms to nineteenth-century prehistorical thought, which introduced the idea of a "Neolithic Revolution." This term captures the momentous nature of the adoption of agriculture and stock-breeding, which made possible an economic surplus, the material foundation of advanced civilization. Interestingly, the scientific community, especially after 1950, generally rejected this position. Experts viewed this development as evolutionary instead of revolutionary in nature. However, the original nineteenth-century position has recently been vindicated. As Gowlett observes, "The view has begun to emerge again that the developments were after all relatively sudden: it is difficult to find much firm evidence of domestication 10,000 years ago, but by 7,000 years ago farming villages, cultivated crops and domestic animals had appeared over large areas of the Old World, and similar developments were beginning in the Americas." However, Spengler's argument that language, a cultural achievement necessary in his scheme to enable hitherto relatively isolated people to engage in coordinated and planned activities, sprang up at this time must be dismissed as very improbable. Although a complete system of writing did not come into being until about 3100 B.C. in Mesopotamia, it is widely believed that language has a long history. Some contemporary experts maintain that language developed during the last 100,000 years, together with the modern cranial form. Others argue that its origins were very much earlier.[29]

Clearly, according to the contemporary state of knowledge, there are considerable inadequacies in Spengler's treatment of human evolution and prehistory. Nonetheless, he does advance powerful ideas of a historical-philosophical nature, to which we now turn our attention. A key idea in his revised philosophy of history is that world history since the fifth millennium B.C. manifests accelerated civilizational development. This challenging thesis acquires even greater power if one applies it to the entirety of world history, which he failed to do because of his rejection of the idea of an extended process of prehistoric biological and cultural evolution and his argument that changes in prehistory were sudden, abrupt, and epochal in nature. The Acheulean period, stretching from 1,500,000 to 200,000 years ago, is known for an unchanging form of large stone tools we call hand axes. This period saw very modest cultural advances, so much so that it is often looked on by experts "as a long standstill, associated with a

29. Gowlett, *Civilization*, 156, 182, 74.

slightly dim-witted *Homo erectus*." The advent of the last Ice Age 100,000 years ago, to which mankind adapted with considerable success, forms a great dividing line. As Gowlett notes, we find "enormous evidence for cultural advance during the last 100,000 years, and acceleration within the last 40,000 years." The last major Ice Age phase, which ended abruptly about 10,000 years ago, is a milestone. Indeed, as Gowlett emphasizes, "most of the spectacular technological achievements of mankind have been made since the start of the subsequent warm period known as the Holocene." Human cultural development accelerates with the rapid transition from early village life toward full civilization in the Middle East, Anatolia, Iran, the Indian subcontinent, and China. It is all completed in the astonishingly brief period of only about 5,000 years, from about 8000 B.C. to 3000 B.C.[30]

Spengler expresses his deepening pessimism about the character and direction of world history, identifying it far more with tragedy than previously. Although the history of each culture in *The Decline of the West* was governed by a tragic logic, it was nonetheless ultimately one of awe-inspiring splendor and harmony. Now, Spengler describes the entire sweep of human history as profoundly tragic. "Every high culture is a tragedy; the history of mankind *as a whole* is tragic."[31] But history is not merely deeply tragic for the last great German cultural pessimist, the heir to Schopenhauer, Burckhardt, and Nietzsche. It is ultimately apocalyptic. In this regard, Spengler decisively goes beyond his three forerunners.

The very opposite of a rational process of progress, accelerated civilizational development is irrational. History's acceleration culminates in cataclysm; the successive high cultures manifest the tempo of "final catastrophes." As Spengler peers through the murky mists of the future, he formulates, years before the fiery dawn of the atomic age at Hiroshima, the Copernican thesis that human history will soon tragically climax. "World history looks very much different than even our own time permits us to dream. The history of man is, measured by the history of the plant and animal world upon this planet, to say nothing of the life span of stellar worlds, short, an abrupt rise and fall of a few thousand years, something of no account in the destiny of the earth, but for us, who have been born into it, from tragic greatness and power."[32]

30. *Ibid.*, 80, 118, 148, 174.
31. *MuT*, 52.
32. *MuT*, 42, 8.

In his sketch of prehistory and early civilization Spengler advances a bleak theory of the origins of the state. He operates in political philosophy in the German tradition of opposition to Anglo-Saxon social contract theories. Political organization (the state) first arises along with embryonic civilizational forms in Neolithic times. For Thomas Hobbes, man is egoistical and conflictual. However, Spengler inverts the Hobbesian social contract. Social peace is not established by a Hobbesian Leviathan in order to liberate man from the fear of being murdered or robbed by his compatriots but emerges to facilitate the defense of the newly constituted community against external enemies. "Such a peace also exists *within* the tribe, in order to keep at its disposal its powers for external tasks: *the state is the internal order of a people for the external purpose.*" The pacification of the community so that it can assert itself in the dangerous world of external relations is a fundamental political task. For "history is the history of *war*, then as it is now." Inverting Karl von Clausewitz's famous epigram on the relationship of war and politics, Spengler asserts, "Politics, as a struggle with more intellectual weapons, is only the temporary substitution for war."[33]

An unresolved tension exists in Spengler's philosophical anthropology that borders on outright contradiction. Individuals, despite their egoism and conflictual tendencies, band together with others. They develop a binding sense of community in order to assert themselves against adversaries of their emergent society. A similar problem exists more acutely in Spengler's idealized portrait of modern Germany. Man is likened to a beast of prey, yet he is enjoined by Spengler to cultivate the civilized virtues of duty, honor, and patriotism. Nonetheless, Spengler's stress on the central role of foreign policy considerations in the origin of the state is a healthy corrective to much of Western political philosophy, which tends to downplay them.

Conflict for Spengler sets the tone not only for political relationships between human communities organized as states but for man's relationship with nature as well. He ponders modern science and technology and the industrial civilization they have made possible from a broader perspective. He reflects on them within the larger context of how man has interacted with his fellow man and the environment in order to survive and progressively assert himself from prehistoric times to the twentieth century. Thus he examines technics, *i.e.*, techniques, practices, procedures, and methods practiced by humans in order to achieve diverse goals in a

33. *MuT*, 37.

world of self-assertion and struggle. He does not restrictively use the term *technics* to refer only to modern technology.

Like Nietzsche, Spengler passionately opposed the English utilitarian tradition. He asks: What is the purpose of Western man's scientific and technological activity? The purpose is not, as is commonly maintained by utilitarians in the Anglo-Saxon tradition of political and social thought, to further the happiness of the greatest number. Instead, the purpose is to satisfy the spiritual longing of Faustian man to conquer the infinite, to dethrone nature, and to elevate himself as a deity above its exploited, prostrate form.

The late Spengler developed an interest in the issue of the nature and implications of the interchange of mankind with the natural environment. His second philosophy of world history provides a useful frame of reference for contemplating the global ecological crisis, of which the visionary thinker deserves recognition as a prophet. Spengler, who considered modern Western civilization to be distinctively dynamic, expansive, and transformative of its environment, did not completely ignore the question of its impact on the ecosystem in *The Decline of the West.* In its final pages, he argued that modern civilization was exhausting the planet's energy resources and would, after its decline, leave the face of the earth permanently altered.[34] Yet Spengler, who was socialized during a period of explosive industrial growth in Germany, went on to conceive an alarming vision of the interchange between mankind and the natural environment throughout history.

Nature is the "background, object, and means" of man in the process of civilizational development. The ability to create his own technics distinguishes man in the Promethean struggle against nature. An inventive and resourceful upstart, man is a "revolutionary" against the world of nature. "Artificial, *contrary to nature* is every human work from the lighting of fire to the achievements that we in high cultures designate as actually artistic. The *prerogative of creation* is torn from nature." World history is the saga of the tragic and hopeless struggle between man, "*the inventive beast of prey*," and nature, one that will be waged to its bitter end.[35]

In revolting against nature by creating civilizational forms, man surrenders the rude freedom of his simple prehistoric existence. He imprisons himself in the hot-house of culture. "Culture, the sum of artificial, per-

34. *UdA* II, 623 ff.
35. *MuT*, 22, 20–22, 39, 24, 18, 25.

sonal, self-created life patterns, develops into a cage with narrow bars for this irrepressible soul."[36]

Fundamental to every philosophy of history is the concept of historical time; Spengler radically changes his. In *The Decline of the West* he portrayed world history as being virtually eternal. Cultures rose and declined in an apparently endless, grand procession. Now he envisions historical time as likely reaching its terminus as terrible crises overwhelm the modern world. Moreover, in *The Decline of the West*, historical change occurred in each cultural cycle at its own distinctive tempo. For example, the dynamic West pressed onward in allegro con brio. Spengler now argues that world history itself flows in an accelerating tempo, clearly observable with the emergence of the first cultures. The quickening pace of world history takes on tragic dimensions as it rushes forward toward its climactic end. "At the latest, two millennia later, the high cultures in Egypt and Mesopotamia already begin. One sees that the tempo of history assumes tragic dimensions. Earlier, millennia played scarcely a role; now every century becomes important. The rolling stone approaches in tearing leaps the abyss." Moreover, in contrast to his major work, where cultures arose aimlessly, they now grow up "in a sequence that points from South to North."[37]

In the following passage, Spengler reiterates the argument made in *The Decline of the West* that the roots of industrial civilization lay deeply embedded in the rich, spiritual humus of West European culture. He claims to have uncovered the "religious origin" of Western technical thought in the meditations of early Gothic monks, who in their prayers and fastings wrung God's secrets from Him.[38]

> One was tired of contenting oneself with the services of plants, animals, and slaves, and stealing from nature its resources—metals, stones, wood, fibrous materials, its water in canals and wells—to conquer its resistance through ship transport, roads, bridges, tunnels and dams. No more was she to be *plundered* in her materials, but *her energy itself put into harness*, performing slave labor, in order to multiply the strength of man. This monstrous idea, so foreign to all other cultures, is as old as Faustian culture. Already in the tenth century we encounter technical constructions of a totally new kind. Already Roger Bacon and Albertus Magnus have speculated about steam en-

36. *MuT*, 39.
37. *MuT*, 27, 44.
38. *UdA* II, 622.

gines, steamships, and airplanes. And many pondered the idea of *perpetual motion* in their monastery cells.[39]

The awesome struggle between man and nature forms a central theme of Spengler's historical cosmos. With the industrial revolution, this struggle escalates into a veritable war. The machine is "the most cunning of all weapons against nature that is at all possible." The war man wages against nature achieves its tragic apex in Western civilization. Since the West has audaciously challenged nature by extracting its secrets in order to exploit it thoroughly, it is the most tragic of all civilizations. "The Faustian, West European culture is, *perhaps*, not the last, but *certainly* the mightiest, most passionate, through its inner contrast between comprehensive intellectualization and deepest spiritual turmoil the most tragic of all. It is possible that a feeble straggler comes along yet, somewhere on the plain between the Vistula and the Amur and in the next millennium. But here the struggle between nature and man, who through his historical existence rebelled against her, has been *practically fought to its end.*"[40]

Spengler addresses the role of ecological and climatic conditions in the development of the spirit of modern Western science and technology. "The Nordic landscape had forged the breed of man in it through the harshness of the conditions of life, the cold, the constant adversity, into a tough race, with an intellect sharpened to the most extreme degree, with the cold fervor of an irrepressible passion for struggling, daring, driving forward."[41]

While bourgeois exponents of the idea of progress and Marxists in the nineteenth century extolled the quintessential rationality of Western science and technology and benignly viewed man as controlling nature, Spengler christens him *"the inventive beast of prey."* Man "plunders," "rapes," and "poisons" nature through modern scientific and technological processes.[42] Adherents of the idea of progress picture world history to be, in large part, the story of the development of progressively sophisticated techniques for the control of nature and the phenomenal growth of mankind's productive capabilities. For Spengler, world history becomes in his late work a record of man's tragic and ultimately disastrous effort to gain the upper hand over the natural world.

39. *MuT*, 48.
40. *MuT*, 6, 51, 52, 44.
41. *MuT*, 44.
42. *MuT*, 18, 48, 34, 55.

In a moment of historical prescience, Spengler virtually anticipates the unfolding, global ecological crisis that first gained public attention in the 1970s. He argues, "Everything organic succumbs to the spreading organization. An artificial world penetrates and poisons the natural one." He grasps the dangerous quality of the extraordinarily sophisticated, yet ultimately brutal, mastery of the environment the human race has won. "The *mechanization of the world* has entered into a stage of most dangerous, excessive tension. The face of the earth with its plants, animals, and people has been altered. In a few decades most of the great forests have disappeared, have been transformed into newspaper, and consequently climatic changes have occurred that threaten the agriculture of entire populations; countless species like the buffalo have been completely or almost completely wiped out, entire races of men like the North American Indians and the Australian aborigines have been brought virtually to extinction."[43]

At the beginning of the twenty-first century, one can easily fill in this very rough sketch of a global ecological crisis with alarming details. The list of critical ecological problems is already depressingly long. It includes threats to biodiversity, acid rain, the death of forests in Europe, desertification, the destruction of the Earth's tropical rain forests, depletion of the ozone layer, the greenhouse effect, and the dilemmas of safely disposing of toxic chemicals and nuclear wastes. They all confirm the significance of Spengler's visionary thesis of the irrational, environmentally destructive qualities of modern industrial civilization. Environmental protection has become a salient feature of domestic public policy not only in Spengler's native Germany and the West as a whole but virtually throughout the entire world and increasingly in recent years a high-priority item on the agenda of international politics. For example, in 1990 a host of signatory nations and the European Commission committed themselves to phase out chlorofluorocarbons, culprits in destroying the atmosphere's ozone layer and in global warming. Moreover, the historic Earth Summit in 1992 produced a convention combatting the threat of global warming, the Convention on Climate Change, and another convention aiming to preserve the world's diversity of life forms, the Convention on Biodiversity.

Placing the prefiguration of ecological catastrophe in *Man and Technics* in its intellectual historical context requires a cursory review of some aspects of the opposition to industry and technology in German culture. As the industrial revolution in Germany gathered momentum, the years from

43. *MuT*, 55, 54–55.

1850 to 1890 witnessed widespread enthusiasm for technological advancement and faith in progress. However, alarming signs of ecological disfigurement and cultural disintegration in the face of modernization gradually appeared and after 1890 became the subject of intellectual discourse in Wilhelmine Germany. The debate intensified during the Weimar period, under the hammer blows of military defeat in an appalling conflict, socialist revolution, inflation, and global economic depression.[44]

Prominent German intellectuals critical about industrialization did not generally adopt as extreme a position as Spengler did. Wilhelm Heinrich Riehl, perhaps the most radical among his contemporaries during the years from 1850 to 1890 in his critical stance toward modernization, argued that the deleterious effects of industrialization could be partially compensated for through state intervention to preserve wilderness areas. Ernst Rudorff pioneered the movement for the protection of the countryside against the effects of industrialism (*Heimatschutzbewegung*). With his aesthetic critique of ecological destruction, he was hopeful that the unspoiled beauty of the romantic German countryside could be maintained through a consequential limitation of tourist excursions. Werner Sombart, despite his insight into the "demonic nature of technology," believed that industrialization could be intelligently managed, minimizing its negative consequences.[45]

Spengler's achievement was twofold. First, he sensed the gravity of the threat to the global environment posed by industrialization. Second, he grasped the centrality of the struggle between man and nature in all of world history, not merely in modern Western civilization, though it is here that this struggle has climaxed. The global ecological crisis has raised the question of whether the industrial revolution has a profoundly dark and irrational side to it. The luminaries of the German tradition of historical philosophy, who emphasized differently the rationality of modern civilization, Kant, Hegel, Ranke, Marx, and Weber, all failed to sense the baneful effects of mankind's forceful reshaping of the environment—effects that preoccupy many intellectuals today.

Inspired by the *amor fati* of Nietzsche, Spengler did not espouse flight into misty agrarian-romantic utopias. Nor did he harbor that which may ultimately prove to be an illusion, namely, the notion that the destructive

---

44. Rolf Peter Sieferle, *Fortschrittsfeinde?: Opposition gegen Technik und Industrie von der Romantik bis zur Gegenwart* (Munich: C. H. Beck, 1984).

45. *Ibid.*, 149 ff., 161 ff., 215, 281 n. 76.

ecological effects of modern production and consumption can be reduced to tolerable levels. Spengler attributes to this tremendous, violent transformation of the environment through the course of world history an apocalyptic character. His argument tragically seems more compelling as our consciousness of global ecological crisis has grown.

The idea of the incompatibility between modern industrial civilization and the Earth's environment is implicit in Spengler's tragic account of man's struggle with nature since his origins. This idea constitutes a notable contribution to the tradition of European cultural pessimism. In the contemporary debate about the global environmental crisis, one can discern two basic positions. According to one perspective, industrial civilization and a healthy environment are incompatible. Industrial civilization cannot be sufficiently modified to prevent the long-term destruction of the ecosystem, especially given the synergistic interaction of the ecological crisis and the population explosion. The ongoing population explosion in the developing world, combined with the imperative to promote robust economic growth, increases the consumption of raw materials and energy resources, placing additional severe burdens upon the global environment. According to an alternative perspective, the very civilizational instrumentalities that have given rise to the ecological crisis in the first place, that is, modern science and technology, offer hope. They can be refined and utilized in a manner that ultimately renders industrial civilization and the ecosystem compatible. One cannot escape a sense of paradox in this reassuring position.

From a Spenglerian perspective, it is impossible to believe that citizens of what we call today the North, the developed world, will radically adjust their life-styles so that they will live within their means on this planet. First, a very high standard of living is the necessary precondition for intellectual, technical, and artistic achievement. Second, and more important, human technics fails to reduce work because every wish fulfilled awakens countless others.[46]

Spengler certainly was not, in a direct way, a precursor of the environmental movement. Although he adumbrated a global ecological crisis, he did not champion conservation or alternative technology measures, which he never contemplated and would have been far ahead of his time anyway. Quite the contrary, Spengler remained true to his heroic, tragic philosophy of life and world history, which glorified struggle and power. Modern

46. *MuT*, 43, 39.

Western man, he believed, must further develop applied science and technology, irrespective of their environmentally destructive features. For they are expressive of his dynamic and transformative civilizational ethos. Furthermore, scientific and technological prowess may enable the West to defend its interests longer in the arena of power politics.

Spengler addresses another issue in world affairs that attracted renewed attention in the seventies, a decade of oil crises and inflation in commodity prices. That issue is the finite quantity of natural resources and its ramifications for the future of industrial civilization. He argues that the collapse of industrial civilization will not result from the exhaustion of natural resources, as it will occur long before this critical point is reached. Spengler addressed this issue in the context of the turn-of-the-century debate over the implications of the hypothesized exhaustion of the coal fields for the long-term prospects of European industry. "It is foolishness, as was the fashion in the nineteenth century, to talk about the impending exhaustion of the coal fields in a few centuries and its consequences. . . . It is not a question at all of such spans of time. The West European-American technology will reach its end *earlier*."[47]

Industrial civilization is a magnificent expression of the human intellect. Its maintenance and continued development depend on a dedicated and self-disciplined scientific and technocratic elite.[48] Spengler's views on Western youth are largely consonant with such sociological phenomena as the countercultural revolution of the 1960s and the continuing crisis in American scientific education at the primary and secondary levels. He argues that the leading intellects of future generations will turn to new life-styles at odds with the furtherance of industrial civilization. Youth reverts to "simpler life-styles that are closer to nature." He pursues sport instead of scientific studies, hating the great cities and the cold atmosphere of technological organization. Youth interests himself in occultism and spiritualism and Christian and pagan metaphysical speculation. Sadly, one could add, since the sixties, he turns to alcohol, drugs, and cacophonous music. "*The flight of the born leaders from the machine begins.*"[49]

Industrial strength is of critical importance to the state in the nineteenth and twentieth centuries. "The extraordinary superiority of Western Europe and North America in the second half of the [nineteenth] century

47. *MuT*, 56.
48. *MuT*, 56.
49. *MuT*, 57.

in power of every kind, economic, political, military, financial power, rests upon an uncontested *monopoly* of industry." Spengler rejects the idea that the diffusion of Western technology in the non-Western world is a thoroughly desirable and progressive historical phenomenon. He presents his challenging thesis, foreshadowed in a lecture delivered in 1926, that the modernizing economies of the non-West will undermine the economic paramountcy of the developed West. The Western export of technology to the non-West is the "*betrayal of technics*."[50] This loss of a priceless treasure occurred through the export of industrial secrets, processes, methods, engineers, and economic organizations. Indeed, this technology transfer has markedly increased during the post–World War II, American-led liberal international economic order. It has contributed to the deindustrialization of the United States and the erosion of its undisputed economic and technological supremacy from its early post–World War II apex.

Western technology will be utilized by the non-West as a mighty weapon against the West in the growing power struggle that has assumed international economic forms. Spengler prophesied an inexorable shift in the center of gravity in industry from the Occident to the non-Western economies. They will mount a "deadly competition" against the Western economies. This stunning decline in Western economic competitiveness will result from three factors: first, the eventual leveling off of the steadily rising scientific and technological niveau of the West (caused largely by an increasing disinterest among the younger generation and its turning to new life-styles); second, much lower wage-scales and a strong work ethic in the non-West; and third, the proliferation of technology by the West in the non-West ("the betrayal of technics").[51]

Spengler's speculations on Japan and East Asia are largely consistent with the emergence of the Pacific Basin as an economic marvel in the 1970s. Although the protracted economic slump in Japan and the Asian contagion of the 1990s appear to invalidate audacious predictions of a Pacific Century under Japanese or Chinese hegemony, the stiff economic competition generated by East Asia does account for most of America's chronic trade deficit. Already, in 1933, Spengler foresees the West meeting its match in economic competition in modernizing non-Western countries. "The opponents have reached the level of their models, perhaps sur-

50. *MuT*, 59; WW, 333 ff.; *MuT*, 58–59.
51. *MuT*, 56–60.

passed them with the craftiness of the colored races and the overripe intelligence of ancient civilizations.''[52]

Few analysts of world affairs in Spengler's generation ever envisioned that the non-Western economies would mount a grave threat to the political and economic hegemony of the West. The strength of Spengler's analysis is his remarkable prognosis of the inevitable, dangerous erosion of Western economic preeminence in large measure through non-Western competition. The weakness of his line of argument is that he believes the non-West is already on the verge of overtaking the West in international economic competitiveness. Symptomatic of Spengler's premature vision of the economic decline of the West is that he views the mass unemployment in Western Europe and in North America during the Great Depression not as a crisis but as *"the beginning of a catastrophe."*[53] Because he came to doubt seriously the capacity of the United States or Germany to forge a universal empire, he does not foresee that the United States would establish a global, liberal, international economic order after World War II. American dynamism and leadership lifted the capitalist world out of the depressed economic conditions of the 1930s and facilitated the continuation of Western global economic supremacy, though some cracks in the edifice were observable as the century ended. Spengler does presciently single out the Japanese, who created after World War II the world's second largest economy, as the outstanding example of the capacity of the non-West to challenge the West's economic dominance. Yet he does not differentiate between the potential of various modernizing non-Western countries to compete economically with the West.

Although a non-Western power like Japan will catch up with the West in economic competitiveness, its achievement will have only a limited significance for modern civilization. For the non-West will not be able to underwrite an enduring modern civilization; the scientific and technological age will be a transitory one. Spengler gives essentially three reasons for this, and his position merits consideration particularly in light of Asia's dream of making the twenty-first century an Asian one. First, the assimilation of Western science and technology by non-Western peoples is not motivated by inner spiritual or cultural necessities but is simply a "mechanical" act of imitation. Moreover, this process of cultural adoption originates solely from the need to copy the West in order to shake off its

52. *MuT*, 60.
53. *MuT*, 61.

oppressive colonial domination. This argument does highlight the role that power-political factors played in the calculations of those members of non-Western elites who espoused modernization reforms, for example, in Meiji Japan and in Manchu China. When one contemplates Japan's meteoric rise from the ashes of defeat in 1945 through an aggressive, neo-mercantilistic policy and the progress of post-Maoist China in modernizing since 1978, then, clearly, power-political considerations continue to play a central role in the aspiration of non-Western elites to modernize.

Spengler does not adequately emphasize, however, that the modernizing drive of non-Western countries responds not merely to power-political competition between the West and the non-West but, indeed, to that obtaining among all the major powers of the world, irrespective of their civilizational heritage. Moreover, he overlooks the obvious fact that historically, as the process of modernization has gathered momentum in the non-West, interest has grown in raising the standard of living for its own sake.

The second reason Spengler gives is more provocative. He expresses his historicist conception of history as a Heraclitean world of constant flux, of mutability. The development of modern science and technology is not merely a reaction to material needs and thus at a certain level rational, as Adam Smith, Marx, and Weber contend. Science and technology are fundamentally cultural products of the West and therefore transitory, like all cultural forms. Thus, despite the spectacular global diffusion of industrial civilization, the possibility that a non-Western people, like the Japanese, can succeed in establishing an enduring modern civilization, is effectively ruled out. No matter with how much virtuosity they imitate the complex civilizational forms of the Occident, they have adopted forms that have virtually completed their process of cultural evolution and are not susceptible to ongoing improvement. They are end forms. "This industrial technology will reach its end with Faustian man and will some day lie demolished and *forgotten*—railroads and steamships just like once the Roman roads and the Great Wall of China, our enormous cities with their skyscrapers in the same way as the palaces of old Memphis and Babylon. The history of this technology is rapidly approaching its ineluctable end. It will be consumed from within, like all great forms of any culture. When and in what way we do not know."[54]

There is a third reason in support of Spengler's thesis of the demise of

54. *MuT*, 61.

the scientific and technological age, despite impressive modernizing efforts in the non-West. The reason is implicitly contained in Spengler's philosophy but not explicitly presented. The highly vulnerable, fragile, globally interdependent nexus of scientific and technological processes and activities may very well disappear amid the cataclysmic disintegration of international political and economic order. The post–Cold War world shows more signs of spiraling downward into the politics of chaos instead of progressing upward to the politics of expanding democratic order, capitalist prosperity, and peace as the crisis of modernity deepens.

Notwithstanding the focus on human evolution and technics, Spengler concludes *Man and Technics* with a romanticized description of the proper ethical stance for denizens of the West to assume, imprisoned as they are in a crisis-ridden civilization. Having experienced Germany's military collapse and socialist revolution, hyperinflation, the onset of economic depression, and social and political turmoil during the Weimar period, Spengler became deeply pessimistic about the future of Germany and the West as a whole, as we will later discuss. The stirring closing lines of *The Decline of the West* sought to inspire its readership to sally forth from the comfort of their studies and accomplish grand civilizational and imperial tasks as dictated by the Zeitgeist. Spengler can now only recommend fatalistic fortitude. *Man and Technics* ends with a macabre death vision. The peoples of the West are enjoined to persevere with heroic tenacity at their "lost posts." They should emulate the Roman soldier who, according to Spengler, remained dutifully on guard at a city gate as the eruption at Vesuvius buried him, along with the city of Pompeii, because his commanders forgot to grant him permission to leave his post.[55]

This distressing death scene strikingly illustrates his deepening pessimism in the interwar years. No longer is a *Realpolitik*, grounded in a philosophy of world history, confidently conceived as aiding visionary statesmen to construct a Western universal empire. The chief function apparently now remaining for *Realpolitik* is to illuminate the necessity for a civilization doomed to destruction to carry out a strategy of protracted siege prolongation against the rising tide of internal chaos and external pressure.

The intellectual community from Spengler's death in 1936 until the mid-1960s, remained virtually completely ignorant of the fact that he had transformed his philosophy of world history. This was not true of some

---

55. *MuT*, 62.

contemporaries who had received complimentary copies of *Man and Technics* directly from its author. Hans Erich Stier, professor of ancient history at Berlin and Münster, enjoyed both professional association as well as friendship with the reclusive private scholar. He was to offer Spengler a forum in the final years of his life for publishing an article extracted from his investigations of prehistory and early civilization in the journal he headed, *Die Welt als Geschichte* (*The World as History*).[56] Stier held Spengler in the highest regard, claiming in 1939 that he had produced a richer and more insightful vision of world history than had any of his most distinguished predecessors in the nineteenth century, including Barthold Niebuhr, Ranke, Droysen, and Meyer. Stier's recognition of a metamorphosis in Spengler's philosophy of world history was recorded in an excursus to an article he published after Spengler's death.

> The actually interesting thing about the little book was the admission that the West European culture was not one among many, but that the path of historical man has reached its climax in her, which at most could still be followed by a "feeble straggler," but not a culture of equal rank, "somewhere on the plain between the Vistula and Amur and in the next millennium." And thus the consequential relativism of *The Decline of the West* was left behind and the old basic idea of a continually running world history, which Spengler had once so vehemently renounced, became once again visible.[57]

Wolf Goetze, author of a dissertation on the historical philosophy of Theodor Lessing and Spengler, also perceived significant changes. Goetze sent a detailed letter concerning this matter to him. Instead of responding in writing to the points Goetze raised, Spengler put him off with a coun-

56. The article in question is "Zur Weltgeschichte des zweiten vorchristlichen Jahrtausends," which appeared in *Die Welt als Geschichte* in 1935. Articles by Spengler that were posthumously published in this journal include "Plan eines neuen Atlas Antiquus," "Altasien: Aufgaben und Methoden," "Das Alter der amerikanischen Kulturen," and "Der Streitwagen und seine Bedeutung für den Gang der Weltgeschichte." All the aforementioned articles were previously published, except for "Altasien." Based on extensive archival material, his sister Hildegard Kornhardt, and his niece, Dr. H. Kornhardt, published also in *Die Welt als Geschichte* a posthumously reconstructed article entitled "Achäerfragen." All the aforementioned articles, with the exception of "Achäerfragen," were reprinted in *RuA*.

57. Hans Erich Stier, "Exkurs: Zur Geschichtsanschauung Oswald Spenglers," excursus of the article, Hans Erich Stier, "Der Aufbau der Weltgeschichte und die Probleme der Zukunft," *Die Welt als Geschichte* 5 (1939): 228–29, 232.

terproposal for a conversation.[58] He stubbornly denied that he had changed his historical philosophy. "I only would like to say to you that, of course, no change has entered into my views on the destiny of high cultures and that the brief arguments in the new book expressly derive from *The Decline of the West*."[59]

Despite its brevity and shortcomings, *Man and Technics* is an important work in the Spengler corpus. It enables the attentive reader to perceive many of the major changes he made in his historical philosophy. Although the little book only outlines broadly his second philosophy of history, we will gain a fuller picture of it when we turn our attention in the next chapter to posthumously published material from the Spengler Archive.

58. Goetze's letter is unfortunately missing; K-Sp, 417 n. 3.
59. Spengler to Goetze, 24 September 1931, *B*, 640.

The Transformation of Spengler's
Philosophy of World History

IN THE TWILIGHT YEARS OF HIS LIFE,
Spengler pursued two related projects. In the second volume of *The Decline of the West*, he had declared his intention to produce a tome on metaphysical questions concerning the human experience of world history.[1]
The second project involved composing a major work on prehistory and
early civilizational history. He aspired to illumine the mysterious origins of
the cultures whose pattern and personalities he had already investigated.
He hoped that these projected works, in combination with *The Decline of
the West*, would constitute a bona fide universal history.

A deterioration in Spengler's health frustrated his parallel-running efforts at completing these projects. He suffered a mild cerebral hemorrhage
in July, 1927, which temporarily impaired his memory and broke his spirit.
A recuperative vacation in Spain led to his recovery the following spring.
Nonetheless, he remained plagued by recurrent health problems until his
death eight years later.[2] Spengler was unfortunately never able to finish
these undertakings, not only because of his stubborn ailments, but more
likely because of the extraordinarily ambitious nature of these twin projects.

Spengler's extensive notes on prehistory, early civilizational history, and
his metaphysical speculations about world history, collated and edited by
Koktanek, were published in the mid-sixties in two separate volumes, *Fundamental Questions* and *Early Period of World History*. Both tomes are
structured in conformance with provisional outlines found in Spengler's
literary estate. His Nietzschean aphoristic reflections and fragmentary
writings on these subjects have been faithfully presented by Koktanek in an

1. *UdA* II, 3 n. 1.
2. K-Sp, 379–80, 389, 395, 423.

accessible format. It appears that Spengler intended these notes to remain aphoristic in style, pithy reflections on prehistorical, early civilizational, and historical-philosophical questions of a more general nature. Despite the unfinished flavor of these twin volumes, these fascinating works, which still await translation into English, command the attention of those who, like their author, ponder the meaning of world history.

In his intellectual odyssey Spengler deepened his pessimism about the nature and direction of history. In 1921 he had protested to his critics that he was not a pessimist. Twelve years later he performed a volte-face, proudly calling his philosophy "*strong* pessimism" and "*brave* pessimism."[3] He also far more closely identifies world history with tragedy than he did in *The Decline of the West*.

The idea that tragedy is a part of historical experience is a commonplace of Western historiography. Yet it is one thing to maintain that tragedy intrudes now and again into the grand sweep of history and quite another to assert that tragedy virtually suffuses history. Spengler is the first thinker to advance the provocative thesis that the whole of human historical experience forms a tragedy of catastrophic proportions. In an age of apocalyptic potential, it would be imprudent to dismiss summarily his philosophy simply because it is unsettling.

That from Germany's cultural soil has sprung a grand vision of the tragedy of world history seems somehow fitting. Tragedy has sadly left its mark on German history more than on that of any other Western nation. And although Spengler died in 1936, before the tragedy of modern German history culminated in the final years of Nazism, he sensed the impending doom more vividly than most of his contemporaries.

In *The Decline of the West* Spengler had boldly designated his comparative historical morphology as the most advanced approach to historical analysis of his era, tantamount to a "*Copernican discovery*." By the time he writes the introduction to one of his final publications, Spengler implies that he has recognized the possibility of surpassing the historical philosophy of his major work. As he observes, "world-historical vision, only emerging among us during the last hundred years, has not yet attained its possible heights."[4]

Underscoring the tragic quality of modern man's interaction with the en-

3. *JdE*, 9, 13.
4. *UdA* I, 23; Oswald Spengler, "Zur Weltgeschichte des zweiten vorchristlichen Jahrtausends," in *RuA*, 159.

vironment is only one of the major differences between the philosophy of history in *The Decline of the West* and the greatly altered philosophy of his late work. He reverses his position on the meaning of history. In attacking the idea of progress, Spengler sought to refute the post-Enlightenment notion that humanity was moving toward a supreme goal, whether it be reason, enlightenment, material advancement, peace, democracy, or what have you. In *The Decline of the West* he took issue with the proposition that world history had any grand or overarching meaning. There was only the sublime "meaninglessness" of an eternal and naturalistic rise and decline. The meaning of history was relativistic and fragmented. It had its locus only within each of the essentially independent cycles of *Kultur* and *Zivilisation*. The late Spengler still considers world history to be composed of distinctive civilizational traditions. Yet he is now convinced that they are ultimately subsumed within the comprehensive and meaningful process of world history itself. History as a whole has meaning.

In studying prehistory and early civilizational history, Spengler contemplates their place in the totality of human existence. He seeks to ascertain the overall pattern of history, the forces that produce it, and the underlying meaning of world history behind the phenomenal façade of historical events. World history, in the narrow sense of the word, encompasses the time span of the high cultures and the preparatory phase, about ten thousand years. Continuing to reject cause-and-effect analysis, Spengler goes further than mainstream German historicism does on the role of intuition in understanding history. He argues that the creative act of immortal poets, like Aeschylus and Shakespeare, in applying poetic insight to explore the human condition can be duplicated in historical philosophy. It is the enormous ambition of this thinker, who composed unfinished historical dramas on Christ, Tiberius, and Napoleon, to be the dramaturge of world history itself. Spengler aspires to achieve full poetic consciousness of the terror and wonder of the entire range of human historical experience. The task of the philosopher of universal history is to capture the greatness and tragedy at the heart of humanity's historical destiny.[5] In a piercing metaphor, he conceptualizes world history as "a great saga of the fortune and end of Icarian man."[6]

In *The Decline of the West*, Spengler drew the distinction between two major periods in world history, that of the high cultures, beginning

5. *FdW*, #8, p. 4.
6. *FdW*, #61, p. 26.

around 3000 B.C., and that of primitive culture or prehistory, which, in his estimation, began with the last Ice Age.[7] In that work he evidenced little curiosity and knowledge about prehistory. "Primitive man has history only in a biological sense," he dogmatically asserted. Moreover, human beings, prior to a cultural cycle, had supposedly wallowed in the "primaeval spiritual condition of an eternal-childlike humanity."[8] This is, to say the least, an unsatisfactory treatment of this vital phase in human cultural development. Nonetheless, Spengler later became one of the first historical philosophers to survey not only recorded history but prehistory as well. His growing conviction that world history formed not a discontinuous but an essentially interconnected and teleological process necessitated a more thorough investigation of the prehistoric and early civilizational basis of subsequent cultural development.

Periods in human cultural development are conventionally classified according to materials and objects collected from archaeological finds. Spengler disapproved of this approach. He maintained that cultural development should be understood instead as a succession of epochs of human spiritual or psychological existence.[9] He now advances a stage theory of history in which mankind traverses four stages of human spiritual or psychological existence and cultural development. They all sequentially unfold after the remote dividing line at which man spiritually emancipated himself from the animal kingdom. The first three periods he had simply lumped together in *The Decline of the West* into one lengthy age of primitive culture. Now he labels them simply "a," "b," and "c," corresponding to the Paleolithic, the Late Paleolithic and Neolithic, and the Late Neolithic and early civilization respectively. Spengler concentrated most of his research effort on the "c" phase of prehistory, which laid the foundation for the early civilizations. The final and fourth stage of world history according to this categorization is that of the high cultures or civilizations. Their typology remains that presented in *The Decline of the West*.

It is beyond the scope of this book to check meticulously the empirical

---

7. *UdA* II, 38, 40. In *The Decline of the West* Spengler normally uses the term *Kultur* to designate what in Anglo-Saxon historiography is typically called a civilization. When he contrasts a *Kultur* with the primitive culture of prehistory, he switches to the term *hohe Kultur* (high culture). In his late work he introduces the term *Hochkultur* (high culture), which is likewise equivalent to the *Kulturen* of his major work. *UdA* I, 23 ff.; *UdA* II, 38; Oswald Spengler, "Plan eines neuen Atlas Antiquus," in *RuA*, 103.

8. *UdA* II, 57; *UdA* I, 142.

9. *FdW*, #67, p. 29, #1, p. 1.

accuracy of Spengler's published writings and extensive notes on prehistory and early civilizational history. Besides, it is more fruitful to focus our attention on the striking changes in his historical philosophy the material reveals. Spengler exhibits here a penchant for evocative nomenclature. He conceives the symbols of lava, crystal, and amoeba to illustrate the character of the prehistoric cultural periods. According to his chronology, the age of lava spans the years from approximately 100,000 to 20,000 B.C. The era of crystal stretches from about 20,000 to circa 6500 B.C., whereas the period of amoebas extends from circa 6500 to around 3000 B.C.[10] The first two periods of primitive culture do not develop organically. Consequently, Spengler assigns them names derived from mineralogy instead of biology. The epoch of "a" culture, or lava, is one of first beginnings. The first humans are dramatically expelled upon the earth's surface like lava in a volcanic eruption. The human psyche then awakens psychologically during the age of "b" culture, or crystal. Man experiences the birth of instinctual comprehension, the transition from formless into form, as light penetrates into the human soul. Next, in the era of "c" culture, this coming-to-consciousness deepens. Man becomes aware of himself as an individual, languages arise, tribes of a couple of thousand people take shape, and collective human enterprise emerges.[11] The "c" cultures participate in, as wandering cultures (*Wanderkulturen*), substantial cross-cultural interaction. Like amoebas, they are extremely mobile, expansive, and flowing. Spengler differentiates between three amoebic cultures, each standing out for its exemplary development in the prehistoric record in comparison with those obscured by the passage of time. He declines to give them geographical names because of their mobility and changing boundaries. Instead, he christens them with colorful names from ancient legend and mythology: Atlantis, Kasch, and Turan. They each have a lifespan of roughly 3,500 years. Just as Spengler emphasized cultural pluralism in the history of civilizations, he underscored, in historicist fashion, cultural variety in prehistory. "But actually, there has never existed a human culture in general, but only independent cultures of individual form, consequently also, at all times, separate developments."[12]

The primitive western culture of Atlantis, a maritime one that built

10. See Koktanek, introduction to *FdW*, ix–x; Koktanek's "Comparative Table of the Four Cultural Stages" (*FdW*, 492–93).
11. Koktanek, introduction to *FdW*, xvi–xvii.
12. *FdW*, #35, p. 217, #41, p. 219, #72, p. 76, #69, p. 30.

megaliths, was centered in Spain, Morocco, and the northern Sahara. It flowed north to Orkney and Denmark, and eastward to Egypt, Sudan, and Akkad.[13] The early southern temple-building culture of Kasch had its center of gravity in the area demarcated by the Persian Gulf, Oman, Baluchistan, and Hyderabad.[14] The primitive northern culture of Turan stretched from Scandinavia to Korea. Turan is the heroic, martial culture of the three, the home of the war-chariot.

The high cultures are organisms like their primitive amoebic progenitors. With their diverse styles of magnificent urban culture, the high cultures are rooted plantlike in a specific geographical area. Atlantis and Kasch fuse to form the origins of the high cultures of Babylon and Egypt.[15] The invasions that took place about 1500 B.C. of the nomadic warriors of Turan, who swept down from the north upon the civilized peoples of Egypt, Minoan Crete, Babylon, the Indus valley, and early China, laid the foundations for the "half-Nordic" Graeco-Roman, Aryan Indian, and Chinese high cultures.[16] Having sketched out Spengler's imaginative portrait of prehistory, we can now consider its philosophical significance. The most important result of his investigation of prehistory is his development of a provocative philosophical anthropology and a tragic teleology of world history.

In his twilight vision of world history, Spengler retains many elements of the theory of cyclically developing cultures from *The Decline of the West*. However, he introduces new ideas that have important consequences for his interpretation of the history of civilizations. Historical philosophers frequently make use of analogies to express their interpretation of the nature of history. Since the analogy was for Spengler the indispensable tool of the historical philosopher, a brief consideration of the analogies he formulated to illustrate his key historical-philosophical ideas will economically capture the nature of the metamorphosis of his philosophy. The prime analogy in *The Decline of the West* is that drawn between a culture and a plant. They each undergo a cyclical process of birth, growth, maturation, and decay. Moreover, like different representatives of the same species of plant following each other in the eternal cycle of nature, cultures do not collectively yield a grander meaning. World history does not manifest a

13. *FdW*, #1, p. 204, #41, p. 219, #52, p. 223.
14. *FdW*, #41, p. 219.
15. *FdW*, #40, p. 219.
16. Spengler, "Zur Weltgeschichte," in *RuA*, 159; Oswald Spengler, "Der Streitwagen und seine Bedeutung für den Gang der Weltgeschichte," in *RuA*, 150–52.

significance transcending the finite life-span of a culture. Furthermore, the analogy has positive overtones. Nature is fecund, life-giving, eternal.

In his late work Spengler came to appreciate fully the self-destructive potential of the unparalleled dynamism, expansionism, and transformative energy of Western civilization. Moreover, as we have seen, he concluded that the tempo of civilizational development in world history accelerates. In the latter stages of his intellectual career, Spengler crafts an arresting analogy to describe world history, capturing these two important ideas. Now the history of civilization is likened to a thoroughly destructive, irreversible, and accelerating process. It is typified by an increasing magnitude of energy and mass and driven toward a terminus, like the natural disaster of an avalanche. "What distinguishes every late and early one [high culture] is the degree of intellectual tension, which leads to catastrophe. The division in life between element and spirit grows. The birth of culture already is accomplished under terrible internal convulsions and everything that emerges in forms, [including] political, religious, and economic, is laden with increasing fatality. It drives something that began around 5000 B.C. toward the end like an avalanche."[17]

The use of the term *catastrophe* above, which in the original Greek means "to overturn," is suggestive. A catastrophe is the concluding event of the dramatic action of a tragedy. As a disastrous ending, it emphasizes finality. The impressive articulation of increasing rationality in human civilization, which mesmerized Kant, Hegel, Marx, and Weber, is overturned in a catastrophic climax. The external, rationalistic expressions of civilization merely masked the underlying irrationalism and destructive vitalism at the heart of human existence. At the end of world history, the comforting illusion of the rationalism of civilizational development collapses under the weight of profound contradictions.

In *The Decline of the West*, Spengler had criticized the traditional modern European understanding of history. History was understood to be progressive. It was neatly divided up into ancient, medieval, and modern phases, leading to a rationally ascertainable end. Spengler's original Heraclitean theory of relatively self-contained, naturalistic historical cycles is, in this context, eminently classical and non-Faustian. With the conceptualization of the sweep of world history, from the beginning around 5000 B.C.

17. *FdW*, #147, p. 485. The analogy between civilizational development and an avalanche is also employed in *Man and Technics*: "The rolling stone approaches in tearing leaps the abyss" (*MuT*, 27).

of a preparatory phase and then on to the rise of the great early civilizations and finally to the modern age, as being comparable to an avalanche, Spengler finally develops a truly Faustian vision. History culminates not in a zenith of progress but in catastrophe.

Spengler's untranslated treatise "Concerning the World History of the Second Millennium Before Christ" sheds additional light on the transformation of his philosophy of world history.[18] He extracted the piece from his major unfinished work on prehistory and early civilizational history and published it in 1935. In this work, he further develops an idea introduced in *The Decline of the West*, that the environmental stimulus of a more rigorous climate exerts a profound impact on cultural development. The notion that a revolutionary new kind of culture might conceivably emerge someday and supersede the high culture as the highest form of human collective existence—a notion that he toyed with in his major work—is abandoned. High cultures are unambiguously the ultimate stage in civilizational development. They are now rather ominously termed "final cultures" (*Endkulturen*). Moreover, Spengler observes in passing that Western culture is "perhaps the final one" in world history. Furthermore, he implicitly retracts his trailblazing, anti-Eurocentric thesis in *The Decline of the West* that each of the eight cultures is of equal cultural significance.

> The second millennium B.C. was *decisive* in the destiny of world-historical man. The old, hot southern cultures, Egypt and Babylon, come to an end. The center of gravity of great events shifts toward the colder, more intense and highly spiritually refined, harder struggling North, and this movement has *continued*. Here, in a colossal sweep from Western Europe up to East Asia, arise inwardly related, new forms of human spirituality, to which the languid world-feeling of the South is foreign. Here one begins to experience life as a riddle, because it is not easy and is not completely self-evident anymore. Thinking, which turns away from proximity and instantaneousness and from directness and immediacy of action, acquires first here a great form. The concerns of life, the deed, become more important than mere physical existence. And now the feeling and reflection of the individual is directed toward the deed. Upon this foundation, in struggle against that older world-feeling, there arise next to each other the Graeco-Roman, Indian, and Chinese high cultures, all three half-Nordic, more individualistic, more domineering, grappling with more profound experiences, proud of these ex-

18. "Zur Weltgeschichte des zweiten vorchristlichen Jahrtausends," in *RuA*.

periences instead of avoiding them, but in the South burning oneself out in the southern climate.[19]

In this passage Spengler reevaluates the ethos of Graeco-Roman culture. In *The Decline of the West* he attempted to overcome European intellectuals' celebration of the classical world by drawing a brilliant yet exaggerated portrait of antiquity, undervaluing its individualistic, creative qualities. He now properly attributes a greater sense of individualism and creative energy to the classical world. Apollonian culture is promoted to the rank of "half-Nordic," whereas Egypt and Babylon are demoted to "the languid world-feeling of the South." This reappraisal of the ethos of these high cultures smooths the way for his formulation of an upward-spiraling model of civilizational development.

In his second philosophy of world history, Spengler has enriched his evaluation of the human condition. He now describes the entirety of man's historical existence as profoundly tragic. The history of mankind is merely an episode in the destiny of the world, an idea foreshadowed in his main work. The brief history of the high cultures constitutes no longer a discontinuous series of unrelated scenes but the final act in the epic tragedy of mankind. "[Man] is an element of all-living nature that rises in rebellion against nature. He will pay for this defiance with his life. Through this act of defiance man distinguishes himself from all other living things, which as pure nature are blended into the tapestry of the natural universe. [Mankind] is the hero of this tragedy, [world history] the final act of the tragedy itself."[20]

Spengler sketches out a provocative philosophical anthropology. Man rises in defiance of the natural world because of a primordial contradiction in his makeup. He is animated with the spirit of a proud beast of prey (*Herrentier*), like that of an "eagle, lion, [or] tiger." Yet he is distinguished by a degree of physical weakness on a par with that of an animal comprising the prey of carnivores (*Beutetier*). This constitutional incongruity is the source of his tragedy. Primitive man finds himself in a condition of relative corporeal "powerlessness," which contrasts sharply with his high intellectual aptitude. Through civilizational development, man strives to resolve this existential dilemma. He compensates for his physical weakness and vulnerability by cultivating and using his powerful intellect.

19. Spengler, "Zur Weltgeschichte," in *RuA*, 158–59.
20. *UdA* II, 32; *Ufr*, #1, p. 337.

"The entire existence of the human race is [directed toward] the overcoming of its powerlessness." Thus, culture is not the harmonious teleological end of history as Kant had sanguinely speculated but "the weapon of the weak against nature."[21]

The progressive bias in Darwin's theory of human evolution aroused Spengler's opposition. In his writings on prehistory and early civilization, he envisions man as being something more than merely the highest stage in the conflictual but ultimately progressive Darwinian process of evolution. Thus, Spengler sees man as not being driven to engage merely in a Darwinian struggle for existence. Possessing more significance than that, life responds to an inner spiritual directedness. Man in his interchange with nature seeks not merely the perpetuation of existence but the achievement of victory (*Siegen*): "*The soul strives to shape the world.*"[22]

The subjugation of nature is an act of hubris with grave implications for man.[23] The technics, which his intellect allows him to develop and refine, are not enduring triumphs of rationality. Technics are counternatural Promethean means that ineluctably lead to man's destruction. It is the great irony of world history that man's intellectual and creative powers are the source of both his transitory glory and his downfall. Man is a proud beast of prey (*Raubtier*) who regards the natural environment as his booty and assaults it. Man "climbed high" but "ends so tragically."[24]

The history of mankind is rapidly approaching its ineluctable end. "Man is an episode, a moment in the destiny of the world. The greatest part of the tragedy of culture is already past. The end dawns." In *Man and Technics*, Spengler, who had intermittently dabbled in playwriting throughout his life, employs metaphors drawn from the milieu of theater. The three stages of prehistory and the fourth stage of civilizational history reach a dramatic finale in the modern age. He assigns the time when he is writing, the 1930s, to the start of the fifth act. The unfolding denouement brings to a dramatic conclusion the four stages of world history. "We stand today at the climax, there, where the fifth act begins. The final decisions will be reached. The tragedy comes to a close."[25]

The "heaven-storming" cultures raise man to a pinnacle where he ex-

---

21. *Ufr*, #19, p. 343, #22, p. 344, # 21, pp. 343–44.
22. *Ufr*, #88, p. 27.
23. *FdW*, #8, p. 4.
24. *Ufr*, #21, #19, p. 343.
25. *Ufr*, #43, p. 350; *MuT*, 52.

periences the extreme consciousness of tragedy.[26] In modernity's twilight the black storm clouds of world history ominously billow on the brooding horizon. A searing moment of lucidity is granted so that man may comprehend the terribleness of his fate. "What distinguishes culture and high culture altogether is the greatness of man. The height and depth of the soul grows in desire and in suffering up to the high noon of world history in the onset of heroism. The great cultures are [history's] battles: [we mistake them for] victories until the redness of sunset and then the look over the battlefield into the terrible in vain of it all."[27]

In this tragic and irresolvable struggle between civilized man and nature, he brings about an ecological catastrophe, mutilating the earth from which he sprang. "Higher man is a tragedy. With his graves he leaves behind the earth a battlefield and wasteland. He has drawn plant and animal, the sea and mountain into his decline. He has painted the face of the world with blood, deformed and mutilated it. But there was greatness in it. When he is no more, his destiny will have been something great."[28]

Spengler now argues that the will to power suffuses the entirety of civilizational development. "The tragedy of human will [constitutes] the imperative of [man's] entire existence until the end."[29] However, the will to power is most powerfully expressed in the Faustian West. The Occident is the creator of modern science and technology and of a politically and economically interdependent world. It is not only the greatest of all civilizations but the last great one of world history.

Spengler's concern with the meaning of world history had important consequences for his earlier views on cross-cultural influences. World history retains certain cyclical qualities for the late Spengler. Its final stage, that of the high cultures examined in his main work, still manifests phases of cyclically developing *Kultur* and *Zivilisation*. However, he evidences a willingness to drop his controversial claim that cross-cultural influences are not of major importance in world history. Indeed, in an unpublished note, West European culture is now acknowledged to be a synthesis indebted to its predecessors. "During the golden age of classical literature, the Teutons had only hunted and worn animal skins. A culture is actually a synthesis of several cultures."[30] Unfortunately, Spengler never goes ahead and really develops this idea of a high culture as the product of cultural synthesis.

26. *Ufr*, 360.
27. *FdW*, #70, p. 30.
28. *FdW*, #20, p. 9.
29. *FdW*, #132, p. 480.
30. Politica II, 84, Lld.

The late Spengler conceives of world history as having an overarching line of development spanning the individual cultures. The plurality of high cultures in *The Decline of the West* is emplaced within a larger framework in which world history forms, to a large degree, a unified process. The emergence of high culture as a stage in civilizational development was a mere accident in his main work. Now, it is a necessary act in the awesome spectacle of man's alienation from nature and his revolt against it. In his late work, Spengler retains his basic pattern of cycles of cultures. Yet instead of merely existing autonomously and in a more or less random sequence, they combine to form a pattern. Integrating the two historical-philosophical paradigms of *The Decline of the West* and his late work, he emerges with an upward-spiraling model of world history that climaxes in catastrophe. The future, according to our Cassandra, holds not merely the end of civilization as we know it but probably the end of any form of fully developed civilization at all. World history is characterized by an accelerating tempo of development, an increase in the dimensions of the catastrophe, and a tragic intensification of human consciousness. Thus, the decline of the West is no longer to be understood as merely an isolated event, as an impressive, macrohistorical phenomenon to be sure but one without earth-shaking ramifications for the course of world history. The decline of the West is its ultimate phase.

This profound change in his thought enabled Spengler to jettison finally a significant and implausible feature of his early philosophy of history. I am referring to the notion that the successor culture to the West, that of Russia, would in a vaguely described manner reject the scientific and technological obsession of the modern West and create a nonscientifically and nontechnologically oriented culture. "The Russian looks with fear and hatred upon this tyranny of wheels, pulleys and rails, and if he yields today and tomorrow to necessity, yet he will one day *strike all of that from his memory and his environment* and build an entirely different world around himself, in which nothing of this devilish technology exists."[31] While it is conceivable that the decline of the West could be followed by a high culture with a comparatively primitive science and technology, virtually all contemporary societies are attempting to adopt Western science and technology. I believe Spengler was initially constrained to defend this curious position because of his thesis that each culture had its own distinctive ethos. Consequently, modern science and technology, hallmarks of

31. *UdA* II, 626 n. 1.

Western civilization, had to disappear with the demise of the culture that gave birth to them. Such a position is unconvincing. Western science and technology are of great utility in the struggle for power among states and in satisfying human material needs.

Not surprising, Spengler eventually revisits this question. He retains the plausible thesis that Western science and technology are materialistic, mechanistic, and utilitarian manifestations of the dynamism and trans-formative energy of the West and could only be conceivably created by such a culture. Yet now he conceives man's struggle with the natural environment, from his earliest origins to the modern age, as forming an integrated process in which man attempts to reshape nature through the refinement of his technics. His treatment of the future of technology is transformed into a profound analysis in *Man and Technics* because of two significant arguments. Spengler is perhaps the first thinker in the Western intellectual tradition to advance the controversial but plausible thesis that industrial civilization is incompatible with the environment. Man "plunders," "rapes," "poisons," and "mutilates" nature through modern scientific and technological processes.[32] In addition, he advances the vaguely formulated, yet nonetheless powerful, historical-philosophical idea that modern man may very well destroy himself through his technology. Indeed, the destruction of human civilization is seen as being perhaps, at one and the same time, the ineluctable consequence of the terrible process by which the most dynamic culture that has ever existed will perish and, in a larger sense, the ultimate expression of the telos of world history.

Spengler was ambiguous about whether or not the end of modern civilization would be tantamount to the demise of mankind. At times he uses language that conveys the image of the approaching end of world history as a distinct possibility, more often as an inexorable outcome. At a minimum, our Cassandra does maintain that it is quite possible that the decline of the West represents no longer the isolated decline of a great culture but the ultimate phase in world history and the destruction of civilization as we know it. In retrospect, his ambiguity is unintentionally well-grounded, for the reason that if modern civilization suffers devastation with the eventual breakdown of international order, it is eminently possible that a new civilization, however deformed, may emerge phoenixlike from the ashes of the old. At one point in his contemplation of the end of civilized man, which one shouldn't forget he engaged in before the dawn of the nuclear

32. See *MuT*, 48, 34, 55; *FdW*, #20, p. 9.

age, Spengler speculates that the world could witness a return to the very low population levels of prehistoric times.[33] However, he does unequivocally indicate that he believes that the great line of accelerated civilizational development, stretching from the southern civilizations of Egypt and Babylon to the northern, "harder-struggling" Graeco-Roman world and the West will be brought to a close in the chaos of the decline of Western civilization.[34]

Spengler has come to see Western culture, the most northern one, as the most advanced that has ever existed and will ever exist yet not in terms of shallow, utilitarian, and materialistic criteria but in terms of the extraordinary and tragic intensification of human spiritual and mental refinement. His philosophy of world history in the twilight of his life is a remarkable vision of tragedy. The line of civilizational development in world history soars upward, spiral-like, striving to reach ever higher levels of spiritual and mental refinement (*Durchgeistigung*), until the crescendo disintegrates in an apocalyptic finale. The greatness of man resides not in his purported capacity to use his intellectual abilities to form enduring "rational" modalities of civilization. His greatness lies in his transitory, Nietzschean, heroic experience of extreme vitalism and creativity.

In *The Decline of the West*, Spengler went too far. He overreached himself in his daring effort to discredit the widely accepted idea that world history was largely a linear process of exceptional progress. In his later work, he recaptures the idea that he originally negated, that world history does have an interconnectedness and a grand line of development. Simultaneously, he deepens his pessimism about history.

Tragedy is the leitmotif of Spengler's daemonic ring cycle of world history. Since conflict and suffering form indispensable elements of tragedy, tragic compositions are cultural products of the harder-struggling, deed-oriented northern cultures. "There is a Nordic world-feeling—stretching from England to Japan—full of joy especially at the severity of the human destiny. One defies it in order to conquer it. One proudly goes to ruin if destiny proves itself to be stronger than one's own will. Such was the outlook in the old, genuine parts of the Mahabharata, which told of the struggle between the Kurus and Pandus, in Homer, Pindar, and Aeschylus, in the Germanic epic poetry and in Shakespeare, in many songs of the Chinese Shuking, and in circles of the Japanese samurai."[35]

33. *FdW*, #80, p. 34.
34. *MuT*, 44.
35. *JdE*, 13.

In *The Decline of the West* Spengler differentiated between what he regarded as the Greek and what he regarded as the West European understanding of tragedy. In the Hellenic world, tragedy was seen as a cruel expression of fate, an accident, and in the West European tradition it is viewed as the necessary developmental expression of an individual's personality. His embrace of the concept of tragedy in his twilight years illustrates how he visualizes the tragic dissolution of world-historical man not to be the result of a mere accident of history (the contemporary mind might think in this connection of the accidental outbreak of nuclear war). Instead, man's ruin is the ineluctable consequence of his existential dilemma, played out in the process of civilizational development.

Hellenic and West-European culture brought tragedy to its highest level of artistic excellence. Spengler singles out Aeschylus and Shakespeare as preeminent tragedians whose works captured much of the tragic nature of world history. However, because of the phenomenal dynamism of Western civilization, which has exacerbated the tensions in the historical process in the last two centuries and converted the entirety of the earth's surface into their immense stage, the tragedy of Western man is greater than what Aeschylus and Shakespeare ever summoned forth from their poetic consciousnesses.[36]

Despite his failure to write a world history that spanned all of human historical experience, Spengler has succeeded in evoking a bold vision of world history. He has given us the dramatic plot, the spirit of the tragedy, and an incomplete, rough framework of acts and scenes. A true history of the world that examines in detail man's climb from his prehistoric origins through various forms of civilizational experience to the twentieth century of crisis and beyond exceeds perhaps the ability of any scholar working individually.

Klemens von Klemperer observed that Spengler, who was born in central Germany, the birthplace of many outstanding German mystics and romantics, "was himself possibly the greatest mystic of modern Germany."[37] Indeed, his twilight vision of world history is mystically articulated in evocative, metaphorical language and provocative analogies.

Spengler's vision of world history as apocalyptic stands in opposition to the image of history and man's future advanced by various luminaries in

---

36. *FdW*, #8, p. 4; *MuT*, 52.
37. Klemens von Klemperer, *Germany's New Conservatism: Its History and Dilemma in the Twentieth Century* (Princeton: Princeton Univ. Press, 1968), 170.

German intellectual history. Kant speculated that history was providentially guided in a grand teleological process. He optimistically believed that man would create stable conditions for the further progress of enlightenment. History would culminate in the advance of culture, democracy, and world peace. Not to be outdone, Marx sanguinely prophesied for the West, after the trials of proletarian revolution, the triumph of socialism, the withering away of the state, and ultimately world peace. Weber was somewhat more restrained in his optimism. Yet he refrained, unlike Spengler, from placing at the centerpiece of his philosophy of history the idea of the tragic nature of human existence, instead maintaining that the advance of human rationality forms the overarching theme of world history.

Hegel's philosophy also offers an interesting contrast with the late Spengler. For Hegel, world history is the triumphant march of the World Spirit (*Weltgeist*); for the late Spengler, it is the march of the World Will (*Weltwille*), the tragic, irrational odyssey of the human will toward catastrophe. Whereas for Hegel the rationality of history increases as the drama of world history progresses from east to west, the irrationalism of world history deepens for Spengler as its theater of action moves from south to north. "The human will (of high cultural man), led by his thinking, imagines to be able to form the world according to his ideals—that is optimism. But history realizes itself completely independently of our wishes and desires. We think in one way, and the World Will [*Weltwille*] in us drives otherwise."[38]

Spengler's vision of history is deeper and more tragic than that of Schopenhauer, who rejected the historicist insight into the central importance of history for understanding the human condition. The manifestations of the will in the phenomenal world do not achieve an endpoint in Schopenhauer's philosophy; world history is not catastrophic. His view of the flow of history is one of an unending continuum of time as it was later for Nietzsche, who taught the eternal return. Schopenhauer maintains that historical time is "infinite" in its reach backward, extending to an "infinite future."[39] According to Spengler, man's will, his instinctual energy, powers world history toward its ineluctable end.

Nietzsche's pessimism approximates most closely Spengler's. Yet his du-

---

38. *Ufr*, #39, p. 349.
39. Arthur Schopenhauer, *Die Welt als Wille und Vorstellung*, vol. II, *Sämtliche Werke*, ed. Wolfgang Frhr. von Löhneysen (Darmstadt: Wissenschaftliche Buchgesellschaft, 1968), 566.

bious notions of eternal return and the superman are sonorous strains of hopefulness absent from Spengler's catastrophic tone poem of the end of civilized man. Nietzsche idealistically strove to become "the physician of culture," reinvigorating the decadent West with new tellurian values. Spengler, more unswerving in his realism than Nietzsche, was impelled toward a deeper and deeper vision of cultural pessimism.

With his historicist commitment to history as the indispensable foundation of a modern world view, Spengler, far from being Nietzsche's epigone as is often asserted, succeeds in going beyond him.[40] He brings the grand tradition of German cultural pessimism to a thundering Wagnerian conclusion. He gives to the philosophy of Nietzsche what it lacked most, a grand historical-philosophical perspective and systematization, liberates it from the dubious aforementioned qualities of hopefulness, and brings to full consciousness, in a magisterial manner, the catastrophic qualities of the will to power in world history as both a civilizational and international political force.

Spengler's reflections on world history constitute a masterful, two-stage critique of the idea of progress. This problematic thesis virtually dominated modern Western historical thought before World War I, succeeding, for the most part, in drowning out the occasional dissenting voices of Vollgraff, Lasaulx, Burckhardt, and Brooks and Henry Adams. In *The Decline of the West*, Spengler critiqued the idea of progress by advancing a model of essentially independent civilizations undergoing a cycle of rise and decline. However, he overreached himself in his daring effort to discredit the widely accepted thesis of historical progress by denying the elements of civilizational continuity that do exist and the consciousness of the onward driving power of world history, which has become a fundamental part of the Western historical outlook since the Enlightenment. In his late work Spengler recaptures the idea that he originally negated, that world history, despite its cultural pluralism and complexity, may be profitably conceived as a largely interrelated series of events. Yet he simultaneously markedly improves his critique of the idea of progress. No longer relying exclusively on the traditional argument of civilizational decline, he ingeniously fashions a vision of world history as a largely integrated, upward-spiraling process climaxing in catastrophe.

40. See, in this regard, the section "Spengler als Epigone Nietzsches" in Detlef Felken, *Oswald Spengler: Konservativer Denker zwischen Kaiserreich und Diktatur* (Munich: C. H. Beck, 1988), 164–69.

Of course, Spengler's historical pessimism is not immune to criticism. The stance he recommends that the individual should adopt in a tragic world is a case in point. He maintains that the man of worth seeks the path of glory as did the noble Achilles, who refused a long and tranquil life bereft of heroic achievement. Spengler projects this image upon the entirety of world history. Man, despite the fact that he is doomed as a collectivity to failure and ruin, is great because he dares to accomplish much. However, an Achilles heel renders his line of reasoning vulnerable to sharp criticism. Man's greatness requires historical consciousness. In this way, the memory of epic struggle in the face of the tragic conditions of life can be preserved. Yet once world history achieves its dramatic climax and man vanishes from the stage, does he remain of heroic proportions when the consciousness of his greatness is obliterated? Spengler fails to address the Wittgensteinian dilemma of whether the existence of tragic greatness requires a human ear to hear the lines of epic verse celebrating heroic deeds mellifluously recited by the blind bard.

If Spengler had given appropriate emphasis in his cosmology of historical philosophy not only to the agonistic qualities of man but to his solidaristic ones as well, his vision of the tragedy of world history would have been richer. His extremely one-sided stress on the primacy of struggle in world history lacks balance. He ignores the very real positive social qualities of human beings, which numerous thinkers properly view as fundamental features of mankind. Indeed, it is precisely because man frequently behaves as a social and loving creature instead of as a mere "beast of prey" that his inability to extricate himself from what may ultimately prove to be the runaway locomotive of self-destructive civilizational development is freighted with such gripping pathos.[41] The tragedy of man, in its world-historical dimensions, would be far more bearable than it actually is if he were merely a beast of prey, as Spengler relentlessly hammers home. Nonetheless, even if one accepts the proposition that man in the course of world history evidences both a conflictual as well as a cooperative side in his behavior, it is quite possible that the conflictual side, manifested in the struggle between classes, between nations and states, and between man and nature, is ultimately of greater weight in determining man's fate.

The preceding analysis of the metamorphosis of Spengler's philosophy

41. Metz touches on this theme as well. See Karl H. Metz, "Faust und Chronos: Das Problem der Technik in der Zivilisationstheorie Oswald Spenglers," *Archiv für Kulturgeschichte* 75, no. 1 (1993): 170.

of world history shows how he underwent an odyssey from an amalgam of pessimism and optimism in *The Decline of the West* to the deep, unadulterated pessimism of his twilight years. Spengler's original position, as elaborated in *The Decline of the West*, displays both optimistic and pessimistic features. On the one hand, his vision of the decline of the West certainly has a pessimistic quality in that he prophesies the demise of the modern world. On the other hand, the nonapocalyptic and cyclical qualities of his vision of the decline of the West express compensatory optimism. A new culture, that of Russia, will rise to replace a moribund West. World history moves on majestically in cyclical fashion. Moreover, although modern technology will have permanently altered the face of the earth after the West has disappeared as a civilizational force, Spengler does not initially consider it as endangering the global environment. His original vision of transformation in international politics is pessimistic in that it foresees the eruption of a terrible struggle for global hegemony and the eventual collapse of the West as a result of decadence and external pressure. Yet it is optimistic from a Germanocentric perspective. For Germany will be the architect of a Pax Germanica. The philosophy of world history Spengler expressed in his late work is uncompromisingly pessimistic. He envisions the apocalyptic end of modern civilization through irresistible historical forces.

By virtue of the transformation of his philosophy of world history, Spengler has illuminated what may ultimately prove to be the awful blackness of the demise of modern civilization. In a century compelled to be more conscious of the ofttimes irrational nature of historical forces by the hammer blows of two world wars, genocide, and global economic depression and the specters of nuclear annihilation and global ecological crisis, his vision of world history is a powerful one and of great timeliness despite the relative obscurity to which the dictates of academic fashion have condemned it. Given that historical pessimists, including Vollgraff, Lasaulx, Burckhardt, and Brooks and Henry Adams, treated the civilizational crisis of the West in the less drastic categories of decline, decadence, sterility, and exhaustion, Spengler merits recognition as the first historical pessimist of the modern West to conceive of world history in truly apocalyptic terms. The accelerating process of civilizational development spanning the end of the last Ice Age around 9000 B.C. to the global diffusion of modern Western civilization in the twenty-first century may eventually reveal itself to be, not a wonderful and reassuring tale of human progress, but a movement perversely comparable to an avalanche driven toward a cataclysmic terminus. The proliferation of weapons of mass destruction; the threat of the breakdown of the global economy; the widening North-South development gap and the ongoing population explosion in many parts of the developing world; the global environmental crisis; and the ineradicability of cultural, ethnic, and nationalist conflict around the globe: Taken together, these potential dangers to world order might someday herald the end of history in a profoundly irrational, Spenglerian sense. Modernity may prove to be, not the vestibule of a new age of global peace and prosperity as Toynbee desperately hoped, for it is only under such conditions that mankind can perhaps negotiate the obstacle-laden passageway through this new millennium, but instead the exit chamber from the laboratory of the "failed" experiment of man that discourse with Spengler strongly suggests.

Spengler and the Approaching Second World War

AMID THE TURBULENCE OF THE INTER-
war years Spengler conceived his catastrophic vision of world history. His
interest in politics had subsided with the Weimar Republic's stabilization
in 1924. That same year he abandoned his political ambitions and rededi-
cated himself to scholarship. However, the world economic crisis, signaled
by the New York stock market crash in October, 1929, swept over Germany in the winter. Mounting economic hardship destabilized the Weimar
democracy. The *Reichstag* elections of September, 1930, catapulted the
Nazis overnight from the political fringe to center stage; they were now
the second most powerful political party in Germany. These stunning
events had restimulated in one stroke Spengler's dormant interest in politics. To be sure, his interest in domestic and international politics remains,
in comparison with the early twenties, theoretical. He does not aspire to
hold a political office or position.[1]

Roderich Schlubach, a prominent member of the business establishment in Hamburg, belonged to Spengler's circle of friends. At his invitation Spengler delivered a lecture, entitled "Germany in Danger"
("Deutschland in Gefahr"), in the port city to guests of the Patriotic Society on March 2, 1930, at the Overseas Club.[2] In November, 1932, he
brought out a new book, *Political Writings*, a compilation of lectures and
previously published political works. The preface to this volume resounds
with Spengler's imperious tone. He audaciously claims that in his analysis
of major political and economic issues over the years, he has "not erred in
any essential point." Spengler voices disdain for ideological utopias and

1. K-Sp, 413.
2. K-Sp, 391–92.

optimistic programs. He stresses his commitment to communicating the hard facts of politics. As speculation was mounting in the early thirties that Hindenburg would call on Hitler to form a government, Spengler pointedly observes that he does not see a future leader for Germany on the political scene. He criticizes the fanatical passion of young Germans for the colorful fanfare of Nazism in an era of growing dangers in world politics for the German ship of state. "Things are bad on a ship when the crew is intoxicated during a storm," Spengler warns. What Germany needs, he declares, are "statesmen, not party leaders and fanatics for a Third Reich."[3]

Another book soon followed. Spengler finally expanded the Hamburg lecture into a volume entitled *Years of Decision: Germany and the World-Historical Development*.[4] His last book, which addresses political matters, was published in August of 1933, which was the fateful year of Hitler's rise to power and three years before Spengler's untimely death. The book constitutes a tragic twilight chapter to the life and work of this unusual thinker. Instead of the idealistic synthesis of Prussianism and socialism that he had first preached for Germany in his book by that very title, a vulgar, terrorizing, racist mass movement headed by a plebian leadership was extending its domination over German civil society. The resumption of conflict between the Anglo-Saxon world and Germany for global hegemony and the potential aggravation of the Russian danger to the West, which Spengler had prophesied in 1920 in *Prussianism and Socialism*, were to become historical reality. The United States helped to turn the tide against Germany in World War II and established the *imperium Americanum*. Hitler's bold gamble to hammer together the *imperium Germanicum* ended in the rubble of his Berlin bunker. The German Caesar, who Spengler had foretold in 1920 would someday dominate German politics, turned out to resemble Nero more than Augustus.

Spengler's final political work was widely read and sparked much controversy. Initially more copies were sold than had been the case with his previous bestseller, the first volume of *The Decline of the West*. Within a mere ten weeks of its appearance, 100,000 copies of *Years of Decision* were printed. Although ever mindful of the danger of censorship, the aspiring

3. *PSch*, v, x, xi.
4. The title was translated by Charles Francis Atkinson as *The Hour of Decision*. See Oswald Spengler, *The Hour of Decision, Part I: Germany and World-Historical Evolution*, trans. Charles Francis Atkinson (New York: Knopf, 1934).

236 / *Prophet of Decline*

praeceptor Germaniae advances in this work a politically courageous criticism of the Nazi leadership. Indeed, *Years of Decision* is one of the few regime-critical works and the most sensational to appear during the Third Reich.[5]

Spengler criticizes the racial ideology of the Nazi party and its anti-Semitism. He boldly dismisses the idea of a Third Reich as an "'Aryan' utopian vision." Furthermore, he voices severe anxiety that the foreign policy skills of the Nazi leadership, which under Hitler aspired to found a millennial empire, were deficient and would lead Germany to disaster. To the indignation of Nazi ideologues, such as Alfred Baeumler, who along with others launched a polemical assault against *Years of Decision*, published the very year that the Nazi movement noisily celebrated its triumphal rise to power, "neither the name Hitler nor the words National Socialism appear in this book." Instead, adding insult to injury, in a daring affront to the Führer and his cronies, Spengler characterizes Germany as "a nation without leaders and weapons."[6]

It is difficult to give a balanced evaluation of Spengler's critical stance toward Nazism because of his intransigent opposition to Versailles and the Weimar Republic. The common ground shared by him and the Nazis, notwithstanding the significant differences that made collaboration impossible for Spengler, was the antagonism of the brown revolution to the two principal objects of his loathing, the Versailles Treaty and the Weimar regime. In this context, one must interpret, yet certainly not condone, the fact that he voted twice for the Nazis apparently out of what his biographer refers to as "tactical reasons." Moreover, this was certainly not done without mixed feelings. As Spengler caustically remarked after casting his ballot for Hitler in the second presidential election of April 10, 1932, "Hitler is an idiot, but one must support the movement."[7] It should be noted that the word *movement* refers not to the Nazi movement as such but to the broader, right-wing national movement against the Weimar Republic, of which Nazism was, to be sure, the driving force after its electoral success of September, 1930.

5. Detlef Felken, *Oswald Spengler: Konservativer Denker zwischen Kaiserreich und Diktatur* (Munich: C. H. Beck, 1988), 195.

6. *JdE*, 3; Alfred Baeumler, quoted in Clemens Vollnhals, "Oswald Spengler und der Nationalsozialismus," *Jahrbuch des Instituts für deutsche Geschichte* 13 (1984): 283; *JdE*, 56.

7. K-Sp, 435, 427.

Spengler had a private talk with Hitler in Hitler's Bayreuth quarters on July 25, 1933, during the annual Wagner festival. The meeting had been arranged by an intermediary. Spengler did not revise his very low opinion of the Führer's potential as a statesman after the one-and-a-half-hour discussion. Ernst Hanfstaengl, the German-American chief of Nazi foreign press relations until 1936 and a friend of Spengler, had attempted for a long time to arrange the meeting. Hanfstaengl summarized the private conversation in his memoirs. "Hitler criticized in Spengler the fundamental conservative stance and the failure to recognize the significance of the race issue, while Spengler expressed to me completely undisguised his contempt for Hitler. He is a fantasizer, a numbskull who is wedded to [Alfred] Rosenberg's myth." According to the diary of Spengler's sister Hildegard, his reaction was not as negative as Hanfstaengl noted. Although Spengler was certainly unimpressed by Hitler, he added, "but he wants something and he does something and one can say something to him." Interestingly, in further remarks recorded by his sister, he more clearly showed that he did not share the feeling of many contemporaries that a powerful magnetism emanated from Hitler's personality. On the contrary, some time after the meeting he is reputed to have remarked, "When one sits across from him, one does not have even one single time the feeling that he is significant."[8]

In his private papers, Spengler's criticism of Hitler and Nazism is understandably both more personal and more biting than that which he dared to set forth in *Years of Decision*. He condemns Nazi terrorism and its aim of perpetuating totalitarian rule. "Only through continuous murder [can] the domination over the Germans be maintained." He lambastes Hitler's personality as "a lot of talk, incapable, externally shallow, internally empty." Spengler denies that the Führer can ever become a competent statesman: "Who has grown up in the dumb and dirty atmosphere of agitation—public meetings and editing, is once and for all spoiled in being a *statesman*." The anti-Semitism of Nazi ideology is psychoanalyzed as compensating for an innate sense of inferiority. "And how much envy of the capability of other people in view of one's own lack of it lies hidden in anti-Semitism!" Moreover, the persecution of German Jewry is a self-

8. Ernst Hanfstaengl, *Zwischen Weißem und Braunem Haus: Memoiren eines politischen Außenseiters* (Munich: Piper, 1970), 281; Hildegard Kornhardt Diaries, quoted in K-Sp, 441.

inflicted wound on German society. "When one would rather destroy business and scholarship than see Jews in them, one is an ideologue, *i.e.*, a *danger* for the nation. Idiotic."[9]

Spengler's concern that his political writings would be suppressed was justified. The patent anti-Nazi qualities and commercial success of *Years of Decision* provoked official condemnation of the book as an anti-revolutionary tract, the forbidding of the mention of Spengler's name in the press, and measures to stop the sale of the book. Not surprising, under such adverse conditions, he abandoned his original intention of writing a second part to *Years of Decision*. As Spengler explained in response to inquiries about the projected sequel, "[I] do not write books for confiscation." Joseph Goebbels, whom he had boldly slighted, was the source of his difficulties. Goebbels had sought to win the support of leading conservative opponents of the defunct Weimar Republic for the fledgling Nazi regime. However, the propaganda minister's courting of Spengler had gone awry. In March, 1933, Spengler declined Goebbels' invitation to deliver a radio speech on "the day of Potsdam." This propaganda event symbolically celebrated the reconciliation of traditional Prussia with the Nazi movement two days before the crucial vote on the notorious Enabling Act (whose passage surrendered the authority of the *Reichstag* to Hitler with his dictatorial ambitions). A theatrically staged handshake between Hitler and Hindenburg was arranged at the gravesite of Frederick the Great. In the fall of 1933, Spengler again refused to give the victorious brown revolution a Prussian stamp of approval. He rejected Goebbels' request to prepare a short essay endorsing Hitler in the upcoming November, 1933, plebiscite for his ministry to distribute through Nazi press channels. As Spengler wrote Goebbels, "I have never taken part until now in electoral propaganda and I will also not do it in the future."[10] In resisting Nazi overtures to lend ideological support to the regime in exchange for a share of the public limelight, Spengler, a highly principled man, after publishing *Years of Decision* retired dejectedly to political limbo. He devoted himself again to the study of prehistory and early civilizational history. However, he did occasionally pen notes for the originally projected second volume of *Years of Decision*, which would have been obviously impossible to publish under the circumstances.

9. Politica I, 75, G1–99; Politica I, 54, B3–46; Politica II, 131, B3–65; Politica I, 54, B3–63; Politica II, 131, B3–150.

10. K-Sp, 454; Spengler to Goebbels, 3 November 1933, *B*, 710.

The thirties brought to Spengler not only Nazi censure of *Years of Decision* but recognition by the German intellectual community.[11] In June, 1933, he declined the offer of a professorial chair and the prestigious directorship of the University of Leipzig's Institute for Cultural and Universal History, which had been founded by Karl Lamprecht. Shortly thereafter, he turned down an offer of a professorship by the University of Marburg. In September, 1933, he was honored with membership in the Senate of the German Academy. Yet these welcome events did not diminish his preoccupation with the deepening tragedy of his fatherland, which remained a leitmotif of the final years of his life. Hitler's brutal eradication of the leadership of the *Sturmabteilung* (Nazi storm troopers) and several conservative opponents of the regime in the notorious Night of the Long Knives in June, 1934, prompted Spengler to divorce himself completely from the brown revolution. Potentially compromising correspondence was destroyed. Friends advised him to travel abroad or to emigrate; he refused to leave his beloved homeland. The following year Spengler resigned his position on the board of directors of the Nietzsche Archive, an honor conferred upon him in 1923. He was appalled at the manipulation of Nietzsche's ideas into ideological support of Nazism.[12]

Unlike opportunistically minded conservatives, Spengler refused to collaborate with the Nazis. However, the question of whether he was a precursor of or ideological groundbreaker for Nazism is another matter. Ideologically, opposition on the right to the Weimar Republic had crystallized around the twin poles of the Nazis and the luminaries of the so-called conservative revolution: Spengler, Moeller van den Bruck, Jünger, Schmitt, Freyer, and Niekisch. In the early thirties, fundamental differences existed between many of Spengler's political ideas and those of Hitler. Spengler's somber vision of the inevitability of German cultural and societal decline fueled his unconcealed scorn for the millenarianism of Nazism. Like Heidegger, he unequivocally rejected the tenets of racism and anti-Semitism in Nazi ideology. Unlike Heidegger and many others,

---

11. After the controversy over *Years of Decision* subsided, the authorities relented and did not interfere in the republication in 1934 of a collection of his political writings entitled *Politische Schriften*. These writings antedated the Nazi seizure of power and thus, with the exception of a few parts of the introduction to the work, a couple of passages from "Reconstruction of the German Reich," and the selection entitled "Political Duties of German Youth," did not represent much of a provocation to the totalitarian regime.

12. K-Sp, 457 ff.

Spengler refused to collaborate in any way with the "providential" leader of a racially based, one-thousand-year Reich. He regarded Hitler, the demonic driving force of the Nazi movement, as a plebian figure unfit to lead Germany, particularly in a crisis-ridden age demanding consummate foreign policy skills. Spengler was deeply skeptical about Germany's purported need for *Lebensraum*. The genocidal campaign against European Jewry and the destruction of the Soviet Union were pillars of Hitler's ideological program antithetical to Spengler's position. Spengler championed German resurgence through elitist and conservative forces instead of the popular ones that Hitler's demagoguery whipped into a frenzy of nationalistic and racialistic irrationality. These differences between their politics were not mere matters of nuance but constituted an unbridgeable chasm. However, Spengler's implacable hostility to Versailles, his corrosive assault on the political legitimacy of the Weimar regime, and his Nietzschean glorification of war and vitalist energies were major points of commonality he shared with Hitler.

Spengler's political writings and activities in his career utterly failed in their core aspiration. His dream in the Weimar years of contributing to the founding of a Prussian, conservative, semi-authoritarian polity capable of executing a very successful foreign policy remained an unfulfilled one that turned into a nightmare under Hitler. Spengler's politics of cultural despair helped to generate an intellectual climate receptive to Nazism's ideology and radical goals and thereby inadvertently helped Hitler, once the Great Depression had reduced the German people to desperation, to destroy Germany's first democracy. Spengler thereby indirectly assisted a dangerous political movement in coming to power. The Nazis erected a political system that was, to be sure, not a "Prussian-socialistic" system of noble care and duty, as Spengler at the beginning of the Weimar period naïvely hoped from the Caesaristic figure whom he prophesied. Instead, the Nazi regime was one of appalling criminality and enslavement. Furthermore, Hitler bore responsibility for the annihilation of Prussia.

Spengler did not live to experience the agony of World War II and the destruction of German national unity he so deeply feared. His sudden death during the night between May 7 and 8, 1936, of a heart attack in his home in Munich came exactly nine years before Nazi Germany's capitulation. He was laid to rest with a copy of Goethe's *Faust* and Nietzsche's *Zarathustra;* his favorite books when traveling in the temporal world accompanied him on his journey into the next one. For his gravestone, his close friend, the Ruhr industrialist Paul Reusch, made an appropriate choice for the foremost historical pessimist of the twentieth century. He selected a block of black porphyry, upon which distinctively only the name SPENGLER was etched.

In *Years of Decision* Spengler alerts his countrymen to the dangers they face in the 1930s and beyond in international politics. For a scholar who had spent the last decade absorbed in the study of prehistory and early civilizational history, he presents what is, despite some deficiencies, a sophisticated analysis of major historical trends in world politics. This book sets forth the final formulation of Spengler's ideas on the historical and international political form in which the decline of the West would transpire.

Spengler reaffirms his lifelong commitment to historical reflection as the means par excellence to enhance the capability of statesmen to conduct sound foreign policy. "It is the great task of the *connoisseur* of history to understand the facts of his time and out of them to sense the future, to indicate, to sketch out that which will come, whether we desire it or not." He accurately foresees the extraordinary and tragic nature of the coming years. "We live in a most fateful time. The most magnificent historical epoch is dawning, not only of the Faustian culture of Western Europe with its colossal dynamism, but, precisely because of that, of the whole of world history, greater and far more terrible than the ages of Caesar and of Napoleon."[13]

This passage makes abundantly clear that Spengler has abandoned the idea of the strict equality of cultural cycles. In *The Decline of the West*, in an appeal for objectivity on the part of the historian with respect to the time and culture in which he lives, Spengler had asserted that no historical period outweighed in significance any other.[14] Now, the awesome and terrible nature of the titanic struggle for mastery of the planet is properly appreciated as the unique era it represents.

Six years before the invasion of Poland in 1939, Spengler senses the imminence of World War II. "We stand perhaps already close to the onset of the Second World War with an unknown alignment of powers and military, economic, revolutionary means and goals that cannot be foreseen."[15] This statement illustrates his recognition of the insurmountable limits on any historical thinker in the twentieth century trying to foresee in detail the future in international politics. By contrast, he had audaciously claimed in *The Decline of the West* to be able to forecast history.

13. *JdE*, vii, 1.
14. *UdA* I, 125–26.
15. *JdE*, xi.

The unprecedented complexity of world politics in the twentieth century demands statesmen equal to the challenge. For it is a "rapidly growing impossibility for most people still to have an overview of the more and more complicated and opaque events and situations of high politics and international economics and to understand the forces and tendencies at work in them, to say nothing of mastering them." However, "genuine statesmen are becoming rarer and rarer." And compounding the dilemma, in an age of mass politics, ignorant voters might very well frustrate the efforts of a talented leader to pursue the right course of action.[16]

Spengler prefaces his analysis of the approaching world war with a discussion of the evolution of the international states system. The European great-power system spanned the period from Peter the Great to the outbreak of World War I. Important changes in international politics had occurred in the second half of the nineteenth century. The founding of the German Empire by Bismarck in 1871 laid the seeds of the inevitable self-destruction of the state system of Europe. The Meiji Restoration of 1868 and the rise to dominance of industry and finance in the United States after the American Civil War foreshadowed the emergence of Japan and the United States as major actors in international politics.[17]

World War I was an unavoidable tragedy for the peoples of Europe, nearly eviscerating them in the struggle with the non-West. Spengler interprets World War I from a nationalistic perspective as being caused by the aggressive encirclement strategy of Alexander Izvolsky, Raymond Poincaré, and Sir Edward Grey. Spengler concedes that none of these statesmen would have wished to see the outbreak of the war if they had been able to anticipate its profoundly debilitating impact on their countries. However, he insists, the Great War was inevitable. To be sure, the specific way it unfolded could have been avoided. Yet only "the *form*" and "the *tempo* of the catastrophe" of the terrible conflict would have been altered. The debacle "was the *necessary* conclusion of a century of Western development, which was propelled toward that end in growing excitement since Napoleon."[18]

Spengler recognizes the importance in international relations of the beggar-thy-neighbor economic struggle that had originated with the Diktat of Versailles, with its Carthaginian reparations provisions, and had as-

16. *JdE*, 4–5.
17. *JdE*, 19, 20.
18. *JdE*, 16.

sumed new forms and wider scope since the onset of the Great Depression. In the future, scholars looking back at the economic nationalism of the post–World War I period may refer to it as "the Second World War."[19] This economic nationalism will culminate in global conflict.

Most political idealists in Britain and the United States in the interwar years dreamed that the League of Nations could play a vital role in securing world peace. They lost their optimism when the League of Nations failed in 1935 to halt Mussolini's aggression in Abyssinia. This failure exposed the dubiousness of their dreams of revolutionizing international relations. Spengler disdains the idea of promoting international harmony through disarmament or collective security. He lambastes the aspiration to international understanding as "cowardly and *dishonest* optimism." He sarcastically dismisses the League of Nations as a "swarm of summer vacationers who sponge off others at Lake Geneva." Yet Spengler's approving attitude, conveyed in his correspondence, toward Hitler's decision to withdraw Germany from the League of Nations in 1933 was politically most imprudent, as this act marked a major step in Hitler's disastrous expansionist program. Spengler's antagonism toward the League of Nations derived not only from his aggrievance against Wilson and the Allied powers after Versailles but from his conviction of the immutably conflictual nature of international politics. Although it is very doubtful that international law and organization could have engendered in the interwar period an enduring moderation of the struggle for power as hoped for by political idealists, nonetheless, Spengler showed poor judgment by inflexibly opposing international law and organization. Hintze argues that opposition to these institutions of international society by Spengler and his fellow conservative nationalists prevented Germany from trying to use them as tools for patiently and incrementally rectifying its condition of power-political impotence after the Diktat of Versailles.[20] Spengler's philosophy of statecraft does, however, properly acknowledge the terrible primacy of conflict and great-power rivalry in modern history.

The Soviet Union has become a pivotal force in world history. Russia is "the *decisive* factor for Europe since 1812, when it still belonged to it

---

19. *JdE*, 40.

20. *JdE*, 11; Spengler to Goebbels, 3 November 1933, *B*, 710; O. Hintze, review essay of *Der Staat (Das Problem der Stände, Staat und Geschichte, Philosophie der Politik)*, *NdR*, and *PP*, by Oswald Spengler, and *Die Staatslehre Oswald Spenglers: Eine Darstellung und eine kritische Würdigung*, by Otto Koellreutter, *Zeitschrift für die gesamte Staatswissenschaft* 79 (1925): 546–47.

politically, since 1917 for the entire world." The Soviet Union has from its founding a "burning hatred for Europe" and forms the vanguard of the "barbarian" onslaught against the West.[21] Spengler had no illusions about Soviet Communism. He understood that the aim of the Bolsheviks was not to construct social democracy but to use the levers of state power, a command economy, and propaganda to pursue an imperialistic foreign policy. His argument that propaganda is a key weapon of the Soviets is consistent with the massive disinformation and propagandistic offensive of the former Soviet Union in the Third World, particularly in the post–World War II era.

The Bolshevik revolution symbolized the reconquest of Russia by Asia and the Soviet state's emergence as a dangerous opponent of the West. Spengler presciently predicts that the Soviet Union, in trying to increase its weight in world affairs through economic modernization, will require foreign participation not only to develop but to sustain a significant economic base.[22] Indeed, importing technology was important to Soviet economic development during Lenin's New Economic Policy, Stalin's first Five-Year Plan, the détente period, and the Mikhail Gorbachev era. Yet not only did economic superpower status elude the Soviet Union from 1917 to 1991, but economic crisis helped cause its collapse.

Many leading figures in American politics espoused isolationism and neutralism in the interwar period. Spengler recognizes that the United States has reached a turning point in its relationship to the rest of the world. He declares, well before Morgenthau's post–World War II appeal for an American statecraft infused with political realism, that it is imperative for America to conduct its foreign policy in conformance with the principles of power politics. For world history is propelling the United States toward increased involvement in international politics. "[America has become] a sea power that is beginning to become stronger than England and now dominates two oceans. Colonial possessions have been acquired—the Philippines, Hawaii, islands in the West Indies. And due to commercial interests and English propaganda it has been dragged deeper and deeper into the First World War to the point of military participation. However, with that the United States has become a leading element in world politics, whether it knows it or desires it or not, and it must now

21. *JdE*, 43, 149–50.
22. *JdE*, 44.

learn to think and act *statesmanlike* in domestic and foreign affairs or disappear in its present form."[23]

In his *tour d'horizon* of the great powers, Spengler insightfully argues that Britain is a gravely weakened power. Indeed, the true extent of Britain's power-political debilitation was only widely recognized after its Pyrrhic victory in World War II. The country he had rated in 1915 so highly as a leading contender for global hegemony is now reduced in rank to a mere "power from yesterday." England is "tired" and no longer strong, young, and healthy enough to face with confidence the international political crises of the thirties. The age of British industrial and commercial supremacy has passed forever. Australia and Canada will gravitate away from England into a closer relationship with the United States. Spengler also foresees eventual imperial withdrawal from India and the abandonment of positions east of Suez. In *Prussianism and Socialism*, England and the United States were portrayed as allies coordinating their drive to attain "absolute economic world domination." Now he emphasizes the rivalry in their relationship, indeed excessively so. Thus, Spengler overreaches himself, foolishly arguing that British resentment at the eclipse of their national power by the United States might, despite the irreversibility of British decline, culminate in an Anglo-American conflict.[24] Nonetheless, Spengler obviously sensed something, for British concern about the impending overshadowing of their empire in world affairs by the United States was considerable. Neville Chamberlain's ill-fated appeasement policy was designed, through the accommodation of German revisionism and the stabilization of Europe, to frustrate any American ambitions to global hegemony. For it would have reduced England to the unacceptable status of a mere junior partner. Spengler's analysis of Britain's position in world affairs captures important elements of its decline in the twentieth century.

Germany's prospects for global hegemony come in for radical reevaluation. Spengler reckoned German success to be virtually a certainty before the armistice of 1918. Quickly thereafter, he scaled down his enormous optimism. Germany, he argued, would perhaps prevail in the struggle against Britain and the United States to forge a universal empire. In *Years of Decision*, this guarded optimism has given way to apprehension. Indeed, Spengler fears the destruction of Germany in the approaching world war. Why this remarkable change in outlook? One can only surmise that his re-

23. *JdE*, 49.
24. *JdE*, 52–54; *PuS*, 88; *JdE*, 56.

246 / *Prophet of Decline*

flections on the tumultuous history of the Weimar Republic, particularly the hyperinflation of 1923–1924 and the Great Depression, his insight into Germany's geopolitical vulnerabilities, and his acute concern that Germany's leadership would not have the requisite skills for the sagacious conduct of statecraft were the source of this profound change in attitude.

Pessimism about the future of the West, not only culturally, socially, economically, but power-politically as well, sets the tone for most of the book. Yet he still defiantly hopes that somehow the "Prussian" ethos can revitalize Western Europe. As I noted in the preceding chapter, Spengler's philosophy of history profoundly changed from a blend of optimism and pessimism to a philosophy bordering on unadulterated pessimism. Now he embraces the label "pessimist." His willingness to face the tragic realities of world history and politics is *"strong pessimism,"* is *"brave pessimism."*[25]

Unquestionably, it is a sign of realism that Spengler rejected Hitler as a suitable modern Caesar for Germany. Nonetheless, his vision of Caesarism was idealistic. What were the desired qualities of the twentieth-century Caesar he envisioned for his crisis-ridden land? This man of action should be an intellectually superior, coldly calculating, if necessary, ruthless, power politician. He should manipulate the masses so that the state will enjoy the freedom of action to advance resolutely and prudentially its interests in the dangerous arena of international politics. Spengler is keenly aware that a politically realistic leader might very well be prevented from crafting a sound foreign policy insulated from fractious interest groups and popular passions. However, superior leadership is imperative given the mounting danger in international politics. As for Hitler, Spengler scorned him as a racist demagogue who would be an incompetent statesman. Although history ultimately confirmed his judgment, despite Hitler's initial successes, history also proved Spengler wrong in his high regard for Mussolini, an opinion widespread among right-wing intellectuals in Germany.

Spengler did not prophesy in 1933 that Hitler, who in his early years as Germany's Führer skillfully misrepresented himself abroad as a peaceful statesman, would become synonymous with aggressive militarism. Nonetheless, Spengler anticipates the outbreak of a world war. Moreover, throughout *Years of Decision* he expresses serious doubts about the competence of the Nazi elite in foreign policy. "And the National Socialists believe that they can deal with the world either by ignoring it or by oppos-

25. *JdE*, 9, 13.

ing it and that they can build their castles-in-the-air without an at least silent but very noticeable reaction from abroad."[26]

Not only is Germany insecure in world politics, but its very existence hangs in the balance. Indeed, it might emerge from the impending war a permanently occupied land, he asserts. "But I am talking here about Germany, which in the storm of facts is more seriously threatened than any other land, whose *existence*, in the alarming sense of the word, stands in question." His startling, interwar odyssey from exuberant optimism (Germany will dominate the world) to pessimism about its future prospects as a great power is complete. Hitler, a bold gambler in foreign policy, had coined the slogan in *Mein Kampf*: "Germany will either be a world power or not exist at all."[27] In contrast, Spengler cautioned against a wildly expansionary foreign policy, fearing Germany's destruction. Thus, the proper approach for Western statesmen, as he sees it, is to pursue vigilantly a strategy of siege prolongation against the internal and external forces of chaos threatening their societies.

One weakness in Spengler's analysis of the coming world war was his failure to anticipate the rise to superpower status by the United States. We have already encountered this defect in his vision of international political transformation in *The Decline of the West, Prussianism and Socialism*, and his correspondence. In *Years of Decision* he maintains that several deficiencies detract from America's ability to become the hegemonic power of the West. First, the American people lack homogeneity. Second, America's enormous size has precluded the development of a sense of genuine national danger, rendering a powerful central government unnecessary. Third, America has historically enjoyed comparative freedom from the power-political realities weighing down upon European statesmen, with the consequence that the United States lacks a tradition of genuine *Realpolitik*. In American politics the pursuit of commercial interests overshadows the determined pursuit of foreign policy objectives. Finally, Spengler is repelled by American society in the thirties. He perceives it as a mix of superficiality, rampant materialism, widespread criminality, and corruption. The American people may very well lack the strength of national character necessary to bring Western civilization to its final hegemonic

---

26. *JdE*, 3.

27. *JdE*, 2; Adolf Hitler, quoted in Andreas Hillgruber, *Deutschlands Rolle in der Vorgeschichte der beiden Weltkriege*, 2d rev. ed. (Göttingen: Vandenhoeck & Ruprecht, 1979), 67.

phase. Here we hear an echo from Ranke's *The Great Powers*, wherein he had argued that power in international politics derived from a people's moral and cultural energies, a problematic argument that greatly influenced German international theory. Moreover, Spengler's distaste for American civilization is compounded by his irrepressible pride in European culture. To a European, the idea that the United States could supplant the Old World, the cradle of modern Western civilization, is a most disagreeable one. This mixture of some interesting observations and a cultivated European's disdain for American culture and society yields a superficial underestimation of the awesome civilizational power slumbering in the American people on the eve of Pearl Harbor. True, Spengler acknowledges that America manifests "the Faustian will to power." But the United States is not to be taken too seriously as a candidate for global hegemony. It grates against his strong sense of aristocratic tradition and his refined cultural sensibilities. For in America the Faustian ethos has been "translated from the organically grown [the culture of the Old World] into the soulless mechanical."[28]

Nonetheless, the continued rise of the United States in the hierarchy of great powers is possible. Yet Spengler leans strongly toward rejecting it as the architect of universal empire. Indeed, he erroneously speculates that the United States, lacking a strong central government in the Continental tradition and traumatized by the Great Depression, might perhaps fragment into its constituent regions.[29] However, a process of ethnic cultural fragmentation with potentially grave consequences has been accelerating in the United States since 1965, though the political disintegration of the United States is unlikely in the first half of the twenty-first century.

Earlier Spengler had been struck by the success of the United States in preserving its national unity under Abraham Lincoln, the rise to prominence of industry and banking following the North's victory in the Civil War, and the debut of the ascendant superpower on the world stage in 1917, so much so, apparently, that he wrote a few lines in *The Decline of the West* that imply that America was on the way to global hegemony. In a remarkable sentence in the second volume, published, one should recall, in 1923, he observes that "the rise of New York to a world city through the Civil War of 1861–1865 is perhaps the most momentous event of the last century." When one bears in mind that in Spengler's philosophy, the

28. *JdE*, 49.
29. *JdE*, 51.

world cities, London, New York, and Berlin, symbolize the civilizational energy and the power-political ranking of the West's principal great powers, Britain, the United States, and Germany, it becomes clear that the sentence implies, though this may very well not have been his conscious intention, that the United States and not Germany might be destined to global primacy. If Germany were to create the solid foundation of an *imperium Germanicum* in the twentieth century, the international political idea that animated Spengler when he composed *The Decline of the West*, then Bismarck's unification of Germany in 1871 and the eventual advancement of Berlin to the status of a world city, not the ascendance of New York after the Civil War, would clearly be the most momentous event of the nineteenth century. However, in *Years of Decision* this fascinating ambiguity is finally laid to rest. Spengler portrays the rise of the United States to world-power status as being an impressive but probably transitory development. America's momentum is finally spent in the economic debilitation and social and political unrest of the Great Depression. "The magnificent episode of the dollar domination and its social structure, commencing with the end of the Civil War in 1865, appears to stand before the end."[30]

Unwisely, Spengler never supplemented his historical-philosophical analysis of the transformation of world politics in the twentieth century with empirical studies of the power resources of the great powers. His erroneous evaluation of the power-political prospects of the United States reflects his lack of appreciation for its unparalleled economic potential, which, despite the immense setback of the Great Depression, could still be translated into tremendous military power. Hanfstaengl, a man very knowledgeable about American conditions, regularly dined alone in the privacy of his home with Spengler. Hanfstaengl recorded in his memoirs how surprised he was to learn that the "universal world picture" of Spengler, whom he greatly admired, was "not free from blind spots." He noted with astonishment how his guest overestimated the significance of the Ruhr in international politics while overlooking that of America's industrial heartland. This decisive development in international politics in the early forties, the conversion of American economic potential into colossal military power, was foreseen by German military experts. General Georg Thomas, in a report of the Economics Staff of the German High Command in the fall of 1939 on American armaments capacity, concluded that

30. *UdA* II, 117; *JdE*, 130.

in the event of the unexpected outbreak of war the United States only "needed about a year to convert its industry in order to produce large quantities of military equipment, particularly airplanes, tanks, and motor vehicles," and that "after a one to one-and-a-half year starting period could achieve in virtually all armament areas a production capacity that would exceed by far that of all countries."[31]

The center of global power, in Spengler's view, has bifurcated and gravitated outward from Europe to Russia and the United States. However, he does not foresee the emergence of American-Soviet bipolarity (in which the Soviet Union is clearly the inferior of the two superpowers). He fails to anticipate this development largely because he rejects America as the future global hegemon, for it may not weather the crisis of the thirties in his estimation. But he erroneously believes that Western Europe may somehow summon up the strength to create a grand neo-imperial structure. Despite his apprehension about Germany's future and the ominous revolt of the non-West against the West, he is desperately hopeful that Europe under German leadership may contain Soviet power and in a very vague and undefined manner preside over the concluding, imperial form of Western civilization.

> It appears that Western Europe has lost its decisive significance, but apart from politics it only appears to be so. The *idea* of Faustian culture has developed here. Here it has its roots and here it will achieve the final victory of its history or rapidly pass away. . . . But in the meantime *power* has shifted to the outlying areas, toward Asia and America. There it is the power over the largest interior land mass of the earth, here—in the United States and the English Dominions—the power over both the world-historical oceans joined by the Panama canal.[32]

Although Spengler fails to forecast the dawn of the American Century, he was prophetic about the Soviet Union. He foresaw that it would sustain a wartime economy in the event of the loss of its European territories. Thus, he warns that a German invasion of the Soviet Union in the coming world war would be madness. The preparatory strategic study for Operation Barbarossa was drafted by Major General Erich Marcks in 1940. He

31. Hanfstaengl, *Zwischen Weißem und Braunem Haus*, 206; General Thomas, quoted in Andreas Hillgruber, *Deutsche Großmacht- und Weltpolitik im 19. und 20. Jahrhundert* (Düsseldorf: Droste Verlag, 1977), 205.

32. *JdE*, 42.

overconfidently expected victory within nine to seventeen weeks. He erroneously maintained that the conquest of the Soviet Union up to the line of advance demarcated by the lower Don, middle Volga, and northern Dvina would place in Germany's hands "the most important areas for military production," as in the report's own words the "eastern industrial regions [were] not yet sufficiently productive." It is not known whether Hitler ever read the following haunting lines cautioning in the strongest possible terms against a German invasion of the Soviet Union. After all, Spengler had boldly sent a complimentary copy of his book about the impending world war to the man who was to be largely responsible for starting it.

> The population of this mightiest of the interior lands of the earth, is unassailable from without. Vastness is a *power*, politically and militarily, that has never yet been overcome; that Napoleon had already learned. Of what use would it be to an enemy if he possessed such great areas? Moreover, in order to render the attempt ineffective, the Bolsheviks have shifted the center of gravity of their system farther and farther to the east. The power-politically important industrial areas have all been constructed east of Moscow, in great part east of the Urals as far as the Altai, and south as far as the Caucasus. The entire area west of Moscow, Byelorussia, the Ukraine, once from Riga to Odessa the most vital part of the tsar's empire, constitutes today a fantastic glacis against "Europe" and could be given up without the system falling apart. Consequently, every idea of an offensive from the west has become absurd. It would be a thrust into empty space.[33]

Not merely Hitler and the German General Staff, but expert opinion in the United States and Britain as well, expected the collapse of the Soviet Union within a matter of weeks after the German panzers knifed into Russia in June, 1941.[34] In the preceding passage, Spengler presents what is, in his view, the chief strategic rationale for a containment strategy vis-à-vis Soviet expansionism as the principal long-term goal of German foreign policy. The boundless imperialism of Spengler during the Great War, when he had envisioned in 1918 after Brest Litovsk a German protectorate up to the Urals, was to be replaced in the East by a sober and cautious defensive posture.

The Soviet Union and Imperial Japan posed, according to *Years of Deci-*

---

33. Hillgruber, *Deutschlands Rolle*, 106; *JdE*, 43–44.
34. Hillgruber, *Deutschlands Rolle*, 127.

sion, the two principal power-political threats to the West. On the one hand, many Western observers of world affairs, in the interwar atmosphere clouded with racial and cultural prejudices, tended to dismiss Japanese military personnel as "little yellow men" who couldn't match up with their purportedly superior Western counterparts. Spengler, on the other hand, an admirer of the bushido tradition, appreciated the fighting prowess of the Japanese Imperial armed forces. Indeed, he overestimated the ability of the Japanese to hold their own against the United States in Japan's bid for domination over East Asia.[35]

Predictions about the tactical and strategic conduct of World War II are interspersed in Spengler's analysis. He foresees the extensive, highly effective use of air power against battleships. He brilliantly anticipates the successful application of the German military doctrine of *Blitzkrieg*. He predicts that in the future airplanes and tank squadrons will play a decisive role in a new kind of warfare, one of rapid movement, in contrast to the static trench warfare of World War I. Spengler's negative appraisal of French morale, while exaggerated, is nonetheless consistent with the dramatic fall of France in June, 1940.[36]

The coming conflict is merely another phase in a marathon struggle for global hegemony. "We have entered into the *era of world wars*. It begins in the nineteenth century and will outlast the current century and probably also the next one. It means the transition from the states system of the eighteenth century to the *imperium mundi*." The era of world wars in the West corresponds in Roman antiquity to "the two terrible centuries between Cannae and Actium, which led from the form of the Hellenistic states system including Rome and Carthage to that of the *imperium Romanum*."[37] Spengler considers the nineteenth century as having been marked both by armed conflict and the pursuit of power-political goals by alternative means, particularly by economic competition, arms races, propaganda, and diplomatic maneuvering. In contrast to most theorists of international relations, he views the latter phase of the European peace of 1815–1914 as having been characterized by an accelerating arms race and such extreme tensions that it was an integral phase in the Western struggle for global hegemony. The arms race after the Congress of Berlin in 1878

35. Paul Kennedy, *The Rise and Fall of the Great Powers: Economic Change and Military Conflict from 1500 to 2000* (New York: Random House, 1987), 298; *JdE*, 47.

36. *JdE*, 36, 37, 38.

37. *JdE*, 16.

had a prophylactic effect on the outbreak of a general conflict in Europe. European statesmen dreaded the catastrophic physical damage and political and social upheaval that would result.

In Spengler's philosophy the dynamic West, alone among all civilizations, was capable of transforming the planet into an integrated network of international political and economic relations. The most striking idea in *Years of Decision* is that, paradoxically, such a remarkable civilization is considered to be possibly incapable of giving birth to an *imperium mundi*. The crowning imperial form of the West might never see the light of day. "Imperialism is an *idea*, whether it enters at present the consciousness of its agents and executors or not. It will perhaps in our case never become full reality, perhaps be frustrated by other ideas, which are increasing in vigor outside the world of the white peoples, but it is situated as a *tendency* of a great historical form, in everything now advancing."[38]

Before 1918 Spengler envisioned Germany as an ascendant power destined to universal empire. Now Germany is vulnerable to destruction in the imminent world war. Britain, formerly a prime contestant for global hegemon, is disqualified as a result of its rapid decline. The United States is erroneously rejected as the leading candidate for establishing the *imperium mundi*. Not only does Spengler have serious doubts about the capability of any of the Western great powers to create a modern counterpart to the Pax Romana, but he prematurely argues that the economic supremacy of the West is being undermined by the non-West. Given his erosion in confidence, it is not surprising that a disjunction arises between his philosophy of world history, which calls for the formation of an *imperium mundi* as a historical necessity, and his evaluation of the international political scene. Basically, he becomes very vague and confused about it. He is pulled in opposite directions by his apprehension about Germany's future and his fervent hope that somehow Europe can be reinvigorated and reassume its traditional primacy in world politics. Thus, he hopes that Germany, with its Prussian virtues of duty, honor, and patriotism and steeled by its martial ethos, can serve as "the educator," perhaps "the deliverer" of the West.[39]

Keenly aware of the decline in European influence in world affairs after the internecine struggle of 1914–1918, Spengler completely changes, as we saw earlier, his interpretation of the historical significance of World War I.

38. *JdE*, 17.
39. *JdE*, 146.

Consequently, he commits a major error. He drops the key thesis of *Prussianism and Socialism,* which forecast irreconcilable rivalry between Germany and the Anglo-Saxon powers for the establishment of a vast economic empire, one that is consistent with the actual course of twentieth-century history. In this book he celebrated the Great War as the opening phase of this hegemonic struggle. Now, he condemns the war as having transpired in "a completely senseless form."[40] Spengler fails to advance in *Years of Decision* the argument flowing logically from *Prussianism and Socialism* that a resurgence of German national power in the thirties would culminate in a resumption of armed struggle between the United States and Germany for the right to create and preside over a global economic empire as prophesied in *The Decline of the West.*

In light of the centrality of the Cold War in post–World War II history, Spengler does, however, show good judgment in retaining the corollary of this thesis, that Russia threatened to overpower a Western universal empire. Thus, in *Years of Decision,* Russia, not the Anglo-Saxon world, is now regarded as the prime antagonist of Germany and its chief strategic concern. Moreover, Spengler believes that Russian hostility is directed not only toward Germany but toward the entire West. Consequently, he emphasized in the preface to *Political Writings,* penned roughly at the same time as *Years of Decision,* that mastering the problem of Russian expansionism should be the highest priority of German foreign policy. "The Russian nationality was then and is today and in the future in every sense the *most immediate* problem for us. . . . We are no longer the leading state in 'Central Europe,' but the *border state against 'Asia.'* "[41] Indeed, *Years of Decision* conveys the impression that Spengler desires to see a genuine détente develop among the European powers. They can then collectively concentrate their energies on a defensive containment strategy against the Soviet Union, with Germany in the vanguard.

The Decline of the West had been written in a mood of soaring optimism about Germany's ability to forge a universal empire. Such an empire would purportedly luxuriate for a couple of centuries in a debilitating affluence before being eventually overwhelmed presumably by the Russian hordes. Scant attention was devoted to the "barbarian" threat because it was not seen as being immediate. The only passage in his major work touching on this concern sternly warned the peoples of the West to avoid the suicidal

40. *JdE,* 22.
41. *PSch,* viii.

folly of unilateral disarmament. The admonition is a timely one in a post–Cold War world in which so many young men recoil at the thought of military service. Once Spengler began to appreciate in the mid-twenties how World War I had undermined Europe's traditional primacy in world politics, he became very concerned about the threat to Europe emanating from the non-West.[42] After the Great Depression had further weakened Europe, his concern about the menace posed by the revolt of the Soviet Union and the colonial world against the West became acute.

I believe that Spengler's cyclical, historical-philosophical framework of the decline of the West is largely valid. However, I remain skeptical about his almost-glacial time frame. One can plausibly argue that the *imperium mundi* of modern Western civilization was hammered together by the United States in 1945, well before the twenty-first or twenty-second century conjectured by Spengler. Furthermore, this neo-imperial world order is already eroding. Although his comparative analysis of the decline of Roman civilization and the modern West is a noteworthy achievement, he is too mechanical in claiming, as he does about the barbarian conflict with Rome, that the historical phenomena are congruent to an extreme degree. Moreover, Spengler asserts that since the struggle for hegemony in the Roman world lasted approximately two hundred years, the contemporary epoch in modern Western history will be of similar duration.[43] However, he thereby arguably ignores the value of his own idea that history in each cultural cycle flows according to its own tempo. Thus, the allegro con brio of Faustian civilization should translate into a quicker movement of historical events than the andante of classical antiquity. The final stages of the decline of the West should then occur considerably earlier than Spengler anticipates.[44] Moreover, his argument in his late work that world history accelerates in tempo suggests that historical change will be remarkably rapid in the twentieth century and beyond. Indeed, the rapidity with which Germany reunified in 1990 and with which the Soviet Union collapsed in 1991, to cite merely two recent, notable examples from international history, substantiate this thesis. Finally, Spengler's preoccupation in *Years of Decision* with the onslaught against the West of non-Western

42. See WW, 333 ff.

43. *JdE*, 148, 16–17.

44. In the "Table of 'Contemporary' Political Epochs," included in the first volume of his major work, Spengler forecasts that the final stages of the decline of the West, featuring barbarian incursions culminating in imperial collapse, would occur after 2200 A.D.

peoples well over half a century before the *imperium mundi* was supposed to be finally established implies that he himself was not confident in the accuracy of his timetable.

According to Spengler, Western civilization is imperiled by two world revolutions: class struggle and race struggle. An additional key factor in history and politics is the " 'horizontal' struggle between states and nations." Class conflict has its roots, not in socialism or Bolshevism, but in rationalism, the proud philosophy that destroyed the theological system of Christianity and subverted the social structure of the ancien régime.[45] Racial conflict is the much more dangerous revolution of the two. It constitutes the assault on the whites by the colored population of the globe, which has become conscious of a sense of community. Spengler's term the " 'coloreds' " refers to all the peoples of the world outside the European-American cultural zone. The term includes even technologically advanced peoples such as the Japanese and Russians.[46] His exclusion of the Russians from the category of white nations demonstrates the civilizational as opposed to the racialistic content of his concept of racial struggle.

Spengler clarifies his views on race. Ever conscious of Nazi censorship, he criticizes the Nazis in moderate language. "But when here the talk is about race, so is that not meant in the sense as it is today fashionable among anti-Semites in Europe and in America, namely, Darwinistically, materialistically." In his unpublished papers, his uncompromising opposition to the Nazi dogma of a master race is pithily formulated. "There are not any noble races. There are only noble specimens of *all* races." Race is for Spengler not a racialistic and zoological concept, as is the case for Arthur de Gobineau, Chamberlain, Rosenberg, and Hitler, but a matter of ethos. Race for Spengler means having "strong instincts," a deep sense of realism, and the urge to rule. Men of strong race accept life as filled with challenge, risk, and struggle.[47]

The Western universal empire, if it ever sees the light of day, will face a mounting assault of the colored peoples, just as the Roman Empire was beleaguered by waves of barbarians. This scenario is the standard, international-political, final phase that every civilization undergoes. "The 'revolution from the outside' had arisen against each of the now-defunct cultures." The anti-Western revolt of the colonized peoples broke out in

45. *JdE*, 147, 58, 75 ff.
46. *JdE*, 58, 150.
47. *JdE*, 157; Politica I, 75, G1–33; *JdE*, 42.

the nineteenth century with the Taiping revolution in China, the Sepoy insurrection in India, and the rebellion against Emperor Maximilian in Mexico.[48]

When he compares contemporary non-Westerners to barbarians, Spengler is not being derogatory. Indeed, he admires their energy and hardiness. The term *barbarian* expresses the foreignness, the externality to Western civilization, of peoples outside the West European-American world. It is used the way the Romans did, as a designation for all peoples other than those under Graeco-Roman influence and domination. Interestingly, in his unpublished papers, Spengler occasionally referred in an unequivocally disparaging context to denizens of the declining West as barbarians.[49]

The mainstream bourgeois and the classical Marxist traditions of political and historical thought idolized the scientific and technological achievements of modern civilization. Moreover, they optimistically christened imperialism a progressive historical force in fostering the modernization of "backward" peoples. Spengler, to the contrary, without illusions or hypocrisy, considered imperialism to be exploitation and, from the perspective of its victims in the non-West, a largely negative and destructive historical experience. He poses this damning question: "How many hundred years had whites shamelessly endangered and insulted colored races?" The counterpart to the decline of the West is the revolt of the non-West. This powerful revolt issues from a "teeth-gnashing hatred, evoked by the unassailable superiority (based on fully mature political, military, economic, and intellectual forms and methods) of a group of cultured nations surrounded by the hopelessly downtrodden, the 'savages' or 'barbarians,' the unjustly exploited." Ironically, the non-Western peoples are schooled by the West in the very weapons that will eventually help them to overpower it: the military arts, science and technology, economics, and diplomacy.[50]

Years of Decision highlights the historical dynamic of the revolt of the non-West against the West. Unquestionably, it is one of the most significant features of world politics from 1800 to the present. Furthermore, Spengler perceives that competition and conflict will occur among non-

48. *JdE*, 147, 156.
49. For example, "We have become barbarians, late posthumous barbarians" (Politica I, 75, G1–184).
50. Politica II, 84, L; *JdE*, 147–48.

258 / *Prophet of Decline*

Western powers, *e.g.*, between the Soviet Union and Japan and the Soviet Union and China. Nonetheless, in an era characterized by strong anticolonial sentiment and fixated on upholding Western primacy in world politics, he inadequately emphasizes the frequency and significance of rivalry among non-Western states. Thus, he fails to probe sufficiently how geopolitical competition among non-Western powers will interact with the conflict between the West and the non-West in the coming decades and beyond.

Although Spengler rejects outright racialistic theories of civilizational evolution as propounded, for example, by Gobineau, Chamberlain, and Rosenberg, his expression " 'coloreds' " is offensive by contemporary standards. Nonetheless, his crude concept of the onslaught of the colored peoples captures the epochal significance of the rebellion of the non-West against Western dominance in the modern age. Hedley Bull identifies five "phases or themes" in the revolt against Western dominance: the fight for equal sovereignty, the anticolonial revolution, the struggle against white supremacism, the struggle for economic justice, and the striving for cultural liberation.[51] As Spengler argued, the non-West has, with varying degrees of success, imitated Western science, technology, military arts, and political concepts in order to compete in power politics against the West. The wave of anticolonial revolutions in modern history and the culmination of the process of decolonization in the post–World War II period is consistent with his historical philosophy.

In the postcolonial age significant tensions have troubled relations between the West and the non-West. They persist and will function as important factors shaping world affairs in the twenty-first century. Of the many serious problem areas in contemporary relations between the West and the non-West, mentioning two will suffice to indicate their difficulty. Although their campaign to redistribute radically wealth and power from the North to the South failed, developing countries are sending waves of economic migrants to the North. This vast migration has stimulated the countermovements of European xenophobia and American anti-immigrant sentiment. Moreover, Europe and the United States watch with dismay the danger of Islamic fundamentalism. Discourse with Spengler strongly suggests a deterioration of relations between the West and the

51. Hedley Bull, "The Revolt Against the West," in Hedley Bull and Adam Watson, eds., *The Expansion of International Society* (Oxford: Clarendon Press, 1984), 220 ff.

non-West as international economic and political order in the post–Cold War world erodes.

Spengler envisions the Soviet Union and Japan as the two powers in the forefront of the revolt against Western supremacy in the twentieth century. The Soviet Union challenged the West in the exhausting struggle of the Cold War, which lasted over four decades. Moreover, despite initial hopes of a strategic partnership between post-Communist Russia and the United States, a strained relationship is increasingly likely. After crushing defeat in World War II, Japan shifted from imperialism and militarism in its struggle with the West to economic expansionism. As we have seen, *Man and Technics* showed a keen appreciation of the potential of Japan to modernize successfully and compete economically with the West.[52]

Speculations about the power-political future of China and India expose how Spengler's concept of "fellaheen" peoples is problematic. He does predict that China and India will liberate themselves from Western colonialism. However, he considers non-Western peoples like the Chinese and Indians, who have created great cultures and then declined to the abject condition of being subjugated for centuries, as incapable of resurgence. They supposedly cannot muster the inner strength to reconstitute themselves as major, autonomous factors in world politics. "Ancient fellaheen peoples like the Indians and the Chinese can never again play an independent role in the world of the great powers."[53]

In briefly considering the case of China, it would be imprudent to dismiss Spengler's view on China's future, when he articulated it, as sheer nonsense. One should not forget that if the United States had not liberated East Asia from Japanese militarism during World War II, then mainland China might still find its major cities under foreign occupation and Manchuria permanently lost to Japan.

The economic boom following Deng Xiaoping's reforms has stimulated much speculation about China's future in the hierarchy of nations. For example, Paul Kennedy argued that China may possibly emerge as a superpower in the twenty-first century after successfully modernizing.[54] However, it is premature to conclude that China will attain superpower status. After the turmoil of the Asian economic crisis of the late 1990s, China's future is murky.

52. *MuT*, 60.
53. *JdE*, 156, 46.
54. Kennedy, *The Great Powers*, 447–58.

While the Chinese and Indians are categorized as "fellaheen" peoples, the Russians and Japanese are not. Spengler had once been convinced that the Russians would initiate the ninth cultural cycle of world history, while he viewed the Japanese as imitators first of Chinese and then of Western civilization. Thus, these peoples have never exhausted themselves by traversing the grand cycle of high culture.

In the 1930s Spengler presciently forecast that the Soviet Union posed a threat not only to Europe itself but to the Western presence in the developing world as well. As he predicted, the Soviet Union served for decades as the standard-bearer of the indigenous, anti-Western movement in the Third World. Its adventurism there was a leitmotif of its Cold War foreign policy from the mid-1950s until 1989.

Years of Decision forecast that the Soviet Union would seek to inflame and exploit instability in the non-West in order to undermine the West. Marxism-Leninism is a propagandistic instrument for the exploitation of conditions of Third World instability. "One still maintains the Marxist face only on the exterior, in order to unleash and direct the revolt against the white powers in South Asia, Africa, and America." Soviet foreign policy Spengler sees as inherently different from traditional European statecraft. "Its strongest weapon is the new, revolutionary, genuinely Asiatic diplomacy, which acts instead of negotiates, acts from below and behind by means of propaganda, murder, and insurrection, and consequently is far superior to the great diplomacy of the white countries."[55]

The sensational collapse of the Soviet Union in 1991 posed yet again the question of the future of Russia's relations with the West. Spengler recognized that the point of departure for understanding Russian domestic and international political behavior since Peter the Great remains the historic debate between Westernizers and Slavophiles ignited in the early nineteenth century. This debate about the existential question of Russia's national identity persists to the present day. Post-Communist Russia faces a stark choice. The first alternative is the Westernizers' cosmopolitan path of quasi-democratization, free-market capitalism, and the abandonment of dreams of imperial restoration. The second alternative is the anti-Western, Slavophile prescription of authoritarianism, a market economy with a strong role reserved for the state, and an effort to restore Russia to its imperial greatness. Discourse with Spengler's philosophy strongly suggests that post-Soviet Russia will not succeed in modernizing by importing

55. *JdE*, 150, 152, 153.

Western political and economic models. Russia will not help undergird the Pax Americana.

The following question naturally arises: How strong an actor on the world stage will this post-Soviet Russia be? Russia, despite its nuclear arsenal and residual military-industrial complex, will not prove to be a durable, powerfully expansionary world power whose armed forces are steeled to pursue victory whatever the cost. As Benjamin Lambeth noted in 1995, "Russia's armed forces, only a few years ago the vaunted Soviet juggernaut, are now in shambles." Even allowing for a recovery from this nadir, the debacles of Afghanistan and Chechnya and not the heroic triumph at Stalingrad are indicative of Russia's power-political future. Spengler underscored that great imperial powers are in fit condition for only a transitory phase of their history, a couple of centuries or so.[56] Despite ebbs and flows, Russia's long period of power-political greatness spanned the historic battles of Poltava in 1709, Borodino in 1812, and Stalingrad in 1942–1943 and appears to have reached its end.

Interestingly, the Western *imperium mundi*, if it is ever established, will turn out to be more difficult to defend than the *orbis terrarum* of Rome. Spengler's argument actually supports my thesis that the power-political decline of the West will occur at a quicker tempo than he anticipated. "But nonetheless, through the centuries a coordinated defense . . . was possible, because the *orbis terrarum* of the Roman Empire was an integrated territory that had *boundaries* that could be defended. Much more difficult is the situation of today's empire of the white peoples, which encompasses the entire surface of the earth and *includes* within it 'the coloreds.' "[57]

Roman imperial strategy, as Spengler observes, became essentially defensive after the annihilation of Varus' legions in the struggle against the Germanic tribes and the first great rebellion of the frontier legions after the death of Augustus.[58] Spengler's insight in the 1930s, that the West would adopt a defensive strategy vis-à-vis the non-West, captures the essence of America's overall foreign policy in the post–World War II era and toward the Soviet Union in particular. The strategy of containment, the centerpiece of American national security policy, notwithstanding the empty posturing about "rollback" by Secretary of State John Foster Dul-

---

56. Benjamin S. Lambeth, "Russia's Wounded Military," *Foreign Affairs* 74, no. 2 (March–April, 1995): 86; *UdA* I, 48.

57. *JdE*, 149–50.

58. *JdE*, 149.

les, has been a thoroughly defensive one since its inception. After the proclamation of the Truman Doctrine in 1947, the United States became the architect and hegemonic leader of an extensive system of alliances in order to contain Soviet expansionism. The defensive orientation of American foreign policy since 1945 was, for the most part, arguably prudential. This defensive posture is reflected in American acquiescence in the Soviet conquest of eastern Europe, Harry S. Truman's cautious pursuit of the status quo antebellum in Korea after General Douglas MacArthur's debacle in his drive to the Yalu River, John F. Kennedy's toleration of the existence of a Soviet Communist ally ninety miles from the American coastline as part of the agreement ending the Cuban Missile crisis, and American unwillingness to go beyond strategic bombing in taking the war to North Vietnam. The defensive orientation of American foreign policy persisted in the postcontainment era, as was demonstrated most strikingly in George Bush's controversial decision to terminate abruptly the war against Iraq, leaving Saddam Hussein in power. The defensiveness of American foreign policy has been aggravated since the trauma of Vietnam semiparalyzed the resolve of American political leadership to utilize the instruments of force in the pursuit of imperial maintenance. The spectacular victory in Operation Desert Storm in 1991 has not reversed this trend.

During the interwar period, most international relations theorists were championing the ideals of world organization and collective security in a futile effort to transcend the tragic nature of world history and politics. Spengler, by contrast, emphasized the central role of war in world history. He exhorts Westerners to surmount their debilitating pacifism so that they will be in form to combat the rising tide of anti-Western power. The warring instinct lies deeply implanted in the psyche of civilized man. It must be awakened and constructively channeled into support for a visionary statecraft. This is the rationale for the Nietzschean espousal of "the eternal-warlike in the type man, the beast of prey."[59]

The analysis of the sociological features of decline in *Years of Decision* remains unchanged from that elaborated in *The Decline of the West*. Spengler attempts to inspire his readers to resist the very process of societal degeneration he predicts is inexorable. He paints an alarming character study of Western societies. The decline in the birth rate, the "graying" of the population, feminism, male liberation from traditional social obligations, the deterioration of the family unit, and hedonism mark the ongoing de-

59. *JdE*, 163–64, 161.

mographic and sociological decline of the West. Rampant speculation by unscrupulous financiers, greedy and undisciplined trade unions, and rising non-Western trade competition will undermine the economic strength of Western countries. Mediocrity in political leadership, demagoguery, plutocratic tendencies, and pacifism will render them unequal to the challenges of international politics. The decline of the West will not be accompanied by heroic Wagnerian fanfare. The peoples of the West will try to alleviate their *taedium vitae* with decadent popular music and sexually explicit dances that will "celebrate the death march of a great culture."[60]

One might object that the purported triumph of democratic and free-market principles, spreading through much of the world with the terminal crisis of Communism, discredits Spengler's prophecy of the decline of democracy. Yet the future of democracy is uncertain, as a cursory regional survey suggests. It is debatable how durable the fledgling democracies of Latin America and the former Soviet empire will prove to be if their economic problems deepen. In addition, the process of democratization appears to be suffering reverses in sub-Saharan Africa and making little headway in the Middle East. While democracy enjoys a turbulent existence in India, it remains an unfulfilled aspiration in China. Moreover, the capacity of democracy to endure in advanced industrialized countries for centuries to come, which Spengler sharply called into question, is still very much a matter of debate. Mature democracies face serious problems: political apathy, the fiscal crisis of the welfare state, self-serving interest groups, the power of plutocratic elements, worsening socioeconomic inequalities, and stubborn ethnic and racial tensions. Fukuyama's proclamation in the late 1980s of the global triumph of democracy will prove to be embarrassingly premature.

We conclude our analysis of *Years of Decision* with a discussion of Hitler's statecraft. Nazism, as the principal variety of European fascism, was, along with liberal democracy and Communism, one of the three major ideologies of the twentieth century. Nazism was crushed in a vicelike grip between the Communist leviathan of the East and the Western democracies in World War II. Hitler's movement represented in one sense a disastrous attempt to combat the decadence of the modern West, of which Spengler was a consummate analyst in German intellectual history, by adhering to a faulty racialistic diagnosis and employing a nihilistic treatment. Thus, it should come as no surprise that, according to one of Hitler's inti-

60. *JdE*, 163.

264 / *Prophet of Decline*

mate party comrades, Herr Otto Wagener, during the period 1929–1935 alone, Hitler, an optimist of sorts, voiced his opposition to Spengler's philosophy on many separate occasions.

The first time, he declared, with emphatic words, "I *am* not a fan of Oswald Spengler! I do not *believe* in the decline of the West. No, I consider it to be my task, set for me by Providence, to be instrumental in preventing it." He continued with a rejection of Spengler's idea of the rise of a Russian high culture, employing a core Hitlerian racialistic argument. "I do not *believe* in the birth of a new Slavic culture. Never have cultures been born yet under Jewish leadership, rather, only some have been destroyed!" Wagener also relates Hitler's plans to "revitalize" German education, adumbrated in a conversation with the future Bavarian state minister for education in his regime. Hitler defiantly boasted, "So we will awaken a new storm and stress period in the youth of our people, which rejuvenates the entire people and overcomes the stagnation of Western culture! In this way the defeatist prophecy of Oswald Spengler of the decline of the West will be censured as lies!" A long-winded harrangue on Spengler's thesis of cultural decline by Hitler in a discussion with a business magnate contains the following assertions: "Without a doubt! Our culture has gone into stagnation, it looks like old age. But the reasons for this do not reside in the notion that it has really already passed beyond its manliness but rather: that the bearers of this culture, the Germanic-European men, have neglected it and have turned to material tasks, to mechanization, to industrialization, the devotion to material possession, to greediness."[61] Naturally, the discourse ends on the "optimistic" note of cultural regeneration through Nazism.

Hitler articulated his opposition to Spengler's philosophy on another occasion in a most dramatic public fashion. In 1935, before a May Day rally attended by 1,500,000 people at Tempelhofer Field, the Führer declaimed, "A writer summarized his impressions of the time [before 1933] in a book, which he entitled: *The Decline of the West*. So, should that really be the end of our history and with it of our peoples? No! We cannot believe that! It must not be the decline of the West but the resurrection of the peoples of the West!"[62] Hitler then expressed his conviction that the

61. H. A. Turner, Jr., ed., *Hitler aus nächster Nähe: Aufzeichnungnen eines Vertrauten 1929–1932* (Frankfurt am Main: Ullstein, 1978), 290, 432, 387–88.
62. Max Domarus, ed., *Hitler. Reden und Proklamationen, 1932–1945*, vol. I, bk. 2 (Wiesbaden: R. Löwit, 1973), 502.

founding of the Nazi regime proved the reality of the regeneration of the German people.

Hitler, far from preventing the decline of the West, promoted Germany's ruin; he unleashed the world war predicted in *Years of Decision*. He rejected Chamberlain's final bid to preserve the peace in Europe by proposing to apply British pressure on Poland for concessions to the Third Reich in exchange for the renunciation of German expansionism by aggressive means in the future. Hitler's determination to resort to force led to the invasion of Poland in September, 1939, and the ensuing ferocious conflict between the German and Anglo-Saxon world for global hegemony, which Spengler had correctly identified in *Prussianism and Socialism* as one of the great historical tendencies of the twentieth century.

Anti-Semitism and anti-Bolshevism occupied a central position in Nazi ideology. Nonetheless, Hitler believed that the struggle in world politics would be between the Nazi gamble to establish a Pax Germanica and the American drive to create a Pax Americana, which historically took form under Roosevelt in response to the German challenge. Spengler prudently considered Germany's chief task in international politics to be conserving its strength for a containment strategy toward the Soviet Union.

Spengler grasped that World War I had marked a turning point in the development of the modern international states system. The war had ended the Eurocentricity of international politics since the Age of Discovery. In world politics the Soviet Union, Japan, and the United States had emerged as major forces that were supplanting the traditional European great powers. Yet Spengler desperately hoped that somehow this momentous development could be reversed. Hitler, contemptuous of the Soviet Union, had considerably more confidence in the prospects of German resurgence than did the cultural pessimist he decried. From a perspective of extreme Social Darwinism, Hitler defiantly believed that Germany could racially and martially reinvigorate Europe and frustrate the United States' bid for global hegemony, which had been foreshadowed in Wilson's diplomacy, notwithstanding his idealism. In his desperate struggle, Hitler destroyed Germany as a traditional great power (its core, Prussia, was abolished, and the truncated, reunified Germany of 2001 has a downsized military that is not autonomous), a disastrous development Spengler presciently foresaw as a possible outcome of the impending world war.

Hitler calculated that the rapid conquest of the Soviet Union west of the Urals would enable him not only to crush Bolshevism and destroy European Jewry but to provide the resource base required for Germany to stand up to America's tremendous economic and military potential. The Führer aspired to forge an *imperium Germanicum*, which would be strong enough to prevail over the United States if it obstinately refused to tolerate such an enormous increase in German power.

Hitler unquestionably achieved some striking early diplomatic and military successes. However, he failed to grasp the implications of the most cardinal fact of modern German diplomatic history, namely, that virtually any expansionary move by Germany provoked the formation of a formidable, opposing coalition of great powers. So elemental was this tendency in world politics that it had been earlier foreshadowed in the process of German unification itself. The tortuous process of the unification of Germany by Bismarck had succeeded because Russia, exhausted from the Crimean War, had adopted a noninterventionist stance toward Prussia's drive to unite Germany against Austrian and French resistance. After the achievement of German unity in 1871, the "Is War in Sight?" crisis of 1875, the Moroccan crises of 1905 and 1911, and the July crisis of 1914 all demonstrated the natural tendency for a powerful anti-German coalition, embracing the principal European great powers, Britain, France, and Russia, to coalesce when Germany became too self-assertive. Moreover, the United States showed its readiness to join this latent, anti-German coalition when it finally took shape during World War I. In a letter written in July, 1915, Spengler stressed the importance of this tendency of hostile coalitions to frustrate Prussia's and later the Second Reich's drive to power and the enormous difficulties faced by its diplomats in countering this danger. He emphasized the immense difficulties that Germany had faced in seeking to triumph against a hostile coalition in a bid to attain Continental hegemony when he soberly observed in 1924 that Germany's prewar position was "perhaps already hopeless" before the war began.[63]

Hitler appreciated the existence, but not the gravity, of this geostrategic predicament. Thus, he fatuously believed that it could be solved by combining three unrealistic approaches. His grand strategy called for a far-reaching accommodation with Britain; for brief, localized military campaigns against a restricted number of opponents; and finally and most absurdly, because of his obsession with radical Social-Darwinist ideas, for the breeding of a master, martial race. Hitler failed to understand that the prevention of European hegemony was an axiom of the British diplomatic tradition. He believed that he could gain British toleration of German

63. Spengler to Klöres, 14 July 1915, *B,* 42–43; *NdR,* 191.

Continental hegemony by offering a guarantee of the British Empire. The short wars Hitler envisioned degenerated into a death struggle once the Americans, the British, and the Russians joined forces in the Grand Alliance. Moreover, the idea that short, localized conflicts would establish German hegemony from the Atlantic to the Urals before the following generation might slug it out with the Americans was an absurd notion when one recalled that World War I had strikingly revealed the tendency toward the rapid internationalization and intensification of armed conflict. The United States had patiently sat on the sidelines a mere three years before intervening in World War I. Why should it wait twenty or thirty years, despite its interwar isolationism, before finally throwing its weight again onto the scales against a bid for German mastery of the Continent?

The unrealistic nature of Hitler's foreign policy objectives for Germany and his reckless attempt at their implementation resulted in the very destruction of German national integrity that Spengler feared. This places into bold relief the politically imprudent and dangerous nature of Spengler's influential opposition to the Weimar Republic. Despite its inability to obtain substantial revisions of the harsh provisions of the Versailles Treaty, except for a belated resolution of the reparations question, the Weimar Republic was a far superior government for Germany than that of the Nazis, viewed exclusively from the perspective of the primacy of foreign policy, the critical standard for Spengler. The very foreign policy impotence of the Weimar Republic, its painful lack of self-assertiveness, was eminently preferable to the fanatical devotion of Hitler to unattainable and ultimately self-destructive dreams of the conquest of an *imperium Germanicum*. Moreover, if Hitler had not succeeded in destroying the fledgling republic in the turmoil and despair of the Great Depression, it is probable that the inconstant leadership of Weimar Germany would have built upon Stresemann's modest achievements and eventually made significant foreign policy gains, given Britain's predisposition to appeasement in the thirties. A patient, steady, peacefully oriented German foreign policy would have enjoyed good prospects for securing German territorial integrity and provided the basis for a position of great weight in world affairs for the duration of the twentieth century, particularly in light of the economic potential of Germany, so impressively demonstrated in the post–World War II economic miracle. The superiority of the Weimar Republic to the Nazi regime in the area of domestic politics, particularly in respecting fundamental civil liberties, is so obvious as to render discussion superfluous.

The most significant development in Spengler's philosophy of politics during the interwar period was his growing pessimism about the future of the power-political relationship of the West to the non-West. He became skeptical about the capacity of any of the great powers of the West to create a modern counterpart of the Roman Empire, which would secure the global primacy Western civilization had enjoyed since the Age of Discovery. Given his disdain for American culture and certain Eurocentric features of his international political thought, he desperately hoped that Europe under German hegemony, and not the United States, would serve as the power-political anchor of Western civilization for generations to come. He vainly hoped that German national energies might somehow rejuvenate the West. At the same time, he feared that the West, mired in the Great Depression, was undergoing a lengthy, quite possibly irreversible process of power-political decline. One observes in his political thought, before and during the Great War, the transition from a buoyant optimism about Germany attaining global hegemony to a deepening pessimism during the twenties, which intensified still further in the thirties after the onset of world economic crisis. This transition in his political thought has its parallel, in even more pronounced form, in the development of his historical philosophy. His philosophy of world history begins as an amalgam of optimism and pessimism, only to end as unadulterated pessimism.

Conclusion: Spengler and Political Realism

THE FIRST PART OF THIS CHAPTER EXAM-
ines Spengler's significance as a philosopher of international relations. The
second part explores how his philosophy ultimately transcends the tradition of political realism in international relations theory. The final section
elucidates the ramifications for this tradition of his tragic vision of world
history and politics.

The discipline of international relations arose at the end of World War
I. Spengler's period of activity as the exponent of a distinctive political realism grounded in a philosophy of world history, from 1918 to 1936, is
contemporaneous with the idealist phase in international relations theory.
Political idealism's interwar dominance stemmed from the discrediting of
secret diplomacy and balance-of-power politics by the disaster of World
War I, the longing for world peace in Britain and the United States, and
the debut of the League of Nations as a focus of idealistic aspirations for
the institutionalization of collective security and general disarmament.
However, the rise of strident revisionist powers, Nazi Germany, fascist
Italy, and militarist Japan; the failure of the League of Nations to resolve
the Manchurian and Abyssinian crises; and the absence of firm international support for the principle of collective security all stimulated a gradual but distinct shift from political idealism to political realism in
international relations theory.[1] During the interwar period, there were two
main currents of scholarly study in international relations: current events
courses, which had superseded the study of diplomatic history, and the
idealistic preoccupation with world peace, reflected in courses on interna-

---

1. Reinhard Meyers, *Die Lehre von den Internationalen Beziehungen: Ein ent-
wicklungsgeschichtlicher Überblick*, rev. ed. (Düsseldorf: Droste Verlag, 1981), 25–26.

tional law and international organization.[2] Spengler's sui generis approach to the study of international relations sharply contrasted with both mainstream modes of inquiry. Employing a philosophy of world history made possible a more searching inquiry into the mainsprings of international political change in the twentieth century than did the superficial fashion of current events study. Enthusiasts of this fad venerated the *New York Times* as their bible and examined contemporary phenomena removed from their deeper historical roots.[3] Spengler's stern political realism, his recognition of the primacy of power and conflict in international politics, clashed with the faith of idealists in international law and organization to achieve world peace.

Any student of Spengler's thought is struck by his abrasive rejection of idealistic and ideological approaches to the major problems of world politics, which one finds in different form later in Morgenthau. Spengler anticipates the concern of international relations theorists since the publication of E. H. Carr's seminal work *The Twenty Years Crisis, 1919–1939* with the differentiation between realistic and idealistic perspectives on the critical problems of international relations. His opening argument in the section "Philosophy of Politics" in *The Decline of the West*, that we should seek to comprehend how statecraft "really has been made in the entire course of history" and not succumb to the illusion that "politics exists, in order to shape the course of the world according to an idealistic plan," can be easily placed alongside Morgenthau's thesis in *Politics Among Nations* that the realist must strive to understand international politics the way it is and not the way he wishes it were.[4]

Morgenthau and other realists typically ascribe man's inability to realize his dreams of transforming international relations to its unchanging character and realities and human nature. Spengler, emphasizing the primacy of necessity over freedom in world history, attributes this inability both to these conventional realist considerations and to the supreme indifference of the march of history to idealistic visions of radically improving international politics as well. The acerbity of Spengler's condemnation of idealism derives from his conviction of the power of necessity in world history and his pessimism about the future.

2. Kenneth W. Thompson, "The Study of International Politics: A Survey of Trends and Developments," *Review of Politics* 14, no. 1 (January, 1952): 434 ff.

3. Kenneth W. Thompson, "The Empirical, Normative, and Theoretical Foundations of International Studies," *Review of Politics* 29, no. 2 (April, 1967): 150.

4. *UdA* II, 544.

Spengler tries to discover what amounts to objective laws of history. He claims the statesman must adjust to them to be successful. For Spengler, history determines the bounds of the politically possible. The paramount task of the statesman is to grasp the direction of the flow of history, Bismarck's "stream of time."

The realist approach, which superseded the modes of inquiry based on diplomatic history or current events, increasingly concerned itself with "the possibility of recurrence."[5] Spengler anticipates the keen interest of twentieth-century political realists in investigating the possibility of theoretically significant recurrent phenomena in international politics. Indeed, in *The Decline of the West*, Spengler elaborates a system of recurrences and similarities in civilizational development and international politics more rigid than what most theorists of international relations would dare to propound.

Spengler's philosophy of world history and politics eminently fulfills the need in the discipline for a global perspective. As Charles McClelland noted, "any conceptual framework adequate for the field of international relations must have the dimensions of a world view." At the dawn of the third millennium A.D., in an increasingly complex and interdependent world undergoing accelerating change, there is a compelling need for wide-ranging, historically informed thought about world politics. Spengler's reflections on history admirably respond to this imperative and are quite relevant to the concerns of international relations theory. As James Joll observed, Spengler serves to "remind us of the grand sweep of history and enlarge our field of vision beyond the historical provincialism into which we all too easily fall." His philosophy of international relations is anticipatory and oriented to the future, responsive to the intellectual demands of an age of explosive global change and crisis. Indeed, as Harold and Margaret Sprout observed about the sphere of international relations, "in no sector of human affairs is it more imperative to be future-oriented."[6]

Interestingly, several foreign policy practitioners and international rela-

5. Thompson, "Study of International Politics," 458.
6. Charles McClelland, "Application of General Systems Theory in International Relations," in James N. Rosenau, ed., *International Politics and Foreign Policy: A Reader in Research and Theory* (New York: Free Press of Glencoe, 1961), 416; James Joll, "Two Prophets of the Twentieth Century: Spengler and Toynbee," *Review of International Studies* 11 (1985): 103; Harold Sprout and Margaret Sprout, *Toward a Politics of the Planet Earth* (New York: Van Nostrand Reinhold, 1971), v.

272 / *Prophet of Decline*

tions scholars evidenced varying degrees of interest in Spengler's ideas. They include George Kennan, Henry Kissinger, Paul Nitze, Louis Halle, Morgenthau, Toynbee, Shotwell, Carr, Raymond Aron, Reinhold Niebuhr, Adda Bozeman, and Joll.[7] Kennan waded persistently through *The Decline of the West* "with the help of a dictionary" during a vacation in Germany when he was a young man. Harvard seemed to attract its share of young "Spenglerians." Kissinger produced a massive undergraduate thesis at Harvard on Spengler, Toynbee, and Kant. One of Kissinger's biographers relates that "Spengler also fascinated Paul Nitze, who in the late 1930s quit his Wall Street job to go to Harvard and study *The Decline of the West*." Halle reported receiving poor grades at Harvard as he neglected his class assignments to devote himself to "a course of reading that represented the interest in Spengler's vision" aroused by his high school German teacher.[8] Morgenthau apparently always kept his copy of Spengler's major work within easy reach on his bookshelf.[9] Toynbee was so awed by the experience of reading the first volume in German of *The Decline of the West* that he related how he "wondered at first whether [his] whole inquiry [into world history] had been disposed of by Spengler before even the questions, not to speak of the answers, had fully taken shape in [his] own mind."[10] Yet despite the interest in Spengler among several foreign

7. See the following: James T. Shotwell, "Spengler," chap. in *The Faith of an Historian and Other Essays* (New York: Walker, 1964); E. H. Carr, "Die Geschichte wiederholt sich nicht: Oswald Spengler und Arnold Toynbee," *Die Kultur* 5, no. 92 (1956–57); with respect to Aron, Gilbert Merlio, *Oswald Spengler: Témoin de son temps*, 2 vols. (Stuttgart: Akademischer Verlag Hans-Dieter Heinz, 1982); Kenneth W. Thompson, "Reinhold Niebuhr," in *Masters of International Thought* (Baton Rouge: Louisiana State Univ. Press, 1980), 27; Adda B. Bozeman, "Decline of the West? Spengler Reconsidered," *Virginia Quarterly Review* 59, no. 2 (Spring, 1983): 181–207; Joll, "Two Prophets of the Twentieth Century," 91–104.

8. George F. Kennan, *Memoirs, 1925–1950* (Boston: Atlantic Monthly Press, 1967), 19; Henry A. Kissinger, "The Meaning of History: Reflections on Spengler, Toynbee and Kant" (A.B. thesis, Harvard University, 1951); Walter Isaacson, quoted in Neil McInnes, "The Great Doomsayer: Oswald Spengler Reconsidered," *National Interest*, no. 48 (Summer, 1997): 70 n. 2; Louis J. Halle, *History, Philosophy, and Foreign Relations: Background for the Making of Foreign Policy* (Lanham, Md.: University Press of America, 1987), 394.

9. Related to this author in a conversation with Christoph Frei, author of an intellectual biography of Morgenthau, *Hans J. Morgenthau: Eine intellektuelle Biographie* (Bern: Haupt, 1994).

10. Arnold J. Toynbee, *Civilization on Trial* (New York: Oxford Univ. Press, 1948), 9.

policy practitioners and international relations scholars, the question of his place in modern international theory has received relatively little attention in the literature.[11] His contribution to international theory has remained largely unknown and his challenging ideas have not been reformulated into a theoretical stance on international relations.

With his argument of the indispensability of historical knowledge to the analysis of world politics, Spengler certainly must be assigned to the ranks of the traditionalists, notwithstanding his unusual approach to international theory. Nonetheless, his quasi-positivism, propensity for "model-building," and aspiration to predictive theoretical power all have an undeniable "scientific" flavor. Spengler's philosophy, despite his rejection of "scientific methods" to study history, foreshadows by over half a century the passion of representatives of the behavioral/quantitative or scientific orientation in international relations to develop theories conferring predictive capabilities. As McClelland observed, "The frank objective of the scientific approach is to learn about patterns and trends in order to be able to predict what is *likely* to happen in international relations." Spengler rapidly came to appreciate the impossibility of predicting with any precision the future contours of international politics and instead sought, more modestly, to ascertain dimly general lines of development. Interestingly, so have many of the later "scientific" theoreticians of world politics wisely abandoned their grandiose predictive modeling attempts.[12]

The taxonomy of levels of analysis in international relations conventionally consists of the individual, the state, the region, and the international system.[13] Discourse with Spengler suggests that this classificatory scheme is incomplete. He champions the idea that the ultimate (and, one hastens to add, the inevitably most speculative) macrolevel of analysis in international relations is that of the process of world history itself. For international relations, notwithstanding the gravity and complexity of the

11. Indicative of the inattention to Spengler are the following works: James E. Dougherty and Robert L. Pfaltzgraff, Jr., *Contending Theories of International Relations: A Comprehensive Survey*, 3d ed. (New York: Harper & Row, 1990); F. Parkinson, *The Philosophy of International Relations: A Study in the History of Thought* (Beverly Hills: Sage Publications, 1977).

12. Charles A. McClelland, "International Relations: Wisdom or Science?" in James N. Rosenau, ed., *International Politics and Foreign Policy: A Reader in Research and Theory*, rev. ed. (New York: Free Press, 1969), 4; Reinhard Meyers, *Weltpolitik in Grundbegriffen*, vol. I, *Ein lehr- und ideengeschichtlicher Grundriß* (Düsseldorf: Droste Verlag, 1979), 89.

13. See Reinhard Meyers, *Weltpolitik*, 207 ff.

developments it encompasses, is subsumed within the process of world history. Spengler is the first thinker to develop fully world history as a level of analysis for the study of international relations.

Spengler offers a panoramic vision of transformation in international relations in the twentieth century and beyond. He enriches our understanding by demonstrating how world politics transpires on the shifting tectonic plates of civilizational development. His philosophy of history illuminates many major events in international relations in the nineteenth and twentieth centuries. Notwithstanding certain imperfections of his historical and international relations analysis, our understanding of key developments such as the destruction of the European balance-of-power system, two world wars, the Great Depression and later crises of the global economy, decolonization and the North-South conflict, Soviet expansionism, the end to European primacy in world politics and the creation of the Pax Americana, and the emergence of quasi-pacifism in the West are all enhanced by his philosophy of world history. The failure of specialists in international relations to have built upon the foundation provided by Spengler's reflections on the tragedy of world history and politics in the twentieth century has impoverished theorizing about international relations.

Discourse with Spengler also prompts one to regard skeptically American optimism about promoting the economic modernization of the developing world. From his perspective, the modernization of the non-West through the diffusion of the civilizational achievements of the Occident will not result in the creation of a stable and reasonably prosperous ecumenical world order, given the deep-seated cultural and power-political antagonisms between the West and the non-West and the tenuous stability of the global economy. Tragically, efforts to modernize the non-West will ultimately undermine the economic preeminence of the West. This bold thesis was enunciated in 1931 and is of striking relevance in the twentieth and twenty-first centuries.

Modern political realists have persisted in a restrictive Rankean focus on diplomacy and balance-of-power politics. In contrast to Spengler, they have also not sufficiently reflected, with the exception of Carr, on the dangers to international political stability posed by untoward economic developments.[14] Spengler's political economy of the decline of the West is a

14. See Samuel P. Huntington, "Why International Primacy Matters," *International Security* 17, no. 4 (Spring, 1993): 72; Robert G. Gilpin, "The Richness of the

significant, and hitherto unappreciated, implicit critique of the premises of neoliberalism. Neoliberalism rests upon the debatable assumption that the universal embrace of free-market policies and the implementation of such measures as trade liberalization, privatization, and fiscal austerity will help promote enduring international economic stability. Spengler boldly argues that the global economy will eventually collapse as part of the grand process of civilizational decline.

Spengler's philosophy of world history sheds light on the spread of quasi-pacifism in the West and the martialness of important states of the non-West, such as Iran and Iraq. The West has undergone a remarkable transition from nationalistic and, at times, bellicose great powers in the decades before World War I to quasi-pacifistic states. This metamorphosis is not merely a rational reaction to the horrendous human suffering of two world wars and anxiety about the destructiveness of weapons of mass destruction. This profound change also reflects the proliferation of quasi-pacifism in societies in the twilight of their civilizational evolution.

Spengler foresaw the fall of Communism in Russia, an event that caught most international relations experts by surprise. Indeed, virtually none of them predicted it when Gorbachev assumed power. Spengler envisioned the Soviet Union in the vanguard of the revolt of the non-West against the West. Thus, he emerges, after a fashion, as a major prophet of the Cold War, which dominated international relations from 1947 to 1990. He believed that the antagonism between Russia and the West was deep and enduring. The end of the Cold War and the demise of the Soviet empire precipitated optimism in the early 1990s in the United States that a new era of cooperative relations between the two former adversaries was dawning. This dream has proven to be unfounded. The strains in American-Russian relations and the formidable difficulties Russia confronts in attempting the dual transition to a free-market economy and full-fledged democracy are consistent with Spengler's understanding of Russian history and culture.

Spengler's relationship to modern political realism deserves more in-depth exploration. The hallmark of political realism, indeed its theoretical justification for providing counsel in the chambers of power, is its rationalism. In Morgenthau's formulation, "politics is engaged in by rational men

Tradition of Political Realism," in Robert O. Keohane, ed. *Neorealism and Its Critics* (New York: Columbia Univ. Press, 1986), 310.

who pursue certain rational interests with rational means."[15] Although Spengler is an important figure in the German tradition of *raison d'État*, he evidences, in contrast to other political realists, greater insight into the oft-irrational qualities of foreign policy and the irrational nature of modern civilization and the milieu in which statesmen function.

Traditionally, the state is regarded optimistically by political realists as a rational actor in international relations. Robert Keohane identifies this purported rationality of state behavior as one of the "three key assumptions" of realism: States "behave in ways that are, by and large, rational, and therefore comprehensible to outsiders in rational terms." Neorealists readily incorporate this problematic idea into their theories. Kenneth Waltz adopts the "assumption of rationality" in analyzing state behavior, and Robert Gilpin argues that "states make cost/benefit calculations in the determination of foreign policy and that a goal of a state's foreign policy is to change the international system in ways that will enhance the state's own interests."[16] Nonetheless, Spengler attacks in three ways the assumption that the state is a rational actor, which is ultimately the justification for the Rankean doctrine of the primacy of foreign policy he himself adopted. First, he describes how even the "prudent" statesman can be compelled to pursue lines of policy by powerful urges he cannot resist. For example, modern Western imperialism is an irrational and irresistible force that seizes hold of even the "prudent" statesman. Thus, Spengler highlights the ineluctability of the two world wars. Second, he underscores the danger posed by the irrational and self-destructive urge of the West to disseminate its invaluable technology in the non-West, which thereupon exploits it to undermine the economic preeminence of the West. Third, his apocalyptic vision of world history raises the specter of the rational international political actor, the state, being impotent to prevent the destruction of civilization as we know it. It matters little the resolution and skill with which the "national interest" may be pursued by each of the various statesmen in power in the world's capitals and the extent of the resources at their disposal. The thoroughgoing historical pessimism of Spengler's

15. Hans J. Morgenthau, "The Nature and Limits of a Theory of International Relations," in Ernst Otto-Czempiel, ed., *Die Lehre von den Internationalen Beziehungen* (Darmstadt: Wissenschaftliche Buchgesellschaft, 1969), 69.

16. Robert O. Keohane, "Realism, Neorealism and the Study of World Politics," in Keohane, *Neorealism*, 7; Kenneth N. Waltz, "Reflections on 'Theory of International Politics': A Response to My Critics," in Keohane, *Neorealism*, 331; Robert Gilpin, *War and Change in World Politics* (Cambridge: Cambridge Univ. Press, 1981), 50.

late work threatens to hollow out the main theoretical justification for the primacy of foreign policy, namely, that the state can pursue "rational" and reasonably successful foreign policy. This has been a fundamental principle in the German tradition of power politics from Frederick the Great to Meinecke and a central tenet of American political realism.

The diplomatic style and wisdom of the great tradition of European statecraft earned Spengler's respect. However, his variant of *Realpolitik* also stands out for its heretical rejection of confidence in balance-of-power policies, a cardinal tenet of political realism in the twentieth century. The principle of the balance of power was revived after World War II by American political realism. Reflection on Spengler underscores a serious weakness in Morgenthau's core argument that a statesman should always pursue a foreign policy consonant with the salubrious operation of the balance of power. For the organic process of the development and self-extension of a civilization may dictate at times, not balance-of-power policies, but the opposite, namely, hegemonic policies. These may facilitate the construction by a rising power of an international political structure conducive to the realization of the aspirations of a dominant, expansive civilization. Politics among nations is more than a struggle for power and peace. It is also an intense competition for the necessary influence and resources and the requisite territory or space to develop civilizational potential fully.

The mainstream European tradition of statecraft was committed to the preservation of the European balance-of-power system. Spengler brilliantly perceived, in contrast to the Neo-Rankeans, the historical inevitability of its destruction by hegemonic struggle and its replacement by a universal empire. Displaying insight into the revolt of the non-West against its subordination in world affairs, he maintained that the Western universal empire would fail to establish an enduring balance of power between itself and its non-Western adversaries.

Intellectual conversation with Spengler supports the argument that international hegemony is an important theoretical alternative to the balance of power in the management of power in international affairs. Under "favorable" historical circumstances, an architecture of hegemony can be erected after opposition to it has been overcome. Hegemonic policies can provide a temporary but nonetheless valuable and substantial measure of world order. The benefits of the Pax Romana in antiquity and the Pax Americana immediately spring to mind. Spengler's espousal of international hegemony as the organizing principle of world politics in the twentieth century and beyond derived in part from his being pessimistic, on the eve of World War I, that the classic balance-of-power system of Europe, under the volcanic pressure of nationalistic and imperialistic passions, could be maintained or transformed, as the Neo-Rankeans had hoped. He is unusual in the tradition of modern political realism for his compelling argument that the strongest power of the West should consciously strive, not to shore up or globally expand the European balance-of-power system, but boldly to create a structure of hegemony facilitating the attainment by modern Western civilization of its ultimate potentialities. He initially overrated Germany's capacity to fulfill this historic mission and failed to perceive America's stronger claim to accomplish this task. His philosophy, purged of its Germanocentricity, would have greatly aided American statesmen in the twentieth century in founding and securing the Pax Americana. That such counsel would have fallen on deaf ears in the United States, given the powerful isolationist, nativistic, and idealistic-internationalist strains in American political culture, reflects the aimlessness and drift of American foreign policy before Pearl Harbor.

Spengler was aware of the difficulty any great, empire-building nation in history faced in maintaining over a long span of time a high level of military performance. For, as he argued, was not imperial Rome truly in form only in its "*classic* wars" against the Samnites, Pyrrhus, and Carthage? "There is no people that remains majestic through the centuries," he observed in his reflections on the exhaustion of national strength in the drive to world empire.[17] The same can be said of the United States, whose people displayed courage, tenacity, and the unshakable will to victory in the Revolutionary War, the Mexican-American War, the Civil War as a divided people, and the world wars. Such magnificent demonstrations of national resolve were followed by the stalemate of Korea, the humiliation of Vietnam, the comical exercise of Grenada, and embarrassment in Bosnia. A key lesson one can draw from Spengler's works is that the Pax Americana, while arguably a historical necessity conforming to the logic of civilizational self-articulation, is nonetheless a transitory phenomenon, a mutable concentration of power that demands an exemplary statecraft to retard its inevitable decay. His thought illustrates the necessity of strategic vision in foreign policy combined with moral regeneration to husband a hegemonic power's energies for executing a strategy of siege prolongation against its external foes and competitors, both military and economic. American for-

17. *UdA* I, 48.

eign policy has suffered in the post–World War II era from idealism about the capacity of man to surmount power politics and hubristic faith in America's enduring supremacy in world affairs. Spengler counseled the inability of man to transcend power politics and the transitory nature of the strength of any great power. Moreover, he was cognizant of the primacy of economic factors in world affairs in the twentieth century. Admiring the phenomenal modernizing drive of the Japanese, he recognized decades ago the need for the West to foster and maintain vigorously scientific, technological, and industrial leadership and to minimize technology transfer to non-Western economic rivals.

Despite his commitment to imperialism and hegemonic policies, Spengler was not without a sense of appreciation for the role of prudence and compromise in power politics. We have seen how he retrospectively voiced support for the idea of Imperial Germany courting Tsarist Russia with her ambitions in the Balkans at the expense of the Austro-Hungarian Empire on the eve of World War I. Cassandra-like, he cautioned against the idea of a Nazi invasion of the Soviet Union, eight years before Hitler launched the disastrous Operation Barbarossa. Moreover, his original Germanocentric vision of the final imperial form of the West was based less upon outright conquest and more upon the achievement and maintenance of global economic hegemony. Spengler, unlike Pan-German imperialists, rightfully esteemed British statecraft, whose hallmarks were cosmopolitan sophistication, prudence, compromise, and unidealistic commitment to power politics, as the most superb tradition of foreign policy, along with that of Rome, in world history.

Political realism is a self-congratulatory term. Thus, when one appraises a political realist's thought, one must be sensitive to the distinction between the presence of the traditional philosophical characteristics of political realism and the realism of the so-called realist. The key question is whether the international political analysis of the political realist in question is truly realistic or not. Spengler's orientation is unquestionably in the modern realist tradition of international relations theory. His pessimism about human nature; his opposition to the projects of political idealism, particularly disarmament and collective security, as solutions to the dilemma of war in international politics; his emphasis on the central role of power; his thesis of the recurrent nature of great-power conflict in history; and his endorsement of the primacy of foreign policy all attest to his being a political realist. However, the actual content of his political realism, his specific analysis of world politics, is, on occasion, erroneous, at times unexceptional, and at times remarkably insightful.

Spengler simultaneously made contributions to three major intellectual traditions in Germany: historical philosophy, *Kulturpessimismus*, and *Realpolitik*. He is primarily a philosopher of world history and a *Kulturkritiker* and secondarily a philosopher of international relations. Yet this creative, interdisciplinary thinker merits recognition as a philosopher of international relations of the first rank. Spengler deserves this distinction for two reasons. First, he understood that insight into world history and the flow and direction of modern civilizational development facilitates a deeper understanding of international relations in the twentieth century and beyond. Second, he provides a very useful framework for trying to understand the major trends and the forces at work in modern history and politics and illuminates the apocalyptic potential of modernity.

Strictly speaking, Spengler is clearly more significant as a philosopher of world history than as an analyst of international relations. For example, unlike his rival Toynbee, he was not a specialist in world affairs, despite his keen interest in the subject. Spengler unquestionably devoted far more of his time and energy to the study of world history than he did to international politics. While the capacity of historical knowledge to provide insight into international political developments has matured in the twentieth century, the complexity of such developments has simultaneously dramatically increased. Indeed, as Kissinger observed of the post–Cold War world, "the emerging international system is far more complex than any previously encountered."[18] Decades earlier Spengler achieved only partial success in illuminating the course of development in international politics. One major constraint was that it is impossible for a solitary scholar to acquire an encyclopaedic knowledge of the immense fields of both universal history and international relations.

Discourse with Spengler leads to the conclusion that, at some point in the future, political realism will be at a loss in counseling statesmen on how to face the challenges besetting a civilization in terminal crisis. Ultimately, world history, in Spengler's view, will reach its tragic climax. The saturninity of his historical pessimism at this approaching juncture of history completely eclipses his hopes for constructive statecraft. It is at this indeterminate point, as we try to peer through the brooding mists of the future, that Spengler's historical pessimism can provide no counsel on how

18. Henry Kissinger, *Diplomacy* (New York: Simon & Schuster, 1994), 833.

to formulate effective foreign policy. For, eventually, political realism will be exhausted in the face of the overpowering tragedy of world history and politics. His philosophy of world history in his late work illuminates what virtually the entire spectrum of international relations theory desperately struggles to deny, the ineluctability of the destruction of modern civilization. It is at this final crossroads of history, as he argued in the conclusion of *Man and Technics*, that the hour of heroic fortitude strikes. All that is left to denizens of a disintegrating world is to resist the temptation to abandon themselves to nihilistic self-indulgence and instead to retain their culturally fostered ethos of self-worth, to remain resolutely at their posts to the bitter end, to go down doing their duty.

Now that we have drawn some conclusions about Spengler's significance as a philosopher of international relations, we can consider further the matter we have just touched on, how his philosophy ultimately transcends the tradition of political realism, and elucidate the ramifications of his tragic vision of world history for modern political realist thought. In two ways Spengler sought to counteract politically idealistic approaches to statecraft in the interwar period. First, he tried to demonstrate that human freedom has much less latitude in shaping the course of history than idealists commonly assume. Second, he attempted to delineate the nonprogressive nature of history, particularly in its civilizational and international political dimensions. According to Spengler, world history is ultimately irrational, destructive, and uncontrollable. Man cannot control the forces of history, steer them in a desired direction, or turn back or freeze the process of history. The great reserves of human freedom in history that the idealist imagines to be the mighty Archimedean lever that he and his fellow-believers can use to ensure global stability and world peace are a chimaera. However, the deepening of Spengler's historical pessimism in the interwar years undermined his attempt at a realist critique of idealism. For in his cosmology of world history and politics, statecraft, of both the idealist and the realist variety, is, in the long run, incapable of mastering the forces of chaos in the twentieth century and beyond.

It should come as no surprise to the reader to learn that prominent interwar political idealists who had perused Spengler's major work opposed his historical pessimism. James T. Shotwell, in an essay written in 1929, argued that the uniqueness of Occidental civilization, its scientific achievements, its development of a global interdependent economy, its purported capacity to attain general social justice, and the supposed staying power and invigorating energy of democratic institutions will enable the West not only to endure but quite possibly to experience dramatic progress in the future.[19]

Toynbee, a temperamental optimist, rejected Spengler's pessimism about the fate of the West. In 1948, after the most terrible war in human history and the dawn of the nuclear age, Toynbee manifested imperturbable confidence in human progress, asserting, "our *post mortem* examination of dead civilizations does not enable us to cast the horoscope of our own civilization or of any other that is still alive. *Pace* Spengler, there seems to be no reason why a succession of stimulating challenges should not be met by a succession of victorious responses *ad infinitum*."[20]

Political realists, like theorists of international relations in general, run the risk of their normative hopes and wishes diluting the force of their theoretical analyses. Discourse with Spengler suggests that it is probably unrealistic to believe that statesmen, particularly in the future, are and will be truly capable of managing the predicaments of world politics. Did not their predecessors prove woefully incapable of preventing two world wars, a crippling world economic crisis, and the Cold War? And are not the burdens on statesmen potentially much greater today, given that international relations are more complex and the pace of change more rapid? The core normative aspiration of modern political realism, to improve, within limits, the world, has at a theoretical level impaired recognition of the possible existence of an irresistible movement of modern civilization toward a cataclysmic climax, which Spengler's philosophy illuminates.

Spengler's philosophy of world history was originally conceived as the bedrock of an innovative form of political realism. Ironically, because of its dialectical development in his later years, it metamorphosed itself into a philosophy whose radical theses raised the very question of the utility and potency of political realism. The irrationalism of modern civilization, illuminated by his deepening cultural pessimism and his tragic vision of world history, will overwhelm the limited capacities of "rational" statecraft. The statesman would ultimately prove powerless to withstand the historical forces that would irresistibly propel civilized man to his doom.

The main challenge to modern political realism is traditionally regarded among international relations theorists as issuing from political idealism. With their grandiose but uplifting schemes for transforming the conflictual nation-state system through international law and organization, idealists

19. Shotwell, "Spengler," 228–29.
20. Toynbee, *Civilization*, 12.

advanced a visionary approach to world politics that the realists sought to discredit with their skepticism and seemingly depressing ideas. The axiom in the discipline that equates political realism with pessimism is a questionable one. Gilpin maintains that "unlike its polar opposite, idealism, realism is founded on a pessimism regarding moral progress and human possibilities." Keith Shimko stressed that classical realism's "entire outlook on international politics rested on an unflattering view of man," a "pessimistic view of man." Keohane spoke of realism's "pessimistic assumptions about individual and state behavior," and Joseph Grieco emphasized its "gloomy understanding of world politics."[21]

Yet political realism, as espoused by Carr, Niebuhr, Morgenthau, Kennan, Kissinger, and others, can be subjected to searching criticism from a far different perspective, that of deep historical pessimism. Indeed, from this unorthodox, Archimedean standpoint, political realists are revealed not to be authentic pessimists despite the fact that they are universally identified as such in the literature. On closer inspection, the "pessimism" of realists—a pessimism associated with their opposition to the historical optimism and grand designs of idealists, with their insight into the power instincts of the human psyche, and with their insistence on the recurrence of struggle and conflict in world politics—is not all that pessimistic. For their pessimism is greatly diluted by their dubious hopefulness and guarded optimism that statecraft infused with their "realism" can weather the storm of civilizational crisis that ensued with the Great War.

Spengler envisions the tidal flow of world history pushing mankind in the twentieth century and beyond toward shipwreck. He offers a unique perspective for critiquing the hopefulness and guarded optimism of modern political realism. The simplistic and debatable characterization of political realism as a pessimistic philosophy of international relations has hindered recognition that it incorporates significant elements of hopefulness and guarded optimism. American realists embrace the questionable belief that if policy makers rely on them for policy prescription, they will facilitate the continued primacy of the United States in the international arena and the growth and development of Western civilization in the

21. Gilpin, "Tradition of Political Realism," 304; Keith L. Shimko, "Realism, Neorealism, and American Liberalism," *Review of Politics* 54, no. 2 (Spring, 1992): 283, 287; Robert O. Keohane, *After Hegemony: Cooperation and Discord in the World Political Economy* (Princeton: Princeton Univ. Press, 1984), 245; Joseph M. Grieco, "Anarchy and the Limits of Cooperation: A Realist Critique of the Newest Liberal Institutionalism," *International Organization* 42, no. 3 (Summer, 1988): 486.

twentieth century and far into the future. The phenomenal dynamism and tensions unleashed by the civilizational energy of the West have made a cataclysmic climax to world history, unfortunately, quite plausible. The entire tradition of political realism expects the perpetuation of the international states system, while Spengler's historical philosophy anticipates its slide into chaos.

A philosophy of political realism, committed to the ethical responsibility of political action, of statecraft, is, by its very nature, incapable of acknowledging the arguable inevitability of the end of modern civilization. Yet, ironically, has not this civilization, despite its patina of rationality, created the most alarming sense of international political crisis in the entirety of human history? Indeed, modern political realism shares with theories of international relations, in general, the explicit or implicit assumption—an assumption that is ultimately of normative origin and thus of questionable analytical potency—that mankind will not succumb to the severe crises it faces. Modern political realism is unwilling to acknowledge the remarkable depth of the tragedy of world history and politics, claiming instead to be capable of ameliorating it through resourceful policy prescription.

Our critique of political realism should not be misconstrued as a depreciation of its accomplishments. The contributions of political realism to international relations theory are of major significance. Twentieth-century political realists have probed the weaknesses of idealist solutions to the dilemmas of world politics. They have enriched our appreciation of the wisdom of the classic European tradition of power politics. Morgenthau's construction in *Politics Among Nations* of a systematic theory of international relations remains, despite its flaws, an enduring achievement in international relations thought in the twentieth century. Finally, political realists have, at times, contributed to the formulation of prudent foreign policy.

Twentieth-century political realists believed that moderation, skillful diplomacy, and balance-of-power policies would not only promote national security but help safeguard modern civilization as well. Political realists did not appreciate sufficiently the irrationality and exceedingly problematic nature of modernity as did the German tradition of cultural pessimism, represented by Schopenhauer, Burckhardt, Nietzsche, and Spengler. The fundamentally irrational nature of modern civilization, its powerful self-destructive tendencies, may make it resistant to efforts to preserve it by the principal actors in international relations.

The modern tradition of political realism has lacked a sense of the profound irrationality of modern civilization and of the decline of the West as an inevitable phenomenon. Morgenthau, for example, did not appreciate Spengler's vision of the irrational nature of Western civilization when he disparagingly observed, "Spengler, with that Hegelian consistency which takes absurd conclusions in its stride as long as they follow logically from premises, forces the history of civilizations into the biological straitjacket and, again not unlike Hegel, finds in the apparent trends of the contemporary scene experimental proof for the pseudoscientific premise of biological necessity." However, Toynbee's heartening thesis of the capacity of human freedom to enable Western civilization to endure, a success he denied to more than twenty earlier civilizations, is given the stamp of approval by Morgenthau, being "a measure of philosophic sophistication."[22]

Carr published a short article in German on the philosophies of world history of Toynbee and Spengler in 1957. He dubiously claims that man's intelligence and his knowledge of the past prevent history from repeating itself and invalidate the necessity of civilizations to experience decline. Niebuhr explored Spengler's thought during the thirties and was influenced by it, yet his evolving tragic sense of history was not as deep as that of Spengler and did not induce the Protestant theologian to abandon faith in man's future. As Kenneth W. Thompson notes, while Niebuhr's "anxious concern for man's fate was constant . . . so was his unquenchable faith that mankind has a future deriving from the Christian vision and the organic view of society." Philosophy of history formed the foundation of Kissinger's political realism. In his treatment of Spengler's philosophy of history in his B.A. thesis, Kissinger objects to Spengler's argument of the limited role of human freedom in history and in statecraft. Kissinger boldly asserts, "Necessity describes the past, but freedom rules the future."[23] He rejects Spengler's pessimism as unsuitable for the formulation of statecraft.

In *Diplomacy*, Kissinger elaborates his philosophy of statecraft as he surveys the evolution of international relations in modern times. In the conclusion, he speculates about the likely future threats to international peace and stability, the shifting rankings in the hierarchy of the great powers, and America's prospects for building an architecture of world order for the third time in the twentieth century. Not surprising, Kissinger sounds

22. Hans J. Morgenthau, "The Rediscovery of Imagination and Religion: Arnold Toynbee," in *The Restoration of American Politics* (Chicago: Univ. of Chicago Press, 1962), 59.

23. Carr, "Die Geschichte"; Thompson, "Niebuhr," 27–28; Kissinger, "The Meaning of History," 24.

rather optimistic that the United States can help create and maintain a reasonable measure of international order in the post–Cold War world. He recommends that the United States exercise a leadership role that blends the spirit of Wilsonian idealism to motivate the masses with a calculating, elitist *Realpolitik* concern for upholding a balance of power. Yet his book, notwithstanding its merits, is too nostalgic for the moribund past of European cabinet diplomacy and too moderate in tone. He doesn't offer much insight into our civilizational crisis, which imperils the prospects for the very kind of constructive grand strategy he confidently prescribes.

Although many of the leading political realists of the twentieth century were exposed to Spengler's philosophy of world history, his cultural pessimism seemed to exert little influence on their ideas. Thus, modern political realism insulated itself from the boldest and historical-philosophically most profound contribution to the European tradition of cultural pessimism.

The end of the Cold War formed a watershed in international history. Yet again, the United States was the only viable candidate to construct, multilaterally with the assistance of its principal allies, some semblance of world order. In the words of Walter Russell Mead, the Cold War's end found "the United States facing for the third time in a century the daunting prospect of creating order out of a chaotic global situation." But if the human race is indeed "confronting all the terrors of the apocalypse," it is illusory to expect visionary statecraft from Washington.[24]

Our world is plagued by critical problems in international relations, all of which are adumbrated in Spengler's philosophy of world history and politics. They include the danger of a severe global economic crisis, foreshadowed in the Asian contagion; the threat of an exacerbation of the North-South conflict; the population explosion in developing countries; the recrudescence of cultural, ethnic, and nationalistic conflict as exemplified by Bosnia and Rwanda; the proliferation of weapons of mass destruction; and the crisis of the global environment. From a neo-Spenglerian perspective, neither political realism nor idealism, nor more trendy approaches in international relations theory, can help statesmen resolve the crisis of world politics. This mounting crisis should not be understood as a manifestation of the interaction of manageable international political factors on the surface of an essentially rational world civilization, as analysts

24. Walter Russell Mead, "An American Grand Strategy: The Quest for Order in a Disordered World," *World Policy Journal* 50, no. 1 (Spring, 1993): 36, 37.

of international relations are wont to do. Instead, it should be understood as a fundamental expression of the irrational nature of modern civilization. Thus, the crisis of world politics is in the long run impervious to rationally conceived methods of political adjustment or management. It would have been most painful for Spengler, a conservative advocate of tough, "realistic" policies, to acknowledge that a logical consequence of the metamorphosis of his philosophy of world history and politics is arguably a grand apolitical perspective. Such a perspective would mean a turning full circle to the positions of his German cultural pessimist forerunners, Schopenhauer, Burckhardt, and Nietzsche. For Spengler, the aspiring *praeceptor Germaniae*, philosophy had to serve life, and this meant the *vita activa* of politics. His main work had been directed, above all else, to the elite *homo politicus.* "Every line that has not been written in order to serve the active life seems superfluous to me." For him to acknowledge that his twilight philosophy of world history arguably culminated in apoliticism would have been unthinkable. Apoliticism would have meant forsaking his major work, the source of his fame, which sought to create "a *world-picture, in which one can live,* and not a *world system, in which one can ponder.*"[25] Yet how can one live, as an engaged political actor, with the cataclysmic world picture that he sketched in his later years?

We have seen in this study how Spengler's passionate commitment to developing a politically engaged form of cultural pessimism ultimately did not yield success. In the final analysis, fidelity to his deepening cultural pessimism threatened to develop dialectically into apoliticism, a fact he stubbornly refused to acknowledge. Spengler's grand attempt to merge the insights of three major intellectual traditions of modern Germany, historical philosophy, *Kulturpessimismus*, and *Realpolitik* ironically miscarried. For his own pathbreaking contributions to the first two traditions were incapable of reconciliation with the latter.

In 1989, in the twilight of the Cold War, Fukuyama generated worldwide interest in the provocative idea of an end of history and the dawn of an age of peace, liberal democracy, and increasingly diffused capitalist prosperity. Spengler's catastrophic vision of an end of history is diametrically opposed to the dubious, optimistic, neo-Hegelian one Fukuyama advanced. Fukuyama asserted that Spengler did not achieve "the degree of seriousness of . . . [his] German predecessors" like Hegel and Marx and that historical pessimism "is contradicted by the empirical flow of events

25. P, 64.

in the second half of the century."[26] In his essay "The End of History?," and the subsequent book that provides much elaboration, he attested to his faith that liberal democratic societies and free-market economies can preserve sufficient vitality in a perpetual era of post-history. He expressed his confidence in the capacity of the industrial democracies to sustain international economic order, to keep within manageable limits the North-South development gap and minimize conflict, and to help the planet avoid ecological crisis. *Pace* Fukuyama, instead of greeting the dawn of an eternal post-historical epoch, I fear the cataclysmic disintegration of international order and a tumultuous end to the modern age. Our extraordinarily complex and fragile global civilization is presently at risk. It rests perilously upon the tectonic plates of international politics, which threaten to shift violently and bring it crashing down.

The end of the Cold War and the purported triumph of the Western principles of free-market capitalism and democracy temporarily bred optimism. New life was breathed into the Wilsonian dream that the dynamic and supposedly largely benign process of world history would generously provide the durable foundation for a new age of spreading democracy, capitalist prosperity, and world peace. The political idealism of the interwar period, whose leading light among statesmen was Wilson, represents the predecessor of contemporary liberal internationalism, whose idealistic vision of world order in the 1990s and beyond anticipates more and more democratic nation-states living in harmony with each other in a stable and interdependent global economy. As democracy broadly spreads in the developing world, it contends, global peace will be achieved. Such a vision is based on the presumptions that democratic states are peace-loving and refrain from waging aggressive war against each other and that an enlightened and powerful global public opinion will help civilize the conduct of nations. An interdependent global economy, operating according to the beneficent principle of free trade, would diffuse prosperity, thereby reinforcing the democratic propensity to peaceful interstate interaction.[27]

The Spenglerian paradigm challenges all these optimistic assumptions of contemporary liberal internationalism. It foresees the persistence of aggression, given the formidable barriers to consolidating democracies in the

26. Francis Fukuyama, *The End of History and the Last Man* (New York: Free Press, 1992), 68, 70.

27. This discussion of liberal internationalism draws on Stanley Hoffmann, "The Crisis of Liberal Internationalism," *Foreign Policy*, no. 98 (Spring, 1995): 159–77.

non-Western world and the reality of human warfare since the dawn of re-corded history. Moreover, the nation-state, the building block of world order according to liberal internationalism, finds itself under stress both in the West, where multiculturalism erodes societal coherence, and the non-West, where ethnic, cultural, and religious conflict has already fragmented several states. The Spenglerian paradigm envisions not merely growing poverty and a widening of income inequalities in both developed and de-veloping societies but the eventual breakdown of international economic order, a pillar of world order in the liberal internationalist scheme of things. Liberal internationalism's vaunted principles of democratization, national self-determination, and economic interdependence sadly do not offer a feasible solution to the deepening global crisis of modernity. Stan-ley Hoffmann, who criticizes realism as promising "only the perpetuation of the same old game" and as being "no better equipped to face the poli-tics of chaos than is liberalism," hopes for a thoroughgoing reconstruction of liberal internationalism, "the only comprehensive and hopeful vision of world affairs." His Harvard colleague, Joseph Nye, foresees an imperfect yet attractive form of liberal world order already slowly emerging. In his contemplation of the prospects for world order since the end of the Cold War, Nye declares hopefully but unconvincingly, "The transition to a lib-eral vision of a new world order is occurring, but not smoothly," and "is a matter of decades and centuries."[28] Although the aspirations of liberal internationalism are noble, they will most likely prove to be severely disap-pointed.

Spengler's deep historical pessimism does assist us in better appreciating the darker side of international relations, which political realism arguably underestimates. Failing to adopt his historical pessimism has prevented modern political realists from getting into closer touch with some of the key, deeply depressing features of international relations in the twentieth century. Conversation with Spengler's ideas raises the question of whether it is truly realistic to entertain confidence in the capacity of statesmen to manage world affairs in light of numerous formidable problems. In the post–Cold War world the efficacy of statecraft will be severely tested. The hopefulness and guarded optimism of realism may be ultimately grounded less in the realities of international politics than in a laudable but theoreti-cally problematic, normative aspiration to change the world modestly for

28. *Ibid.*, 177; Joseph S. Nye, "What New World Order?," *Foreign Affairs* 71, no. 2 (Spring, 1992): 93.

the better. Realists may be temperamentally incapable of acknowledging the anguishing profundity of the tragedy of international politics in the twentieth century and beyond. Carr underscored the immense difficulties a political thinker would encounter in embracing a fatalistic perspective toward international politics when he wrote, "In politics, the belief that certain facts are unalterable or certain trends irresistible commonly reflects a lack of desire or lack of interest to change or resist them. The impossibility of being a consistent and thorough-going realist is one of the most certain and most curious lessons of political science."[29]

In the face of a possibly inevitable apocalyptic climax to world history, not only political realism but the entire spectrum of international relations theory as well, despite its rich diversity, clings almost desperately to the questionable core belief that the destruction of modern civilization is in some way an avoidable phenomenon. One should not forget that modern international relations theory has been largely dominated by Anglo-Saxon scholarship, with the American contribution being of greater weight, and thus has been implanted in political cultures strongly biased toward optimism and pragmatism.[30] Spengler's philosophy of world history and politics is a cultural product of the most tragic nation-state of Western civilization. His thought illumines the arguably unrealistically hopeful nature of international relations theory in this specific and vitally important context, despite the intellectual sophistication of some of its content. Ironically, Spengler's philosophy of world history and politics represents, in the final analysis, an unintentional but provocative critique of the very tradition of political realism, from Thucydides to Weber, he sought to enrich. Spengler advances a plausible, albeit admittedly ultimately speculative, philosophy of world history. His Copernican thesis of the tidal movement of world history toward a catastrophic conclusion is of decisive importance to historical and international relations thought. When the complacency of the West is shaken someday by the sight on the horizon of the rumbling storm clouds of apocalypse, Spengler's philosophy will provide illumination.

29. Edward H. Carr, *The Twenty Years' Crisis, 1919–1939: An Introduction to the Study of International Relations* (New York: Harper & Row, 1964), 89.
30. Meyers, *Die Lehre*, 10–11.

INDEX

the International Economy and World Politics" (Spengler), 183–87

Copernicus, 199

Corelli, Arcangelo, 47

Cortés, Hernando, 30

Coss, John, 161

Costello, Paul, 18

Craig, Gordon, 134, 178

Crimean War, 266

Croce, Benedetto, 107, 108

Cuba, 262

Cultural pessimism. *See* Historical/cultural pessimism

Cultural pluralism, 29, 35, 43, 45, 105, 230

Cultures: in Spengler's *Decline of the West*, 28–44, 98–99, 108–109, 168, 199, 216–17, 217n7, 219, 221, 225; cycles of, 30–31, 37–40, 49, 53, 54, 84, 93, 108, 216, 219, 225, 230, 241; as organism, 30, 104, 108, 219; spiritual essence (soul) of, 31, 41, 79, 85, 96; and climate, 34, 221–22; and "mother landscape," 34; civilization stage of, 37–38, 41, 44, 45, 54, 61, 66, 84, 216; life-span of, 38; influences of foreign cultures on, 41–42, 224; and pseudomorphosis, 41–43, 42n65; development of, as unique, 43, 79–82, 97, 105, 107, 189–90; and meaning of history, 43, 43–44; aesthetic forms of, 45, 46–47; and cities, 54–55; climacteric of culture, 56; decline of, 74–75; Herder on, 79; and *Volk*, 79, 80; idea of, 82; as individuals, 82, 85; primitive cultures, 190, 218–19; nature versus, 201–207, 223; birth of, 220; *Endkulturen* (final cultures), 221; high cultures, 221, 224. *See also* Civilization; and specific cultures

Cycles: of world history, 18, 27, 37, 44, 49, 61, 84, 97–98, 220–21, 224, 227; of cultures, 30–31, 37–40, 49, 53, 54–55, 84, 93, 108, 216, 219, 225, 230, 241; of nature, 44; grand political cycles, 57–58; grand economic development cycles of, 66–67, 69–71; of scientific knowledge, 73; Lamprecht on, 83–84; Goethe on, 97; Joachim of Floris on, 97–98; Vico on, 97–98; Danilevsky on, 98; Machiavelli on, 98; Polybius on, 98

Dahlmann, Friedrich, 140

Danilevsky, Nikolai, 98–99

Darwin, Charles, 9, 195–96, 223

Decadence, 55–56, 95, 127, 263

Decline of the West (Spengler): and German tradition of historicism, 2, 77–90, 92; prose style of, 3–4, 91–92, 100; on Jesus, 7; significance of, 7, 17–19, 75–76, 89–90, 96, 112, 169, 190, 191, 272–73; and Agadir crisis (1911), 12, 19–20, 21; title of, 12, 17, 167; composition of, 13, 145; popularity and success of, 13–14, 21, 101; publication of, 13, 21, 56, 146, 159, 167; on philosophy of world history, 15, 21–26, 44–54, 227; on philosophy of statecraft and politics, 20–21, 25–27, 52–53, 87–88, 159, 270; preface of, 20, 93; critical reactions to and controversies regarding, 21, 92, 100–113, 166–69, 183, 189, 212; and comparative morphology of world history, 22–23, 215; and forecasting of history, 22, 26, 40, 186, 241, 255n44; goal of, 22–23; and historical methodology, 23–24, 111; imperfections of, described by Spengler, 23; on imperialism, 23, 50–55, 57–63; analogies in, 24–25, 29, 111, 219–20; on cultures, 28–44, 98–99, 108–109, 168, 199, 216–17, 217n7, 219, 221, 225, 241; dismissal of prehistory in, 28, 188, 190, 216–17; on cultural pluralism, 29, 35, 43, 45, 105; on time and history, 29–30, 202, 255; depreciation of classical antiquity in, 35–37, 39–40, 222; on civilization, 37–39; on meaning of history,

technology, 72, 224; and cultural transmission from past cultures, 105–107; and wars, 147, 149–50; and catastrophe, 220–21, 225, 227, 230, 232–34, 290. *See also Decline of the West* (Spengler)

Felken, Detlev, 114

Fennelly, John F., 191, 192, 193

Fernández-Armesto, Felipe, 19

Fichte, Johann Gottlieb, 96

Fischer, Klaus P., 191, 192

Flaubert, Gustave, 9

Fontane, Theodor, 9

Ford, Henry, 187

Forecasting of history, 22, 26, 40, 186, 241, 255–56, 255*n*44

Foreign policy. *See* Imperialism; International relations; Wars; and specific countries

Fox, William T. R., xi

Fraenkel, Ernst, 161

France: Spengler's trips to Paris, 9; and Agadir crisis (1911), 19–20; and French Revolution, 54, 57, 60, 123, 149; and Napoleonic Wars, 60, 137, 149; in World War I, 118, 150; rivalry between Germany and, 131, 155, 266; Pan-Germans on, 142; socialism of, 154; occupation of the Ruhr by, 155, 174, 182; as world power, 155, 174; economy of, after World War II, 164; in World War II, 252

Frank, Ludwig, 133

Frederick the Great, 25, 238, 277

Freedom, 15, 52–54, 107, 108, 270, 281, 285

Freud, Sigmund, 59, 99

Freyer, Hans, 145, 239

Friedrich Wilhelm, 140

Frobenius, Leo, 188–89

Fukuyama, Francis, 1–2, 263, 287–88

Fundamental Questions (Spengler), 192, 214–15, 223–24

Genghis Khan, 169

German Oriental Society, 189–90

Germany: and Agadir crisis (1911), 19–20; imperialism and power politics of, 20–21, 23, 50–54, 58, 60–61, 86–88, 117, 124, 133–34, 137, 140, 142, 158–59, 179, 180, 181, 277; Second Reich of, 20, 51, 88–89, 92, 113–34, 136, 139–40, 166, 177–80, 266; defeat of, in World War I, 21, 57, 88, 101, 130, 145, 154–55, 166, 177; in World War I, 37, 117–19, 121, 124, 125, 131, 141–42, 147–48; and Pax Germanica, 50, 139, 232, 265; overthrow of Hohenzollern monarchy in, 57, 101, 148; socialist revolution of 1918 in, 57, 101, 145, 146, 147–48, 176; Spengler's early support of partial democratization of, 113–32, 149, 166; Social Democratic party of, 115, 119, 121–22; conservatism in, 116–17, 119–20; divisiveness in politics of, 117–18; National Liberal party in, 119–20, 126; and nationalism, 127–28; cultural achievement of, 128–29; as "second America," 128–29; parliamentarism in, 130, 154, 179–80; unification of, 133, 139, 140–41, 177, 249, 266; and *Weltpolitik*, 133–37, 139; *Deutschtum* (German national character), 143–44; and French occupation of the Ruhr, 155, 174, 182; economy of, after World War II, 164, 267; and Versailles Treaty, 166, 236, 240, 242, 243, 267; and relations with Russia, 169, 171–72, 265, 266, 279; interwar politics and German youth, 172–74; Spengler's anxiety about, after World War I, 174, 177, 211, 245–46, 247, 253; as world power, 175, 176–77, 187, 247, 249, 253; nobility in, 176–77; education in, 180–81; economy of, after World War I, 186, 205, 211, 234, 240, 246; in World War II, 235; reunification of, in 1990, 255, 265. *See also* Bismarck, Otto von; Hitler, Adolf; Nazism; Weimar Republic